The past as prologue

In today's military of rapid technological and strategic change, obtaining a complete understanding of the present, let alone the past, is a formidable challenge. Yet, the very high rate of change today makes study of the past more important than ever before. *The Past as Prologue* explores the usefulness of the study of history for contemporary military strategists. It illustrates the great importance of military history while revealing the challenges of applying the past to the present. Essays from authors of diverse backgrounds – British and American, civilian and military – come together to present an overwhelming argument for the necessity of the study of the past by today's military leaders despite these challenges. The chapters of Part I examine the relationship between history and the military profession. Those in Part II explore specific historical cases that show the repetitiveness of certain military problems.

Williamson Murray is Professor Emeritus of European Military History at Ohio State University and a Senior Fellow at the Institute of Defense Analysis. He is the author of a number of books, including *The Changes in the European Balance of Power, 1938–1939*; *The Path to Ruin*; *Luftwaffe*; *German Military Effectiveness*; *The Air War in the Persian Gulf*; *Air War, 1914–1945*; *The Iraq War: A Military History*, with Major General Robert Scales, Jr.; and *A War to Be Won: Fighting the Second World War*, with Allan R. Millet. He also coedited numerous collections, including *Military Innovations in the Interwar Period* (1996), with Allan R. Millet, and *The Dynamics of Military Revolution, 1300–2050* (2001), with MacGregor Knox.

Richard Hart Sinnreich is a former director of the U.S. Army's School of Advanced Military Studies. His writings include "The Changing Face of Battlefield Reporting," *ARMY*, November 1994; "To Stand & Fight," *ARMY*, July 1997; "In Search of Victory," *ARMY*, February 1999; "Whither the Legions," *Strategic Review*, Summer 1999; "Conceptual Foundations of a Transformed U.S. Army" with Huba Wass de Czege, The Institute for Land Warfare, March 2002; "Red Team Insights from Army Wargaming," *DART*, September 2002; "Joint Warfighting in the 21st Century" with Williamson Murray, IDA, 2002; and "A Strategy by Accident: U.S. Pacific Policy 1945–1975," National Institute of Defense Studies, March 2004. He writes a regular column for the *Lawton Constitution* and occasional columns for *ARMY* and the *Washington Post*.

The past as prologue

The importance of history to the military profession

Edited by

WILLIAMSON MURRAY
Institute of Defense Analysis

RICHARD HART SINNREICH
Carrick Communications, Inc.

CAMBRIDGE
UNIVERSITY PRESS

CAMBRIDGE UNIVERSITY PRESS
Cambridge, New York, Melbourne, Madrid, Cape Town, Singapore,
São Paulo, Delhi, Dubai, Tokyo, Mexico City

Cambridge University Press
32 Avenue of the Americas, New York, NY 10013-2473, USA

www.cambridge.org
Information on this title: www.cambridge.org/9780521853774

First published 2006
Reprinted 2008

A catalog record for this publication is available from the British Library.

Library of Congress Cataloging in Publication Data
The past as prologue : the importance of history to the military profession / edited by
Williamson Murray and Richard Hart Sinnreich.
p. cm.
Includes bibliographical references and index.
ISBN-13: 978-0-521-85377-4 (hardback)
ISBN-10: 0-521-85377-X (hardback)
1. Military history – Study and teaching. 2. Military art and science. I. Murray,
Williamson.
II. Sinnreich, Richard Hart. III. Title.
U27.P28 2006
355.009 – dc22

ISBN 978-0-521-85377-4 Hardback
ISBN 978-0-521-61963-9 Paperback

To Andrew "Andy" Marshall and Theodore "Ted" Gold –
two servants of freedom who have made a difference.

Contents

Contributors

Jonathan B.A. Bailey, M.B.E., A.D.C.
Major General
British Army (Retired)

John Gooch
Leeds University

Andrew Gordon
Joint Services Staff College

Colin S. Gray
University of Reading

Christopher C. Harmon
Marine Corps University

J. Paul Harris
Royal Military Academy

Francis G. Hoffman
Defense Consultant

Michael Howard
Professor Emeritus
Oxford University

John P. Kiszely, M.C.
Lieutenant General
British Army

Williamson Murray
Senior Fellow
Institute for Defense Analysis

Paul A. Rahe
University of Tulsa

Richard Hart Sinnreich
Colonel
United States Army (Retired)

Paul K. Van Riper
Lieutenant General
United States Marine Corps
(Retired)

1

Introduction

WILLIAMSON MURRAY AND RICHARD
HART SINNREICH

If recent events are any guide, an unacknowledged conviction of too many of those responsible for national security decisions, civilian and military, is that history has little to offer today's defense policy maker. Beset by accelerating change, current senior leaders seem to have neither the time nor the inclination to look to the past for help. Events crowd one another too rapidly. Technology matures too quickly. Crises succeed each other too abruptly. Coping with a demanding present and confronting an ominous future, few current civilian and military leaders seem willing to indulge in systematic reflection about the past.

Too harsh a judgment? How else to explain political and military assumptions preceding the 2003 invasion of Iraq that largely ignored the history of the region, planning that discounted postconflict challenges that had arisen even in the much less complicated overthrow of Manuel Noriega's corrupt Panamanian regime a mere thirteen years earlier, and the slowness only thirty years after Vietnam to recognize and deal with the insurgency that followed the collapse of Saddam Hussein's regime?[1] Overconfident in their ability to control the future, those responsible for planning the invasion chose deliberately or by oversight to ignore history. The future, unfortunately, turned out to look all too much like the past. As Yogi Berra might have put it, Iraq was déjà vu all over again. That, too, is a dismally familiar historical phenomenon.[2]

---

[1] In fairness, some notables warned of these difficulties. Former national security adviser Brent Scowcroft and retired regional combatant commanders Anthony Zinni, Wesley Clark, and John Shalikashvili come to mind, as does then Army Chief of Staff Eric Shinseki, the only active duty senior officer willing publicly to dispute the administration's optimistic estimates. For their trouble, they were ignored or vilified.

[2] For the checkered performance of political and military leaders and their bureaucracies in the making of strategy through the ages, see Williamson Murray, MacGregor Knox, and Alvin Bernstein, *The Making of Strategy, Rulers, States, and War* (Cambridge, 1996).

Indeed, political and military leaders' tendency to discount history is neither novel nor peculiarly American. Throughout history, leaders and institutions have repeatedly manifested an almost willful ignorance of the past.[3]
One of the great myths of the twentieth century is that armies study only
their last war and thus do poorly in the next. That, for example, is the conventional explanation for the Franco-British allies' military defeat of 1940.
According to the argument, French and British armed forces based their
force development throughout the interwar period on their experiences of
the First World War, whereas the Germans, unfettered by their defeat in
1918, searched for new methods to prevent a repetition of the deadlock that
had frozen the Western Front for four years.[4]

Nothing could be further from the truth. It was rather the Germans who
systematically and with brutal honesty reviewed the tactical failures of the
First World War,[5] and then exploited that knowledge to create the military juggernaut that won such decisive battles in the early years of World
War II. The British blandly ignored the lessons of the First World War until
1932 and thereafter applied them indifferently, while the French deliberately
reinterpreted their own experiences in the last years of the war to satisfy
preconceived political and military preferences.[6]

Some 2,400 years ago, perhaps the greatest of all military historians,
Thucydides, declared that he had written his history of the Peloponnesian
War to inform "those who want to understand clearly the events which happened in the past, and which (human nature being what it is) will, at some
time or other and in much the same ways, be repeated in the future."[7]

The trajectory of human history over the centuries since he wrote his masterpiece has more than confirmed his prognosis. Notwithstanding, successors
of the Hellenic soldiers and politicians about whom he wrote have repeatedly
chosen to believe that they are different and that the lessons of the past are

---

[3] Many of history's most successful soldiers were students of military history and not a few
wrote it themselves, including Thucydides, Julius Caesar, Ulysses Grant, and William Slim.
The reverse correlation between historical ignorance and military incompetence is likewise
too consistent to dismiss as accidental.

[4] Defeat certainly can be a more effective engine of change than victory. Our own military's
response to defeat in Vietnam is a case in point. But the records of the French and Italian
militaries in the twentieth century, among others, suggest that even defeat doesn't guarantee sensible military transformation. For a detailed treatment, see Allan R. Millett and
Williamson Murray, *Military Effectiveness*, 3 vols. (London, 1988).

[5] Though not, unfortunately, its strategic lessons. See, e.g., Holger H. Herwig, "Clio Deceived:
Patriotic Self-Censorship in Germany after the Great War," *International Security*, Fall 1987.

[6] Three useful treatments are James S. Corum, *The Roots of Blitzkrieg, Hans von Seeckt and
German Military Reform* (Lawrence, KS, 1992); Harold R. Winton, *To Change an Army:
General Sir John Burnett-Stuart and British Armored Doctrine, 1927–1938* (Lawrence, KS,
1988); and Robert Doughty, *The Seeds of Disaster: The Development of French Army
Doctrine, 1919–1939* (Hamden, CT, 1986).

[7] Thucydides, *History of the Peloponnesian War*, trans. Rex Warner (London, 1954), p. 48.

irrelevant to their unique circumstances.[8] Why this is so remains one of the mysteries of the human experience. Perhaps the most compelling explanation is simply generational transition, the conviction of each new crop of leaders assuming power that they are different from their predecessors and immune from their errors. To paraphrase an old saying, what is new is not necessarily interesting and what is interesting is not necessarily new. Yet, political and military leaders seem driven to repeat the blunders of their predecessors. It is the very repetitive quality of many of military history's worst disasters that can make reading it so depressing.

Thus, in 1940 and 1941, not a single senior German military leader expressed the slightest qualm with Hitler's plans for Barbarossa, the invasion of the Soviet Union. Even Franz Halder, chief of the general staff and the most analytical among its number, saw no reason to reflect on the unhappy results of earlier such invasions, whether Charles XII's or Napoleon's. Only as winter's darkness descended on the battle lines in front of Leningrad, Moscow, and Rostov in December 1941 did some senior German officers belatedly began to consult Caulaincourt's sobering memoirs of Napoleon's disastrous Russian campaign.[9]

All in all, considering that war is the most demanding and consequential of human endeavors, it is astonishing how cursorily it tends to be studied by its practitioners. It is even more surprising given that most military organizations spend the majority of their time at peace, which one might suppose offered leisure if not incentive to study the past. Instead, modern militaries are consumed with the recruitment and training of generations of young men, the management of large military bureaucracies, and the routine administrative burdens of command. In the day-to-day business of peacetime soldiering, systematic study of the past all too easily becomes a luxury that busy commanders and their subordinates cannot afford.

That is the more true because the serious study of history is difficult. It is no simple matter to extract what is relevant and important from the wealth of recorded military experience. Often, what appears relevant is trivial and what appears significant is not easily transferable. Nor does history furnish straightforward and comfortable answers to contemporary questions.

Beyond the desire of each generation to chart its own course and the competition of peacetime routine, one should also note the natural human distaste for upsetting evidence, especially when it challenges cherished

---

[8] Herodotus's earlier history of the great war between the Persians and the Greeks underlines that little in the behavior of the latter had changed fifty years later when Thucydides wrote his history of the Peloponnesian War.

[9] For the best account of the 1941 German campaign against the Soviet Union, see Horst Boog, Jurgen Förster, Joachim Hoffman, Ernst Klink, Rolf-Dieter Müller, and Gerd R. Ueberschär, *Das Deutsche Reich und der Zweite Weltkrieg*, vol. 4, *Der Angriff auf die Sowjetunion* (Stuttgart, 1983).

convictions. Not all leaders find intellectual debate congenial, and even fewer relish challenges to their own ideas and assumptions.[10] Immersion in history inevitably invites both. History raises more questions than it answers. It suggests unpleasant possibilities. It demolishes preferred theories. It often forces leaders to recognize unpalatable truths. Yet, it also suggests possible paths to the future, no matter how uncomfortable. Perhaps most important, it compels them to think dispassionately about potential opponents – their nature, worldview, aims, and options.

It is this understanding of the "other" – the adversary – that has repeatedly proved most difficult for civilian and military leaders to acquire, an understanding that history suggests is crucial to success in war. Thus, the failure of European rulers in the early nineteenth century to recognize the magnitude of the sociological changes wrought by the French Revolution and of their commanders to understand the military implications of Napoleon's expropriation of it goes far to explain the terrible series of defeats suffered by France's enemies between 1792 and 1811. As Carl von Clausewitz commented:

> Not until statesmen had at last perceived the nature of the forces that had emerged in France, and had grasped that new conditions now obtained in Europe, could they foresee the broad effect all this would have on war.... In short, we can say that twenty years of Revolutionary triumph were mainly due to the mistaken policies of France's enemies.[11]

Still another of the obstacles to acquiring and using historical knowledge littering the policy landscape is the bureaucratic nature of modern governments. Bureaucracies often conserve the past but rarely examine it critically. Such examination would challenge the routines that smooth the bureaucratic process. We already noted the impact of peacetime routine on the willingness and ability of military organizations to study history seriously. That routine is even more pronounced in the civilian bureaucracies that drive modern governments.[12] It is easy for bureaucrats to become imprisoned by it. The past then becomes a nuisance, and its qualifiers and warnings merely a threat to their projects. For too many, potential adversaries are merely a convenient justification for funding, not real people we might actually have to fight one day. Their history, when cited at all, serves only as a source of aphorisms,

---

10 Considerable evidence confirms that the rejection, if not outright suppression, of competing views has preceded more than one of history's most egregious military blunders. For example, see Williamson Murray, *The Change in the European Balance of Power, 1938–1939: The Path to Ruin* (Princeton, NJ, 1984).

11 Carl von Clausewitz, *On War*, ed. & trans. Michael Howard and Peter Paret (Princeton, NJ, 1986), p. 609.

12 One might recall that the report of the 9/11 Commission commented that a principal reason for the failure to anticipate the September 11 catastrophe was a uniform lack of imagination in the intelligence bureaucracy, this despite ample prior evidence of al Qaeda's general intentions, if not their specific plans.

not a means of deciphering the complex interrelationships that are likely to affect their future behavior.[13]

Finally, of course, bureaucracies, military and otherwise, are hostage to the political sensitivities and prejudices of those they serve. History has a bad habit of upsetting both. During the last few decades, American defense policy making especially has been afflicted by politically appealing but historically unsupported assumptions about the nature of war and the sacrifices, material and moral, required to prosecute it. As they percolate through the organizational apparatus, such assumptions gain acceptance despite lack of evidence. The result, only too visible in today's defense establishment, is an endless effort to find easily marketed and preferably inexpensive solutions to the most complex and difficult of national enterprises.

In such a climate, history at best is an inconvenience and at worst an outright embarrassment. A contemporary historian captured the problem all too succinctly in relation to the challenge of designing strategy in the twenty-first century:

> In this bewildering world, the search for predictive theories to guide strategy has been no more successful than the search for such theories in other areas of human existence. Patterns do emerge from the past, and their study permits educated guesses about the range of potential outcomes. But the future is not an object of knowledge; no increase in processing power will make the owl of history a daytime bird. Similar causes do not always produce similar effects, and causes interact in ways unforeseeable even by the historical sophisticated. Worse still, individuals – with their ambitions, vanities, and quirks – make strategy. Machiavelli's Prince is sometimes a better guide than Clausewitz to the personal and institutional vendettas that intertwine unpredictably around the simplest strategic decisions.[14]

One of the great ironies in today's America is that its civilian policy makers will for the most part be even more ignorant of the past than the military officers who serve them. The latter at least are compelled by the professional military education system to confront history at various points in their careers, however infrequently. Their political masters are under no such compulsion. Perhaps this is inevitable. Political leaders invariably reflect the prejudices and attitudes of the citizens they defend, and Americans are by birthright prone to dismiss history as a brake on their ambitions. Even in the military,

---

13 A classic example was the inability of advocates of German appeasement in the late 1930s to recognize how extraordinarily different the norms and aims of Nazi Germany were from their own. For the need to understand other cultures in planning and conducting war in the twenty-first century, see Major General (Retired) Robert H. Scales, Jr., "Culture-Centric Warfare," *Naval Institute Proceedings*, October 2004.

14 Macgregor Knox, "Continuity and Revolution in Strategy," in Williamson Murray, MacGregor Knox, and Alvin Bernstein, eds. *The Making of Strategy, Rulers, States, and War* (Cambridge, 1996), p. 645.

there will always be some who from loyalty or discretion accept without challenge the cavalier assumptions of political leaders unwilling to consult the past and unable to hear its echoes.

At present, moreover, even in the military, what too often takes the place of serious historical analysis is an intense but historically undisciplined theorizing. Indeed, the surfeit of "transformational" concepts currently besieging senior civilian and military leaders is incredible. Some seek to demolish the institutional traditions believed to prevent the separate military services from harmonizing their activities and resources effectively; others seek to expand the scope of civilian influence on historically military concerns; whereas still others seek the technological means of eliminating the inherent ambiguity and friction of war.[15]

Forward thinking is necessary. But what characterizes too much of it today is an almost complete disconnection from the past, surprising as that may seem in a military with an almost uniformly successful tradition. Part of the explanation lies in the dominance for almost a half-century in American policy-making circles, military as well as civilian, of political science and management theories exhibiting an almost theological aversion to history as a source of insight and evidence. But the broader explanation is simply that military organizations and their leaders are too consumed by immediate pressures to examine the past in a serious and critical way. New concepts are both less onerous to justify and easier to market to a defense industry hungry for new business and to politicians seeking less materially and politically expensive solutions to war's complexities.

Many have warned of the risks associated with such ahistorical theorizing. Attacking military theoreticians of his own time, Clausewitz was especially blunt. His comments on the writings of some of his colleagues in the nineteenth century might just as cogently be applied to many of today's conceptual efforts:

> It is only analytically that these attempts at theory can be called advances in the realm of truth; synthetically, in the rules and regulations they offer, they are absolutely useless. They aim at fixed value; but in war everything is uncertain, and calculations have to be made with variable quantities. They direct the inquiry exclusively toward physical quantities, whereas all military action is intertwined with psychological forces and effects.[16]

---

[15] Examples unfortunately are legion, but for one representative concept, the reader might examine Joint Vision 2010, an extraordinary collection of historically unsupported dicta produced in the early 1990s, which set the tone for many of the concepts that followed over the next decade and a half. The contrast with earlier military concepts could not be more apparent. For notable examples, consult the 1982 and 1986 editions of the Army's Field Manual 100-5, "Operations," and the Marine Corps' 1989 FMFM 1 "Warfighting" and its 1997 successor MCDP 1, each of which relied heavily on historical analysis.

[16] Clausewitz, p. 136.

Conceptualization and experimentation certainly have their uses. But only history records the reactions of real people to real events in the context of the real pressures that policy making and war making inevitably impose. Again, Clausewitz:

> [Theory] is an analytic investigation leading to close acquaintance with the subject; applied to experience – in our case to military history – it leads to thorough familiarity with it. The closer it comes to that goal, the more it proceeds from the objective form of a science to the subjective form of a skill, the more effective it will prove in areas where the nature of the case admits no arbiter but talent. It will, in fact, become an active ingredient of talent.[17]

The central purpose of this book is to illustrate the qualities that make the study of history so important to military leaders, and at the same time, consider what makes it so difficult and challenging for those who choose to engage in it. Not long after the seizure of Baghdad in April 2003, a Marine Corps instructor at the National War College wrote to his former boss, then Major General James Mattis, commanding the 1st Marine Division during the invasion, asking how Mattis would reply to officers who discount history as having little relevance or utility to their military careers. Mattis wrote back:

> Ultimately a real understanding of history means that we face nothing new under the sun. For all the "Fourth Generation of War" intellectuals running around today saying that the nature of war has fundamentally changed, the tactics are wholly new, etc., I must respectfully say: "Not really." Alex the Great would not be in the least perplexed by the enemy that we face right now in Iraq, and our leaders going into this fight do their troops a disservice by not studying (studying, vice just reading) the men who have gone before us. We have been fighting on this planet for 5000 years and we should take advantage of their experience. "Winging it" and filling body bags as we sort out what works reminds us of the moral dictates and the cost of competence in our profession.[18]

No one who knows James Mattis well would ever mistake him for an ivory tower intellectual. On the contrary, he is the epitome of a combat commander, a leader who consistently leads from the front. But like so many successful military commanders before him, from Alex the Great to George Patton, Mattis also is a committed student of war. For Mattis, as for his celebrated predecessors, to be a student of war is first to be a student of military history.

This book reflects the same conviction. The authors of its various essays believe the study of military history plays an essential role in the educational development of future military and civilian leaders. In addressing what

[17] Ibid, p. 141.
[18] Unpublished e-mail, quoted by permission of the author.

America's war colleges should teach their students, Admiral Stansfield Turner, former president of the Naval War College and the author of its widely praised educational reforms of the early 1970s, noted:

> War colleges are places to educate the senior officer corps in the larger military and strategic issues that confront America in the late twentieth century. They should educate these officers by a demanding intellectual curriculum to think in wider terms than their busy operational careers have thus far demanded. Above all the war colleges should broaden the intellectual and military horizons of the officers who attend, so that they have a conception of the larger strategic and operational issues that confront our military and our nation.[19]

Without attention to history, there can be no such professional broadening of officers beyond the immediate scope of their duties. Apart from the conduct of war itself, the only comprehensive evidence of the demands it places on those who fight it and their leaders is the evidence of history. Written from a number of different perspectives, the essays in this volume illuminate the extraordinary richness of that evidence, as well as the extent to which its study can inform military innovation in peacetime and adaptation in war. Some focus on war's enduring features and challenges, whereas others suggest the insights furnished by particular historical cases. Still others examine the sometimes troublesome relationship between those who make military history and those who record it.

All are products of an extraordinarily pleasant and productive Anglo-American scholarly collaboration during the summer and fall of 2003. Each was originally written and presented at "Past Futures," a conference on military history at the Royal Military College, Sandhurst, sponsored by the British Army's Directorate of Ground Development and Doctrine, the British counterpart of the U.S. Army's Training and Doctrine Command. Subsequently, all but Sir Michael Howard's were presented at a follow-on conference at Marine Corps University, Quantico, sponsored by the Marine Corps University Foundation. The authors reflect a broad diversity of backgrounds and interests – British and American, civilian and military, scholars and practitioners. Whatever their professional credentials and orientation, all share the conviction that studying military history is a crucial prerequisite to understanding the nature and future of war.

It is certainly not the only prerequisite. Other ingredients, from familiarity with emerging technologies to awareness of cultural differences to actual battlefield experience, contribute to that understanding. But the authors in this volume uniformly believe these other ingredients are ultimately sterile unless grounded in a careful and thorough examination of the past.

---

[19] Quoted in Williamson Murray, "Grading the War Colleges," *The National Interest*, Winter 1986/1987, p. 13.

Their essays reflect that view. Sir Michael Howard's generous permission to use his keynote address to the first Past Futures conference as the introductory essay is a special gift. Perhaps the most distinguished military historian writing today, Sir Michael has been a mentor and model for every other contributor in the book. His essay eloquently reminds us that, whatever its many other contributions may be, military history and war studies are in the final analysis about war, and that, although much modern historiography rightly and usefully examines war in its broadest context, the study of war finally is about fighting. Classic military history – the study of military operations and campaigns – thus remains a *sine qua non* of the study of war.

We have divided the remaining essays into two groups. Those in Part I examine various aspects of the relationship between history and the military profession. To a considerable extent, they seek to elucidate how one might think about the possible and potential uses of history within the framework of professional military education and the careers of officers. The essays in Part II examine specific historical cases that illuminate recurring military problems. For convenience, we have grouped the essays in this section chronologically.

Lieutenant General John Kiszely, British Army, begins the first section by reminding us that using military history superficially can be more dangerous than ignoring it altogether. In particular, he urges that its study be imbedded in a broader and deeper commitment to professional self-education, a commitment that requires deliberate encouragement by military institutions. His chapter is followed by that of Lieutenant General Paul Van Riper, USMC retired, whose autobiographical essay describes how a lifelong progressive engagement with military history, largely self-driven and managed, helped shape a distinguished military career in peace and war.

In the third essay, Colonel Richard Sinnreich, U.S. Army retired, traces the evolution of historical study in America's formal military education, a relationship marked by episodic advances and retreats driven by both scholarly and military fashion. The final essay in this section, by Williamson Murray, professor of military history emeritus at The Ohio State University, underlines that, too often, soldiers' engagement with military history is distorted by an unhappy congruence between historians' need to simplify a phenomenon suffused with ambiguity and uncertainty and soldiers' yearning for didactic guidance.

Indeed, Murray argues, for history to be of any use, its very complexities demand skeptical inquiry rather than reliance on a smattering of inevitably oversimplified historical anecdotes. As General Mattis suggests, therefore, military history, not to mention history in general, is of little value unless it is studied, not merely read.

The essays in Part II address more directly recurring military phenomena and the ability of history to illuminate them. The first two examine the writings of two seminal thinkers about war and the human condition. Paul Rahe, professor of history at the University of Tulsa, examines Thucydides. His essay demonstrates that studying war in its wider social context is far from a modern preoccupation, in the process reaffirming the contemporary relevance of the first, and in many ways still most important, military historian to the study of war and its impact on civil society. Professor Colin Gray of the University of Reading offers a spirited defense of Clausewitz. His essay is a refreshing and much-needed antidote to those British and American academics who over the past several decades have spilled much ink arguing the irrelevance of the Prussian theorist to the conditions of the modern world (in a few cases, apparently, without having bothered to read him).[20]

The third essay, by John Gooch, Professor of History at Leeds University, examines what history has to say about strategy. Both Thucydides and Clausewitz would approve of Professor Gooch's careful distinction between history as a source of not always reliable maxims and as a means of diagnosing and understanding recurring patterns of strategic behavior, a distinction too rarely acknowledged by strategic practitioners.

The next three essays in Part II apply the lens of historical analysis to the very contemporary problem of how military institutions cope – or fail to cope – with major technological changes. Andrew Gordon, lecturer at Britain's Joint Services Staff College, describes the impact on the Royal Navy of a prolonged period without major maritime warfare, during which the technology of war at sea underwent rapid and massive changes, while it managed to forget almost entirely the principles on which its great victories in the early nineteenth century had rested. Major General Jonathan Bailey, chief of the British Army's Directorate of Ground Development and Doctrine, examines the failure of Western armies to learn from the experiences of the 1904–1905 Russo-Japanese War, in every way the harbinger of the nightmarish Great War that followed barely a decade later and came close to destroying Europe. Paul Harris, lecturer of War Studies at the Royal Military College, offers a thoughtful rebuttal of the conventional view that early British defeats in the Second World War reflected professional military myopia, instead locating many of the prewar British Army's difficulties in broader political, economic, and intellectual obstacles that began by hindering innovation before the war and ended by retarding adaptation to its actual conditions.

The last two essays examine military challenges that transcend particular historical eras, having arisen repeatedly over the course of the centuries

---

[20] In Britain, there is a long tradition of criticizing Clausewitz, beginning with B. H. Liddell Hart. Americans' rejection of Clausewitz's work is more recent, and reflects both emotional distaste for Clausewitz's merciless realism and insistence on the power of modern information systems to dissipate the fog and friction of war. For the latter view, see Admiral Bill Owens with Ed Offley, *Lifting the Fog of War* (New York, 2000).

without enduring solution. Chris Harmon, professor at Marine Corps University, dissects the use of terrorism as an alternative to classic inter-state warfare. His essay at once clarifies the terrorist threat confronting the democracies today and underlines some of the inherent vulnerabilities to which such unconventional enemies are prey. Frank Hoffman, a defense consultant in Washington, DC, analyzes American civil–military relations in their historical context. In the process, he identifies some of the perceptual differences that make that vital relationship so persistently problematic.

In the end, like the phenomenon it studies, military historiography is a human enterprise, with human attributes and flaws. Military and civilian institutions can and should contribute to its development, improvement, and exploitation, but all three finally depend on the personal intellectual commitment of scholars and soldiers to their vocations and successors. Just as the younger essayists in this volume are all, in one way or another, Sir Michael Howard's intellectual heirs, and before him of military historians reaching back to Thucydides, so too, serving military commanders like Jim Mattis are Paul Van Riper's intellectual heirs and before him of historically literate military practitioners reaching back to Clausewitz and earlier.

Young soldiers and marines, as well as scholars, take their cues from the leaders of their profession. Today, in a period of accelerating strategic and technological change, it is all the more essential that soldiers confront the future with a firm understanding of war's continuities, and that scholars furnish them the best historical analysis of which they are capable in which to ground that understanding. The moral dictates and cost of competence cited by General Mattis thus apply equally to both professions. It is in explicit recognition of that joint responsibility that we offer this volume.

2

Military history and the history of war

MICHAEL HOWARD

When the first university chair in our subject was established at Oxford in the first decade of the twentieth century, its field was defined simply as "Military History," and it took two world wars to broaden this to the "History of War." I have no firm evidence for this, but I suspect that the change was made to make it clear that the incumbent was expected to cover naval and air matters as well.

The same enlargement occurred in the scope of the only other similar chair in this country, which was established after the First World War at King's College London for Lloyd George's nemesis, General Sir Frederick Maurice, and about this I can speak with greater authority. The people responsible for reviving it after the Second World War were not military men; they were academics in the University of London who had been involved in the civilian conduct of the war – economists like Lionel Robbins, social historians like Sir Keith Hancock, diplomatic specialists like Sir Charles Webster. They knew from personal experience that the conduct of war was too serious a business to be left to the generals and believed in consequence that the study of war was too important to be left to military historians. The scope that they had in mind was so wide that they were not sure how to define it.

I recall a meeting of the great and the good in the early 1950s, where the title of the chair was being debated. Because its subject matter was not confined to history, they adopted that usefully vague term "studies"; one that was then in its infancy and today provides cover for innumerable soggy nonsubjects. But how were these "studies" to be defined? If they were not "military," what were they? "Defense Studies" was deemed too mealy mouthed. "Strategic Studies" was too narrow. "Conflict Studies" was too broad. One learned scholar suggested, in desperation, "Polemelogical Studies." At last Sir Charles Webster, a blunt and massive Yorkshireman, hit the table with a fist the size of a large ham and demanded: "It's about war isn't it? So what's wrong with War Studies?"

So, War Studies it became and has remained ever since. I was put in to hold the fort until they could find someone more eminent to occupy the chair (which I am glad to say they never did), and they genially made it clear to me that there were no limits to the claims I might stake out. I myself might teach the history of war, which was all I knew about, but I was to recruit as widely as possible among other disciplines: international relations, naturally; strategic studies, a subject whose birth had just been precipitated by the invention of nuclear weapons; economics, and the social sciences in general; law, both international and constitutional; anthropology; theology – indeed anything that I could think of and whose practitioners I could interest. If black studies, gender studies, gay studies, or media studies had then existed, I would certainly have colonized them as well. In short, I laid the foundation for that vast empire over which Professor Sir Lawrence Freedman now presides on both banks of the Thames.

I am myself always a little uneasy when described as a "military historian." Until very recently, the great majority of professional historians found it hard to think of the term in anything but a rather pejorative sense: "military history is to history," as I think someone once said, "what military music is to music." To dismiss it in this way is of course grossly unfair, but for doing so I think there have been two good reasons. "Military history" was equated with "operational history," and most of it – at least, before the twentieth century – was written, and studied, to enable soldiers to be better at their jobs. This was and remains a quite legitimate function. Past wars provide the only database from which the military learn how to conduct their profession: how to do it and even more important, how not to do it.

Good, accurate military history serves a necessary purpose so long as we have a military profession at all. Clausewitz warned of the misuse of military history, of expecting it to provide "school solutions" rather than to educate the minds of the military commander to expect the unexpected, but his warnings have all too often been ignored. One does not, or anyhow should not, study the past in order to discover the "school solutions" – that is the first "lesson" that professional historians have to drum into the heads of their pupils. Nevertheless, however intelligently it may be studied, military history has preserved for many of its readers and writers a distinct didactic purpose to which few other branches of historical studies would lay claim and one which they regard with understandable suspicion.

The second characteristic of much – indeed I would say most – military history is its parochialism. It has all too often been written to create and embellish a national myth, and to promote deeds of derring–do among the young. I would like to be able to say that this is a characteristic that military historians have now outgrown, but we have only to step into any bookshop to see that this would not be true. Leaving earlier history aside, the First World War in British historiography focuses almost exclusively on the British Army's heroic sufferings and achievements on the Western Front. The Second World War is ransacked to provide material for the glorification of our past, while shelves are still being filled with scrapings from barrel bottoms about the Gulf and Falklands Wars.

Heaven knows that we are not the only ones to be parochial: American military historians, with a few brilliant exceptions like Carlo d'Este, seem unaware that the United States had any allies in the Second World War at all, in either Europe or the Pacific, and I doubt whether the Russians are any less oblivious either, although they have better reason. No wonder bookshops have special sections on "military history" carefully quarantined from history proper. Some of my colleagues refer to it as "pornography": This is going a bit far, but I understand what they mean.

This parochialism is particularly marked in the case of British military history because of the peculiar introversion of the British Army itself. The wars fought by the great continental powers, at least since the French Revolution, have been genuine "wars of nations" fought by peoples in arms, as often as not on their own soil. So were the great formative conflicts of the United States – the War of American Independence and the Civil War. In the two World Wars, the British Army did expand briefly to become "a people in arms," but it did so reluctantly and inexpertly, and went back afterward to "proper soldiering" as soon as it decently could. It was a club, or rather a congeries of clubs, whose activities were a private matter and took place a long way from home. Its historiographical tradition is that of regimental history writ large, a rather selective regimental history at that. The regimental historian – and I have been one myself, so I should know – is expected to chronicle triumphs, not disasters. His purpose is morale building, not dispassionate analysis, which rather limits its didactic value.

Furthermore, one would not learn from most histories of the British Army that, throughout the first half of the nineteenth century, one of its major functions was repressing social conflict within the United Kingdom or, in the twentieth, policing Ireland. Accounts abound of colonial or imperial conflicts overseas, but few deal with the most remarkable achievement of the British Armed Forces: getting to where they had to fight, wherever it might be in the world, and remaining there. The amazing logistic network created primarily by the Royal Engineers, the ports, railroads, and depots that provided the skeleton of the British Empire, the feats of exploration and cartography that put so much of India, Africa, and the Middle East quite literally on the map – none of this was chronicled by Fortescue or indeed, as far as I know, by anyone else until Daniel Headrick drew attention to it in his *Tools of Empire* written twenty years ago. If we are now beginning to learn more about the political and social context of the Army at home and its adjustment to the weapons revolution of the nineteenth century, much of this is due to the work of Hew Strachan and his fellow practitioners of what our American colleagues call the "New Military History."

Before going any further, I must say a word about naval history. This is even more of a specialization than military history and remains shamefully isolated even from that. But naval history cannot be studied in isolation from maritime history as a whole – no naval historian can get very far without using the resources of the National Maritime Museum – and maritime history demands a grasp of very complex technologies that lie as far beyond the range of the average military historian as they do of his political and social colleagues. But naval history has been distorted even more than has military history by parochialism and nationalism. Its study peaked at the turn of the nineteenth and twentieth centuries as part of a general campaign of imperialist propaganda.

Indeed, until chairs of naval history were recently established at King's College London and Exeter University, the only relevant post in any British university was that of, significantly, "Imperial and Naval History" at Cambridge, and that has been sanitized for the last half-century by being held by a succession of highly respectable economic historians. But they could have done worse. Like maritime history as a whole, naval history is sterile unless studied in association with economic history. The emphasis laid on operational naval history by traditional British naval historians, the glorification of Nelson and his triumphant battles, is understandable; but as Julian Corbett (our finest naval historian, one who was neither a sailor nor a professional academic) pointed out, we cannot appreciate the importance of Nelson's victories unless we devote equal attention to the ten years of humdrum blockade and minor actions that followed his death.

In fact, the finest picture of British naval activities during the Napoleonic Wars that we have to date is that given in the superb novels of Patrick O'Brien. It remains a standing reproach to British historians that until very recently the best, if not the only studies of the economic dimension of the Napoleonic Wars, have been by foreign historians, Eli Hecksher the Swede and Francois Crouzet the Frenchman. We had to wait for Paul Kennedy's *Rise and Fall of British Naval Mastery* to see the sweep of British naval history set in its appropriate economic context, and this pioneer work still awaits a successor.

In the era of so-called "limited wars," it was possible to study military and naval operations in isolation, although even for that era it remained a pretty sterile and impoverished approach. But we should recall how comparatively brief, in the sweep of world history, that era was. I remember the amazement and amusement with which my colleagues in the Department of Classics at King's regarded me, when I rather naively asked them to tell me who were the major current authorities on warfare in classical antiquity whose help I should try to enlist. *Any* historian of the classical era, they explained kindly, had to be an authority on warfare: war was what the classical era was all about. I knew enough to avoid a similar humiliation at the hands of my medievalist colleagues, who would have told me the same about European history between the fifth and the fifteenth centuries.

As for the Renaissance, the late John Hale was already reminding us in his work how intrinsic a part warfare played in the molding of its entire culture. Only for three centuries of European history at the most, between the sixteenth to the nineteenth, was it possible to regard warfare as an intermittent activity, conducted by a class of specialists, that could be studied in isolation, before in the twentieth there dawned what has been called "The Age of Total War"; war not only total but global. In that century, war – preparing for it, waging it, deterring it – became a dimension of human history that no historian can neglect. As Trotsky is alleged to have put it, "You may not be interested in war, but war is very interested in you." The military historian can no longer write about it without understanding that "military history" is only one dimension of the history of war that is of little value if not studied in its social and political context. Today, even the most unregenerate of military historians feels uneasy unless his or her work is legitimized by the rubric "War and Society."

The concept "War and Society" is as significant in its way as "War Studies." If "War Studies" represented an attempt by military historians to extend their territory to cover the nonmilitary aspects of warfare, "War and Society" was the enterprise of social historians exploring the impact of war on the whole structure, initially on industrial and postindustrial society, but eventually on social development throughout the ages. Something of the kind had been pioneered in the early twentieth century by a few German historians like Werner Sombart and Hans Delbruck, but otherwise it had been widely neglected. It had no didactic value for military historians, while the first generation of British social historians was temperamentally hostile to the whole idea that war could have anything but a negative impact on the development of mankind. The overlap between these two approaches has been vast and immensely fruitful; but, for "War and Society" in particular, the catalytic moment was probably the fiftieth anniversary of the outbreak of the First World War in 1964 and the celebrations of that event in the media.

"Celebrations" is perhaps not the right word to describe the remorseless emphasis given at the time, and ever since, to the worst ordeals suffered by the British Army on the Western Front. In the eyes of the general public, the experience of the "Great War" is encapsulated in two words, "Somme" and "Passchendaele." The reasons for fighting the war, and the fact that we actually won it, passed almost unnoticed. A suggestion that I made a few years later that the victorious "Battle of a Hundred Days" in 1918 was at least as deserving of national celebrations as the ordeals of the Somme sank like the proverbial stone. Perhaps this was not to be regretted. Anything that diminished the mindless glorification of war was certainly to be encouraged, although I have observed very little of such glorification in my own lifetime.

But what needed to be recalled was not so much the operational events of the war, whether triumphant or disastrous, as the social mobilization of the entire community; the massive and willing national participation in the war effort; and the birth, if only through an accumulation of individual tragedies across barriers of class and wealth, of a new sense of popular self-consciousness that transformed British, and indeed, European society. The proliferation of work published during the past forty years, in this country and in Germany, in particular, has shown how successfully the concept of "War and Society" has extended its sway in the academic, if not yet the popular, mind.

I discovered this – if I may again be self-referential – when I was commissioned by the Oxford University Press to contribute a volume on the First World War in their series of "very short introductions" to such enormous subjects as philosophy, religion, or art. I was asked to submit a synopsis to be sent to anonymous referees, and their comments were revealing. What, they asked, was I going to say about civil–military relations? About high and low culture? About industrial mobilization? About the changing role of women in belligerent societies? About the historiography of the war and its reflection of national bias? About the function of war in catalyzing revolution? About the memorialization of the war? About the development of mass media and its influences on public opinion? All this was very helpful but a little bewildering, given that I had only 40,000 words to play with. Fortunately, cutting through this clamor of advice, I seemed to hear the voice of Charles Webster thundering "It's a book about war, isn't it? So write about the War!" So I did.

The comments of the referees were gratifying in that they showed how widely accepted the concept of "War and Society" has now become. But they also illustrated what might be termed a kind of historiographical "flight to the suburbs." A populous and lucrative industrial estate has grown up around the old center of military history, populated by social and economic historians who – rather like the inhabitants of Los Angeles – feel no necessity to visit that center, and are barely aware that it exists. Their reluctance is not altogether surprising. For at least a generation, it was inhabited mainly by a sleazy and shifting population of popular and impressionistic writers of the "lions led by donkeys" school, earning a fast buck before going on to some more lucrative racket. They found it unnecessary to go through the tedious business of working from contemporary documents, analyzing the technical problems that staff officers and commanders in the field had to solve, and assessing in any scientific and scholarly fashion the causes of their success or failure.

Only gradually was the inner city reoccupied by serious professionals: Trevor Wilson and Robin Prior, preeminently; Tim Travers, Paddy Griffiths; Gary Sheffield, Ian Beckett: scholars patiently illuminating, by their detailed and well-documented studies, why the war was fought, and perhaps had to be fought, in the way that it was. Even so, the failure even by the most eminent of "general historians" of the war to take account of their work was starkly illustrated by Sir John Keegan's astonishing description of it as a "pointless waste."

Nonetheless, if we are to understand why the war was such a catastrophe for the generation that fought it, why it bankrupted all its European participants and destroyed four empires, it is to the despised military historians that we have to turn. It was the demands of the military that resulted in the total mobilization not only of men, but also of industry and the transformation of the social order, whether peacefully or by violent revolution. Why did the military make such insatiable demands? Why were their expectations of a short war falsified? Was there a "Schlieffen Plan," and if so, why did it fail? Why were those huge battles on the Eastern Front so indecisive? Why were the attacks on the Western Front for long such bloody failures? Much can be made of the inexperience of the British High Command and the slowness of its "learning curve," but why were the French no better? And if the Germans were better – as I think they were – then why was this so?

The only way to answer these questions is to plough through the military documentation: the training manuals, the operational orders, the war diaries, the plans for operations as they developed at every level of command, the after-action reports, the organization of logistics, all the huge mass of paper always engendered by armies generally known as "bumf"; paper without which not a single soldier can be recruited, paid, fed, armed, trained, posted, punished, promoted, sent into battle, hospitalized if wounded, decorated if deserving, and buried with his next of kin informed, if he gets killed. Not all of this is necessary to the understanding of what happens in battle and why, but it helps, if only because it reveals the vast complexity of the conduct of war in the industrial age and the demands that the maintenance of even the most efficient armies made on the national economy. When the armies were not efficient – and the inefficiency of the Russian and Austro-Hungarian armies beggars belief – the sheer effort of their maintenance and replacement was enough to stretch their national economies beyond the breaking point. At least, it was if the war went on for long enough, as in 1914–18 it did. But why did it?

For the answer to these questions, we have to turn in the first place to the lowly military historians. They will start with the development of railways and telegraphs that made possible the deployment of *Millionenheere*, armies numbering millions, a development disastrously some fifty years in advance of that of the radio communications needed for the tactical control of armies in the field. They will go on to describe the huge advantage given to the defense by the development of breech-loading firearms and the attempts to counter it by intensifying artillery fire. They will explain the problems to which this gave rise in coordinating fire and movement – the essence of all military operations – in the absence of reliable battlefield communications. They will show how, on the Western Front, each side gradually learned from its mistakes, but often applied that learning only to find that its adversary had learned a little more. They will trace the evolution of weapons systems until by 1918 – on the Western Front at least – the war was being fought by armies using doctrines and techniques that would have been impractical and inconceivable four years earlier. It is only by studying this technical operational history in some detail that we can understand how this happened and answer the question, whether this transformation could have occurred any more rapidly and any more effectively than it did, and judge the performance of the high commands accordingly.

Any historian who tries to tackle the history of the war without first dealing with these basic questions is ill qualified for his task, to put it very mildly. War is too serious a business for its history to be tackled without first learning how to use the basic tools of the military historian. But we must go on to ask further questions for which these tools can provide little help. Why did civil society respond so readily to the demands of the military and not collapse under the strain? Was blockade as effective a weapon as the British Admiralty had expected, and why was Germany able to withstand it for so long? How did the strain of operations affect the political and social structure of the belligerent powers? All these are immense questions that will occupy historians for many years to come. But they would not have even been raised if the war had not lasted for so many years, and only the military historian can explain to us why it did.

Interestingly, the same questions do not arise, or do not arise with the same urgency, when we consider the Second World War. That war itself did not transform the belligerent societies that were fighting it. In the First World War, the defeat of the Habsburg and Russian Empires can be attributed directly, and that of the Hohenzollens indirectly, to the strain on their economies. There were no "decisive battles" in the First World War – not even Tannenberg. The outcome of the so-called "battles" on the Western Front – Verdun, the Somme, Passchendaele – still has to be judged in terms of the grisly statistics of attrition.

But that did not apply in the Second World War. It was defeat in the field that destroyed both the Nazi and Japanese Empires, not internal revolution. Both remained politically intact to the bitter end. Military victory, if anything, strengthened the political systems of the victorious powers, Soviet communism and Anglo-American democracy. Britain certainly emerged impoverished, but with its parliamentary system intact, and from

the perspective of half a century it is hard to believe that the two most evident results of the war – the growth of social democracy at home, the loss of
Empire abroad – were anything more than the acceleration by a few decades
of long-term and inescapable trends. As a result, we do not have to study
that war in such depth as we do the First World War if we are to understand
its outcome: the military historians can on their own provide us with very
satisfactory answers. The Blitzkrieg of 1940, the Battle of Britain, the Battle
of the Atlantic, Japan's conquest of Southeast Asia, the great naval battles
in the Pacific, the bombing offensive against Germany, the Normandy landings, and above all, the German invasion of the Soviet Union and its repulse –
these were the events that cumulatively determined the outcome of the war,
and they were undoubtedly events military historians are most competent
to analyze and describe. Military history is inescapably the core of the history of the First World War. For that of the Second World War, it must be
dominant.

Where operational history is dominant, so also is the element of the *contingent*, the counterfactual, something that most historians prefer to consign
to the most obscure pornography shelves. Whether they are right to do so is
perhaps debatable. Maybe we should consider legalizing it for personal use,
in private, among consenting adults, and under strict medical supervision, if
only because, for military historian at least, the temptation to take an occasional snorter is sometimes overwhelming. My own obsession, I must admit,
is 1940. What if Göring had not prematurely switched the Luftwaffe from
tactical to strategic targets, from airfields to ports and cities, thus leaving
radar installations intact and giving Fighter Command a chance to recover?
What if Hitler had not abandoned "Operation Sealion" and given priority
instead to the invasion of the Soviet Union? What would have happened
if Germany had successfully invaded the United Kingdom? What, not least
important, would have happened to me?

How far the history of either world war is relevant to the conduct of present
or future wars is for our colleagues in staff colleges to discuss. They will probably prefer to dig deeper into the past to find relevant wisdom. The Russian
conquest of the Caucasus? Britain's campaign on the Indian Northwest
Frontier and Afghanistan? The American pacification of the Philippines?
Perhaps even the Third Crusade? I would prefer to not speculate. I can only
reemphasize my message, that despite the flight to the suburbs, despite the
growth of "war studies" and "war and society" – a growth that I have myself
done my best to stimulate and encourage, and whose growth I regard with
some parental pride – at the center of the history of war there must lie the
study of military history – that is, the study of the central activity of the
armed forces, that is, *fighting*.

Part I

The influence of history on the military profession

3

The relevance of history to the military profession: a British view

JOHN P. KISZELY

Although the extent to which history in general is relevant to the military profession is a matter for debate, I doubt that there is much argument to be had that, in principle, a knowledge and understanding of *military* history is at least of some relevance and, indeed, use. But to what extent has the British military, in particular the British Army, recognized and exploited this relevance? And if we have a *use* for military history, do we still have a *need* for it in the twenty-first century? If so, how much? This chapter sets out to answer these questions from the personal perspective of a British military professional.

The military profession in the United Kingdom has had a highly variable attitude toward military history over the past century or so. Of course, the services have contained many individuals with a love of military history and many who have found in it some utility in their profession. There are those who have studied military history at university, and some who have continued to study it throughout their careers, although it is impossible even to estimate their number. Rather easier to quantify would be the number of those who have made important written contributions to the subject, either when retired or while still serving, but it is striking to note the low proportion in the latter category. The attitude to military history of the military *establishment* has been particularly variable, surprisingly so given what appears to be the rather obvious potential contribution that a study of military history offers to a better understanding of the military profession. Taking the Army as an example, although there have certainly been professional heads of the Army – the Chiefs of the General Staff, and their predecessors, Chiefs of the Imperial General Staff (CIGS) – who have sought to emphasize and

The views expressed in this chapter are purely personal and do not necessarily reflect British government policy.

encourage this professional link, there have also been many who appeared indifferent about it, and some who appeared downright hostile. The CIGS from 1933 to 1936, Field Marshal Sir Archibald Montgomery-Massingberd, railed against "those who think that because they have read a little military history, everyone else is an ignoramus."[1] This, of course, was a rebuke, probably justified, against arrogance; but I doubt that, while Montgomery-Massingberd was still serving, too many officers were to be heard admitting to reading military history, let alone encouraging others to do so. The Army has not been alone here. Some twenty years earlier, Admiral Sir John Fisher, the First Sea Lord (the professional head of the Royal Navy), had made his views plain on the subject: "Whatever service the past may be to other professions, it can be categorically stated in regard to the Navy that history is a record of exploded ideas. Every condition of the past is altered."[2]

But retaining the focus on the British Army, a number of factors appear to have been at play here. First, the early twentieth-century Army was not a literary or intellectual army in any sense. It believed spare time was best occupied, not in reading – one of the most damning epithets an officer could attract was "bookish"[3] – but in physical activities such as hunting, and playing games and sports, the latter memorably described by J. F. C. Fuller as having "no more military value than playing fiddles or painting postcards." Second, the opportunities to study military history as part of the military curriculum were few and far between. Because only a small proportion of officers attended staff college, officer cadet training was the first and last formal instruction in military history that most received. Moreover, such study often tended to be highly factual and antiquarian in nature,[4] either following the Victorian and Edwardian traditions of celebrating imperial triumphs, or else indulging in what was claimed to be science, but of the type graphically described by Sir Basil Liddell Hart as "enumerat(ing) the blades of grass in the Shenandoah Valley."[5] Moreover, those who did indulge in military historical studies of a critical nature, such as Fuller and Liddell Hart, were perceived to be undermining good order and military discipline by so doing. A similar view continued in the War Office and the Ministry of Defence to the close of the twentieth century, with officers strongly discouraged, not least by bureaucratic censorship, from publishing anything that could possibly be construed as contentious.

In the past thirty-five years or so, the period of my service, military history in the British Army has received a stronger profile. When I joined, most officer cadets entering the Army had the benefit of the outstanding military

---

[1] J. F. C. Fuller, *Memoirs of an Unconventional Soldier* (London, 1936), p. 434.
[2] Jay Luvaas, *The Education of an Army* (London, 1965), p. 275.
[3] Ibid.
[4] J. F. C. Fuller, *Generalship: Its Diseases and Their Cures* (London, 1938), p. 81.
[5] B. H. Liddell Hart, *The Remaking of Modern Armies* (London, 1927), p. 170.

history department at the Royal Military Academy, Sandhurst, and its small group of distinguished and inspiring instructors, which, when I was there, included John Keegan and Brigadier Peter Young, the latter occasionally to be seen in the full military uniform of a Cavalier general from the English Civil War. In the days of the two-year program at Sandhurst, there was a high course content of military history, with the time to read and reflect – a luxury that, despite the continuing quality of instruction at Sandhurst, few of today's officer cadets would claim to have. Both of the Army staff courses, which existed for captains and majors, had some military history content, but it is noteworthy that a resident historian at the Army staff college was only appointed in 1987, after a gap of some eighty years. I do not remember having time on either course for much extracurricular study, let alone reflection, although I certainly did have such time as an instructor at the staff college and subsequently as a student, and later director, of the Higher Command and Staff Course (HCSC).[6] Although that course lays considerable emphasis on military history and its part in the education of a senior commander, the whole course was, and remains, only three months long. I doubt that Gerd von Scharnhorst would consider such a course to be anything more than a little light entertainment.

What the HCSC certainly used to achieve, and I hope still does, is to inspire in its graduates the further study of military history. An addition to mainstream staff training in the last decade, though, is a master's degree in War Studies, albeit for only about half of those Army students attending. There has also been increasing use throughout the Army of battlefield tours and staff rides. But all this instruction in military history amounts to a very limited total; and it has always surprised me how few officers – senior ones, too – have seen the need to supplement this instruction with continuous and systematic study. There is also a paradox here: the potential penalty of a poor understanding of military history increases with rank; yet, contrary to popular belief, the time available for the necessary study decreases with rank. Such understanding is not something a general officer can leave until he or she arrives at that rank. One can only acquire a proper understanding of history through continuous and systematic study in one's own time, and over a considerable period of time. In short, it is easy to underestimate the degree to which, in the British Army at least, military education is a question of self-education.

In analyzing how a study of military history can be of practical use to the military professional, we need to have ringing in our ears the warnings of Professor Sir Michael Howard in his 1961 lecture, "The Use and Abuse of Military History," that military history should be studied with care, and

---

[6] The equivalent of the U.S. Army's SAMS Course and the U.S. Marine Corps' SAW.

specifically "in width, in depth and in context."[7] There are certainly dangers of drawing false lessons in not doing so, just as there are in believing that, for the participant, the battlefield is as some historians depict it – a neat, ordered place in which it is always possible to determine precisely not only what happened and where, but why. As well as studying military history within the context of wider historical studies – for example, political, economic, and social history – the military professional can usefully study military history as part of the much wider context of war studies alongside more contemporary strategic and social studies.

But this argument can be taken to extremes. In the late 1960s, some advocates of war studies were proposing that military professionals should strictly limit their study of military history to that which was deemed to be "relevant." They argued that

> Military history necessarily deals with a past which is in many ways tactically, strategically, politically, economically and certainly technically irrelevant to the military present and future of any contemporary major industrial power ... and that ... nuclear weapons and delivery systems, modern surveillance and communications techniques, guided missiles, the growth of super-powers and the emergence of the phenomenon known as People's Revolutionary War have rendered a great deal of pre-1945 warfare of no more than antiquarian interest.[8]

Similar voices are to be heard at the start of the twenty-first century. They claim that the nature of warfare has been fundamentally changed by the pace and scale of technological development; that, as Admiral Fisher argued, "Every condition of the past is altered"; and that, as a result, history is, indeed "a record of exploded ideas." Certainly, major technological changes – and, indeed, social and political changes – should cause us to apply particular circumspection when drawing conclusions from military history. In seeking to identify from our studies the constant and variable factors, we should be prepared to find that more of the constants have become variables.

But even if the technological change amounts, as some claim, to a revolution in military affairs, this does not invalidate a study of military history or even reduce its relevance. Similar claims of the irrelevance of the past were made at the advent of other major technological developments, such as the introduction of gunpowder and the aeroplane, as well as nuclear weapons; and in retrospect history has underlined that such claims were simply misguided and erroneous. Taking the long view, we may conclude that warfare adapts to circumstances, that its development is evolutionary rather than

---

[7] Michael Howard, "The Use and Abuse of Military History," *Journal of the Royal United Services Institution*, vol. CV II, no. 625, 1962, p. 8.

[8] Lt. Col. (later Major General, and Director of the Royal Army Education Corps) A. J. Trythall, "What Are War Studies?" *British Army Review*, no. 35, August 1970, pp. 21–4.

revolutionary. As Clausewitz observed, "All wars are things of the same nature."[9]

The military professional is, however, likely to approach the subject of military history in a rather different way from the historian. The latter seeks to find out, as Leopold von Ranke famously put it, "[w]hat really happened."[10] The military professional is likely to want to go further and to study the subject with an eye to the future – that is to say, to seek insights, gain an understanding of warfare, and draw conclusions that may be of professional use later in his or her career. This, of course, requires a particularly critical and skeptical approach, an understanding that such an approach may distort the clarity of historical vision, and an awareness that false insights, unsound conclusions, and erroneous lessons offer themselves everywhere like fools' gold to the unwary prospector. Furthermore, sound judgment in this matter requires reflective analysis. As Frederick the Great observed, "[w]hat is the good of experience if you do not reflect?"[11] Clausewitz said much the same point: "The knowledge needed by a senior commander is distinguished by the fact that it can only be attained by a special talent, through the medium of reflection, study and thought."[12]

This does not sit easily with the practice, all too prevalent in staff colleges, of "learning against the clock." The concept of speed-reading a voluminous book list has limited value and is often counterproductive. Time for reflection, study, and thought is essential if insights are to be gained and valid conclusions drawn. Some combat experience can be of benefit in this process. It allows one to recognize on the printed page a proposal or conclusion that chimes exactly with one's own operational experience, or what one recognizes as a truth as a result of that experience. Experience thus becomes a sounding board. The inherent danger, of course, is that one's own errant judgment and prejudices can thus become reinforced, or that one seeks to generalize from the particular without taking due account of changing circumstances. This points toward the necessity for military professionals to be guided and mentored in their study of military history by historians, and for this process to be conducted face to face rather than by correspondence course. Too often the latter results in oversimplistic formulae, templated solutions, and erroneous lessons.

It does not take a lifetime's study of military affairs to sense a warning about trying to master the profession of arms without study of military history. Take the necessity to recognize and understand Clausewitzian friction – "the countless minor incidents, the kind you can never really

---

[9] Carl von Clausewitz, *On War*, ed. and trans. Michael Howard and Peter Paret (Princeton, NJ, 1976), p. 606.

[10] Howard, "The Use and Abuse of Military History," p. 5.

[11] Fuller, *Generalship*, p. 79.

[12] Clausewitz, *On War*, p. 146.

foresee – (which) combine to lower the general level of performance, so that one always falls far short of the intended goal . . . the only concept that distinguishes real war from war on paper."[13] To his own question, "[I]s there any lubricant that will reduce this abrasion?" Clausewitz's clear answer was, "[o]nly one, and a commander and his army will not always have it readily available: combat experience." But combat experience – direct experience of the sharp end of the battlefield – is a commodity in increasingly short supply. And we should note Scharnhorst's warning that "[n]othing is more dangerous . . . than using personal experience without regard for that experience which military history teaches us."[14]

Although it cannot be a full substitute, military history can at least give some understanding of the phenomenon of friction, how it affected other commanders, and how they sought to deal with it. True, simulation and operational analysis can be most useful tools in this respect, but I would suggest that without military history, both are remarkably two-dimensional and shallow. We should beware the scientific purists, all too prevalent in operational analysis, who reject the inclusion of military history because its data are difficult, if not impossible, to quantify. In this respect, we may have something to learn from the former Soviet Army – an avid advocate of the use of military history for the purposes of operational analysis.[15]

The same applies to understanding the human dimension of warfare, the psychology of the soldier, sailor, and airman. In the absence of combat experience, how can you possibly understand this critical dimension of the military profession without studying military history? I found that on the battlefield I recognized in my company many of the characters I had met before in first-hand accounts about warfare, not only in the twentieth century but also in the accounts – all too rare accounts – of private soldiers of earlier times, such as Edward Costello in the Peninsula,[16] Thomas Morris at Waterloo,[17] and Rifleman Harris retreating from Corunna.[18] Circumstances may have been different, but the psychology of participants on the battlefield remains much the same; learning, for example, how soldiers on other battlefields in other times viewed their officers is not without utility for the officer of today.

Military history also warns us of the pressures on commanders and the remarkably low tolerance that commanders have for each other. There are famous examples of such personality clashes; not for nothing is Norman

[13] Ibid., p. 119.
[14] Charles White, *The Enlightened Soldier. Scharnhorst and the Militärische Gesellschaft 1801–1805* (New York, 1989), p. 9.
[15] See, for example, Christopher Donnelly, "The Soviet Use of Military History for Operational Analysis," *British Army Review*, no. 87, December 1987.
[16] Peter Young, ed., *The Peninsula and Waterloo Campaingns: Edward Costello* (London, 1967).
[17] John Selby, ed., *The Napoleonic Wars: Thomas Morris* (London, 1967).
[18] Henry Curling, ed., *Reflections of Rifleman Harris* (London, 1848).

Gelb's book on Eisenhower and Montgomery subtitled *Generals at War*.[19]
Indeed, it is far easier to find similar examples of serious discord among
senior commanders, and not just multinational ones, than it is to recollect
a campaign in which commanders were all in harmony. Without a study of
military history, this phenomenon would not be apparent – exercises simply
do not produce the same pressures – and commanders need to anticipate
that, despite their protestations to the contrary, they too are likely to fall
prey to these pressures and need to take action to prevent such potentially
disastrous, dysfunctional behavior.

A further key attribute of a commander for which military history seems
to me to play a vital role is in the development of intuition or *coup d'oeil*,
which as Clausewitz reminds us "refers not only to the physical, but more
commonly, to the inward eye...the quick recognition of a truth that the
mind would ordinarily miss or would perceive only after long study and
reflection."[20] Many people might think that those Great Captains renowned
for their intuition possessed some sort of second sight. But, surely, few, if
any of them, were born with it. Instead, they built up intuition largely based
on combat experience, over many years. For example, according to John
Keegan, "Wellington's battles were so many that by 1815 even he might
have had trouble enumerating them...sixteen battles and eight sieges as a
commander, several more as a subordinate."[21] His experience is overtaken
by Napoleon's and completely eclipsed by commanders such as Alexander
the Great and Hannibal.

When Rommel said in the Western Desert that "[i]t is given to me to feel
where the enemy is weak"[22] – and this was no idle boast – it was the result,
in large part, of the huge experience that he had acquired as a commander
in combat at many levels in two world wars. Rommel himself might have
disputed this. He said, "It is often not a question of which of the opposing commanders is the highest qualified, or which of them has the greater
experience, but which of them has the better grasp of the battlefield."[23] The
better grasp, surely, was founded on the breadth and depth of his combat
experience, together with a considerable knowledge of military history, of
which Rommel was a serious student. In the absence of extensive combat
experience, an extensive study of military history seems to me an indispens-
able ingredient in the development of battlefield intuition. I find it difficult,
therefore, to see how a commander who has forgone such a study can possess
intuition when he or she encounters the battlefield.

---

[19]   Norman Gelb, *Ike and Monty – Generals at War* (London, 1994).
[20]   Clausewitz, *On War*, p. 102.
[21]   John Keegan, *The Mask of Command* (London, 1987), p. 92.
[22]   David Fraser, *Knight's Cross. A Life of Field Marshal Erwin Rommel* (New York, 1993),
       p. 227.
[23]   Richard Simpkin, *Race to the Swift* (London, 1985), p. 235.

Among examples of the continuing utility of military history to the soldier on the battlefield, it would be remiss to omit that which might appear most obvious to the layman, if most odious to the historian: inspiration. Much military history has been written with this in mind, and the fact that much of it is poor military history makes it none the less inspiring. Reading of heroes who defied the odds but triumphed has sustained many soldiers in difficult situations and inspired them to feats of arms. British regimental histories are particularly rich veins in this genre of hagiography, with never a bad word for the performance of The Regiment in order to sustain the legend, well in the spirit of the critic of the French military reforms in the late nineteenth century who argued that "[t]he man who destroys the legend destroys the faith, and whoever destroys the faith destroys an immeasurable force in which every race, one after another, has sought victory."[24]

I admit unashamedly that on the eve of battle I drew strength from thinking of the many generations of warriors in my own regiment who had kept the faith and preserved the honour of The Regiment, and who were looking down, placing their trust in the present generation to do likewise. But purveying military history for this purpose – preserving the legend to preserve the faith – may, in the longer run, do much more harm than good by delivering false lessons and perverting the course of progress.

It is not only on the battlefield or on operations that a knowledge and understanding of history has continuing potential utility for the military professional. The latter is involved in policy making across the whole spectrum of defense at governmental level – for example, weapon acquisition, strategy, force development, military theory, and doctrine. It is, surely, little short of negligent to make decisions in any of these policy areas without at least testing one's thesis against the experience provided by history. The relationship between, on the one hand, military theory and doctrine and, on the other hand, military history is, or should be, a particularly strong one in this regard.

Not only should military history act as a sounding board for doctrine, against which to test new theories, but also as a catalyst to initiate doctrinal change. Where this link is strong, military theory and doctrine are more likely to flourish – for example, in the nineteenth century, Prussian *Kriegsakademie* and *Militärische Gesellschaft*, and in the Soviet Army, before the 1937 purge and in the last half of the twentieth century. The reverse is also true. The link within the British Army has not been a strong one in the past century, although certainly stronger since the creation a decade ago of the Directorate of Doctrine and Development. Although we tend to congratulate ourselves on the creation of the Higher Command and Staff Course in 1988, perhaps

---

[24] Quoted by Michael Howard, *The Franco-Prussian War* (London, 1981), p. 37.

we should instead be asking ourselves why it was that British Army doctrine took until 1988 to recognize even the existence of the operational level of war, and whether we have taken sufficient steps to ensure we are not quite so far behind the curve in future.

Following on from this, a significant contribution of a knowledge of history is to help our understanding of our own military culture: our nature and ethos, the characteristic way in which we go about our business and think about our profession. Our military culture acts as a prism through which we, as military people, see military affairs, and which shapes our view of them. Armed forces need to be highly aware of this prism, and the distorting effect it may be having on their perspective, if they are to see military affairs clearly and objectively. For example, the British Army's military culture has in the past, and not too distant past, included characteristics such as innate conservatism, parochialism, and a predilection for an attritional approach to warfare. Whatever our military culture today, we would do well to take it constantly into account when making judgments on military affairs. Because military culture is in large part influenced by heritage, a study of history is essential to an understanding of our military culture.[25]

To what extent is a study of military history relevant for peace support operations? There are certainly those who excuse themselves from such study on the grounds that military history has little relevance in an era where the majority of operations are likely to be peacekeeping or peace enforcement. This seems to me to be dangerously short sighted. Failing to study past peace support operations, just as for warfighting operations, risks repeating the errors of the past. Furthermore, there are many generic similarities between the two. For example, the basic need to understand one's opponents, and to work out how best to outmaneuver them mentally is far from confined to combat.

I doubt, however, that the nature of future conflict will allow many campaigns to be neatly categorized as either warfighting or peacekeeping. As General Krulak, former commandant of the U.S. Marine Corps, has indicated with his notion of a "three block war," a single campaign may easily encompass warfighting, peace support operations, and humanitarian operations, possibly simultaneously in different parts of a theatre, and this underlines the degree of breadth with which future commanders will need to study their military history. And a study of history may point them toward the need to understand both the sociopolitical context of their military action, and the dangers of the all-too-prevalent military practice of applying treatments for the symptoms, which serve to exacerbate the causes.

---

[25] See also Williamson Murray, "Does Military Culture Matter?" *Orbis*, Winter 1999, pp. 27–42, and J. P. Kiszely, "The British Army and Approaches to Warfare Since 1945," in Brian Holden Reid, ed., *Military Power: Land Warfare in Theory and Practice* (London, 1997).

Whatever the nature of the campaign, we are also likely to be operating in coalitions, for which military history offers important lessons. It is my experience of multinational operations that those participants with little inclination for the study of other people's history can too easily fail to see the vital need to empathize with – to understand – those with whom they are dealing, whether as allies, opponents, or other involved parties. Without some sense of history, there is also a temptation toward short termism. I recollect during my early service in Northern Ireland seeing well-intentioned commanders who believed they could solve three hundred years of history in a four-month tour of duty, leaving sadder but not always wiser, their actions having actually been counterproductive to the achievement of the long-term goals of the campaign.

In conclusion, though, I would not want to suggest that military history is some kind of magic talisman for the military professional. We should beware, just as Field Marshal Montgomery-Massingberd warned, "those who think that just because they have read a little military history that everyone else is an ignoramus." A little military history may be more dangerous than none at all. Similarly, we should treat with circumspection those who believe the study of military history can in some way substitute for wider professional study. Military history must be part of a balanced diet, alongside, for example, the study of military theory, operational analysis, and training. Not that there is anything new in that thought. Over a century and a half ago, Baron Jomini was asserting, "[c]orrect theories, founded upon right principles, sustained by actual events of wars and added to accurate military history will form a true school for instruction for generals."[26]

Military history thus helps provide the theoretical foundation for the science of war, and continues to do so even in an era of huge technological and social change. Military history also provides the military professional with an aid to judgment, a tool to help test the validity and practical application of new theory or new weapons and equipment. Without some sense and understanding of history, it is too easy to fail to recognize the snake oil salesman for what he is. Our military education and training regimes thus need to provide a balanced program, and one of intellectual rigour.

Given, however, that the instructional courses in all our armed forces are time constrained, often increasingly so, how do we establish and retain this balance while studying our military history in sufficient width, depth, and context? The temptation, it seems, is to attempt to square this circle by forgoing some of the width, depth, and context, with all the potential danger that that entails, and to mistake the study of military history as training rather than education. A particular danger is that because the "output" of the study of military history is impossible to quantify, such study becomes vulnerable

[26] A. Jomini, *The Art of War* (London, 1992), p. 321.

to cuts when resources are tight. But, finally, if the time available for formal instruction is insufficient, we must accept that the necessary education in military history is largely a matter for individual self-education. If this is so, the primary duty of the military history instructor is to enthuse and inspire, and thereby to act as a catalyst in this process.

4

The relevance of history to the military profession: an American Marine's view

PAUL K. VAN RIPER

When I enlisted in the U.S. Marine Corps in 1956, the American military placed little emphasis on nontechnical professional education. The well-developed curricula – much of it based on the study of history – that served World War II's leaders so well no longer existed. In their place stood courses dominated by political science and management philosophies. Fortunately for the United States, the situation altered considerably over the next forty years, although only at great cost. Advancing from private to lieutenant general during those four decades, I found myself initially a victim and later a beneficiary of military schooling.

The weak and uninspiring education system I first encountered might have survived far longer had it not been for the tragedy of the Vietnam War. That conflict and its aftermath provided the catalyst for much-needed change. At the center of the transformation lay a renewed interest in the study of military history. The American military's performance in Iraq during Operation Desert Storm and the major combat phase of Operation Iraqi Freedom, as well as its recent accomplishments in Afghanistan, offer compelling evidence of the value of the improvements made in the American armed forces between 1974 and 1991, none more so than the fundamental alterations in professional education.

In the following pages – after briefly outlining how the American military education system progressed over a century and a quarter only to lose its way in the early Cold War years – I have chronicled my own professional education and its importance to my development as a leader. I close with a cautionary note expressing concern that the gains of the past twenty years may be slipping away in a manner reminiscent of that earlier era.

POST–WORLD WAR II PROFESSIONAL
MILITARY EDUCATION

The American military, along with many European militaries, evidenced a disdain for overt intellectual activities by its officers for much of the nineteenth and twentieth centuries. To most officers, such interests fell short in reflecting the manliness expected of those in uniform. Hard fighting, hard riding, and hard drinking elicited far more appreciation from an officer's peers than the perusal of books. Commenting on a recent study of the nation's military profession, one present-day commentator notes, "[w]e glimpse in finely wrought microcosm the current of anti-intellectualism that has coursed through American arms from its earliest beginnings to the present day."[1] Seeds of this anti-intellectualism remain, despite the efforts of several generations of reformers dedicated to improving professional military education.

Emory Upton, a U.S. Army officer who spent his adult life urging reform of the American military, laid the foundations of officer professional military education in the United States. Others in the early part of the nineteenth century, such as Stephen B. Luce, Tasker Bliss, Alfred Thayer Mahan, and Elihu Root, built on Upton's initial efforts in their own attempts to further the professional development of officers. All met resistance in their time, but by the mid-1920s their ideas guided the study of war in most service academies, staff schools, and war colleges. History formed the core of much of the instruction in such institutions, especially in those courses focused on operations and strategy. During the 1920s and 1930s, Generals George C. Marshall and Dwight D. Eisenhower, Admirals Chester W. Nimitz and Raymond A. Spruance, and a host of other World War II leaders attended classes enriched with military history. Many later attested to the importance of that historically grounded education. In his autobiography, Eisenhower described his time at the Army's Command and General Staff School – from which he graduated first in the class of 1926 – as "a watershed in my life."[2]

---

[1] Lloyd J. Matthews, "The Unified Intellectual and His Place in American Arms," *Army Magazine*, July 2002, p. 1. The book he references is William Skelton, *The American Profession of Arms: The Army Officer Corps, 1784–1861*.

[2] Dwight D. Eisenhower, *At Ease: Stories I Tell to Friends* (Garden City, NY, 1967), p. 200. For a detailed description of Eisenhower's experience at Command and General Staff School (now called a "College"), see Mark C. Bender, *Watershed at Leavenworth: Dwight D. Eisenhower and the Command and General Staff School* (Fort Leavenworth, KS, 1990). Ronald Spector, maintaining that the Naval War College curriculum was too narrow and technically focused, calls into question claims of senior World War II navy leaders that their War College education proved invaluable to prosecuting that conflict. See Ronald Spector, *Professors of War: The Naval War College and the Development of the Naval Profession* (Newport, RI, 1977), pp. 149 and 150. My own interpretation is that war games provided strength to the college's curriculum during this period, although these games focused on refighting past battles, especially Jutland.

Victory in 1945 seemingly validated the content of prewar professional military education; therefore, major changes appeared unlikely. However, a number of defense authorities concluded that the advent of atomic weapons negated any value to be gained from studying the past. In the ensuing years, even some prominent military historians questioned the relevance of their field. In 1961, Walter Millis wrote: "It is the belief of the present writer that military history has largely lost its function.... [I]t is not immediately apparent why the strategy and tactics of Nelson, Lee or even Bradley or Montgomery should be taught to the young men who are being trained to manage the unmanageable military colossi of today...."[3]

Through both design and neglect, those in positions of influence contributed to the virtual elimination of history from the core curricula of nearly every American professional military institution throughout the 1950s and early 1960s. In its place, they inserted courses not only on nuclear war, but also on systems engineering, operations analysis, and management. Senior officers clearly deemed the emerging quantitative methods as far more relevant to the new demands of command in the nuclear age. The shortsightedness of these post–World War II leaders meant that the Vietnam generation of military officers – of which I am one – learned its early professional lessons in programs largely devoid of history. America paid a high price for such myopic views, and the resulting undue emphasis on the science of war to the detriment of the art of war.

AN EARLY INTEREST IN MILITARY HISTORY

My first exposure to military history came in the late 1950s as a squad leader in a Marine Corps reserve unit. Enrolled in a college program with a history-centered curriculum, I found study of the past enjoyable. At the same time, knowledge of history appeared as if it might prove useful if I earned the officer's commission I sought. Not surprisingly, whenever I came across an advertisement for an inexpensive book on military history, I usually invested in a copy. Of the several books I bought during this period, two made notable and long-lasting impressions. The first, S. L. A. Marshall's *Men Against Fire: The Problem of Command in Future War*, cost only $1.35 in paperback.[4] I eagerly read and heavily annotated Marshall's analytical

---

[3] Walter Millis, *Military History* (Washington, DC, 1961), pp. 16–18.
[4] Although initially troubled by allegations concerning Marshall's research raised in several venues in the 1980s, as well as the subsequent controversy, I regained my former confidence when Dr. Roger J. Spiller, who questioned many of Marshall's research methods in the winter 1988 issue of the *RUSI Journal*, said he did not doubt the combat historian's conclusions stating, "Forty years later, as the quest for universal laws of combat continues unabated, Marshall is still right." (Quoted in a review of *Men Against Fire* in the July 1989 edition of *Military Review*, pp. 99 and 100.)

history of recent battles. I discovered much that seemed intuitively correct although not always obvious. In field exercises, I routinely tried to take into account Marshall's insights into leadership and small unit tactics.

The second influential book, T. R. Fehrenbach's *This Kind of War*, graphically detailed the penalties paid by poorly prepared U.S. Army units early in the Korean War. It made an indelible imprint on my mind in regard to the absolute necessity for challenging training and strict discipline in military organizations. The reputation I acquired as a hard-nosed leader found its start not only in the stern lessons taught by my drill instructors at Marine Corps Recruit Depot, but equally in those I drew from this book. I copied many passages from *This Kind of War* and returned to them for inspiration. My favorite was and remains: "In 1950 a Marine Corps officer was still an officer, and a sergeant behaved the way good sergeants had behaved since the time of Caesar, expecting no nonsense, allowing none. And Marine leaders had never lost sight of their primary – their only – mission, which was to fight."[5]

As a newly commissioned second lieutenant and student at the Marine Corps officers' basic course in early 1964, I encountered history only as a means of reinforcing the customs and traditions of the Marine Corps. This instruction involved little more than story telling – often inaccurate when it came to details, as I discovered afterward when I read that the red stripes along the trouser seams of officers' and noncommissioned officers' uniforms, usually referred to as "blood stripes," were not awarded in recognition of the high casualties Marine leaders suffered at the Battle of Chapultepec in the Mexican-American War. Apparently, the stripes served simply as a decorative flourish to officers' uniforms. Fundamentally, these classes offered a narrowly focused review of the organization's heritage – "drum-and-trumpet" military history at its finest – useful for its purpose, but not professionally enlightening.

Arriving at my first operational unit – a 2nd Marine Division infantry battalion – in late summer 1964, I found minimal interest in military history. Those officers who read of past battles and campaigns seldom advertised the fact. They judged it, I imagine, more an avocation than the heart of professional learning. Some bright spots existed. The *Marine Corps Gazette* offered military history books for sale at reduced prices and frequently presented articles examining past battles. A collection of *Gazette* articles appeared in an edited work entitled, *The Guerrilla – And How to Fight Him*, proving reasonably popular. Although more theoretical, Robert Osgood's *Limited War: The Challenge to American Strategy* also attracted attention. The magazine even identified a set of "military history classics" for purchase in a suitably marked box. Several new books on World War II generated moderate

[5] T. R. Fehrenbach, *This Kind of War* (New York, 1963), p. 188.

interest among my contemporaries, including the first two volumes of the
official *History of the U.S. Marine Corps in World War II* and Kenneth
Davis's *Experience of War: The United States in World War II*. Although my
own interest centered on reading and studying books dealing with irregular
or small wars – because we seemed more likely to face such wars in the near
future – I made efforts to at least peruse others. Perhaps most important,
my career-long habit of always having professional reading near at hand as
a guard against wasting unexpected free time began in this assignment.

When it came to small unit fighting, however, nothing surpassed the wisdom I found in *Men Against Fire*. After returning from my initial baptism of
fire in spring 1965 in the Dominican Republic, I re-read Marshall's book and
found my original evaluation reinforced. Over the succeeding thirty years,
I made revisiting his book a habit after each combat episode I experienced.
Always, I came to the same conclusion. This author-historian possessed an
extraordinary understanding of the close fight and wrote about his insights
as clearly and succinctly as anyone before or since.

Interest in reading military history increased among my fellow Marine officers as the war clouds over Vietnam grew darker. Reading about the French
experience in Indochina and the British experience in Malaya became fashionable. Copies of Bernard Fall's *Street Without Joy* appeared on more than
a few officers' desks. Still, many believed that sharpening their tactical and
technical proficiency outweighed the potential of intellectually preparing for
war. I confess to conflicted feelings at this point in my military life. Upon
receiving orders assigning me to an advisory billet with an infantry battalion
of the Vietnamese Marine Corps, I devoted more time to readying my personal equipment, boots, knife, map kit, and survival gear, and to improving
my physical fitness than to professional reading. I did, however, re-read *Men
Against Fire*.

A gunshot wound to the stomach shortened my tour in Vietnam by more
than half and placed me in a series of military hospitals for several months.
Thus, I was offered the opportunity to contemplate recent events. A growing
desire to understand my wartime experience led to a renewed and intense
interest in reading. I mentally created a more expansive and sophisticated
menu of books than the one I had turned to prior to my departure from
the United States the previous summer. I began with a survey of the history
of war with Lynn Montross's *War Through the Ages*. I then revisited the
situation in Southeast Asia with Bernard Fall's *The Two Vietnams*; tried to
understand the new type of war through David Rees's *Korea: The Limited
War*; and looked at the larger issues of war in B. H. Liddell Hart's *Strategy*
and Walter Goerlitz's *History of the German General Staff: 1657–1945*. I
formed no agenda or reasoned plan for my reading. Instead, I simply tried
to satisfy the gnawing feeling that I had known too little about war before
going to Vietnam.

After convalescence, there followed an assignment as an instructor at The Basic School in Quantico, where all the Corps' lieutenants undergo training to become rifle platoon commanders, regardless of their future occupational specialties. Faced with pending postings to Vietnam, these young officers readily sought advice on how to prepare themselves. When they asked how long it took to get ready for combat, my most common response was, "At least 100 years!" I then explained that no one wants to risk his life and those he leads without taking every opportunity to acquire the necessary skill and knowledge to succeed. Thus, any allotted time is always too short. The most frequent follow-up question concerned what to do in the time available. Here, I invariably urged each lieutenant to read, making clear the logic and efficiency of tapping into the collective wisdom of generations upon generations of warriors. I often repeated a quote from Liddell Hart, "There is no excuse for any literate person to be less than three-thousand years old in his mind."[6] By this point, I possessed my own list of recommended books to share, though, in hindsight it was weak in many respects, particularly regarding the nature and character of war.

I soon found myself in a position to follow my own advice, because after completing the instructor tour and attending the Amphibious Warfare School, I received orders returning me to Vietnam in summer 1968, on this occasion to serve as a rifle company commander.[7] My free time before this second tour in Southeast Asia focused on specialized reading instead of overly preparing personal equipment and exercising my body to an extreme. I wanted to know more about what it meant to be a professional warrior, so I struggled through both Morris Janowitz's *The Professional Soldier* and Samuel Huntington's *The Soldier and the State*, devoured Martin Russ's *The Last Parallel* to gain a better appreciation of infantry combat, and sought lessons on irregular war from Samuel B. Griffith's translation of *Mao Tse-Tung on Guerrilla Warfare*. I once again re-read *Men Against Fire* to great benefit. An article by then Captain Allan R. Millett – later to become a noted historian and a reserve "colonel of marines" – supported my notions about the importance of history, so much so that I clipped the piece, "Military History and the Professional Officer." To this day, it remains in my files.[8]

History offers no "lessons" for military officers. It does, though, provide a rich context for understanding the terrible phenomenon that was, is, and

---

[6] B. H. Liddell Hart, *Why We Don't Learn from History* (London, 1946), pp. 7–8.

[7] The use of history by Amphibious Warfare School instructors during my time there as a student appeared selective and primarily designed to support a specific teaching point. I often recalled examples that ran counter to the ones being cited. Such biased use of military history in military schools occurred all too frequently in the 1960s and 1970s.

[8] Allan R. Millet, "Military History and the Professional Officer," *Marine Corps Gazette*, April 1967, p. 51.

will remain war. The vicarious experiences provided through study of the past enable practitioners of war to see familiar patterns of activity and to develop more quickly potential solutions to tactical and operational problems. My several years of professional reading, for example, gave me a sense of confidence on the battlefield that I did not have during my previous tour in Vietnam. To the degree that the word has meaning in such circumstances, I became *comfortable*, whether under enemy fire or pressed to make rapid tactical decisions. "Mike" Company, 3rd Battalion, 7th Marines, soon developed a divisionwide reputation for success in battle, as well as for its ability to handle unique problems. The Viet Cong continue to fire long-range rockets at the Da Nang Airfield: put Mike Company on it. Need to stop North Vietnamese infiltrators: send for Mike Company. Only the inevitable casualties made command less than ideal. I could never identify a direct cause-and-effect relationship between the orders I gave in combat and the books I had previously read, but clearly a symbiotic connection existed. The second-hand wisdom gained from reading thousands of pages of military history synthesized over time in my mind and eventually merged with the experiences of previous firefights in the Dominican Republic and during my first tour in Vietnam. This combination of real and vicarious learning provided the ability to make well-informed judgments despite the inherent stresses of war.

FINDING A WIDER WORLD OF PROFESSIONAL STUDY

Eight years of varied postings after my second tour in Vietnam – instructor at the U.S. Army's Institute for Military Assistance, staff officer at Headquarters Marine Corps, battalion and regimental operations officer, and battalion executive officer in the 8th Marines – allowed sufficient free time to continue reading military history. Although I never doubted the value of my ongoing efforts, my methodology never seemed sufficiently organized. Selection and assignment to the Naval War College's naval command and staff course in summer 1977 soon eliminated this problem. Admiral Stansfield Turner had recognized the harm done to professional military education in the pre-Vietnam era, and upon assuming presidency of the college in 1972, he had completely revamped the curriculum. History became the mainstay of all war-related instruction. At the start of the academic year, students read Thucydides's *Peloponnesian War* from cover to cover with the expectation that they would understand the significance of this ancient text and its relevance to the present day. The admiral believed in the value of the humanities and demanded students cover a minimum of 900 pages of assigned reading each week. His insistence on academic excellence proved intoxicating to those of us who previously had studied in relative isolation. He tossed us into the "briar patch," and individuals who arrived at the college with an appreciation of history loved every minute of it.[9] Nonetheless, some disappointment surfaced within this group when the next major assignment turned out to be the Napoleonic Wars because we leapt over some 2,000 years of history with only a nod to its existence. However, when a school needs to cover the sweep of history in a single trimester, major compromises inevitably occur.

Personally, I resolved in the months ahead not only to work my way through the missing two millennia of military history, but also to return to the classical period of the Greek and Roman world and read in far greater depth. With a growing family and the associated expenses, I welcomed the advantage of soft cover books such as Penguin Books' translations of Xenophon's *The Persian Expedition*, Arian's *The Campaigns of Alexander*, and Livy's *The War with Hannibal*. My endeavor nearly floundered at the outset, when curiosity and an insatiable appetite caused me to expand my horizon even further in attempts to better understand the Greek and Roman civilizations, and then their art and architecture. Tempting as these new venues proved, I soon returned to the "main attack," an effort that continues to the present.

Admiral Turner's introduction of the works of the classical strategists, most particularly Clausewitz's *On War*, proved as important to Naval War College students as his revitalization of historically based instruction. For nearly a quarter-century after World War II, America's military schools failed to ground their students in the fundamental philosophies of war. Few understood the nature of war, much less its underlying theories. Without a basic knowledge of concepts and devoid of any historical context, there is little wonder that the mid-twentieth century officer corps led America into the Vietnam quagmire. Military leaders in the 1950s and 1960s proved quite adept in the science of war – mobilization, logistics, personnel management, and other peripheral activities – but demonstrated an almost complete lack of awareness of the art of war.

Turner insisted on a rebalancing of the equation. Michael Howard and Peter Paret's 1976 translation of *On War* greatly aided the study of Clausewitz's masterpiece, and thus, war itself. No more complete and enduring theory of the subject exists than the one contained in this volume. Clausewitz's complex style of writing means the knowledge enclosed in his tome is extremely difficult to comprehend with simple reading. It requires close reading, aided by an adept teacher. Above all, Turner assembled a

---

[9] I always sensed that officers with a specialty that potentially brings them closer to an actual fight – infantrymen, pilots, artillerymen, etc. – most appreciate the study of history. A study done by a fellow student at the Army War College in 1982 that found combat arms officers "most likely to view military history as highly valuable" supports this thesis. See David W. Hazen, "The Army War College and the Study of Military History," U.S. Army War College, April 19, 1982, p. 22.

first-class faculty, which over time led the American military back to solid intellectual ground. The course of instruction provided me the basis for even more advanced study. Equally important, it prepared me for high-level command.

My next assignment to the United Nations (UN) Truce Supervision in Palestine promised the possibility of again seeing conflict, although as an observer trying to prevent renewed war. In preparation, I refocused my reading from the theoretical to the practical. More knowledgeable now about the wealth of military literature available, I turned to an earlier military-scholar, Ardant du Picq, whose *Battle Studies: Ancient and Modern Battle* in many ways closely paralleled S. L. A. Marshall's book. I had secured this volume earlier as part of the *Marine Corps Gazette's* collections of "classics." However, I had never felt inclined to read it – a huge mistake. Du Picq's observations on the moral effects on men in battle and the importance of cohesion seem in retrospect self-evident, but it took his book to make them so for the soldiers of his time.[10] Marshall carried forward this form of military research and writing, although without the extensive research he claimed. But the close examination of war's sharp end truly came into its own with publication of John Keegan's *The Face of Battle* in 1976. A genre of similar books soon followed, including Paddy Griffith's *Forward into Battle: Fighting Tactics from Waterloo to Vietnam* (and a revised edition entitled *Forward into Battle: Fighting Tactics from Waterloo to the Near Future*) and the works of other lecturers in War Studies at the Royal Military Academy at Sandhurst.

I learned an important lesson reading Keegan's book: not to downplay the ability of those without active military service or actual combat experience to write meaningfully about battle. I nearly went no further than the first sentence in *The Face of Battle*, in which Keegan states, "I have not been in a battle; not near one, nor heard one from afar, nor seen the aftermath." I again thought of closing the book two pages later when the author revealed he had never served in uniform. Luckily, I chose to ignore my prejudices and pressed on. As a result, I learned much from this now-famous military historian, not the least being that it is possible to become schooled in the profession through vicarious means, and in some cases, even more so than those who spend an unreflective lifetime in military attire.

Overall, duty in the Middle East supported my continuing professional reading and opened up a new vista, battlefield studies, or using today's more common term, staff rides. I discovered such a plethora of sites in this region that selecting which to visit presented a huge challenge. Meggido, the location of the first recorded battle of history, won by the Egyptian Pharaoh Thutmosis III in 1469 BC, lay at one end of the time spectrum, while at the

---

[10] Azar Gat provides a valuable critique of du Picq in "Ardant du Picq's Scientism, Teaching and Influence," *War & Society*, October 1990, pp. 1–16.

other lay the various battlegrounds of the 1973 Arab-Israeli War. The Second Battle of Meggido, fought by General Allenby in September 1918, offered another possibility for study at both the original position and over the surrounding area traversed by the likes of Lawrence of Arabia. At the time I visited in 1979, one could imagine the possibility of a future battle between the Soviet Union and the United States at this same spot with the Soviet backers of Syria moving down from the Golan Heights to meet Americans assisting in the defense of Israel. It was certainly an eerie thought at the time because *Har* (hill) Meggido is the location of the biblical Armageddon.

The earlier wars between the Arabs and Israelis – in 1948–9, 1956, and 1967 – offered numerous additional battlefields for examination. Bookstores in the region carried many publications on these wars that imparted viewpoints not elsewhere available. A few of these remain in my personal library. Among those I found most useful were Chaim Herzog's *The War of Atonement* and Mohamed Heikel's *The Road to Ramadan*. Such readings were reinforced by the opportunity to study the campaigns of 1941 and 1942, especially El Alamein. Good map reading skills aided my travels over these positions because the desert looks much the same from horizon to horizon in this part of North Africa.

No nation tends to its overseas battlefield burial sites as well as the United Kingdom. Walking through the El Alamein cemetery along row upon row of gravestones – each inscribed with a message from loved ones at home – invariably caused me to reflect deeply on the terrible costs of war and the immense responsibilities borne by those who practice the profession of arms. No words affected me more than the simple ones from a young son to his departed father: "Goodnight Daddy – Wee John." Such a loss cannot be measured in the normal calculus of war. The safety of one's nation and the sacrifices many pay – some the ultimate – *must* motivate every officer to master his or her profession.

For nearly a year, the United Nations schedule of a week of duty followed by a week off allowed me much time for staff rides accompanied by a handful of equally interested officers from a variety of nations. The chance to explore old battlefields also arose occasionally in the normal course of conducting patrols. I always tried to precede these events with detailed reading of works on the battle of interest. In the first half of my tour I worked out of Cairo, Egypt, where a preponderance of the Soviet observers also served. This meant that normally two out of three patrols I participated in included a Soviet partner.

The arrangement provided a unique opportunity to talk freely with members of a potential enemy nation, while driving over desert routes or relaxing in our small encampments. The subjects ranged from politics and religion to areas of mutual professional interest. The Soviet officers – all from the Army – often gave us copies of history books as gifts, some in Russian, others

English translations. Apparently, their government made these available for free. Although a few consisted of pure propaganda, most contained credible material on the past performance of Soviet forces. The chance to discuss professional military matters with these officers offered a perspective on past and future operations unavailable anywhere else in the world at the time. The course at the Naval War College had prepared me well and allowed me to hold my own in some great debates. When patrols brought us to the scene of a 1973 battle, we usually stopped and walked over it, examining destroyed Soviet equipment and an occasional American tank, always attempting to understand how the particular engagement was likely to have unfolded. On several occasions, our accompanying Egyptian liaison officer described his own wartime experience at or near the site and suggested English translations of books related to the action.

The second half of my tour with the UN took me to southern Lebanon, where ongoing hostilities between various guerrilla factions and the Israeli Defense Force (IDF) often made the work of an observer difficult. I never became comfortable under fire or near small but deadly engagements while unarmed. Nonetheless, professional rewards abounded. Observers normally alternated duty at positions near or colocated with units from the IDF and the Palestine Liberation Organization (PLO). Again, circumstances often allowed professional discussions with the two antagonists. Somewhat surprisingly, I never felt any hostility directed against me from members of the PLO, despite the official American attitude toward that group. Militarily related conversations in these surroundings naturally tended toward various aspects of irregular warfare. As had the Soviet officers, members of the PLO often gave us free literature, usually pamphlets. Approximately 75 percent turned out to be pure propaganda of an incendiary nature; the remainder were well-written features on the history of the region.

The insecure countryside and the reluctance of both sides to venture beyond fixed posts limited opportunities to see old battlefields. Instead, our responsibilities took us to sites of conflicts only minutes or hours old, with the object of separating the warring parties and investigating the circumstances of the action. A few PLO positions located on or near Crusader castles and in the ancient city of Tyre allowed some limited study, however. I left the Middle East with a much-enhanced understanding of warfare over the ages and of the many similarities between armies around the world. The Naval War College experience, coupled with that of a UN observer, served as an unsurpassed professional school that provided an exceptional education.

FORMALIZING MY STUDY EFFORTS

When I returned to the States, I assumed command of a Marine Barracks near Jacksonville, Florida. No Marine duty is undemanding when one is the commanding officer; yet, regular hours and no requirement to spend days away on field exercises provided more time for professional study than I had found in earlier assignments. A combination of formal schooling, overseas travel, and four tours in combat zones over the preceding twenty-four years had widened my reading interests immensely. To continue my tactical education along with my understanding of combat leadership, I turned to the newly published (in 1979) translation of Erwin Rommel's *Attacks* and a reprint of the U.S. Army Infantry Journal's landmark *Infantry in Battle*, originally published in 1934 under the signature of George C. Marshall. These seminal works provided me with a wealth of new and important knowledge. To expand my understanding of strategic thought, I probed Edward Mead Earle's *Makers of Modern Strategy: Military Thought from Machiavelli to Hitler* and Michael Howard's *The Theory and Practice of War*.

In summer 1981, I reported to the Army War College. After a quick review of the program of instruction, I ascertained that this institution at the time failed to offer much of a test for any serious student. There appeared to be little opportunity for the study of *war* at this *war* college. To illustrate, World War I and World War II studies each consumed approximately eight academic hours, whereas instruction in U.S. immigration policy took up nearly twenty hours. Furthermore, reincorporating history into the curriculum remained an ongoing effort with little evidence of any significant impact. I found no surprise in one scholar's earlier observation that, "Perhaps the most conspicuous shortcoming of the lectures offered [in an elective course on military history] is that too few of them deal with conflict."[11]

Finally, the 1981–2 academic year saw the first introduction of Clausewitz's *On War*, a text I felt comfortable with after the rigors of the Naval War College. Determining how to best fill the many hours the college scheduled for personal study – hours obviously not required to meet the limited demands of work outside the classroom – became my immediate mission. Visits to the campus library and bookstore promptly revealed the best way to accomplish this task, and the upcoming months looked considerably brighter as I contemplated the possibilities for personal reading and research. In a few days, I established two goals for my year at the Army War College: first, determine how best to approach the professional study of military history, an issue raised after Vietnam by critics both in and out of uniform; second, create a self-directed study program that could guide officers in their own continuing professional education, a responsibility too few seemed to recognize rested on their own shoulders.

Michael Howard's highly regarded 1961 article, "The Use and Abuse of Military History," looked like a good place to start my research on the role

---

[11] Russell F. Weigley, *New Dimensions in Military History* (San Rafael, CA, 1975), p. 11.

of military history in professional education.[12] I found a treasure trove of advice in this piece beginning with Sir Michael's counsel to study in width, depth, and context. The U.S. Army Center of Military History's *A Guide to the Study and Use of Military History* proved equably valuable.[13] It offered everything from specifics on how a student might approach military history to bibliographic guides on great military writers and military history in specific periods. This became one of the most well-worn books in my library. I uncovered several additional aids to studying history: "timeless verities of combat," "recurring themes," and "threads of continuity." These conceptual schemes help an officer understand a specific aspect or a unique instance of war through the perspective of time. Trevor N. Dupuy explained the use of the timeless verities of combat in *The Evolution of Weapons and Warfare.* The Naval War College and the U.S. Military Academy organized their military history study around recurring themes and threads of continuity, at least in 1982. My research enabled me to write a short paper describing the techniques a student might use to better direct his or her study of history. I shared the ideas in this paper with other officers for the remainder of my career.

At the outset of my studies at the Army War College, a letter to the school's professional journal, *Parameters*, caught my attention. Retired Army Major General David W. Gray suggested "that each officer should set forth the guidelines which he intended to follow throughout his career. These guidelines would encompass principles of conduct as well as skills essential to professional fitness, including not only those of a purely physical or technical nature but also those designed to train and discipline the mind. Presumably these skills would be modified or expanded as the officer progressed in rank."[14] I set out to review studies made of officer education in the recent past, talked with numerous authorities on officer education, and surveyed a variety of literature on the subject. From this endeavor, I concluded it best to divide my proposed self-directed program into three parts, the humanities in general, military history specifically, and communications, that is, reading, writing, speaking, and listening. Broadening the program allowed me to consider the "whole man," while centering on the military characteristics. Over the next months, I wrote a paper describing the importance of each of these categories to an officer's self-education: how he or she might go about studying subjects within these categories. As an unexpected benefit, my paper

---

12   Michael Howard, "The Use and Abuse of Military History," *Royal United Service Institute Journal,* February 1962, pp. 4–8.

13   The Army intended this guide, published in 1979, to serve as a tool for the self-education of officers. However, little evidence existed in 1981 of it accomplishing that purpose. Although the Army War College gave a copy to each student, I never heard it referenced during my time there as a student.

14   David W. Gray, Letter to the Editor, *Parameters,* September 1981, p. 93.

met the requirements of the college for an individual research essay; thus, it performed double duty.[15] More important, it guided my own professional development efforts over the next fifteen years and informed my later work directed at improving professional military education in the Marine Corps.

Classes with Harry G. Summers, author of *On Strategy: The Vietnam War in Context*, certainly counted among the few highlights of my time at the Army War College. In both his book and classroom, he correctly refocused responsibility for failures in Vietnam from the liberal media and antiwar protestors to the real problems: a lack of strategic thinking and realistic understanding of the nature of war. Along with Admiral Turner, Summers forced thoughtful military officers to revisit their own deficient professional educations.

General Robert Barrow, who served as Commandant of the Marine Corps during the year I attended the Army War College, also provided a beacon of light during this period with his scholarly manners. A man of exceptional physical stature and presence, he evidenced an extraordinary intellect. As a serious student of history, he frequently employed historical examples in talks and speeches. In his annual visit to the college, he opened his remarks with a spellbinding story of Admiral Nelson at Trafalgar. In a telephone call the following weekend to my twin brother, a student at the Naval War College, I mentioned the favorable reaction Barrow had received during his visit. My brother indicated that the general's visit to Newport that same week elicited a similar response. I asked about the effect of his historical example, and my brother answered that it clearly motivated the students. We continued our conversation for some minutes, with my assuming that it centered on the same example – Nelson at Trafalgar – only to realize eventually that to the Naval War College audience, Barrow had spoken of Wellington at Waterloo. Unique among senior leaders, the commandant provided a navy example for an army school and an army example for a navy school.

PUTTING MY IDEAS TO THE TEST

Following the Army War College, I returned to the operating forces for six years, first as the executive officer of the 7th Marines and then as commanding officer of the 2nd Battalion of the 7th Marines. From there I went to Okinawa, Japan, and assumed command of the 4th Marine Regiment. Duties as the operations officer and chief of staff of the 3rd Marine Division came afterward. Each of these billets offered the chance to implement my self-directed study program. Among the many books I read during this period, none proved more influential than Martin van Creveld's *Command*

---

[15] Paul K. Van Riper, "A Self-Directed Officer Study Program," student research paper, U.S. Army War College, April 19, 1982.

in War. In the first chapter, he offered an enlightened view of command and control as practiced over the ages. In the following chapters, he expanded on his ideas with clear historical illustrations. From the outset, van Creveld recognized the inherent uncertainty of the modern battlefield. That fact, virtually unacknowledged elsewhere, supplied the underpinning for my own approach to modernizing the command and control of every unit I served in during these and subsequent assignments. I insisted subordinate commanders and staff read the book and held my own command-level workshops to review van Creveld's ideas. In my mind, *Command in War* reached the status of classic almost upon publication. Surprisingly, when I asked Martin van Creveld at a conference in 1989 how he evaluated his many writings, he did not place that book at the top but stated that his then yet to be published *The Transformation of War* would likely hold that honor in the future.

An obscure pamphlet filled with historical illustrations in its first chapter, *Combat Operations C3I Fundamentals and Interactions*, written by Air Force Major George E. Orr, also influenced my thinking on command and control in the mid-1980s. The only other officer I ever encountered in this period who demonstrated familiarity with this little booklet, General Al Gray, Commandant of the Marine Corps at the time, enjoyed a reputation as a prolific reader. One of my fondest memories remains discussing the merits of Orr's book with General Gray, while escorting him through a display of 3rd Marine Division command posts in 1987, as the officers in trail looked on with puzzled expressions. John Keegan's *The Mask of Command*, an analysis of generalship over the ages, became another of my "must read" books on command and control during this time, mainly for the way it dealt with the issue every commander faces in combat – how far forward to go.[16]

By this point in my career, I had organized my reading to ensure I regularly covered the three levels of war – tactical, operational, and strategic. At the tactical level, a number of worthwhile books appeared in the mid- to late 1980s. John A. English's *On Infantry* and a reprint of E. D. Swinton's 1907 edition of *The Defense of Duffer's Drift* serve as excellent examples. English addressed the infantry arm in a scholarly way and to a depth not

---

[16] The commander of the 1st Marine Division provided a traditional answer to this question during operations in Iraq in March and April 2003: "At a time of increasing reliance on sophisticated sensor and communications technologies to paint a 'picture of the battle space' to top generals far from the war front, a key Marine Corps commander last spring opted to lead his troops in Iraq the old-fashioned way: He went there. 'In two minutes at the front edge of the combat zone, you know if the troops feel confident, if the battle's going the way they want it to, [or if] they need something,' said Maj. Gen. James Mattis, commanding general of the 1st Marine Division. 'You can sense it. And you can apply something.'" Quoted from Elaine M. Grossman, "Marine General: Leading from Iraqi Battlefield Informed Key Decisions," *Inside The Pentagon*, Washington, DC, October 2003, 20, p. 1.

previously matched.[17] Swinton used a literary technique whereby a young officer in a series of dreams refights the same battle several times – improving the performance of his unit on each occasion until he finally masters the mission.

Although substantial interest in the operational level of war and operational art arose throughout the American armed forces during the 1980s and generated numerous articles, few books on the subject appeared. The opposite occurred with strategy. Peter Paret's edited *Makers of Modern Strategy: From Machiavelli to the Nuclear Age* and Edward N. Luttwaks's *Strategy: The Logic of War and Peace* gained much attention throughout the defense community. Andrew F. Krepinevich's *The Army and Vietnam* led the way for a more introspective series of works on the Vietnam War. Reprints of Lord Moran's *Anatomy of Courage* and John Baynes's *Morale: A Study of Men and Courage* expanded the available literature on the human element in war. They stood solidly alongside the works of du Picq and S. L. A. Marshall. All became part of my expanding library, and I urged peers and subordinates alike to read them.

Two studies materially aided those seeking guidance on what to read, Roger H. Nye's *The Challenge of Command: Reading for Military Excellence* and Robert H. Berlin's bibliography, *Military Classics*, the latter published by the U.S. Army's Combat Studies Institute. A little pamphlet retitled *Literature in the Education of the Military Professional*, edited by two members of the U.S. Air Force Academy's English Department, encouraged me to venture again into areas and subjects not directly related to war. In his foreword to this booklet, Vice Admiral James Stockdale urged military professionals to study the humanities: "From such study, and from the lifetime highminded reading habit it frequently spawns, come raw material for reflective thought in times of quietude, sixth-sense inspiration in the heat of battle, and a clearer vision of the big picture in peace or war from a philosophic and historical plane high above the buzz-word filled bureaucratic smog layer which can be counted on to contaminate the atmosphere of the nether regions."[18]

MARINE CORPS COMMAND AND STAFF COLLEGE AND THE MARINE CORPS UNIVERSITY

Despite my protest – as far as a serving officer can protest orders – General Gray denied an extension of my tour in Okinawa, and in summer 1988,

---

[17] English's style of writing and his organization of material made *On Infantry* difficult reading for many. A revised edition in 1994 with Bruce I. Gudmundsson proved to be an easier read, although it discarded much useful material.

[18] Donald Ahern and Robert Shenk, eds., *Literature in the Education of the Military Professional* (Colorado Springs, CO, 1982), p. vii.

directed me to report as Director of the Marine Corps Command and Staff
College at Quantico, Virginia. In the midst of his Corpswide effort to enhance
professional military education, he made clear his purpose from my first day
of duty. He said simply, "This school needs changing. My intent is for it to
become the premier institution of its kind in the world. You cannot achieve
that goal in the time I expect you to be here, but you will have time to lay a
foundation that allows it to happen." I received no more guidance, except a
pointed edict to base all instruction on history and the concepts of maneuver
warfare. General Gray wanted no separate classes on military history – he
insisted on weaving history into all the instructions on operations and tactics.
The same admonition followed for "maneuverist's thinking," with a strong
suggestion that I ensure the infusion of Clausewitz and Sun Tzu into the
course. Basically, he wanted the entire course to rest on military history and
established ideas of strategy.

Turning to the faculty, I sought to understand the existing curriculum.
Years of tinkering with the course of instruction made attempts to explain
it confusing at best. Three bodies of thought crystallized concerning corrective actions. One group thought the commandant wrong and argued
against change. A second group recognized and supported the requirement
to revamp the curriculum, but argued that instruction be halted for at least
a year, and perhaps two, to accomplish such a large task. A third, smaller
faction wanted to press ahead. I elected to take my counsel from Timothy
Lupfer's *The Dynamics of Doctrine: The Change in German Tactical Doctrine During the First World War*. I reasoned that if the German Army in a
matter of two months in the winter of 1917–18 could completely alter its
tactical doctrine in the midst of combat, certainly the U.S. Marine Corps
was capable of changing a program of instruction while teaching it. Thus,
in fall 1988, we set out to revise the program of instruction completely
while presenting it. For inspiration, I turned to the example Admiral Turner
had established fifteen years earlier. For new content, I looked to my own
work at the Army War College, the Naval War College curriculum, the
critiques of outside observers and military historians such as Williamson
Murray, and the thorough study of professional military education commissioned by Representative Ike Skelton, member of Congress from the state of
Missouri.

To support professional education within Marine Corps schools as well as
throughout the Corps, General Gray tasked the doctrine writers at Quantico
to prepare a new "capstone" manual that captured the essentials of warfare.
Although many of my contemporaries – experienced colonels – hoped for
assignment to the project, a young captain, John Schmitt, received the mission. In short order, Schmidt gained an understanding of Clausewitz and
Sun Tzu worthy of any war college graduate and transposed their weighty

ideas to simple prose. Drafts of his manual circulated among Command and Staff College instructors, informing them even as they critiqued the material. The final document – *Warfighting* – dramatically influenced education throughout the Marine Corps and in other organizations in the Department of Defense. Moreover, translations appeared in Spanish, Japanese, and Korean within a few years of its publication.

Part way through the year, General Gray announced he wanted a reading program developed for Marine Corps officers. The task eventually found its way to my desk. The mission seemed simple because my self-directed officer study program created at the Army War College already contained a list of recommended readings for officers. I spent several weeks updating and adding to this list, querying other institutions such as the service academies, the other command and staff colleges, the war colleges, and civilian universities. Much to my surprise, the fifteen copies of the initial draft list elicited twenty-one responses. Clearly, some who learned of the list felt compelled to offer their thoughts, although not officially asked. Some respondents wanted every book written by a particular author on the list, while others demanded we include none from the same author. Other equally strong suggestions materialized. Plainly, recommended reading lists bring out deep-seated emotions and prejudices. I sensed in this deep interest a pent-up desire for a Corpswide reading program. Relying on the wisdom contained in the Center of Military History's *A Guide to the Study and Use of Military History*, Nye's *The Challenge of Command*, and Berlin's *Military Classics*, I pressed ahead to produce a list approved by General Gray.

In the midst of the curriculum change and the construction of a professional reading list, General Gray sent out another task: Draw up plans for establishment of a Marine Corps University. Again, primary responsibility for this undertaking fell on the Command and Staff College. Once more, I looked to history. A review of Scharnhorst's efforts to establish the *Kriegsakemie*, Upton's labors to create the schools at Fort Leavenworth, Commodore Stephen Luce's work to establish the Naval War College, and others gave me the grounding for this new endeavor. The work of a dedicated staff created the new organization, and in 1990, I assumed the position as the first President of the Marine Corps University.

My assignment at Quantico ended in summer 1991, with orders to report as the commanding general of the 2nd Marine Division. The work to overhaul professional military education continued under the sure hands of others and reached its culmination before the end of the decade. Perhaps no better manifestation of the results the commandant anticipated exists than the performance of the senior Marine commanders, Lieutenant General Jim Conway and Major Generals Jim Mattis and Jim Amos, during Operation Iraqi Freedom.

BRINGING THINGS TO FRUITION
AS A SENIOR COMMANDER

Senior officers influence subordinates through a combination of direction and example. As a division commander, I was in the position to order and inspire 18,000 marines to make history part of their professional development. As a first step, I added an hour of professional reading to my own official schedule, promulgated daily throughout the division. I reasoned that if subordinates saw the division commander setting aside an hour each day for reading, others might follow. I also issued a memorandum that stated in part: "The professional reading program is a key part of the continuous professional education that is necessary to develop the minds of our Marines. It is most valuable for developing the sound military judgment that is essential for practicing the maneuver warfare doctrine contained in [the *Warfighting* manual]. Just as we expect them to maintain their mental fitness, so should we expect them to maintain their mental fitness through a career-long professional reading program."

In addition, I directed the purchase of more than 6,000 books for unit libraries, ordered the establishment of a historical reading room and the conduct of monthly seminars, required the division's regiments and battalions to sponsor reading groups and hold regular discussions of selected books, sponsored staff rides to Civil War battlefields for the division staff, and asked my units to carry out their own series of staff rides. The closing sentence of my memorandum stated, "Marines fight better when they fight smarter, and a systematic and progressive professional reading program contributes directly to that end." The proof of the value of reading is not straightforward. Performance on the battlefield provides the final test. I have no doubt marines from the division later fought smarter and therefore better because of the wisdom they gained from these various programs.

After an assignment at Headquarters Marine Corps – one that not only allowed me to read more, but also to attend several college-level history and defense-related courses – I received orders to take command of the Marine Corps Combat Development Command at Quantico. That organization is responsible for all Marine Corps training and education, creation of operating concepts, and writing of doctrine. Thus, it possesses considerable ability to affect professional development across the entire Marine Corps. Again, I employed a combination of direction and example to advance the education of marines everywhere. Early on, I took action to ensure history provided the basis for all doctrinal development and the curricula for all schools. I invited noted historians to speak not only to students in formal schools, but also at professional gatherings. Monthly, I hosted a reading group – comprised of officers from lieutenant to major general – at my quarters for dinner and a follow-on discussion. Often, we were fortunate enough to persuade the author or the subject of the book under discussion to join us. Admiral Sandy Woodward, author of *One Hundred Days: The Memoirs of the Falklands Battle Group Commander* and former Army Major Dick Winters, commander of the airborne company featured in Stephen Ambrose's *Band of Brothers*, honored our reading group in this manner. When visiting units or conducting inspections at the various commands around the Marine Corps that fell under my cognizance, I made it a habit to ask questions about publications on the Commandant's Reading List and gave away copies of books to those answering correctly.

I often noted in my two years at Quantico that the primary "weapon" that officers possess remains their minds. I followed with the observation that books provide the "ammunition" for this weapon. Always I cautioned against looking for answers in reading, especially history. Rather, I urged officers to read with the goal of absorbing the material as part of their being. To underscore my meaning, I referenced a scene from the movie *Patton* where the general, in a near trancelike mood, observes an ancient battlefield and replays in his mind how he trod this ground during the original battle. Most viewers, I believe, concluded Patton to be either some sort of mystic or perhaps a little deranged, while I supposed his many years of reading and study gave him the sense of having been there previously. I wanted to impart a simple lesson: a properly schooled officer never arrives on a battlefield for the first time, even if he has never actually trod the ground, if that officer has read wisely to acquire the wisdom of those who have experienced war in times past. My thought was far from original, for Clausewitz observed, "Continual change and the need to respond to it compels the commander to carry the whole intellectual apparatus of his knowledge within. He must always be ready to bring forth the appropriate decision. By total assimilation with his mind and life, the commander's knowledge must be transferred into a genuine capability."[19]

A LOSS OF MOMENTUM

Six years into retirement, my worry grows that the erroneous ideas on military education held by post–World War II military leaders are again creeping back into the system. Evidence of such an unsatisfactory situation appears regularly. The promise of information technology and the rewards that it seemingly offers in terms of automated command and control, surveillance and reconnaissance, and precision-guided munitions holds a place in the minds of many defense leaders similar to the technological advantage allegedly provided by systems analysis, nuclear weapons, and computers in

---

[19]   Carl von Clausetwitz, *On War*, trans. and ed., Michael Howard and Peter Paret (Princeton, NJ, 1976), p. 147.

the 1950s and 1960s. Methodical planning techniques like those currently promised by advocates of "effects-based operations" and "operational net assessment" stand in for Robert McNamara's systems engineering of military decision making. Having been a victim – along with an entire generation of American military officers – of such shallow thinking, I find myself habitually warning those who will listen of the potential for repeating the tragic mistakes of the 1950s and 1960s.

The value of military history to the professional military officer remains incontestable. Those who might urge its reduction or elimination from military schools and colleges are woefully uninformed at best or completely ignorant of the basic underpinnings of their supposed profession at worst. The American military cannot afford to lose a second battle to keep history at the core of professional military education.

5

Awkward partners: military history and American military education

RICHARD HART SINNREICH

The absence of romance in my history will, I fear, detract somewhat from its interest; but if it be judged useful by those inquirers who desire an exact knowledge of the past as an aid to the interpretation of the future, which in the course of human things must resemble if it does not reflect it, I shall be content.
— *Thucydides*, The Peloponnesian War[1]

When the father of military history penned those words in 431 BC, he introduced a question about the practical utility of historical inquiry that reverberates to the present day: How and to what extent can the study of history usefully inform the man of affairs?[2] The question is especially acute for the professional soldier, for whom the opportunity to practice his or her profession happily is episodic. Unlike other human enterprises in which constant repetition allows for a smooth learning curve, war generally occurs at intervals sufficiently great, and in circumstances so diverse and unrepeatable, that military organizations cannot take for granted the useful transfer of experience from one conflict to the next.

Indeed, despite the conventional accusation that militaries invariably prepare to refight the last war, closer examination suggests they are prone more often to ignore history, or at best recall it carelessly, if not disingenuously.[3] That has been the more true during the past half-century of rapid

---

[1] Thucydides, *The Peloponnesian War*, ed. T. E. Wick (New York, 1982).
[2] Some would reserve the title to Herodotus, "The Father of History." It was, however, precisely Thucydide's (unjustified) concern about the "absence of romance" in his work that argues his acknowledgment as the first true military historian. For a more robust argument, see G. F. Abbott, *Thucydides: A Study in Historical Reality* (New York, 1970), chap. 2.
[3] Williamson Murray, "Thinking About Innovation," *The Naval War College Review*, Spring 2001.

technological change, during which the recurring tendency has been to discount the relevance of the past altogether.

Today, fortunately, few soldiers and even fewer historians doubt that military history has an important, even irreplaceable, contribution to make to the education of the military professional. But the desirable nature and extent of that contribution remains a matter of debate in both professions. This chapter explores that discussion. It will argue that, although the infusion of military history in professional military education has made enormous strides since the dark days of the 1950s and 1960s, it still is far from occupying the vital place that its importance to the education of the soldier deserves and the future effectiveness of the U.S. military requires.

EVOLUTION OF AMERICAN MILITARY EDUCATION

In America's military, both ignorance of the past and careless or calculated interpretation of it have deep roots. At the outbreak of the Civil War, for example, few of the professional soldiers who eventually led Northern and Southern armies in battle had recent combat experience. The minority who had fought in Mexico more than a decade earlier had done so as junior officers.[4] Even fewer had fought American Indians. Neither experience was studied systematically.

Instead, at West Point, cadets continued to suffer through Jominian lectures about Napoleon's campaigns of half a century earlier.[5] Once graduated, of course, they received no further formal military education. Hence, it is not surprising that, committed to a struggle on a continental scale that also witnessed the introduction of new technologies as diverse as the Minié ball, the telegraph, the railroad, and the ironclad, many officers found themselves wholly unprepared for what they faced and, in effect, compelled to purchase learning with lives. It was a pattern that would repeat itself in one fashion or another throughout the remainder of that century and the beginning of the next.

The first deliberate effort to break that pattern was the establishment of the Naval War College in 1884. Conceived by its first president, Stephen B. Luce, as "a place of original research on all questions relating to war, and to statesmanship connected with war, or the prevention of war,"[6] from its outset the Naval War College's curriculum reflected a vision of professional military

---

[4] The most senior, Albert Sydney Johnston, was a colonel. Others, among them George McClellan, Robert E. Lee, and U.S. Grant, were company or junior field grade officers.

[5] No less an authority than Grant later commented wryly that he found his last two years at West Point, those in which such studies predominated, "about five times as long as Ohio years." Ulysses S. Grant, *Personal Memoirs* (New York, 1999), p. 19.

[6] Stephen B. Luce, quoted in "NWC History," Official Naval War College Web page; www.nwc.navy.mil/l1/history.htm.

education unprecedented in its expansiveness, together with a commitment to intellectual rigor that, with occasional interruptions, has continued to distinguish the college among its counterparts to this day. Both its vision and rigor rested explicitly in military and naval history and theory. Not coincidentally, the Naval War College's first historian and Luce's successor as president was Alfred Thayer Mahan, generally regarded as America's only world-class military theorist. Under Mahan's guidance, the Naval War College attained an international reputation in both academic and military circles.

It took the Army twenty years to follow the Navy's lead. In 1903, an Army War College finally emerged at the instigation of Secretary of War Elihu Root. Conceived as an adjunct to the newly authorized General Staff, and thus with a much narrower view of its role than its naval counterpart, the Army War College nevertheless provided selected Army officers their first formal advanced education beyond West Point.[7] Early graduates destined to earn distinction included John J. Pershing (1905) and Dwight D. Eisenhower (1927).

In one respect, however, the Army outpaced the Navy. In 1881, General William T. Sherman established a School of Application for Cavalry and Infantry at Fort Leavenworth Kansas, aimed at instructing officers in larger unit tactics for ground forces. Its name changed several times before the adoption of today's Command and General Staff College. So, too, did the diversity and seniority of the student body, the scope of its curriculum, and its duration, which alternated episodically between one and two years. The Command and General Staff College furnished the Army the perfect locus for examining, refining, and propounding evolving tactical doctrine, and a base from which to train the vast accretion of midgrade officers required to staff the Army upon mobilization in both 1917 and 1941. Some of its prewar doctrinal products remain today among the best written of their kind.[8]

In an institutional sense, then, by the outbreak of World War II, the U.S. military had to a considerable extent erased its educational deficit. Both the Army and Navy (and their imbedded Air Corps and Marine Corps subcultures) had at least limited access to a multilevel system of professional military education, beginning with West Point and Annapolis and culminating at the Army and Naval War Colleges, respectively. In the Army, although less extensively in its sister service, the development and dissemination of doctrine had become regularized. The U.S. military thus entered World War II

[7] A status that finally will end later this year, when control of the Army War College shifts from Headquarters, Department of the Army, to U.S. Army Training and Doctrine Command.

[8] For example, the highly regarded 1982 and 1986 editions of Field Manual 100-5, *Operations*, the Army's capstone doctrinal manual (since renumbered FM 3.0), drew inspiration from the Army's 1941 Field Service Regulations more directly than from any more recent doctrinal publication.

better prepared intellectually, if not materially, than for any previous war in its history. The rapidity with which the nation was able to mobilize for war and shrug off early disasters to mount offensive operations on a global scale was at least partly attributable to that preparation.[9]

Judging how much the study of military history contributed to that success is more problematic. At West Point, founded originally to train engineers and artillerists, the curriculum emphasized mathematics and engineering. Humanities were well down the list of academic priorities, and the study of military history tended to be fragmentary and doctrinaire, a condition that persisted even after the war. Leavenworth and the Army branch schools examined the occasional historical case, but only for tactical lessons. The war college provided a broader perspective befitting the seniority of its attendees. Even here, however, pedagogical commitment to the case analysis limited historical study.

At the Naval War College, the Luce-Mahan legacy assured a somewhat broader approach to professional study. Unlike the Army, however, the Navy had established no intermediate professional school, and relatively few naval officers had the opportunity to matriculate at the Naval War College. Even at Newport, moreover, the increasingly technical demands of naval warfare were beginning to impinge on more traditional subjects.[10]

The result was that military history was not studied in a synthetic or comparative way in either service. Prewar military modernization reflected this condition. In a few cases, focused historical inquiry had visible impact. The evolution of Marine Corps amphibious doctrine, for example, owed much to the careful examination of earlier operations, especially the Allies' tragic experience at Gallipoli. Despite some resistance by battleship traditionalists, the Navy likewise managed to apply what little experience of naval aviation World War I offered to the development of carrier operations.[11]

In contrast, myopic interpretation of the Army's (admittedly brief) World War I experience resulted in a stunted approach to armor and mechanization that burdened ground combat operations throughout the war's early years.[12] In the Navy, Mahanian insistence on the centrality of the battle fleet

---

[9]   Williamson Murray and Allan R. Millett, *A War to Be Won* (Cambridge, MA, 2000), chap. 2. The authors are a bit ambivalent on this score, as well they might be. The extent of intellectual preparedness was at best uneven.

[10] For a brief but perceptive appraisal of the professional military education system through the 1950s, see Morris Janowitz, *The Professional Soldier* (New York, 1960), pp. 132–3.

[11] Williamson Murray and Allan R. Millett, *Military Innovation in the Interwar Period* (Cambridge, 1996).

[12] David E. Johnson, *Fast Tanks and Heavy Bombers* (Ithaca, NY, 1998). In contrast, one postwar product, the Infantry School's *Infantry in Battle* (Washington, Inc., 1934) became a small unit classic; and 1919 saw the first official recognition of the importance of history to the Army with the establishment of a historical branch in the War Plans division of the general staff, forerunner of today's Office of the Chief of Military History. See Dennis J. Vetock, *Lessons Learned: A History of U.S. Army Lesson Learning* (Carlisle Barracks, PA, 1988).

tended to obscure the growing threat of the submarine to maritime commerce and power projection.[13] As for the Air Corps, obsession with gaining independence from the Army merely reinforced many airmen's intellectual convictions that military history had little relevance to future warfare in general and the employment of airpower in particular.[14]

Nor did victory in World War II materially alter military appreciation of the value of systematic historical inquiry. On the contrary, especially in the newly created Air Force, the emergence of the nuclear weapon seemed to many to have transformed the nature of war so radically as to render irrelevant any previous battlefield experience.[15] Stalemate in Korea likewise reinforced the convictions of many military professionals and civilian scholars that traditional approaches to the understanding of war had become outdated.

Instead, throughout the late 1950s and early 1960s, professional military discussion succumbed to the allegedly more verifiable prescriptions of political science and systems analysis. Increasingly, military history served only as a convenient anvil against which to hammer theories of future conflict themselves generated almost self-consciously without reference to the past. At the military academies, study of military and naval history surrendered in prestige and resources to the social sciences, while the war colleges largely abandoned traditional campaign studies in favor of strategic policy development.

Vietnam witnessed the apotheosis of this transformation. As the war consumed a generation of officers, residual education in the art of war gave way to training for a single war. Even the post-Korea preoccupation with a potential clash between NATO and the Warsaw Pact could not survive a decade that saw U.S. forces cannibalized across the world to support operations in Vietnam. Conventional military modernization stultified. Meanwhile, increased reliance on the tools of systems analysis, and a resulting obsession with quantitative indicators of military performance, displaced professional interest in classical operational and strategic theory and the history that it reflected.

Concurrently, Vietnam saw the nadir of support for military history in American academia. Just as mounting failure in Vietnam traumatized the military, so too mounting elite opposition to the war delegitimized the study of warfare generally and military history in particular. The discipline always

---

[13] Williamson Murray, "Misreading Mahan," *Military History Quarterly*, Winter 1993, pp. 34–5.

[14] Johnson, *Fast Tanks and Heavy Bombers*. See also Williamson Murray, "Why Air Forces Do Not Understand Strategy," *Military History Quarterly*, Spring 1989, pp. 34–5.

[15] Notwithstanding which the Air Force established its own war college immediately on separation from the Army. Its research orientation, however, was from the outset and (as a review of recent student writing confirms) to a considerable extent remains the examination, articulation, and extension of airpower doctrine.

had been something of a scholarly stepchild in many collegiate history departments, its scholars deprecated as not quite serious. As the war continued, it became an ideological as well as an intellectual target. On one campus after another, military history disappeared from course catalogs and aspiring young historians turned their talents elsewhere.[16]

RECOVERING FROM VIETNAM

In the United States, renewed interest in military history in the decade after defeat in Vietnam paralleled concomitant changes in professional military education so closely that it is impossible not to connect the two. Withdrawal from Vietnam unleashed a surge of interest in the causes, conduct, and consequences of military conflict. Beginning in the mid-1970s, in academic departments across the country, teaching and research in military history rebounded. Undergraduate and graduate courses blossomed. Foundations began opening their coffers to scholars in the field, and new periodicals emerged to provide outlets for their research.[17]

The same period witnessed a revival of scholarly and professional military attention to the classical military theorists and their modern successors. Vegetius, Sun Tzu, Jomini, Clausewitz, Du Picq, De Saxe, Mahan, Corbett, Liddell Hart, J. F. C. Fuller – all were dusted off and reexamined. In 1976, publication of the first new English translation of Clausewitz's *On War* since 1943 was justifiably hailed as a scholarly milestone, and the book itself quickly became (and has remained) an academic and military bestseller.[18]

In the military, meanwhile, bitter criticism of America's performance in Vietnam by highly regarded veterans such as Harry G. Summers[19] and David R. Palmer[20] reflected the cumulative frustration with what many military officers regarded as a professionally uninspired, if not actually incompetent, approach to the conduct of the war. Rejecting earlier critiques holding the military blameless for a primarily political debacle, these and other revisionist treatments lodged at least part of the responsibility for America's defeat in basic professional errors, from persistent failures to link military operations

---

[16] Paul Kennedy, "The Fall and Rise of Military History," *Military History Quarterly,* Winter 1991, pp. 9–12. Kennedy notes that, fortunately for aspiring American military historians, the antipathy to military history did not extend to Britain and Canada or to a few domestic holdouts, such as Duke, Kansas State, and Stanford. See also Robert D. Kaplan, "Four-Star Generalists," *The Atlantic Monthly,* October 1999.

[17] Kennedy, "The Rise and Fall of Military History," p. 10.

[18] Carl von Clausewitz, *On War,* edited by Michael Howard and Peter Paret (Princeton, NJ, 1976).

[19] Harry G. Summers, *On Strategy: A Critical Analysis of the Vietnam War* (Navato, CA, 1974).

[20] David R. Palmer, *Summons of the Trumpet: U.S.–Vietnam in Perspective* (Navato, CA, 1978).

to strategic goals, to pervasive overreliance on quantitative indicators of tactical success unrelated to any coherent operational or strategic objective.

At the heart of many of these critiques was a sense above all that Vietnam reflected a decline in professional literacy. Bemused first by the nuclear weapon and subsequently by systems analysis, the military seemed to have forgotten whatever it formerly understood about the essential ingredients of waging war. Rising alarm about the growth of Soviet military power over the decade only served to reinforce concerns about this intellectual deficit. The 1973 Arab-Israeli War, the swiftness and violence of which stunned American officers conditioned by ten years of single-minded preoccupation with counterinsurgency, also contributed to deep-seated feelings that something was wrong. As they watched engagements consuming in a day more men and materiel than months of action in Vietnam, senior military leaders confronted abruptly and unpleasantly the realization that, but for America's overwhelming air and naval superiority, defeat in Vietnam might have come earlier and even more expensively than it did.

The doctrinal convulsions prompted by all this have been described elsewhere.[21] Central to the military's postwar recovery, however, was a fundamental redirection of attention to conventional military operations. Given that the last American experience of such operations was by then more than twenty years old, it is perhaps not surprising that one result was a renewed interest in history to help diagnose and correct accumulated deficiencies in doctrine, organization, equipment, and training.

This renewed interest in military history influenced all four services, but was most visible in the Army, on which Vietnam had inflicted the most severe professional trauma. Early manifestations included historical research aimed at better understanding the Army's previous preparation (or lack thereof) for war,[22] intensive examination of the German *Wehrmacht*'s experience in Russia from 1942 to 1945,[23] and renewed attention to the "Green Books," the voluminous series of World War II historical studies launched in 1946 under the auspices of the Army's Center of Military History.[24]

---

[21] See John L. Romjue, *From Active Defense to Air–Land Battle: The Development of Army Doctrine 1973–1982* (Fort Monroe, VA, 1984), and Richard Hart Sinnreich, "Strategic Implications of Doctrinal Change: A Case Analysis," in Keith A. Dunn and William O. Staudenmaier, eds., *Military Strategy in Transition* (Boulder, CO, 1984), pp. 42–54.

[22] Culminating in Charles E. Heller and William A. Stofft, eds., *America's First Battles, 1776–1965* (Lawrence, KS, 1986).

[23] In support of which the Army, through contract with BDM Corporation, engaged as consultants several senior veterans of the Eastern Front, including Generals Hermann Balck and Friedrich von Mellinthin. See BDM, *Generals Balck and Von Mellinthin on Tactics: Implications for NATO Doctrine* (McLean, VA, 1980).

[24] Formally *The United States Army in World War II*, and currently up to an astonishing seventy-eight volumes. The U.S. Navy commissioned a similar although shorter series, Samuel Eliot Morison's magisterial fifteen-volume *History of United States Naval Operations in World War II*.

Meanwhile, changes were also taking place at the Army's educational institutions. At West Point in 1969, history finally acquired its own independent department.[25] Under the supervision of its first two directors,[26] legitimate military history courses using contemporary scholarly research gradually replaced superficial courses in "military art" based on what amounted to historical Cliff Notes. In place of dedicated but uncredentialed officer instructors, the department began to recruit visiting civilian historians and sponsor the graduate preparation of uniformed instructors at major universities.

History enjoyed a similar revitalization at the Command and General Staff College, by then responsible for the midcareer education of one out of every two army officers. In 1979, the college established a Combat Studies Institute staffed with both uniformed and civilian historians specifically to conduct and disseminate historical research on military operations.[27] The Combat Studies Institute eventually matured into one of Command and General Staff College's five major academic departments and served as its parent Army Training and Doctrine Command's proponent for historical studies.[28] Military history courses, initially required only of students seeking a Master's of Military Arts and Sciences degree or selected for a second year of study, became accessible and attractive to regular course students as well.

Military history was even more central to the Army's youngest intermediate institution, the School of Advanced Military Studies. Founded in 1985,[29] the school offered a second year of intense study in operational theory and practice to a small number of hand-picked Command and General Staff College graduates,[30] and a one-year fellowship in advanced operational studies for an even smaller number of war college-selected officers.

Military theory and history were central ingredients of the School of Advanced Military Studies' curriculum from the outset. Indeed, the first two permanent faculty were a civilian theorist and historian, both with doctoral

---

[25] Earlier, military history had been taught first in the Department of Law and History and subsequently in the Department of Military Art and Engineering, typically by serving officers without credentials in the field.

[26] Colonels, later Brigadier Generals, Thomas E. Griess and Roy K. Flint.

[27] Instigated by then TRADOC commander General Donn Starry and organized by then Major Charles R. Schrader. Early members included several alumni of West Point's history department faculty. See Roger J. Spiller, "War History and the History Wars: Establishing the Combat Studies Institute," *The Public Historian*, Fall 1988, pp. 65–81.

[28] Among its recent products are two well-received studies of Army operations in the 1991 Gulf War: Colonel Richard M. Swain's *Lucky War: Third Army in Desert Storm* and General Robert H. Scales's *Certain Victory: The U.S. Army in the Gulf War* (Fort Leavenworth, KS, 1993 and 1994, respectively).

[29] The School of Advanced Military Studies' founder, then Colonel Huba Wass de Czege, launched a pilot Advanced Military Studies Program comprising fourteen students in 1984. The school itself was formed and designated a separate college department the following year.

[30] Originally twenty-four, all U.S. Army. The most recent class graduated seventy-nine, including nine sister service and three international officers.

degrees in military history.[31] Historical examination ranged from small unit actions to whole campaigns, deliberately and intricately interwoven with theory, the latter used to formulate questions of history, history in turn used to challenge the assertions of theory. Nor was attention limited to warfighting. Both preparation for war and military operations other than war also received historical and theoretical scrutiny.[32] The resulting educational experience was so compelling that the program subsequently was emulated by the Air Force and Marine Corps, and also contributed to the creation of a similar advanced educational program by the British Army.[33]

At the Army War College, finally, the post-Vietnam period saw the restoration to the basic curriculum of strategic and operational studies largely ignored since the end of World War II. By the mid-1980s, five of the war college's ten core courses focused on strategy and operations, all heavily laced with military history.[34]

Earlier, the Army's Chief of Military History had designated Carlisle as the central repository for the Army's growing collection of historical source materials. In 1971, the Military History Research Collection was renamed the Military History Institute and given pedagogical, as well as archival and research responsibilities. In 1985, acknowledging the institute's growing centrality to the educational process, formal control passed from the Chief of Military History in Washington to the commandant of the war college.

Since then, historical study and research at Carlisle has continued to expand. In 1971, the college launched its own scholarly journal. Throughout the late 1980s, the infusion of military history into the regular curriculum continued, until by the mid-1990s, case studies in twentieth-century strategy comprised nearly one-fifth of the core curriculum.[35] In 1999, at the instigation of a commandant himself a published military historian, and assisted by the Harold K. Johnson Professor of Military History,[36] the college inaugurated an Advanced Strategic Arts Program not unlike the School of Advanced Military Studies' Advanced Operational Art Studies Fellowship. The new course focused on strategic rather than operational issues, but like

---

31 Both still on the faculty today, an uncommon tenure in Army schools.

32 In its early years, the School of Advanced Military Studies devoted considerable attention to tactical and operational issues (except for the Advanced Operational Studies Fellows, study of strategy was deferred to the war colleges). Recently, the school has tended to concentrate more narrowly on operational art, many of its previous tactical concerns having been absorbed by the first-year Command and General Staff College course.

33 The current deputy director of the School of Advanced Airpower Studies, for example, was one of the schools' two original seminar leaders and its second deputy director. Similarly, the officer charged with creating Camberly's Higher Command and Staff Course in 1986 interned at the School of Advanced Military Studies in preparation.

34 Judith Hicks Stiehm, *The U.S. Army War College: Military Education in a Democracy* (Philadelphia, 2002), pp. 114, 122.

35 Ibid., p. 152.

36 Major General Robert Scales and Ohio State Professor Emeritus Williamson Murray, respectively.

its Leavenworth predecessor, it was self-consciously grounded in military history.[37]

Changes in Army professional education accompanied similar changes in the other three services. Perhaps the most significant were the pedagogical and curricular reforms introduced at the Naval War College in the early 1970s by Admiral Stansfield Turner. Turner reorganized the basic curriculum of the college into three blocks, the first of which deliberately resurrected the intensive Luce-Mahan foundation in theory and history that had declined in the intervening years. At his direction, the Naval War College adopted the syndicate method in place of lecture and began recruiting civilian academics to supplement the uniformed faculty. In 1975, the Secretary of the Navy formally enlarged the college's mission to include scholarly research, in support of which the college in that same year established a Center for Advanced Research, subsequently combined with the War Gaming Department and the Naval War College Press into an integrated Center for Naval Warfare Studies.[38]

LINGERING DISCOMFORT

The resurrection of military history in American academia and its renewed importance in professional military education might lead one to conclude that the discipline has entered something of a golden age in the United States. In some respects, that may well be true. Certainly, the general interest in and quality of historical scholarship on military topics has never been greater. Each successive year has seen publication of fresh, readable, and occasionally startling reexaminations of conflicts remote and recent, many reflecting previously ignored or unobtainable evidence.[39] Perhaps as important, a plethora of professional journals subject today's historical scholarship on military subjects to an unprecedented level of peer review.

Moreover, apart from their intrinsic quality, the products of recent military historiography have tended to enlarge on much (although certainly not all) of the scholarship that preceded them. The change is most visible in the breadth of historians' gazes. Traditional campaign studies certainly have not disappeared, nor have appraisals of military commanders from damning to hagiographic. But recent military histories also exhibit both a wider and narrower intellectual aperture than many of their predecessors.

---

[37] The course description is careful to note that the Advanced Strategic Arts Program "is rooted in history; but it is not a course in history." Not coincidentally, the last two Army War College commandants both earned PhDs in history.

[38] "NWC History," Naval War College Web site. See fn. 6.

[39] Examples include Fred Anderson's *Crucible of War: The Seven Years' War and the Fate of Empire in British North America, 1754–1766* (New York, 2001); James M. McPherson's *Battle Cry of Freedom: The Civil War Era* (New York, 1988); and Williamson Murray and Allan R. Millett's *A War to Be Won: Fighting the Second World War* (Cambridge, MA, 2000).

Looking outward, military historians today routinely emulate Thucydides in probing the contextual conditions that have influenced the outbreak, conduct, and termination of wars.[40] Looking inward, they have begun with considerable success to decipher and describe in a more systematic way the messy, confused, and contingent human activities and events too often concealed and as often misrepresented by the red and blue boxes and arrows on traditional battle maps.[41] The result has been a deeper and more sophisticated appreciation of one of society's least attractive, but most compelling and consequential, activities. Meanwhile, the infusion of military history and military historians into professional military education and conceptual development has provided a welcome and necessary counterbalance to the military's post–World War II preoccupation with science and technology.

That said, in the United States perhaps more than elsewhere, the marriage between historian and soldier remains in some ways uncomfortable for both. In academia, lingering suspicion of military historiography as a legitimate scholarly enterprise, as well as ideological aversion to its practitioners, continues to inhibit the growth of the discipline and its attraction to younger scholars.[42] Both especially afflict civilian historians who choose to work in or for the military, whether at military educational institutions or as command historians in line units and operating agencies.[43]

Moreover, academic prejudices apart, the appropriate relationship between military history and professional military education remains unsettled even in purely intellectual terms. In part, that reality reflects America's military culture and in part the question of how military history is written, and, therefore, how it can and should be used.

---

[40] Kennedy, "The Rise and Fall of Military History," p. 11.

[41] The best known may be John Keegan's *The Face of Battle* (New York, 1976), which has become virtually canonical reading in military educational institutions. Others include Paddy Griffith's *Forward into Battle* (Chichester, 1981); Richard Holmes' *Acts of War* (New York, 1985); and Victor Davis Hanson's *The Western Way of War* (New York, 1989).

[42] Kaplan, "Four-Star Generalists." Some of this reflects the popularization of military history, occasional manifestations of which trade accuracy for drama. In contrast, as one historian privately commented to me, for some of his academic colleagues, the worst scholarly sin seems to be writing history that is actually readable.

[43] See, for example, Stanley Sandler, "U.S. Army Command Historians: What We Are and What We Do," *Perspectives*, April 2001. Sandler notes that "While it is a source of some pride to be the professional historian for, say, the Artillery Center and School, there is the feeling among many academics that such historians are little more than 'hired guns' (no pun intended), who basically write and teach what they are told."

Oddly, the problem seems to be less acute with respect to historians in uniform than for their civilian counterparts. Just why this should be so is not clear, inasmuch as both are equally at the mercy of their government employer. It is at least arguable, though, that civilian historians simply because they are civilians are held informally to a higher standard of intellectual independence than their uniformed colleagues, and their objectivity in turn is more likely to be discounted however scrupulous their scholarship. Such an assertion is hard to prove, needless to say, and I offer it only as a hypothesis. However, it is a view shared by several military historians with whom I've worked, both uniformed and civilian.

Concerning the former, one view holds that America's military culture traditionally has been anti-intellectual, a bias shared with other Western armies.[44] Whether or not that is true, today's American military professionals certainly tend to be impatient with abstraction and ambiguity.[45] In part, such attitudes are an almost inevitable by-product of the mission orientation inculcated in soldiers, sailors, airmen, and marines from their recruitment, and the modern military's limited leisure for contemplation. It may also be a reflection of the engineering bias that has characterized American military education from its beginning. The latter in turn is no accident, but rather reflects a national military experience that began with the taming of a continent and has since, with but one exception, required America to project military power abroad as the prerequisite to employment. Both have tended to focus professional interest and education on the measurable logistics of military science rather than the less quantifiable challenges of military art, a predilection merely reinforced by a cultural confidence in technology shared by few other nationalities.[46]

Together, these attributes predispose military professionals toward simplicity and precision in learning. In the extreme, this can become dismayingly reductionist. An old Army joke tells of the NCO required to instruct his subordinates in the finer points of ballroom deportment who promptly transforms the waltz into a drill. The story may be apocryphal, but the military's recurring efforts to rationalize and simplify the processes of learning and judgment through heuristics such as formats, templates, matrices, and other devices certainly are not.[47]

Applied to the study of history, the same cultural predisposition encourages a search for certainty with respect not only to fact, which would be challenging enough, but also to causality, which is infinitely more problematic.[48] For many in uniform, the litmus test of historical utility resides in the presumed ability to draw unambiguous lessons from the past with respect to the future. Indeed, since World War I, few American military operations have taken place without an organized effort to record decisions and events

---

[44] Col. Lloyd J. Matthews, USA (Ret), "The Uniformed Intellectual and His Place in American Arms," *ARMY*, July/August 2002.

[45] Janowitz, *The Professional Soldier*, p. 135.

[46] Russell F. Weigley, *The American Way of War: A History of United States Military Strategy and Policy* (New York, 1973). See also Williamson Murray, "Clausewitz Out, Computer In, Military Culture and Technological Hubris," *The National Interest*, Summer 1997.

[47] At Leavenworth, during my attendance at the Command and General Staff College in the late 1970s, students were required to apply a "battle calculus" that allocated forces in strict mathematical ratios. There is little evidence that the passion for such seductively but also often spuriously exact methods has diminished significantly in the intervening years.

[48] Thus, the preface to the Army's September 1993 Training Circular 25-20, *A Leader's Guide To After-Action Reviews*, notes that soldiers and leaders must understand after every training event "what did and did not occur and why." The same expectation applies to actual combat, which of course is also a training event.

as they occur, and to assemble the results as rapidly as possible thereafter for use in education, training, and combat development. So insistent is the military on this requirement that each service has established organizations whose principal responsibility is to collect, archive, evaluate, and disseminate tactical and operational "lessons learned."[49]

Approached carefully, of course, there is nothing whatever wrong with such efforts to capture experience systematically. On the contrary, as many have pointed out, the doctrinal and organizational reforms that resulted in *Blitzkrieg* reflected just such a thorough review of Germany's World War I experience.[50] But the same example also reveals dangers: the wider the scope and higher the level at which military organizations attempt direct generalization from historical experience, the greater the risk that they will ignore, misinterpret, or accidentally or intentionally distort the essential ingredients of that experience.[51]

Increasing military reliance on advanced technologies only aggravates the danger. On the one hand, it encourages confidence that technology can bypass, if not eliminate, some historically intractable battlefield problems, chiefly those associated with transforming information into knowledge.[52] On the other hand, it tends to place demands on the study of military history that many contemporary historians are intellectually disinclined to satisfy. In effect, it seeks a "scientific" history in which, despite war's intrinsic messiness, officers can reduce its essentials to unambiguous and reliable guides to action.

There is of course a long tradition of just that sort of military history, from Jomini's *Summary of the Art of War* to the late Colonel Trevor Dupuy's efforts to derive quantitative predictions about battlefield relationships from historical research.[53] However, few of today's military historians are willing to follow that path. On the contrary, if contemporary historiography has a professional bias at all, it is quite the opposite.[54] Certainly, few modern historians would be entirely comfortable with British classicist G. F. Abbott's ringing assertion, written in the disillusioned aftermath of the catastrophe

[49] Which is not to say the results invariably are used. The considerable lessons learned output of the Vietnam War, for example, has remained largely (and regrettably) ignored. See Vetock, *Lessons Learned*, pp. 119–20.

[50] James S. Corum, *The Roots of Blitzkrieg: Hans von Seeckt and German Military Reform* (Lawrence, KS, 1992). See also Murray and Millett, *Military Innovation in the Interwar Period*.

[51] Williamson Murray, *German Military Effectiveness* (Baltimore, MD, 1992). See also Holger H. Herwig, "Clio Deceived: Patriotic Self-Censorship in Germany after the Great War," *International Security*, Fall 1987.

[52] Recent discussion of this issue is voluminous. For the leading proponent, see William A. Owens, *Lifting the Fog of War* (New York, 2000). For one of many critiques, see Barry D. Watts, *Clausewitzian Friction and Future War* (Fort McNair, Washington, DC, 1996).

[53] See especially T. N. Dupuy, *Numbers, Prediction, and War* (Indianapolis, IN, 1979).

[54] Lynn Hunt, "Where Have All the Theories Gone?" *Perspectives*, March 2002.

of 1914–18, that "The use of history...is to light the present hour to its duty."[55]

THE PROBLEM OF HISTORICAL UTILITY

Many authors have described at length the intrinsic obstacles to history's ability to teach transferable lessons.[56] Those summarized here seek simply to register the problem, in full awareness that one could say a good deal more about each.

The central objection is that, even at its best, the writing of history intrinsically deforms it. Like the lens of a camera, historiography distorts the past in the very effort to portray it. To begin with, even were every relevant fact bearing on some historical event obtainable – and the word "relevant" presents its own problems – the historian must be selective merely from considerations of clarity. In fact, no one is more conscious than the historian himself or herself that all relevant facts are never obtainable, and that, even if they were, their interconnections would remain in large measure unfathomable.[57]

Moreover, given that history unread might as well not be written, some narrative sequence is essential, and regardless of how carefully chosen, the result is to impose a relational logic on events that is almost always to some degree artificial. Perhaps the most familiar examples are descriptions of Waterloo and Gettysburg, conventionally divided for narrative purposes into distinguishable acts like those of a play, a logical and convenient arrangement that, however, was largely invisible to the participants.

Still another challenge confronting the conscientious historian is the problem of translation. Russell McNeil notes that "The objective facts of...war are difficult if not impossible to document for the very reason that words and ideas change their meanings most during the course of war."[58] Even when original sources are abundant, and putting aside whatever biases, errors, and omissions they may contain, the words in which they were written inevitably reflect assumptions and understandings quite different from our own.

This problem arises even in recent and well-documented conflicts. Soldiers are apt in their reporting, whether officially or informally, to take for granted conditions, procedures, and relationships self-evident to their correspondents, but that are rarely apparent to those attempting later to piece

---

[55] Abbott, *Thucydides*, p. 7.
[56] See, especially, Michael Howard, "The Use and Abuse of Military History" in Michael Howard, *The Causes of War* (Cambridge, MA, 1983), pp. 188–97.
[57] All this quite apart from the deliberate use of history for mythmaking. Ibid., pp. 188–9.
[58] Russell McNeil, "Thucydides as Science," Malaspina University-College, 1996 (Web publication), www.mala.bc.ca/nmcneil/ice18b.htm.

together what they did and why. When the events in question are chronologically or culturally remote, translation is even harder.[59]

Finally, insofar as it affects history's perceived usefulness to the military professional, there is the challenge of establishing causality, about which scholars have spilled whole gallons of philosophical ink. Bertrand Russell in one notorious essay went so far as to insist that "the word 'cause' is so inextricably bound up with misleading associations as to make its complete extrusion from the philosophical vocabulary desirable."[60] Problematic enough even in the physical sciences,[61] establishing causality is even more challenging for historiography, which rarely permits even a rough approximation of the controlled experimentation central to scientific inquiry.[62]

Nevertheless, most soldiers judge history's essential utility according to its presumed ability to explain, if not actually predict, the relationship between actions and events and between one event and another. Military historians, of course, are only too aware of this inclination, whence considerable professional discomfort. As Professor Jay Luvaas complained years ago, "[N]o other field of history is under as much pressure as military history to provide 'practical'answers to some current problem. If military history cannot provide such answers, why study it?"[63] He goes on to warn, as others have, that read incautiously and without meticulous attention to context, history is capable of furnishing precedent for nearly any lesson.

Because, as G. C. Lichtenberg once acidly noted, the most dangerous of all falsehoods is a slightly distorted truth, requiring military history to provide definitive answers to questions that it inherently is ill-equipped to ask is ultimately self-defeating. No one understood that better than Carl von Clausewitz, who devoted much of *On War*'s second book to debunking the scientific pretensions of prevailing military theory and the universal principles of action it claimed to validate. At the same time, however, Clausewitz insisted that "[h]istorical examples clarify everything and also provide the

---

[59] Thus, commenting on accounts of Greek hoplite battle by Herodotus, Thucydides, and Xenophon, Victor Davis Hanson notes that "while each author saw war and battle as the theme of their histories, they also took for granted an understanding of battle practice on the part of their audience, mostly male and veterans themselves." Hanson, *The Western Way of War*, p. 44.

[60] Bertrand Russell, "On the Notion of Cause," in *Mysticism and Logic* (New York, 1957), p. 174.

[61] For one distinguished scientist's exasperated view, see Steven Weinberg, "Can Science Explain Anything? Everything?" in Matt Ridley, ed., *The Best American Science Writing 2002* (New York, 2002).

[62] Which has not prevented at least one writer from claiming that history "comes closest of all the liberal arts to being a hard science." Kaplan, "Four-Star Generalists." For a more conventional view, see John McCannon's rebuttal in Letters to the Editor, *The Atlantic Online*, January 2000.

[63] Jay Luvaas, "Military History: Is It Still Practicable?" *Parameters*, May 1982, pp. 2–14.

best kind of proof in the empirical sciences,"[64] especially as applied to the art
of war. In this apparently paradoxical view of military history lies an answer
to the Hobbesian choice between demanding of it an unachievable precision[65] and renouncing it as irrelevant for the practical education of soldiers.

The Clausewitzian approach to using history rested on two central
postulates: one concerning how such study should be expected to educate,
and the other concerning the kind of history required to underwrite that
study. Regarding the former, Clausewitz largely rejected the use of history
to derive prescriptive rules of action.[66] Anticipating subsequent philosophical objections, he considered history, at least as then written, incapable of
sustaining the burden of proof required to justify such generalizations.

Instead, for Clausewitz, the central utility of history was to enable the
aspiring leader, in effect, to refight battles and campaigns in his mind, in
all their ambiguity, contingency, and danger, and thus begin vicariously to
sense the resulting complex interplay of decisions, actions, and events in
the real world. Theory, he believed, had a place in this process, but not the
simplifying and prescriptive role that contemporaries such as Von Bülow
and Jomini assigned to it. Rather, its vital function was to enable the critical
student to make logical inferences with which to bridge the inevitable gaps
in confirmed historical knowledge.[67]

Above all, Clausewitz believed the purpose of studying war was to hone
judgment before the battle, not dictate decisions during it. He was adamant
that the study of military theory, and by extension military history, should
aim at educating "the mind of the future commander, or, more accurately, to
guide him in his self-education, not accompany him to the battlefield."[68] He
might have been chagrined to learn, as one writer tells us, that "many a Civil
War general went into battle with a sword in one hand and Jomini's *Summary
of the Art of War* in another,"[69] but he would not have been surprised by
the result.

To achieve the vicarious immersion in the turmoil of war that Clausewitz
had in mind also placed stringent burdens and restrictions on the historiography employed for the purpose. Above all, Clausewitz objected to the use
of compressed or summarized examples. "An event that is lightly touched
upon," he insisted, "instead of being carefully detailed, is like an object seen

---

64 Clausewitz, *On War*, p. 170.
65 Used here in the formal sense of generating reliably reproduceable results.
66 At least to the extent of informing the mind of the strategic commander. He was somewhat
    less resistant to the derivation of principles governing what today's military calls "tactics,
    techniques, and procedures."
67 For a more comprehensive argument, see Jon Tetsuro Sumida, "The Relationship of History
    and Theory in *On War*: The Clausewitzian Ideal and Its Implications," *Journal of Military
    History*, April 2001.
68 Clausewitz, *On War*, p. 141.
69 LTC J. D. Hittle, *Jomini and His Summary of the Art of War* (Harrisburg, PA, 1947), quoted
    in Michael Howard, *Studies in War and Peace* (New York, 1971), p. 31.

at a distance: it is impossible to distinguish any detail, and it looks the same from every angle."[70] For Clausewitz, the utility of military history resided precisely in its thoroughness. Nothing less would confront potential commanders with war's contingency and complexity, or offer the richness of description essential to making reliable inferences.

For much the same reason, he discounted the use of multiple examples to compensate for insufficient depth in any one. "There are occasions," he noted, "where nothing will be proved by a dozen examples."[71] Such treatments, he argued, offered merely the "semblance" of evidence, but not its substance. His views anticipated modern science, which likewise has come to understand that the mere multiplication of data points, to use today's jargon, alone guarantees neither unambiguous explanation nor even reliable prediction.

Finally, for Clausewitz, the more recent the experience, the more useful the history. With the passage of time, he noted, history "loses some elements of life and color, like a picture that gradually fades and darkens. What remains in the end, more or less at random, are large masses and isolated features, which are thereby given undue weight."[72]

With this view, if no other, most current historians and even some soldiers might take issue. It is hard to imagine how any military commander could fail to profit from reading Slim's *Defeat into Victory*, Grant's *Memoirs*, or Josephus's *The Jewish War*. Still, one should not dismiss Clausewitz's caution lightly because it is certainly true that most of the challenges associated with both the writing and reading of military history inflate with the remoteness of either from its subject. Commenting on the dilemma, historian Joseph Ellis noted, "Hindsight . . . is a tricky tool. Too much of it and we obscure the all-pervasive sense of contingency, [too little] and we are thrown without resources into the patternless swirl of events. . . . We need, in effect, to be nearsighted and farsighted at the same time."[73]

USING MILITARY HISTORY TO EDUCATE

Moreover, as compelling as they are, Clausewitz's injunctions concerning the proper use of military history present difficulties for historian and soldier alike. For the former, the burdens of thoroughness and accuracy are immense. Clausewitz himself acknowledged as much, admitting that "Anyone who feels the urge to undertake such a task must dedicate himself for his labors

---

[70] Clausewitz, *On War*, p. 172. He would have sympathized with famed gourmet Brillat-Savarin's reported response when offered grapes after dinner: *"Non, merci. Je ne prends pas mon vin en pilules."* ("No, thank you. I don't take my wine in pills.")

[71] Ibid.

[72] Ibid., p. 173. Presumably, he would have applauded today's elaborate efforts to record the events of battle even as they occur.

[73] Joseph J. Ellis, *Founding Brothers* (New York, 2002), pp. 6–7.

as he would prepare for a pilgrimage to distant lands."[74] He likened history's evidentiary standards to those of jurisprudence. It is only too clear from the tenor of his comments that, in his opinion, few historians of his day met those elevated standards.

It may not be thought wholly self-congratulatory (since this writer is not a historian) to suggest that the work of today's scholars comes a good deal closer. In the 170 odd years since Clausewitz wrote, methods of military historiography have matured, the variety and quality of sources have expanded, and, in the United States at least, access to them by historians has significantly improved.[75] Indeed, where once the historian's principal problem was to secure enough reliable information to tell his or her story with some confidence in its essential truthfulness, today's historian is more likely to confront a superabundance of information, in respect to which the major challenge is distinguishing the vital from the trivial.

At the same time, that problem suggests that, although the nature of the burden facing the military historian may have changed, its magnitude has not. Moreover, today's historian confronts a problem his or her predecessors never imagined: the exponential increase in contemporary wartime reporting, which too often has the effect of propagating an understanding of battlefield events that may be both distorted and incomplete. Beyond the traditional scholarly challenges associated with assembling, weighing, and presenting reliable factual evidence, therefore, today's historian also must combat the preconceptions instilled by instant and pervasive media reportage.[76]

Above all, the military historian must avoid the temptation to impose retrospective normative categories and criteria on decisions and actions reflecting very different perceptions of the world. To interpret what they read in the sense suggested by Clausewitz, those who study history must attempt to see events in the same light as the participants themselves, in all their confusion, ambiguity, and occasional stupidity and brutality. That, of course, does not preclude historians from making judgments about the decisions and events described. But the reader must also be able to draw conclusions, and to do so must attempt to the extent possible to see events in context, free of hindsight's inevitable distortion.[77]

---

[74] Clausewitz, *On War*, p. 174.

[75] Progress that may paradoxically be at increasing risk as electronic replaces paper communication. See Fred Kaplan, "The End of History," www.slate.com/id/2083920, June 4, 2003.

[76] We saw a good example during Operation Iraqi Freedom, in which imbedded reporting, although furnishing undeniably gripping coverage of events in progress, also repeatedly distorted their meaning and impact.

[77] Professor Eliot Cohen is not alone in deploring "the journalist's and historian's practice of putting defeated commanders in the dock, as it were, or on the couch to be scrutinized for psychopathologies." Eliot A. Cohen, "Military Misfortunes," *Military History Quarterly*, Summer 1990, p. 106.

For the soldier, the principal challenge associated with the Clausewitzian approach to history is finding time for the immersive study and reflection it requires. Clausewitz, it may be recalled, devoted more than twenty years, off and on, to developing an understanding of war that he himself considered incomplete when he died. No one in U.S. uniform today possesses even a fraction of that time for self-education. Moreover, few would indulge in it if they could. On the contrary, given the variety of professional demands on their time, modern military and naval officers tend inevitably to focus on rapid analysis and problem solving. A venerable West Point faculty adage holds that cadets are not so much overworked as overscheduled. One could easily say the same of most officers, in or out of the professional education system.

Unsurprisingly, the ensuing "learn it quickly, apply it correctly, and move on" approach to knowledge also affects the study of military history. Describing faculty guidance at the Army War College, for example, Judith Stiehm notes: "The need to cover the curriculum without 'wasting time' seemed to be an implicit theme, an informal element of the whole curriculum, even though it was stated explicitly only with regard to strategy."[78] A similar tendency to sacrifice depth to coverage in the interests of time also affects the study of history in other military schools, risking the very "semblance" of historical understanding that Clausewitz was so insistent on avoiding.

Given the operational demands on officers, especially at a time of expanding military commitments, expecting this reality to change without a basic reassessment of educational priorities is simply not reasonable. Some officers will continue to invest their own time in historical study, whether from personal interest or from a sense of professional obligation. A few will continue to have the opportunity to pursue graduate studies in history at government expense. For most, however, caught between professional and family obligations, the incentive to volunteer such an investment will remain limited. Hence, while applauding the well-intentioned exhortations of senior leaders to intellectual self-improvement on the part of their subordinates, one wonders where they expect the latter to find the time and energy. [79]

Military educators might, of course, console themselves with the reminder that, after all, few officers will become senior commanders, and that, for most others, the distillation of history through doctrine, however incomplete, will suffice to meet professional needs. The reality is less comforting. Some junior officers eventually *will* become senior leaders, and current selection processes offer no assurance that historical literacy will be among their intellectual attainments. On the contrary, the institutional bias, if anything, is in the opposite direction. Moreover, if there is a perceptible trend in modern

[78] Stiehm, *The U.S. Army War College*, p. 114 and fn. 36.
[79] Most recently, U.S. Representative and long-time advocate of professional military education Ike Skelton (D-MO). See "War by the Book," *St. Louis Post-Dispatch*, June 12, 2003.

warfighting, at least among developed nations, it is the devolution of leadership responsibility downward. As recent conflicts have underlined, junior officers increasingly confront requirements formerly the province of more senior leaders, and for which prescriptive rules, however thoughtfully developed, will prove less and less useful.

Finally, there is the problem that doctrine itself tends to be written by relatively junior officers. Although it may be reviewed and approved by their superiors, few generals or admirals can afford the time to supervise its production in detail.[80] More important, it is typically taught by officers still more junior. Thus, there is no assurance that it will reflect even a distilled version of relevant and important historical experience, much less experience remote from the writers' and teachers' own time and circumstances.

In short, if Clausewitz were right about the essentiality to the military professional of "thorough familiarity" with historical experience, military organizations simply cannot leave its development to voluntarism. Instead, they must deliberately inculcate it throughout the professional development process. That will require an investment in time and resources, at least to the extent invested routinely and without hesitation in developing and sustaining physical fitness.

The first requirement is to begin inculcating the habit of historical study early, in the precommissioning process. For academy cadets, that already takes place to some extent, but real immersion remains largely limited to those choosing history as their academic concentration. That state of affairs must change. The study of military history should be understood not simply as an area of academic specialization, but rather as a uniform prerequisite of officership. The same requirement applies to officers accessed through ROTC, in which attention to military history is frequently even more cursory. ROTC departments should enlist the assistance of their colleagues in collegiate history departments, and the Department of Defense in turn should be willing to assist those departments financially in recruiting and developing the necessary scholarly talent.[81]

The second challenge is to induce young officers to sustain the habit of historical study after commissioning, despite the myriad routine demands on their time. That will happen only if their superiors invest their own time and energies. Merely publishing recommended professional reading lists will not suffice. Especially for young officers, extracting value from the study of history requires active mentorship. Moreover, junior officers develop their sense of what matters professionally in large measure by observing their superiors.

---

80   In fairness, some will. Development of the Army's 1982 and 1986 editions of FM 100-5, for example, benefited from active involvement by senior leaders, as did the Marine Corps' FMF 1. But such high-level involvement is not common for most doctrinal writing.

81   Which is what the Canadian military does at every major university, despite the relative paucity of defense spending in that nation.

If the latter are willing to invest precious time reading and discussing history, so too will their subordinates, and conversely.[82]

In a perfect world, no officer would arrive at Fort McNair, Carlisle, Newport, Maxwell, or Quantico without a solid base of interest in and familiarity with military history on which to build, a base the stronger for having been sustained not only in an academic environment, but also as a routine feature of military duty. The role of the war colleges, then, would simply be to expand that familiarity by exposure to a broader and more complex range of issues, contexts, and historical treatments.[83]

Finally, there is the question of the application of military history in the war colleges themselves. Here the excuse that not all officers will become senior leaders is moot, even were it otherwise defensible. Their presence at a war college virtually guarantees that matriculating officers will exercise significant influence on both the internal development of the military services and their employment in peace and war. To the extent that historical literacy is material to either enterprise, the war colleges are the places that must ensure the understanding of the wider implications of historical knowledge.

As earlier discussion suggests, to a considerable extent, it already is. All five war colleges – the Marine Corps now operates its own – rely in varying degree on historical studies to supplement and enrich their curricula. All have recruited professionals in the field to monitor, advise on, and occasionally teach historical subjects. All have journals in which historical research and analysis are welcome, and which encourage students to publish. All host distinguished guest lecturers in military history, as well as other academic and professional fields.

Nevertheless, the encounter with military history at the war colleges currently remains distant from the Clausewitzian ideal. As is true throughout the military educational system, the study of history at the war colleges, some more than others, remains fragmentary. Just as at the military academies, at the beginning of professional military education, officers who choose to immerse themselves in history can do so at the war colleges. The resources are there.[84] What are not available are the time and incentive. Rather, as the earlier comment by Judith Stiehm on the Army War College's curricular bias suggests, the war colleges are in many respects more like undergraduate

---

[82] My personal model is the informal military history seminars conducted personally by LTG P. K. Van Riper, USMC retired, during his service as commander of the Marine Corps Combat Development Center.

[83] In effect, satisfying Michael Howard's injunction that military history be studied in depth, breadth, and context. Howard, "The Uses and Abuses of Military History," pp. 195–7.

[84] With the qualifier that the war colleges' ability to attract top-quality scholarly talent is limited not only financially, but also by the disincentives of the military academic environment. See Stiehm, *The U.S. Army War College*, chap. 4.

than graduate institutions, prevented by the sheer quantity of the subjects they insist on covering from concentrating seriously on any.

Here there is room for major change, but such change would require serious reconsideration of the role of the war colleges. Specifically, it would require an acknowledgment that the business of the war colleges, unlike that of intermediate military schools, is to educate, not train. It would require sacrificing curricular breadth to intellectual depth. It would require shifting the emphasis from the classroom to individual study, writing, and research. It would require a similar change in curricular materials from the summaries, extracts, and excerpts that currently undergird the curricula at most war colleges to complete works by leaders in the field. Above all, it would require a change in the prevailing attitude toward war college attendance that selection is a reward for past performance and an opportunity to relax away from operational responsibilities, rather than preparation for future service and an obligation every bit as serious and demanding as command, and treating a casual or lackluster attitude toward that obligation as professionally unacceptable.[85]

CONCLUSION

Is such change likely? The historical record is equivocal. There certainly have been changes in the fundamental direction of professional military education, from the initial establishment of the Naval War College by Luce and Mahan to its intellectual revival under Turner to a similar but too brief flowering of the Air War College in the early 1990s to the Army War College's Advanced Strategic Arts Program. In each case, institutional establishment and reform reflected a commitment by the senior leadership – civilian, military, or both – to the essential importance of military education and the provision of the resources needed to underwrite it. There is no reason it could not happen again.

That it would require such a commitment, however, is not debatable. In civilian academia, revolution from below is possible, if infrequent. In the professional military education system, a hierarchy within a hierarchy, it simply is not. Brilliant and committed faculty can make a difference and often do. But the weight of the military personnel management process limits such impact to the margin. Only senior leaders can make real change, and only a succession of like-minded leaders can sustain it – something that has not happened since World War II.

---

[85] For an elaboration of this argument, see Leonard D. Holder, Jr. and Williamson Murray, "Prospects for Military Education," *Joint Forces Quarterly*, Spring 1998, and Williamson Murray, "Grading the War Colleges," *The National Interest*, Winter 1986/1987.

Today, at a time when too many in America's military look to technology rather than education to offset deficiencies in knowledge, the prospects for significant reform of military education in general and expanded reliance on military history in particular are not altogether encouraging. But military history has proved a determined and resilient survivor. It is simply too early to surrender its crucial role in the education of the military professional to its technology-bemused detractors. Provided historians continue to sustain history's scholarly excellence, concerned political and military leaders will continue to assert its professional relevance.

They should, for their own sake, as well as that of the soldiers they lead and the interests of the nation they serve. For if military history cannot and does not guarantee an answer to every question that may confront America's defenders in a troubled and uncertain future – if, as Maya Angelou rightly said, "History, despite its wrenching pain, cannot be unlived" – still it is true, as she added, that "faced with courage, [it] need not be lived again."[86] That objective alone justifies the enterprise Thucydides launched nearly 2,500 years ago.

[86] Maya Angelou, "Inaugural Poem," Presidential Inauguration, Washington, DC, January 20, 1993.

6

Thoughts on military history and the profession of arms

WILLIAMSON MURRAY

In one of their more infamous skits, the "Frog and the Peach," Peter Cooke and Dudley Moore played a mishapen restauranteur and the food critic from a major London newspaper. Cooke had located his restaurant in the middle of the Yorkshire bogs – no problem with parking, just in extracting the cars afterward. One specialty of the house was "frog á la peche" – a giant frog with a peach in its mouth with boiling cointreau poured over the melange. The other was "peche á la frog" – a giant peach with boiling cointreau poured over it – from which, when cut open, tadpoles swam out. Needless to say, the restaurant was not a success. At the end of the interview, Dudley Moore asked Peter Cooke whether he had learned from his mistakes. Cooke's reply was brief and to the point: "Yes, I have studied my mistakes from every point of view, gone over them again and again, and feel fully confident I can repeat every one of them!"[1]

Unfortunately, that story is all too relevant to the performance of statesmen, military institutions, and generals over the course of the past 2,500 years. If the reader feels such a comparison is overly harsh, the comments of a highly regarded retired U.S. Army general examining the performance of military institutions of the great powers in the first half of the twentieth century should suggest that the comparison is all too apt:

> [I]n the spheres of operations and tactics, where military competence would seem to be a nation's rightful due, the twenty-one [historians'] reports suggest for the most part less than general professional military competence and sometimes abysmal incompetence. One can doubt whether any other profession in these

---

[1] The re-creation of the above dialog is entirely from my fading memory. I heard the skit twice in the early 1970s, when the two comics were performing on Broadway in a show entitled *Good Evening*. I beg indulgence from the shades of those two great comics, both in the tradition of Aristophanes, for my feeble attempt to re-create one of their greatest skits.

seven nations during the same periods would have received such poor ratings by similarly competent outside observers.[2]

My own period of primary academic interest – the interwar period and the Second World War – suggests that military institutions rarely have been interested in studying their own experiences with any degree of honesty. Historians often argue that armies and navies invariably study the last war and that is why they get the next one wrong. Nothing could be further from the truth. In fact, one of the major reasons military institutions get the next war wrong is because they either deliberately fail to study the last war, or do so only insofar as it makes leaders feel good.

Ironically, in view of this myth, only the Germans studied the First World War at the tactical and operational levels with a degree of honesty that allowed them to carry those lessons forward into the next conflict. And because through that study they were able to understand more clearly the possibilities offered by future war, they won a series of devastating victories in the first years of World War II. General Hans von Seeckt, the father of the *Reichswehr*, created no fewer than fifty-seven different committees in 1920 to study the lessons of the last war.[3] In contrast, the British created the Kirk Commission only in 1932 to examine the lessons of World War I, while the French ensured their historical examinations of the last war remained limited to what made their army look good.[4]

Yet for all the honesty with which the Germans examined their tactical and operational performance in World War I, they also deliberately set in motion a massive disinformation campaign to cover over the strategic and political mistakes that had contributed so mightily to Germany's defeat.[5] In the end, their efforts misled not only the victorious powers in the 1920s and 1930s – particularly the Americans and the British – but also the Germans themselves.[6] The fact that the German military, not just Adolf Hitler, managed to repeat virtually every strategic mistake in the next war says much about

---

[2] Lieutenant General Jack H. Cushman, U.S. Army, retired, "Challenge and Response at the Operational and Tactical Levels, 1914–1945," in Allan R. Millett and Williamson Murray, eds., *Military Effectiveness*, vol. 3, *The Second World War* (London, 1988), p. 322.

[3] James S. Corum, *The Roots of Blitzkrieg, Hans von Seeckt and German Military Reform* (Lawrence, KS, 1992), p. 37.

[4] For the British Army, see J. P. Harris, *Men, Ideas and Tanks, British Military Thought and Armoured Forces, 1903–1939* (Manchester, 1995); for the French, see Robert Doughty, *The Seeds of Disaster, The Development of French Army Doctrine, 1919–1939* (Hamden, CT, 1985).

[5] Along these lines, see Holger Herwig, "Clio Deceived, Patriotic Self-Censorship in Germany after the Great War," *International Security*, Fall 1987.

[6] Thus, the German explanation for their final defeat in 1918 – that the Communists and the Jews had stabbed the army in the back – led most German analysts to miss entirely the extraordinarily important psychological and military role that American forces played in the war's last months.

their twisted and dishonest examination of the last war at the strategic
level.[7]

Nevertheless, the chapters in this volume rest on an acceptance of Polybius's statement that "the study of history is in the truest sense an education
and a training for political [and military] life, and ... the most instructive, or
rather the only, method of learning to bear with dignity the vicissitudes of
fortune is to recall the catastrophes of others."[8] Thucydides, the greatest of
all military and strategic historians, simply noted about his own work: "It
will be enough for me, however, if these words of mine are judged useful by
those who want to understand clearly the events which happened in the past
and which (human nature being what it is) will at some time or other and
in much the same ways, be repeated in the future."[9] If Thucydides's claim is
correct, then statesmen, soldiers, and military institutions should have been
able to learn from history. Unfortunately, the record of the past decade, much
less that of the past century, would suggest that with rare exceptions they
have not.

This chapter aims to suggest why it has been difficult for the serving professional officer, much less the statesmen, to learn from the past and why it
may be increasingly difficult for Americans to do so in the future. Then, it will
turn to what history, if properly understood and used, can do for military
professionals in forming a philosophical or theoretical framework within
which to understand better the challenges they will inevitably confront. As
the Prussian theorist, Carl von Clausewitz, noted:

> [Theory] is an analytical investigation leading to a close *acquaintance* with
> the subject; applied to experience – in our case to military history – it leads to
> thorough *familiarity* with it. The closer it comes to its goal, the more it proceeds
> from the objective form of a science to the subjective form of a skill, the more
> effective it will prove in areas where the nature of the case admits no arbiter
> but talent.... Theory then becomes a guide to anyone who wants to learn about
> war from books; it will light his way, ease his progress, train his judgment, and
> help him avoid the pitfalls.[10]

---

[7]   Along these lines, Hitler's decision to invade the Soviet Union was greeted enthusiastically
      by the army and Luftwaffe, whereas Hitler's decision to declare war on the United States
      met with the Kriegsmarine's enthusiastic support, while no one in either the army or air
      force voiced the slightest opposition. Of course, when the Second World War was over,
      the surviving military leaders of the Third Reich claimed otherwise, but the documents
      underline how false their postwar claims were. For further discussion of these issues, see
      Williamson Murray and Allan R. Millett, *A War to Be Won, Fighting the Second World
      War* (Cambridge, MA, 2000), or Gerhard Weinberg, *A World at Arms, A Global History
      of the Second World War* (Cambridge, 1994).
[8]   Polybius, *Polybius on Roman Imperialism*, trans. Evelyn S. Shuckburgh, abridged, Alvin
      Bernstein (Lake Bluff, IL, 1987), p. 1.
[9]   Thucydides, *History of the Peloponnesian War*, translated by Rex Warner (New York,
      1954), p. 48.
[10] Carl von Clausewitz, *On War*, trans. and ed., Michael Howard and Peter Paret (Princeton,
      NJ, 1975), p. 141.

THE DIFFICULTIES OF HISTORY FOR
THE PROFESSIONAL OFFICER

The difficulty that history presents to today's professional officer begins with its place in the intellectual framework of the modern world. Since the Renaissance, it has been an important but, for the most part, a peripheral discipline. Yet, for the ancients, it was central to their understanding of the world. In one of his essays: the great classicist Bernard Knox has suggested how different their conception of the past was from ours:

> The early Greek imagination envisaged the past and the present as in front of us – we can see them. The future, invisible, is behind us. . . . Paradoxical though it may sound to the modern ear, this image of our journey through time may be truer to reality than the medieval and modern feeling that we face the future as we make our way forward into it.[11]

In effect, Western man has set himself on a march into the future with little regard for the past.[12] If this has been true for Europeans, it has been even more so for Americans, bent as they are on reinventing themselves and their world.

Exacerbating such tendencies has been what has occurred over the past several decades with study of history in American secondary schools and universities. American education has turned history into something called social studies in an all-too-successful effort to wash out anything that might offend any racial, religious, or national group. American universities for their part have turned history into a triumph of the politically correct. Quite simply, if one does not work in social, racial, or gender history, then one is not doing "serious" history. In terms of the larger society, as Robert Kaplan has suggested, Americans are educating a generation of elitists, no longer capable of grasping the tragic. In their personal lives, they see little enough of what one might term tragic, and in their education, they no longer read the classics of Sophocles, or Euripides, or even Dostoevsky, much less Tolstoy.[13] The result has been that there are few schools – and they are getting fewer – where serious military or strategic history can engage the future officer in his or her education, and this includes America's military academies.[14]

---

[11] Bernard Knox, *Backing into the Future: The Classical Tradition and Its Renewal* (New York, 1994), pp. 11–12.

[12] If one has doubts about this statement, one might want to consider the whole performance of the Marxist left over the past century.

[13] How much is this affecting the education of the young? Four years ago, I taught a seminar on strategy at George Washington University. Of the twenty-four students from among the best private and state universities in the United States, only one of them had read a Greek tragedy. My experiences at Ohio State, where I taught until the mid-1990s, suggest that this was not an aberration, but rather reflective of what is passing for education these days among the elite graduates of major universities in the United States.

[14] West Point at least seems to be holding the line at teaching serious military and political history.

But there is a larger problem that has emerged since the Vietnam War. Academic history has increasingly been written by those who have *never* done anything in their lives but live in schools and universities. Polybius suggests that one cannot write history unless one has been either a statesman or general, and preferably both. In the end he is wrong, because there have been and continue to be historians who through the sheer power of their imagination manage to reach a deep understanding of how the past unfolded.[15]

Yet, Polybius does have a point. The flight from the study of important historical events or individuals – much less "great" men – suggests that academic historians are so far removed from the real world that they are incapable of discussing events in terms that make sense. The prevailing prejudice in the professoriate that individuals play little role in the course of events, but rather that only great sweeping social forces such as the immutable laws of Marxism determine history, can only be held by those whose entire experience in the external world is embodied in the squabblings of university politics. All this leads intelligent undergraduates, interested in what makes military institutions and governments function, to dismiss history as an exercise in academic self-indulgence. And it is from that population that the future officer corps of the services will come.

If this were not enough to discourage officers from studying history, then how military institutions use the discipline completes the depressing picture. The British Army's attitude toward "inky-fingered" officers surely created a contempt for the study of the past that explains much of the difficulty that army confronted in World War II.[16] As Professor Michael Howard has suggested about that Army's officer corps between the two world wars: "[T]he evidence is strong that the army was still as firmly geared to the pace and perspective of regimental soldiering as it had been before 1914; that too many of its members looked on soldiering as an agreeable and honorable occupation rather than as a serious profession demanding no less intellectual dedication than that of the doctor, the lawyer or the engineer."[17] If anything, matters are even more anti-intellectual in some portions of the current American military than they were in the British Army a century ago.[18]

---

[15] Along these lines, one has only to read James McPherson's *Battle Cry of Freedom, The Civil War Era* (Oxford, 1988); or Fred Anderson's *Crucible of War, The Seven Years' War and the Fate of Empire in British North America, 1954–1966* (New York, 2000) to recognize that Polybius is at times quite wrong.

[16] The most thorough examination of the intellectual failures of the British Army in the interwar period remains Brian Bond, *British Military Policy Between the Two Wars* (Oxford, 1980); see also my discussion of the British military in *The Change in the European Balance of Power, 1938–1939, The Path to Ruin* (Princeton, NJ, 1984), chap. 2.

[17] Michael Howard, "The Liddell Hart Memoirs," *Journal of the Royal United Services Institute*, February 1966, p. 61.

[18] For current trends in the American military, see Williamson Murray, "Clausewitz Out, Computers In, Military Culture and Technological Hubris," *The National Interest*, Summer 1997; "Preparing to Lose the Next War," *Strategic Review*, Spring 1998; "Does
(continued)

But there is a larger problem, because history is not easily accessible to anyone, much less officers in their busy careers with little time to reflect. Here, Thucydides suggests the dimensions of the problem in his description of his own efforts: "And it may be that my history will seem less easy to read because of the absence in it of a romantic element."[19] That may be the crux of the matter: "the absence in it of a romantic element." Useful history is also difficult history, and learning from it takes serious work.

Not least, it demands a certain intellectual breadth. The student of history must possess a knowledge and understanding of the context of events, geography, the figures who act on its stage, how different the political and moral standards may have been from one's own time, and the extraordinary impact that irrational and incalculable factors can have on the course of human events. The student must also bring to an examination of the past a sense of how uncertain and ambiguous the choices were to those who made them – of the fact that those who participated in the historical drama had only a partial understanding of the landscape and that the path to the future was far less clear to them than it is to the historian who later recounts the course of events.

Because historians know the result, they risk seeing clarity where there was none.[20] For the professional officer who lives in a world characterized even in peacetime by ambiguity and uncertainty, the clarity of all too many histories seems unreal – almost like fiction – and therefore unusable. Officers who want to understand the past and how it might be repeated in some fashion in the future must therefore bring a healthy skepticism to their reading and a willingness and knowledge to challenge historians.

In the end, much of the writing of history has rendered its readers a disservice. In analyzing military and diplomatic events, historians tend to simplify and clarify the arguments and difficulties through which governments and bureaucracies muddle in any decision-making process. Often, they look for complex explanations for what may simply be a matter of incompetence or accident.[21] That very clarification of what, to a soldier in war, is inevitably a

---

(continued)
Military Culture Matter?," *Orbis*, Winter 1999; and "Military Culture Does Matter," *Strategic Review*, Spring 1999.

[19] Thucydides, *History of the Peloponnesian War*, p. 48.

[20] Some military historians have argued that Heinz Guderian, whose branch was signals, was picked to work on the Reichswehr's armor program because the his superiors recognized that communications were going to be a key ingredient in the *Blitzkrieg*. For those who understand the hit-and-miss approach that personnel systems use in assigning majors, it is far more likely that a number of combat arms officers turned the assignment down or that Guderian was the one general staff officer who was available for assignment.

[21] The explanation for why one of the most disastrous diplomatic appointments ever was made appears to have been that Robert Vasittart, the head civil servant in the Foreign Office and by and large a competent man, nominated Sir Nevile Henderson to be the ambassador in Berlin because he was a good shot. As to Henderson's qualification and performance in

(continued)

chaotic, terrifying experience and, to the diplomat in peace, a set of confusing and disagreeable choices, brings with it a distortion of the reality within which decision makers must operate and act. That in turn makes what really happened almost inaccessible to those not familiar with history or with how decisions are reached at the highest levels in the real world.

The clearer and more apparently inevitable the story that historians present, the more skeptical students should be. But skepticism cannot be simply a matter of disbelief. It must rest on a solid foundation of the student's own experience as well as his or her wider reading of history, contemporary and ancient. Especially if he has not seen war, the professional officer must also bring an imagination capable of grappling with what it must really have been like on the battlefields of dark and sodden places like Omaha Beach on June 6, 1944. "If no one had the right to give his views on military operations except when he is frozen, or faint from heat and thirst, or depressed from privation and fatigue, objective and accurate views would be even rarer than they are."[22] What the professional officer must supply to all history are his or her own experiences and sense of what is possible or probable in the events someone else is interpreting.

History also suggests a view of the world that is anything but reassuring for those who believe there are basic or simple truths in the affairs of humans. As Winston Churchill suggested about the outbreak of World War I:

> One rises from the study of the causes of the Great War with a prevailing sense of the defective control of individuals upon world fortunes.... The limited minds of even the ablest men, their disputed authority, the climate of opinion in which they dwell, their transient and partial contribution to the mighty problem, that problem so far beyond their compass, so vast in scale and detail, so changing in its aspects – all this must surely be considered....[23]

Thus, there are no simple, easy solutions to be found in the study of history. To search for such answers, as so many in the world of American political science have done, is to remove what small truths history can provide.[24]

(continued)
  the job, the great historian Lewis Namier had the following to say: "Conceited, vain, opinionated, rigidly adhering to his preconceived ideas, [Henderson] poured out telegrams, dispatches and letters in unbelievable numbers and of formidable length, repeating a hundred times, the same ill-founded views and ideas. Obtuse enough to be a menace, and not stupid enough to be innocuous he proved un homme néfast – important, because he echoed and reinforced Chamberlain's opinions and policy." Lewis Namier, *In the Nazi Era* (New York, 1952), p. 162.

22 Clausewitz, *On War*, p. 115.
23 Winston S. Churchill, *The World Crisis* (Toronto, 1931), p. 6.
24 Along these lines, the reader is urged to avoid books such as Barry R. Posen, *The Sources of Military Doctrine, France, Britain, and Germany Between the World Wars* (Ithaca, NY, 1984), where the authors rely solely on works in English, ignore most of the historical literature, and come to the topic with the answer in hand before they even open a book.

How complex the problem of historical causality can be is suggested by the fact that it was only in the 1980s that historians really began to unravel the problems involved in the development of the *Blitzkrieg*.[25] Thus, professional officers must grapple with the reality that history is always more complex than historians make it seem. They must themselves with their own imagination supply the murky and ambiguous context, the roads not taken, the decisions made serendipitously, and the role of sheer human incompetence and bloody mindedness – factors that historians often either miss entirely or minimize to the point of distortion.

In fact, it is the role of sheer incompetence in human affairs with which historians are least comfortable.[26] Twentieth-century historians have tended to regard military organizations as peculiarly incompetent. In the index of Lloyd George's memoirs, there is a revealing entry. Under the entry "military mind," one finds

> Narrowness of, 3051; stubbornness of, not peculiar to America, 3077; its attitude in July, 1918, represented by Sir Henry Wilson's fantastic memorandum of 25/7/18, 3109; obsessed with the North-west Frontier of India, 3119; impossibility of trusting, 3124; regards thinking as a form of mutiny, 3422.[27]

That attitude toward the military finds more than sufficient supporting evidence in the disasters at Loos, Gallipoli, Verdun, the Somme, Passchendaele, and the other terrible battles that populate the history of World War I. Yet, some historians tend to assume decisions in the civilian world are, for the most part, more intelligent, judicious, and farseeing than those made by military institutions. In other words, most historians believe competence underlies most aspects of human affairs.

From this author's point of view, nothing could be further from the truth. In fact, a casual perusal of the twentieth century suggests that shortsightedness, close mindedness, and institutional rigidity are as endemic to civilian

---

25 For a summary of current thought on the development of what can best be termed "the development of combined arms doctrine between the wars see, among others," Williamson Murray, "Armored Warfare," in *Military Innovation in the Interwar Period*, edited by Williamson Murray and Allan R. Millett (Cambridge, 1996). For the initial thrust in altering our understanding of the relationship between developments on the battlefield at the end of the First World War, see Timothy Lupfer, *The Dynamics of Doctrine, The Changes in German Tactical Doctrine during the First World War* (Leavenworth, KS, 1981). See also James S. Corum, *The Roots of Blitzkrieg, Hans von Seeckt and German Military Reform* (Lawrence, KS, 1992); and Harris, *Men, Ideas, and Tanks*.

26 Along these lines, it is worth noting that no less than three major academic works have appeared that attempt to explain away the French defeat in 1940 on the basis of something other than sheer, unmitigated military incompetence. See Jeffrey Gunsburg, *Divided and Conquered, The French High Command and the Defeat in the West, 1940* (Westport, CT, 1979); R. J. Young, *In Command of France, French Foreign Policy and Military Planning* (Cambridge, MA, 1978); and Martin Alexander, *The Republic in Danger, General Maurice Gamelin and Politics of French Defence, 1933–1940* (Cambridge, 2003).

27 David Lloyd George, *Memoirs*, vol. 6 (London, 1936), p. 3497.

societies as they are to military institutions. After all, it was the civilian world that managed to produce the Great Depression, seventy straight years of planned agricultural disaster in the Soviet Union, innumerable stock bubbles, Mao's "great leap forward," and other political and bureaucratic disasters too numerous to mention. The only difference would seem to be that military disasters are harder to hide.

Finally, there is a dark side to history that goes deeply against the basic positivism of the Anglo-Saxon *Weltanschauung* (worldview). Thus, honest history rubs many in egalitarian, democratic societies the wrong way. For example, there is no truth to the myth first perpetrated by Herodotus that free men fight better than the soldiers of tyranny. History's terrible secret, discovered by the Romans – and rediscovered by the Europeans in the seventeenth century – is that disciplined, trained troops, whether in the service of tyranny or a democracy, will win every time over ill-disciplined warriors, no matter how enthusiastic or ferociously devoted to their cause they might be. Napoleon once suggested that God is on the side of the big battalions. He was all too right, as the democratic Finns discovered in 1940 and 1944. Equally depressing is the fact that the divisions of the *Waffen SS* or the Guards units of the Red Army fought with a ferocity that few of the units the democracies placed on the battlefields of World War II could match.

History also underlines that the coin of international relations is power. It can at times wear a glove, but it is power nevertheless. As the Athenian negotiators suggested to the Melians in 416 BC:

> So far as the favour of the Gods is concerned, we think we have as much right to that as you have. Our aims and our actions are perfectly consistent with the beliefs men hold about the Gods and with the principles which govern their own conduct. Our opinion of the Gods and our knowledge of men lead us to conclude that it is a general and necessary law of nature to rule whatever one can. This is not a law we made ourselves, nor were we the first to act upon it when it was made. We found it already in existence, and we shall leave it to exist for ever among those who come after us. We are merely acting in accordance with it, and we know that you or anyone else with the same power would be acting in precisely the same way.[28]

There is nothing in the long dark history of the past 2,400 years to suggest that humans have acted in any fashion contradictory to those dark words, most probably spoken by Socrates's prize student Alcibiades.[29]

The long and short of it is that history is a discipline that one can only access by hard and consistent work. It does not provide clear or simple

[28] Thucydides, *History of the Peloponnesian War*, pp. 404–5.
[29] Thucydides did not name the Athenian negotiators, but Plutarch does indicate that Alcibiades was one of the Athenian negotiators sent to Melos by the assembly.

answers. As one of the most perceptive historians of the Second World War and commentators on the present has suggested:

> The owl of history is an evening bird. The past is unknowable; only at the end of the day do some of its outlines dimly emerge. The future cannot be known at all, and the past suggests that change is often radical and unforeseeable rather than incremental and predictable. Yet despite its many ambiguities, historical experience remains the only available guide both to the present and to the range of alternatives inherent in the future.[30]

In the end, those who want to learn from history must address it in its own terms. The context matters. Details cannot be shrugged off. History offers no simple, clear answers. Historical understanding demands imagination and skepticism. Military professionals must be willing to challenge both the historian's and their own assumptions. History's value often lies in its ability to suggest the possibility of the improbable. Finally, it suggests little that is certain about the road to the future.

THE UTILITY OF MILITARY HISTORY

What then are the "take aways" from history for military professionals, given the considerable difficulties that its study places in their path? The most important has to do with the very nature of their profession. Again, as Professor Howard has pointed out on a number of occasions, the military is the only profession that does not get to practice its profession on a regular basis, a fact for which military professions and the societies they protect should indeed be thankful.[31] The history of past military campaigns, of past military innovation in times of peace, and of the very nature of war is the only reliable source on which we can draw, if we indeed do want to understand what warfare or combat may look like. Thus, any one who wishes to understand the profession of arms *must* study history.

History does suggest a number of things about war. The first is that it is always about politics. Despite the efforts of a number of British critics of Clausewitz, who would appear for the most part not to have read him, the Prussian thinker is right in his comment that "war is not a mere act of policy but a true political instrument, a continuation of political activity by other

---

30 MacGregor Knox, "What History Can Tell Us About the 'New Strategic Environment," in Williamson Murray, ed., *Brassey's American Defense Annual, The United States and the Emerging Strategic Environment* (Washington, DC, 1995), p. 1.

31 In a classic talk in 1962, Professor Howard suggested: "First, his [the officer's] profession is almost unique in that he may have to exercise it once in a lifetime, if indeed that often. It is as if a surgeon had to practice throughout his life on dummies for one real operation.... Secondly the complex problem of running a [military service] at all is liable to occupy his mind and skill so completely that it is easy to forget what it is being run *for*." Michael Howard, "The Uses and Abuses of Military History," *Journal of the Royal United Services Institute*, February 1962.

means.... [War] should never be thought of as *something autonomous*, but always as an *instrument of policy*" [italics in the original].[32] The political and strategic end must be the guiding light in determining the activities toward which military organizations direct their efforts. The Germans in their conduct of two world wars, as well as the wretched results of America's efforts in Vietnam, have made all too clear the results of allowing operational and tactical expediency to drive policy and strategy. "No one starts a war – or rather, no one in his senses ought to do so – without first being clear in his mind what he intends to achieve by that war and how he intends to conduct it."[33]

In the 1990s, for example, a number of senior American military leaders, drawing on theories of air power advocates of the 1930s that history since has largely discredited, argued for an American approach to war that can best be described as "distant attack" – a form of warfare waged by stealth and precision that would hazard the lives of few Americans. Its attraction also reflected America's success in the Gulf War of 1991, in which the air campaign came close to forcing Saddam Hussein to disgorge Kuwait without a ground campaign. What those leaders failed to realize – because they were almost entirely ignorant of history – was that such a "success" would have allowed Saddam to claim to receptive audiences in the Middle East that his armies had stood unbroken and undefeated in the field before an American military too cowardly to risk combat on the ground.[34]

In the most recent war against Iraq, airmen in Washington again raised the possibility of an independent air campaign before the war with Iraq began.[35] In this case, they entirely ignored the fact that such a campaign would have allowed Saddam to manipulate the international environment by setting fire to Iraq's oil fields, dumping millions of gallons of petroleum into the Persian Gulf, and playing on the sympathies of those appalled by any idea of collateral damage. But politics, not military utility, must drive the train, and in the Iraq War it did, at least in the short term. The longer term, with the most inadequate preparations for an occupation and rebuilding of Iraqi society, is another matter. As Clausewitz suggests "even the ultimate outcome of a war is not always to be regarded as final."[36]

The larger point that history and its student Clausewitz make about the importance of politics in the formulation of operational plans is the necessity

---

[32] Clausewitz, *On War*, pp. 87–8.
[33] Ibid., p. 579.
[34] In fact, he essentially made that claim anyway long after the war. Interview with Dan Rather, February 24, 2003, CBS "60 Minutes."
[35] In fairness to the airmen who planned and ran the campaign, the issue of an independent air campaign never appears to have been raised as a serious possibility in the planning at Centcom.
[36] Clausewitz, *On War*, p. 80.

to understand both the political end toward which military operations must point and the importance of understanding clearly the nature of one's opponent. Here, the United States has not had a particularly impressive record during the past forty years. Those who formulated American military policy with regard to South Vietnam in the early to mid-1960s simply failed to understand the nature and tenacity of the North Vietnamese. Here, we are talking not just about the politicians, but also about a substantial portion of America's military leaders.[37] As General William Westmoreland noted in his memoirs, he had Bernard Fall's works and those of a number of other authors dealing with Vietnam beside his bed, but he never had time to read them.[38] Unfortunately, the current difficulties in Iraq suggest that the Bush administration has had a similarly blase attitude toward the period that would come after the defeat of Saddam Hussein's military forces.

History is also quite specific about the fundamental, unchanging nature of war. It is about killing and about the terrible threat of death that hangs over those who fight. The new American way of war, proposed in the 1990s, suggested that technology could entirely remove the elements of friction – chance, uncertainty, ambiguity, and incompetence – from war, at least as far as American forces were concerned. Instead, as U.S. forces have discovered again in Afghanistan and Iraq, the world of the battlefield is one where friction in its widest sense continues to rule every action and operation. As a special forces officer recently wrote about the battle on Takur Ghar Mountain in Afghanistan:

> The U.S. military is fielding some outstanding technologies to support its missions. Many of these technologies saw their first combat use during operations in Afghanistan. The preponderance of the equipment and systems worked exactly as advertised. Although ... the latest technology helped in achieving battlefield dominance, there were instances where over-confidence actually made matters worse.[39]

There are two crucial elements in understanding what the study of history provides the military professional in his or her search for knowledge. The

---

[37] For the most careful examination of how the United States became involved in the Vietnam War, see H. R. McMaster, *Dereliction of Duty, Lyndon Johnson, Robert McNamara, the Joint Chiefs of Staff and the Lies They Told* (New York, 2003).

[38] Westmoreland's comment: "Beside my bed at home I kept ... several books: a Bible; a French grammar; Mao Tse-tung's little red book on theories of Guerrilla warfare; a novel, *The Centurions*, about the French fight with the Viet Minh; and several books by Dr. Bernard Fall, who wrote authoritatively on the French experience in Vietnam and provided insight into the enemy's thinking and methods. I was usually too tired in late evening to give the books more than occasional attention." General William C. Westmoreland, *A Soldier Reports* (New York, 1997), p. 364.

[39] Colonel Andy Milani, "Pitfalls of Technology: A Case Study of the Battle on Takur Ghar Mountain, Afghanistan," unpublished paper, U.S. Army War College, April 2003, p. 42.

first is a sense of the reality of war rather than "war on paper."[40] What military professionals confront in war with its terrifying combination of terror, fear, hatred, and death is the enormous impact of nonlinear factors on their actions. When exposed to battle for the first time, "the novice cannot pass through these layers of increasing intensity of danger" as he or she approaches combat

> without sensing that here ideas are governed by other factors, that the light of reason is refracted in a manner quite different from that which is normal in academic speculation. It is an exceptional man [or woman] who keeps his [or her] powers of quick decision intact.[41]

Only history can give the professional some sense of the interactions that occur on the battlefield, no matter how imperfect and ambiguous those lessons might appear. Only history can provide some sense of how it is that fear can turn armed mobs of *warriors* to jelly and how discipline keeps trained troops on the field. As all great military history underlines, "in the dreadful presence of suffering and danger, emotion can easily overwhelm intellectual conviction, and in this psychological fog it is... hard to form clear and complete insights."[42]

In that respect, the natural sciences have underlined why, despite its ambiguities and uncertainties, history still illuminates the world the soldier and marine will continue to live in more closely than the predictive efforts of the social sciences. Man lives in a world where absolute prediction simply is not possible and where initial conditions – read historical context – provide only a glimpse at the possibilities that can arise from any given interaction, whether political or military. The implications for the understanding of war are profound. As one historian of science recently suggested, the continuing relevance of Clausewitz to understanding war in the modern world reflects the fact that

> *On War* is suffused with the understanding that every war is inherently a nonlinear phenomenon, the conduct of which changes its character in ways that cannot be analytically predicted. [Moreover,] [i]n a profoundly unconfused way, [Clausewitz] understands that seeking exact analytic solutions does not fit the nonlinear reality of the problems posed by war, and hence that our ability to predict the course and outcome of any given conflict is severely limited.[43]

Clausewitz's writings, because they remain so true in their nonlinear framework to what history suggests about his world and our own that technology

---

[40] Ibid., p. 119.
[41] Clauseweitz, *On War*, p. 113.
[42] Ibid., p. 108.
[43] Alan Beyerchen, "Clausewitz, Nonlinearity, and the Unpredictability of War," *International Security*, Winter 1992/1993, p. 61.

has changed so much, provide the second crucial nugget of wisdom for the professional soldier. His "unified conception of a general friction" was undoubtedly his greatest contribution to understanding what makes war so unpredictable, intractable, and difficult to analyze. General friction was Clausewitz's explanation for why "everything in war is very simple, but the simplest thing is difficult. The difficulties accumulate and end by producing a kind of friction that is inconceivable unless one has experienced war."[44] As another commentator on Clausewitz has suggested, we might think of the factors that contribute to general friction even in modern wars in the following terms:

> 1) danger; 2) physical exertion; 3) uncertainties and imperfections in the infor-
> mation on which action in war is based; 4) chance; 5) friction in the narrow
> sense of the resistance within one's own forces; 6) physical and political limits to
> the use of force; 7) unpredictability stemming from interaction with the enemy;
> and 8) disconnects between ends and means in war.[45]

Only to the extent that it accurately reflects these same conditions can history – good history – enhance the professionals' understanding of the difficulties with which military leaders and institutions have had to grapple in the past.

History also underlines that in war soldiers confront enemies who seek to kill them. We in the First World may be able to strike our opponents from platforms distant from their defenses, but we should not forget that they may have unexpected means of striking back, as the attacks on the World Trade Center's Twin Towers and the Pentagon indicated on September 11, 2001. As Americans discovered in Somalia and are now rediscovering in Iraq, even in the Third World there are those capable of using relatively primitive technologies with considerable success against the military forces of the United States.

To add to the contextual complexities of war, history underlines the importance of the imponderables of interpersonal dynamics. "Is there a field of human affairs where personal relations do not count, where the sparks they strike do not leap across all practical considerations?"[46] How could we possibly calculate or predict the influences and dynamics of that factor on the conduct of military operations, even on our side of the hill? On the other side of the hill such predictions are simply impossible, particularly given the inability of First World political, military, and intelligence leaders to understand that the rest of the world runs on very different calculations and beliefs.

---

44 Clausewitz, *On War*, p. 119.
45 Barry Watts, "Friction in Future War," in Williamson Murray and Allan R. Millett, eds., *Brassey's Mershon American Defense Annual, 1996–1997* (Washington, DC, 1997), p. 66.
46 Clausewitz, *On War*, p. 94.

CONCLUSION

History will always present the military professional with considerable difficulties. But the past can suggest how to think about new contexts and different challenges. It is almost never predictive. It can only suggest a range of possibilities in thinking about the future. Thus, the business of professionals is to prepare for the unexpected, knowing, as Michael Howard has suggested on a number of occasions, they will always get it wrong to some degree. A study of the past suggests the importance of understanding the nature of our opponents, their political, ideological, or religious framework, and their goals. All the technological intelligence in the world, all the information dominance, will gain the professional soldier or marine little, if they misunderstand their opponent.

Even more perplexing is the historical lesson that war can take a radical shift in directions entirely unexpected, even by the most professional of officers. As Clausewitz noted about the terrible wars against the French between 1792 and 1815:

> Suddenly war again became the business of the people – a people of thirty millions, all of whom considered themselves citizens.... The people became a participant in war; instead of governments and armies as heretofore, the full weight of the nation was thrown into the balance.... War, untrammeled by any conventional constraints, had broken loose in all its elemental fury.[47]

Recognizing the reality of war and preparing to adapt represent the first step to success on the battlefield. History at least presents to military professionals an understanding of how to think about intractable problems, how to grapple with uncertainty, and how to prepare throughout their careers for the positions of responsibility that they must inevitably assume.

---

[47] Clausewitz, *On War*, pp. 592–3.

Part II

The past as illuminator of the future

7

Thucydides as educator

PAUL A. RAHE

Exiled Thucydides knew
All that a speech can say
About Democracy
And what dictators do,
The elderly rubbish they talk
To an apathetic grave;
Analysed all in his book,
The enlightenment driven away,
The habit-forming pain,
Mismanagement and grief.
We must suffer them all again.
    – W. H. Auden, "September 1,
    1939"

Toward the end of the introductory section of his epic history of the Peloponnesian War, Thucydides advances a claim on that work's behalf that hardly any modern historian, contemplating his own efforts in the privacy of his own study, would have the audacity even to consider. My account of the war, Thucydides observes, "was composed as a possession for all times rather than as a contest piece (*agō*nisma*) meant to be heard straightaway" (1.22.4).[1] This apparent boast he justifies in advance by first remarking on the absence in his writing of "the mythic" or "fabulous (*tò muthō*des*)," arguing that, although this may render his account "less delightful (*aterpésteron*)" to some, it would satisfy his own purpose if his work were "judged useful

---

[1] All parenthetical citations in the text are to Thucydides's history. Unless otherwise indicated, all translations are my own. In this notes, in referring to the classical texts, this chapter uses the standard abbreviations found in N. G. L. Hammmond and H. H. Scullard, eds., *The Oxford Classical Dictionary*, 2nd ed. (Oxford, 1970) and cites by the standard divisions provided by the author or subsequent editors.

by those who want to observe clearly the events which happened in the past and which in accord with the character of the human (*katà tò anthrō*pınon*) will again come to pass hereafter in quite similar ways" (1.22.4).

It is my contention that, although we modern historians really are by and large modest little men with much to be modest about, Thucydides had a just understanding of his proper place in the constellation of things – that he was right to think his past akin to our future and to suppose that, despite the passage of time, generations in the far-distant future would stand to profit from studying his account of the Peloponnesian War.[2] In my judgment, no work written at any time in human history is more essential to the education of a statesman and general officer. Robert Strassler's fine edition of Thucydides's history should be issued to everyone who attends a military academy or staff college, to everyone enrolled in a war college, and to everyone who aspires to a political career. And it should not only be read once, but re-read and reflected on again and again at frequent intervals.[3]

I do not mean to say that perusing an author who penned his book almost 2,400 years ago is a substitute for understanding the role played by modern technology in the conduct of war. That would be, on the face of it, absurd. Nevertheless, no careful reader of Thucydides's account of the failure of Athens' Sicilian expedition at Syracusa can emerge from its study unaware of the role played by technological progress in bringing about Athens' defeat (7.36). Nor do I mean to suggest that reading Thucydides is a substitute for mastering the particulars of time and place, or of terrain and circumstance, because the painstaking attention he pays to detail in providing an account of his war aims at conveying to those who wish to learn from him that they must do the same in their own time and place.

But if Thucydides does lavish attention on the details of his war, these details do not constitute his true subject – that which does not change, the unchanging substrate that underpins and, indeed, drives the changes that are always taking place. His subject is, as he puts it, "the human," and it is his claim that, in a rough and ready way, the patterns visible in the past predict the future. The devil may be in the details, but it is the devil that one needs to discern – and one can do so only by first attending to the details. "The human" rarely, if ever, presents itself to us in the abstract.

---

[2] In the late 1990s, when I asked Anthony Pagden, then of Johns Hopkins University, whom he considered the greatest historian to write in the twentieth century, in a manner both revealing and apt, he sniffed in reply, "It is not at greatness that we aim."

[3] The multitude of maps provided; the superb introduction by Victor Davis Hanson; the brief epilogue completing Thucydides's narrative of the war; the eleven appendices on ancient institutions, customs, and practices by a series of distinguished scholars; the running chronology in the margins of the text; the host of illustrations; the glossary; the bibliographies of ancient sources and modern scholarly accounts; and an encyclopedic index make Robert B. Strassler, ed., *The Landmark Thucydides: A Comprehensive Guide to the Peloponnesian War* (New York, 1996), a treasure beyond compare.

Let me take one example well known to all contemporary students of war. Thirty years ago, while a lecturer at the Royal Military Academy at Sandhurst, John Keegan wrote a justly famous book entitled *The Face of Battle*. In that work, he quite rightly belabored the significance, for our understanding of combat on land, of attending to the experience and concerns of the ordinary infantryman. As he points out, the great bulk of the literature on war focuses narrowly on the commander's craft, treating units and the men who make them up as chess pieces easily moved across the board. The one notable exception to this rule, which Keegan cites, is Thucydides's history, which, in analyzing the battle of Mantineia, pays careful attention to the circumstances in which the individual hoplites ordinarily find themselves and to the manner in which these circumstances shape their concerns and determine the behavior of those occupying the phalanx's right flank (5.66–74, esp. 71).[4] No general officer who has pondered this passage in Thucydides's text will fail to reflect on the situations in which the ordinary infantrymen under his command generally find themselves in combat, on the concerns that drive them, and on the behavior on their part that one can reasonably expect. If one has read Thucydides with sufficient care, one can easily anticipate the questions posed by S. L. A. Marshall and Ardant du Picq, if not also their findings.

Because "the human" rarely, if ever, presents himself of herself to us in the abstract, Thucydides rarely speaks in generalities. For his reticence in this particular, he has another reason as well. The ancients, Greeks and Romans alike, recognized that moral and political persuasion is akin to seduction. Accordingly, it was one of the principles of ancient rhetoric that one must by indirection make one's listener a participant in the process of achieving conviction. As Theophrastus put it,

> It is not necessary to speak at length and with precision on everything, but some things should be left also for the listener – to be understood and sorted out by himself – so that, in coming to understand that which has been left by you for him, he will become not just your listener but also your witness, and a witness quite well disposed as well. For he will think himself a man of understanding because you have afforded him an occasion for showing his capacity for understanding. By the same token, whoever tells his listener everything accuses him of being mindless.[5]

It has long been recognized that the classical historians were schooled in rhetoric and practiced this art.[6] In this matter, Thucydides was no exception: his goal was to educate and not to train.

---

[4] See John Keegan, *The Face of Battle* (New York, 1976) passim, esp. pp. 62–70.
[5] Theophr. F696 (Fortenbaugh).
[6] See, for example, Thomas Gordon, "Discourses upon Tacitus 2.5," in Gordon, *The Works of Tacitus, With Political Discourses upon That Author*, 4th ed. (London, 1770), pp. 149–50.

Training is, of course, what the military does best. Like all large bureaucracies, it has little choice. If great numbers of men and women from diverse
backgrounds are to collaborate on common projects, they must learn a set
of common procedures and protocols. Moreover, in the emergencies that
quite commonly present themselves in war, there is normally little, if any,
time for deliberation. Both the officers and those whom they command must
immediately, as if instinctively, know how to act or react. If unthinking obedience to prescribed protocols is but rarely sufficient, quick decision making
grounded in an intimate knowledge of strategic doctrine and approved tactics is nonetheless requisite.

Military organizations, however, are less effective at education, although
education is no less essential for the accomplishment of their missions. Like
all bureaucracies, they tend to cast a baleful eye on rumination and reflection. They regard the bookish for understandable reasons as suspect. Among
other things, the latter are apt to raise awkward objections and disconcerting
questions. Even in the war colleges, there is a powerful propensity to turn
reading into rote, to reduce complex narrative to lessons easily learned. It is
this propensity that retards innovation and makes it as difficult for military
organizations as for other large bureaucracies to adapt to circumstances forever in flux. Thucydides is the perfect antidote because he resists reduction.
He demands rumination. He requires reflection.

No one understood this better than Thomas Hobbes, who judged it "the
principal and proper work of history...to instruct and enable men, by
the knowledge of actions past, to bear themselves prudently in the present
and providently towards the future." In the preface to the translation of
Thucydides's history that he published in 1628, Hobbes singled out the Greek
historian as "the most politic historiographer that ever writ," explaining his
judgment in the following way:

> [Thucydides] filleth his narrations with that choice of matter, and ordereth them
> with that judgment, and with such perspicuity and efficacy expresseth himself,
> that, as Plutarch saith, he maketh his auditor a spectator. For he setteth his
> reader in the assemblies of the people and in the senate, at their debating; in the
> streets, at their seditions; and in the field, at their battles. So that look how much
> a man of understanding might have added to his experience, if he had then lived
> a beholder of their proceedings, and familiar with the men and business of the
> time: so much almost may he profit now, by attentive reading of the same here
> written. He may from the narrations draw out lessons to himself, and of himself
> be able to trace the drifts and counsels of the actors to their seat.[7]

What Thucydides did not do was openly tell his readers what to think. As
Hobbes would later put it, "Digressions for instruction's cause, and other

---

[7] Thomas Hobbes, "To the Readers," in Thucydides, *The Peloponnesian War: The Complete
Hobbes Translation*, ed. David Grene (Chicago, 1989), pp. xxi–xxii.

such open conveyances of precepts, (which is the philosopher's part), he never useth; as having so clearly set before men's eyes the ways and events of good and evil counsels, that the narration itself doth secretly instruct the reader, and more effectually than can possibly be done by precept."[8]

Hobbes was by no means the last to make this observation. Jean-Jacques Rousseau described Thucydides as "the true model of an historian," adding as an explanation:

> He reports the facts without judging them, but he omits none of the circum-stances proper to make us judge them ourselves. He puts all he recounts before the reader's eyes. Far from putting himself between the events and his readers, he hides himself. The reader no longer believes he reads; he believes he sees.[9]

Put bluntly, Thucydides is less interested in telling his readers what to think than in teaching them how to think. If he is as sparing in spelling out his own analysis of events as he is generous and precise in his provision of detail, it is because he is eager to induce his readers to figure things out for themselves. His goal is to educate citizens and statesmen, not to train automatons.

Thucydides would have been delighted to learn that his book really did become "a possession for all times" and that, nearly two and a half millennia after its appearance, a soldier-statesman, the American Secretary of State and General of the Army, George Catlin Marshall, should look to the ancient Athenian for an understanding of the state of affairs current in his own time and express to a university audience grave doubts as to "whether a man can think with full wisdom and with deep convictions regarding certain of the basic international issues today who has not at least reviewed in his mind the period of the Peloponnesian War and the Fall of Athens."[10] Thucydides would have been no less pleased that, some thirty-six years later, a poet, the Pole Czeslaw Milosz, soon to be awarded the Nobel Prize for Literature, should remark, "People always live within a certain order and are unable to visualize a time when [it] might cease to exist. The sudden crumbling of all current notions and criteria is a rare occurrence...characteristic of only the most stormy periods in history," and then add, with regard to "the rapid and violent changes of" the twentieth century, that the "only possible analogy may be the time of the Peloponnesian War, as we know it from Thucydides."[11]

---

8 Thomas Hobbes, "Of the Life and History of Thucydides," in Thucydides, *The Pelopon-nesian War: The Complete Hobbes Translation*, p. 577.
9 See Jean-Jacques Rousseau, *Emile or of Education*, trans. Allan Bloom (New York, 1979), p. 239.
10 See W. Robert Connor, *Thucydides* (Princeton, 1984), p. 3. Marshall delivered this address at Princeton University on February 22, 1947.
11 See Czeslaw Milosz, *The Witness of Poetry* (Cambridge, 1983), p. 81.

Marshall's words were uttered in 1947; Milosz's words were published in 1983. They could, with equal justice, have been spoken or printed in 1917, 1939, or 1991. For much, if not quite all, the last century, the world resembled that of Thucydides's time. It was a time of profound revolution, as was the fifth century BC. The political universe in each age was bipolar – with a coalition of democracies supreme on the sea at war with or poised for war against a coalition of states less friendly to democratic freedom and supreme ashore. Apart, perhaps, from Winston Churchill in his *Life of Marlborough*, no one has reflected as deeply as Thucydides on the difficulties of coalition management and those associated with a maritime political community's need to project power on land, while deflecting an opponent's attempts to take to the sea.[12]

Thucydides's *modus operandi* is nicely illustrated by a little puzzle he sets for his readers at the end of the first book of his history, where he focuses on the so-called Megarian Decree. He makes us wonder whether the war resulted from the mismanagement of a trivial dispute between Athens and Megara over the precise location of their border, from the latter's harboring of a handful of runaway Athenian slaves, and or from Athens' decision to retaliate by excluding Megarian traders from the ports it controlled (1.139. 1–2).[13] Thucydides leaves it for us to puzzle over Athens' relations with Megara during and after the First Peloponnesian War (1.103.4, 105–8, 114), to ponder what this reveals concerning that city's strategic significance for Corinth and for Sparta,[14] and to notice that, when Athens made a defensive alliance with Corcyra, all cities lying on the Saronic Gulf near Athens that had previously fought with Corinth against Corcyra abandoned the former – apart, that is, from Megara.[15]

Only if we attend closely to these and other details, weighing the significance of information Thucydides has scattered hither and yon, can we then begin to recognize that throughout the period leading up to the war, Pericles was playing a double game, doing everything within his power to antagonize Sparta's restive ally Corinth, while attempting to placate Sparta. Only in this light can we make sense of the fact that while observing to the letter

[12] This magnificent work has recently been reissued in an inexpensive two-volume edition. See Winston S. Churchill, *Marlborough: His Life and Times* (Chicago, 2002).

[13] This was a view widely held in antiquity. It has recently been revived by Donald Kagan, *The Outbreak of the Peloponnesian War* (Ithaca, NY, 1969), pp. 251–356 (esp. pp. 254–72, 309–11, 322–24, 326–30).

[14] After reviewing Thuc. 1.103.4, 105–8, 114, see 1.42.2 along with Hdt. 5.74–5 and 6.89, 108, keeping in mind what Thuc. 2.69.1, 80–92, reveals about the significance of 1.108.5 when read in conjunction with 1.101.2–103.3: at the time of the First Peloponnesian War, Athens' possession of both Naupactus and Megara with the latter's ports on the Saronic and Corinthian Gulfs placed it in a position to bottle up the forces of the Spartan alliance within the Peloponnesus and to cut off Corinthian trade to the West and the East. Given Corinth's dependence on food imported by sea, this was no small matter.

[15] Cf. Thuc. 1.46.1 with 1.27.2.

the terms of the Thirty Years Peace, while offering to submit all disputes to arbitration as that treaty required, and while displaying a keen awareness of the fact that Sparta was not only reluctant to go to war but doubly reluctant to offend the gods by breaking a treaty it had sworn to uphold[16] – Pericles *seemed* utterly obtuse with regard to Corinth: oblivious of the fact that this city was for understandable reasons highly sensitive to Athenian involvement in the affairs of its immediate neighbor Megara, and unconcerned that the Corinthians were no less likely to be distressed when faced with Athens' intervention anywhere along their grain route to the West, which stretched, like an umbilical cord, from Sicily through the Adriatic to Epidamnus and Corcyra and then on to the Corinthian Gulf.[17] Sorting out the puzzles, such as this one, that Thucydides leaves throughout his account requires and then hones the skills essential to statesmanship and military command that are now and have always been prerequisite for the analysis of intelligence and the interpretation of events. If these puzzles remain illuminating to this day, it is solely because, although circumstances are forever in flux, "the human" remains entirely unchanged.

Let me suggest another example. The apparent hero of the first section of Thucydides's narrative is Pericles, the Athenian general and statesman. It is he who guides the Athenians on the eve of the war, it is he who steadies them as war approaches, and it is he who delivers the unforgettable Funeral Address once the war begins. When Thucydides records Pericles's death from the plague in the middle of his second book, he pauses to give him a brief eulogy:

> As long as he presided over the city in time of peace, he led it in a measured manner (*metríōs*) and in safety; and in his time it was at its greatest. When the war broke out, in this also he appears to have foreknown its power. He lived on thereafter for two years and six months; and, when he died, his foreknowledge with regard to the war (*pronoía . . . es tòn polémon*) became still more evident. For he told them that they would prevail if they remained at rest (*hēsucházontas*) and looked after the fleet and if, during the war, they made no attempt to extend their dominion and refrained from placing the city at risk. What they did was the contrary in all regards, governing themselves and their allies, even in matters seemingly extraneous to the war, with an eye to private ambitions and private profit in a manner quite harmful, pursuing policies whose success would be to the honor and advantage of private individuals, and whose failure brought harm to the city in the war. The cause was that Pericles – as a consequence of his standing, his understanding, and the fact that he was clearly impervious

---

[16] Consider Thuc. 1.85.2, 140.2, 141.1, 144.2, 145, in light of 1.78.4; then, consider 5.14.3–15.1, 16.1–17.1, in light of 6.105.1–2, 7.18.2.

[17] Cf. Kagan, *The Outbreak of the Peloponnesian War*, pp. 203–356, who draws a different inference from what, we both agree, are the facts.

to bribes[18] – held (*kateîche*) the multitude under his control in the manner of a free man (*eleuthérōs*) – in short, he led them instead of being led by them; for, since he never came into the possession of power by improper means, he never had to go out of his way to please them in speech, but enjoyed so high an estimation that he could get away with contradicting them even to the point of angering them. Whenever he perceived that they were in an untimely manner emboldened to the point of insolence (*húbris*), by speaking, he reduced them to fear; on the other contrary, if they fell without reason (*alógōs*) victim to fear, he could restore in them again their confidence. What was, in name, a democracy was, in fact, rule by the first man. Those who came later were more on an equal plane with one another, and each desiring to be first, they sought to please the people and to them handed over public affairs. In consequence, as tends to happen in a great city also possessed of an empire, they blundered in many regards, especially with respect to the expedition against Sicily – which failed not such much as a consequence of a mistake in judgment with regard to those against whom it was dispatched, as through the senders' not deciding to make proper provision for those who had gone out, but choosing instead to occupy themselves in private quarrels regarding the leadership of the people, by which they blunted the efforts of those in the camp and became embroiled with one another in matters pertaining to the city. And yet, after losing the better part of their fleet along with their other forces in Sicily, despite the fact that they were also caught up in sedition (*stásis*) in the city, for three years they nonetheless held out against their former enemies, those from Sicily who had joined them, their own allies the majority of whom were in revolt, and later Cyrus, son of the [Persian] King, who provided money to the Peloponnesians for their navy – and they did not give way until they tripped themselves up by means of their private differences. So great were the resources from which Pericles forecast that, in the war, the city could quite easily outlast the Peloponnesians if the latter were fighting on their own. (2.65.5–13)

If one reads this passage once, one is persuaded that Thucydides admired Pericles. If one reads it twice or thrice in isolation, one's conviction regarding the depth of his admiration only grows. It is only when one compares this eulogy with the one provided in the first book of Thucydides's history for Themistocles that one realizes that, in one crucial particular, Thucydides is damning Pericles with comparatively faint praise.

Here is what Thucydides has to say about Themistocles on the occasion in which he remarks on that Athenian statesman's death:

Themistocles was a man who in a fashion quite reliable displayed strength of nature, and in this regard he was outstanding and worthy of greater admiration than anyone else. By his own native intelligence (*oikeía xúnesis*), without the help of study before or after, he was at once the best judge (*krátistos gnō*mōn*) in matters, admitting of little deliberation, which require settlement on the spot,

---

18 Apparently, this fact did not prevent him from being charged with bribery toward the end of his life: see Pl. *Grg.* 516a1–2, Plut. *Per.* 32–33.

and the best predictor (*áristos eikastē*s*) of things to come across the broadest expanse. What he had in hand he could also explain; what lay beyond his experience he did not lack the capacity adequately to judge. In a future as yet obscure he could in a pre-eminent fashion foresee both better and worse. In short, by the power of his nature, when there was little time to take thought, this man surpassed all others in the faculty of improvising what the situation required (*krátistos ... autoschediázein tà déonta*). (1.138.3)[19]

As should be clear from what is said and from what is left unsaid, although Themistocles's well-earned reputation for corruption and deceit rendered him suspect and less effective in guiding Athens than Pericles would be, he was, in all other regards, the younger statesman's superior.[20] To begin with, as Thucydides repeatedly insists, Themistocles's understanding was natural; it was not acquired. The source of Pericles's capacity for foreknowledge remains unmentioned. Thucydides leaves it to us, having read the two eulogies and having noted the oblique manner in which he draws attention to Themistocles's well-known defects as a politician, to wonder whether Pericles had to learn the statesman's art in the hard school of experience.

And once we wonder, we will be induced to review his early career and to discover that, in the wake of Cimon's ostracism and Ephialtes's assassination, the young Pericles appears to have been the statesman in charge when, in the midst of an earlier war with Sparta, Athens – a city of some 30,000 to 50,000 adult male citizens – lost perhaps as many as 250 ships and 50,000 citizen and allied rowers in a quixotic attempt to oust Persia from Egypt (1.104, 109–10).[21] On the eve of the great Peloponnesian War, when Pericles warned his compatriots that "they would prevail" only "if they remained at rest (*hēsucházontas*) and looked after the fleet," and when he told them that "during the war" they should make "no attempt to extend their dominion" and refrain "from placing the city at risk," he knew firsthand of the dangers to which he was alluding.

Moreover, Thucydides indicates that Themistocles's foresight with regard to matters "better and worse" in "a future as yet obscure" was universal in scope. To Pericles, he attributes "foreknowledge" solely "with regard to the war." Was there, we are lead to wonder once we compare the two obituaries, *was there* a sphere in which Pericles was lacking in foreknowledge? In particular, was the Athenian statesman obtuse with regard to future developments in the city of Athens? After all, as Thucydides points out, in the wake of Pericles's death, the Athenians proved incapable of following his advice.

---

[19] For at least some of the events that Thucydides has in mind, see Hdt. 7.143–4, 8.22, 56–64, 74–83, 108–10, 123–5.

[20] What Thucydides conveys by failing to contend that Themistocles was "clearly impervious to bribes" Herodotus makes unmistakable: see Hdt. 8.4, 108–12 (with an eye to 74–5).

[21] For the evidence pertaining to Pericles's achievement of political supremacy at this time, see Arist. *Ath. Pol.* 25.1–28.2, *Pol.* 1274a7–10, Plut *Cim.* 14–18, *Per.* 9–14 (esp. 9–10).

"What they did," the historian tells us, "was the contrary in all regards, governing themselves and their allies, even in matters seemingly extraneous to the war, with an eye to private ambitions and private profit in a manner quite harmful, pursuing policies whose success would be to the honor and advantage of private individuals, and whose failure brought harm to the city in the war."

What Athens did was, in fact, precisely what Wilhelmine Germany did after Otto von Bismarck retired as Chancellor of the Reich. In the wake of German unification, Bismarck had exhorted his countrymen to regard their country as a satisfied power and follow a conservative policy they were temperamentally incapable of following; and, like Pericles, he bore considerable responsibility as a consequence of the example that he himself had set for their incapacity in this regard. Both Pericles and Bismarck had gained glory from promoting expansion. Their daring in this particular had been breathtaking in the extreme. How could either have expected a people whose character he had formed to remain at rest – even for a time? We will return to this question in a moment.

First, however, it is incumbent on me to make clear what it is about "the human" that Thucydides discerns more clearly than anyone since. Obliquely, in fact, I have already pointed it out. But it is best that I approach it in the manner of Thucydides himself. The beginning of Thucydides's history is decidedly odd. In the first paragraph, he introduces himself ("Thucydides the Athenian") and then his topic ("the war between the Peloponnesians and the Athenians"). Then he claims that this war was "most worthy the relation of all that had been before it," citing the fact that its participants were at their acme with regard to equipment (*paraskeúē*) and that the rest of Hellas had already taken sides or was contemplating doing so (1.1.1). This war was, he then adds, "the greatest motion (*kínēsis*) in history – not just in that of the Hellenes but in that of a substantial part of the barbarians and, so to speak, the bulk of mankind" (1.1.2). The remainder of his first paragraph and the next twenty paragraphs Thucydides devotes to proving this claim by showing that the evidence pertinent to all prior history shows that, in earlier times, there was "nothing great in regard to war or other matters" (1.1.3).

This section of the book, which is customarily called the "archaeology," which is to say Thucydides's discourse (*lógos*) concerning ancient things (*tà archaía*), is exceedingly abstract, providing, as it does, a potted history of earlier times inferred from the sketchiest of sources, emphasizing the degree to which those times were characterized by disorder. Thucydides's point is simple and straightforward: in times of general disorder, no one can in a serious manner project power. But he makes this point in a fashion that should occasion reflection, for by dint of his narration and the language chosen, he leads us to conclude that the greatest *kínēsis* or motion in human history follows upon and is contingent upon a species of settling down that he terms *hēsuchía* or rest (1.12.1–4).[22]

What it is that constitutes *hēsuchía* Thucydides does not specify, but he does intimate what he has in mind in what appears to be a colorful, but largely irrelevant digression introducing the two peoples that form the subject of his book. In early times, Thucydides remarks,

> all in Hellas went about armed, their homes being unguarded, and their inter-
> course with one another unsafe, and, just like the barbarians today, they were
> accustomed to go about their daily lives with their weapons ready to hand.
> Those parts of Hellas still organized in this fashion [such as Ozolian Locris,
> Aetolia, and Acarnania] provide an indication of the patterns of daily life then
> similar for all. Among these, the Athenians were the first to put their weapons
> down and take up a mode of daily life less restrained and more luxurious. It
> was not until quite recently that the old men among their wealthy ceased, out
> of a sense of delicacy, wearing tunics of linen and fastening a knot of the hair on
> their heads with a tie of golden grasshoppers – whence also, as a consequence
> of their kinship, this same style of dress long prevailed among the old men in
> Ionia. The Lacedaemonians [at Sparta], on the other hand, were the first to
> make use of a measured style of dressing, more in conformity with the mode
> now current, with the well-to-do altering their behavior in other regards and
> adopting a way of life equal to that of the many. The Lacedaemonians were
> also the first to go naked, stripping off their clothes in the light of day (*es tò
> phanéron*) and rubbing themselves with oil after exercising. In the past, even in
> the Olympic games, the athletes who contended first girded their loins; and it
> is not many years since the practice ceased. Even now among some of the bar-
> barians, especially the Asians, when prizes are set out for boxing and wrestling,
> those engaged in the contest gird themselves. And there are many other respects
> in which one might demonstrate that the ancient Hellenes lived in a fashion
> quite similar to the manner in which the barbarians live now. (1.6)

Although this seems like an inconsequential digression, in fact, it goes to the heart of the matter because the species of settling down and of "coming to rest," which is pertinent to a society's acquiring what Thucydides calls the equipment (*paraskeuē*) for war, is described therein. It is constituted by the emergence of a distinction between internal and external relations, by the invention of what we now call "citizenship," by disarmament at home and the establishment of domestic peace. According to Thucydides, his fellow Athenians pioneered this development, and their setting aside of arms at home and their cooperation in the common defense not only gave rise to an end of piracy on land and at sea, but also occasioned a measure of

---

[22] See Leo Strauss, "On Thucydides' War of the Peloponnesians and the Athenians," *The City and Man* (Chicago, 1964), pp. 139–241.

prosperity. The Spartans completed the process by imposing on their com-patriots a modicum of equality that obviated social tensions. To the extent that rivalry remained, it played itself out in the gymnastic arena in which men set aside all clothing, and with it every indication of socioeconomic distinction, and competed as equals displaying the capacities natural and acquired that underpinned their ability to fight effectively for Sparta on the field of battle.

From Thucydides's perspective, it was not an accident that the greatest motion in history took place in the Hellenic rather than in the barbarian world. Nor would he have been suprised to learn that in the age after his death Greek arms conquered the Persian empire in its entirety. The Greeks were, in his view, superior because they established among themselves by means of institutions such as the gymnasium ("the place of nakedness") an equality conducive to political solidarity. What appears to be the least consequential paragraph in Thucydides's archaeology is, in fact, the most consequential: the key to the projection of power is what Thucydides and his fellow Greeks called *politeía* – the political regime, that set of institutions, mores, and manners that transformed a mass of disconnected human beings into a people possessed of a capacity to reach decisions by public deliberation and act in unison upon those decisions. As it happened, the two best integrated political regimes in Hellas went under the name of the Athenians and the Lacedaemonians.

Thucydides places his "archaeology" at the head of his book to alert his more careful and thoughtful readers to the true foundations of power. But, if the first twenty-one paragraphs of the work have, as their theme, the accumulation of those resources, both moral and material, that make possible the projection of power, the rest of the work has as its concern the gradual dissipation of those resources. In his narrative, early on, Thucydides makes it repeatedly clear that Athens should have won the war. On the eve of the war, for example, Sparta's Corinthian allies tell the Lacedaemonians:

> The Athenians are innovators, keen in forming plans, and quick to accomplish in deed what they have contrived in thought. You Spartans are intent on saving what you now possess; you are always indecisive, and you leave even what is needed undone. They are daring beyond their strength, they are risk-takers against all judgment, and in the midst of terrors they remain of good hope – while you accomplish less than is in your power, mistrust your judgment in matters most firm, and think not how to release yourselves from the terrors you face. In addition, they are unhesitant where you are inclined to delay, and they are always out and about in the larger world while you stay at home. For they think to acquire something by being away while you think that by proceeding abroad you will harm what lies ready to hand. In victory over the enemy, they sally farthest forth; in defeat, they give the least ground. For their city's sake, they use

their bodies as if they were not their own; their intelligence they dedicate to political action on her behalf. And if they fail to accomplish what they have resolved to do, they suppose themselves deprived of that which is their own – while what they have accomplished and have now acquired they judge to be little in comparison with what they will do in the time to come. If they trip up in an endeavor, they are soon full of hope with regard to yet another goal. For they alone possess something at the moment at which they come to hope for it: so swiftly do they contrive to attempt what has been resolved. And on all these things they exert themselves in toil and danger through all the days of their lives, enjoying least of all what they already possess because they are ever intent on further acquisition. They look on a holiday as nothing but an opportunity to do what needs doing, and they regard peace and quiet free from political business as a greater misfortune than a laborious want of leisure. So that, if someone were to sum them up by saying that they are by nature capable neither of being at rest (*hēsuchía*) nor of allowing other human beings to be so, he would speak the truth. (1.70)

In the end, however, after twenty-seven years of war, both hot and cold, it is the slow-poke Spartans, the tortoises of ancient Greece, who defeat the hares of Greece, their quick-thinking, quick-acting cousins the Athenians. They are able to do so for the very reasons that the Corinthians inadvertently identify: the Athenians "are by nature incapable of being at rest." Patience is a virtue that they cannot deploy; and, as Pericles insists, patience is required if they are to defeat the Spartans.

"The fox," says the ancient lyric poet Archilochus, "knows many things; the hedgehog knows only one, a big one." Athens is a fox; Sparta is a hedge-hog. The Spartans are supreme in hoplite battle: that is their only trick. Long before Thucydides's time, they fashioned a series of alliances with cities in or on the margins of the Peloponnesus to supplement their manpower; and, tied down by the threat of revolt on the part of the helots who farmed the land they control, they hunkered down. To defeat them, one had to exploit the fissures in their alliance system. One needed to rally Sparta's ancient rival Argos and turn the manpower of the cities within the so-called Peloponnesian League against the hegemon that led it. Short of that, Athens could do little. Above all, the Athenians needed to await opportunity. If they acted, they needed to act in such a manner as to elicit that opportunity.

Pericles understood that reality. From the beginning, his grand strategy aimed at splitting the Peloponnesian League, and in time, despite the delay occasioned early in the war by the plague at Athens, Pericles's strategy worked. Finding their offensive strategy of no avail when deployed against a maritime city linked to the sea by impregnable walls, the Spartans eventually lost heart and made peace with the Athenians (5.14.3–15.1, 16.1–17.1). Then, in fury, Corinth bolted from the Peloponnesian League, Argos entered the fray, and Mantineia and Elis revolted (5.14–42). The stage was, then, set for a decisive battle to bring Sparta to its knees – but the Athenians lacked the capacity to exploit the situation. Alcibiades, who recognized the opportunity, was not a politician equal to the occasion. He managed to draw together the Argives, Mantineans, and Eleans, and even to force on the Spartans a decision in the field, but he proved unable to rally Athens as a city in support of these allies, and in the absence of whole-hearted support, the result was defeat for the anti-Spartan coalition (5.43–75). The grand strategy devised by Alcibiades's onetime guardian required on the part of their compatriots both patience and a capacity for sudden, focused action that only an Athens led by Pericles could display. To the extent that Pericles encouraged in his compatriots a mad lust for glory, which is precisely what he did in the Funeral Oration (2.43.1),[23] he encouraged in them at the same time an impatience fatal in his absence to the enterprise he conceived.[24]

Consider what Thucydides reports concerning Pericles: The latter told his compatriots "that they would prevail if they remained at rest (*hēsucházontas*) and looked after the fleet and if, during the war, they made no attempt to extend their dominion and refrained from placing the city at risk. What they did was the contrary in all regards, governing themselves and their allies, even in matters seemingly extraneous to the war, with an eye to private ambitions and private profit in a manner quite harmful, pursuing policies whose success would be to the honor and advantage of private individuals, and whose failure brought harm to the city in the war" (2.65.7). A people "by nature incapable of being at rest (*hēsuchía*)" cannot for long be persuaded to "remain at rest (*hēsucházontas*)."

From Thucydides's "archaeology," we learn that the greatest motion in human history presupposes the greatest rest. Domestic tranquillity makes possible the projection of power. But a people who are "incapable of being at rest" are always in danger of succumbing to faction and are forever prone to domestic unrest. As we learn from studying Thucydides's history, Sparta wins the Peloponnesian War because the Lacedaemonians maintain a species of solidarity and a domestic tranquility that the Athenians, absent Pericles, simply cannot sustain. Athens in Pericles's heyday was not a democracy; it was "rule by the first man." Whenever Pericles saw his fellow citizens "in an untimely manner emboldened to the point of insolence (*húbris*), by speaking, he reduced them to fear; on the other contrary, if they fell without reason (*alógōs*) victim to fear, he could restore in them again their confidence."

---

23 To grasp the significance of Pericles's use of a cognate of *érōs* in this passage, one must consider the import of the reappearance of this word and its cognates at 3.45.5 and 6.13.1, 24.3.

24 For an extended discussion of the peculiar form that the daring and restlessness of the Athenians took, see Paul A. Rahe, "Thucydides' Critique of *Realpolitik*," *Security Studies*, 5:2, 1995, pp. 105–41.

After Pericles's death, however, there was a return to democratic normalcy. As Thucydides puts it,

> Those who came later were more on an equal plane with one another, and each desiring to be first, they sought to please the people and to them handed over public affairs. In consequence, as tends to happen in a great city also possessed of an empire, they blundered in many regards, especially with respect to the expedition against Sicily – which failed not such much as a consequence of a mistake in judgment with regard to those against whom it was sent, as through the senders' not deciding to make proper provision for those who had gone out, but choosing rather to occupy themselves in private quarrels regarding the leadership of the people, by which they blunted the efforts of those encamped and became embroiled with one another regarding matters pertaining to the city. And yet, after losing the better part of their fleet along with their other forces in Sicily, despite the fact that they were also caught up in sedition (*stásis*) in the city, for three years they nonetheless held out against their former enemies, those from Sicily who had joined them, their own allies the majority of whom were in revolt, and eventually Cyrus, son of the [Persian] King, who provided money to the Peloponnesians for their navy – and they did not give way until they tripped themselves up by means of their private differences. So great were the resources from which Pericles forecast that, in the war, the city could quite easily outlast the Peloponnesians if the latter were fighting on their own.

Why did Athens lose the Peloponnesian War? According to Thucydides, it was because the Athenians became "embroiled with one another"; it was because they succumbed to "sedition" and "private differences." The narrative confirms what we learn from the archaeology: that the projection of power depends on domestic tranquility, that motion abroad depends on rest at home.

By the same token, if there is domestic discord, if motion does arise at home, all is lost. It is by no means fortuitous that, in the third book of his history, Thucydides interrupts his narrative to describe in dramatic detail the revolution (*stásis*) that took place at Corcyra. Nor is it an accident that, in justifying this digression, for the first and last time subsequent to the initial paragraph of his book, he deploys a cognate of the noun *kínēsis*, observing with regard to revolution that "later" virtually "the entirety of Hellas was subject to motion (*ekinē*thē*) with rival parties in every city – the patrons of the common people trying to bring in the Athenians, and the few trying to bring in the Spartans." In time of peace, he insists, there would have been no opportunity for intervention: it was the war that occasioned the plague of civil strife. "In peace and when matters go well," Thucydides remarks, "cities and individuals are better-minded because they have not fallen into the necessity of doing what they do not wish. But war is a violent teacher; in depriving them of the means for easily satisfying their daily wants, it assimilates the thinking of the many to their present circumstances"

(3.82.1–3).[25] It was this "violent teacher," *motion without*, that brought to Athens *motion within*, and this development Pericles did not foresee. With regard to the city, he did not have the foreknowledge required.

But why should anyone care today? Because, I would submit, George Marshall and Czeslaw Milosz were right. The greatest sustained feat of generalship – i.e., of statesmanship – in human history occurred during the half-century stretching from 1948 to 1989. At no other time did a great power leading a coalition of allies defeat *and dismember* another great power leading a comparable coalition of allies without in the process having to fight a great war. At the heart of the strategy that guided the West in those crucial years was the recognition that the Cold War could be won without catastrophe if, and only if, one could set *in motion* a totalitarian regime, akin in some respects to ancient Sparta, which seemed destined to remain eternally at rest. This struggle could be won without terrible cost if and only if one could somehow manage to embroil its citizens with one another, encourage "private differences," and foment "sedition" not just in communist Russia's satellites but within the Soviet Union itself. It was in the course of wrestling with Thucydides, while ruminating on his account of the Peloponnesian War, that Marshall, Milosz, and the like came to discern what needed to be done. It would in no way be surprising if we, in our own time, had something to learn from the ancient Athenian as well. After all, for a soldier who is also a statesman, training can never be a substitute for education. In politics and war, there is no substitute for what Thucydides instills: the capacity to reflect, to deliberate, and, more generally, to think.

---

[25] Cf. Thuc. 6.38.3, where a city free from *stásis* is said to "be at rest (*hēsucházei*)."

8

Clausewitz, history, and the future strategic world

COLIN S. GRAY

If this were a sermon, Carl von Clausewitz's declamation would be its text: "[A]ll wars are things of the *same* nature."[1] This is the master claim that provides coherence and unity to the argument that follows in this essay.

Writing in approximately 1818, Clausewitz revealed the ambition and pride common to many authors when he declared that "[i]t was my ambition to write a book that would not be forgotten after two or three years, and that possibly might be picked upon more than once by those who are interested in the subject."[2] The heart of the matter is that there are two reasons why military leaders and theorists at all levels are unlikely to forget Clausewitz's work. First, he developed, albeit sketchily in some regards, a theory of war that does not depend for its relevance to a particular time, character of belligerent, or technology. Second, his theorizing was manifestly superior to anything similar written before or since. Christopher Bassford has it exactly right when he claims that Clausewitz's "work survives as a living influence because his approach, overall, comes closer to capturing the complex truth about war than any writer since."[3] In other words, Clausewitz is the best that scholars and soldiers have to help in understanding the nature of war, how it works, and above all, why it works. Even admirers of the great theorist and those who have found his writings of profound practical help on a host of subjects should not confuse *On War's* wisdom with holy writ. Nevertheless, John Keegan is wrong when he asserts that "[t]hose who go for Clausewitz" ascribe to him "a possession of absolute truths – which would make strategy

---

[1] Carl von Clausewitz, *On War*, trans. and ed. Michael Howard and Peter Paret (Princeton, NJ, 1976), p. 606 [emphasis in original].
[2] Ibid., p. 72.
[3] Christopher Bassford, "Book Review," *RUSI Journal*, vol. 148, no. 1, February 2003, pp. 98–9.

unique among the social sciences."[4] To be generous to Keegan, those who are in the habit of deploying favorite Clausewitzian quotations can sometimes inadvertently give the impression that they regard the ever convenient words from *On War* as concluding the debate.

Clausewitz certainly did not write the last words needed for a fully satisfactory theory of war, nor should one deny that some of his analysis could stand improvement, if only one were sufficiently talented to undertake the task. Nevertheless, while the international body of literature on defense subjects and military history is vast, true general theories of war are extremely rare. There are not even many incompetent imitators of Clausewitz. The only theorist of war in the past hundred years who stands even close to Clausewitz is Rear Admiral J. C. Wylie of the U.S. Navy, with his brilliant, and agreeably brief, study, *Military Strategy: A General Theory of Power Control.*[5] It is exceptionally difficult to devise a general theory of war that avoids the minefields of banality, on the one hand, and of an undue, and therefore dating, specificity on the other.

Moreover, the market for general theory is not, and has never been, a lively one. There was good reason, beyond his longevity, why Jomini was more popular than Clausewitz through much of the nineteenth century. Indeed, to this day the American approach to war owes more to Jomini than Clausewitz, not withstanding the near reverence in which soldiers claim to hold the latter. Clausewitz tends to provide insights into questions that policy makers and soldiers have not asked, or which, for all their brilliance, are less than obviously useful today.[6] For example, Andrew Marshall, the Pentagon's long-serving Director of Net Assessment and certainly no foe of Clausewitz, insists that it is virtually impossible to operationalize the complex concept of "friction."[7] Everyone agrees that the concept is among the more glittering achievements of *On War*. But what can one do with it?

Similarly, Clausewitz is unique among theorists in the strength of his emphasis on the fact that "war is the realm of chance."[8] But, as with friction, having grasped the point that chance reigns, if not rules, in war, what are the practical implications? Wylie offers the helpful judgment that "planning for certitude is the greatest of all military mistakes."[9]

A general theory of war, especially one as complex and knowledgeable as that provided by Clausewitz, thus can easily find itself adrift from the

---

[4] John Keegan, "Peace by Other Means?", *The Times Literary Supplement*, December 11, 1992, p. 3.

[5] J. C. Wylie, *Military Strategy: A General Theory of Power Control* (Annapolis, MD, 1989).

[6] This point is well made in Beatrice Heuser, *Reading Clausewitz* (London, 2002), p. 12.

[7] Cited in Barry D. Watts, *Clausewitzian Friction and Future War* (Washington, DC, 1996), p. 122n.

[8] Clausewitz, *On War*, p. 101.

[9] Wylie, *Military Strategy*, p. 72.

working library of those who direct contemporary strategic events. As Bernard Brodie insisted, strategy "is nothing if not pragmatic.... Above all, strategic theory is a theory for action."[10] *On War* is long on the education of the defense and military professional, but relatively short on provision of practical advice. Of course, that also is its principal glory, and a reason why its reputation stands so high after more than 170 years.

That acknowledged, before presenting this essay's argument in detail, the author must register his shock and awe at the title of a 1997 essay by a British scholar, "Strategy in a Post-Clausewitzian Setting."[11] The very idea of a "post-Clausewitzian setting" is an absurdity. One might as well postulate a setting in which the sun ceases to rise. The author of this bizarre piece insists, with a dubious existentialism, that "the crisis in strategic thinking is caused by the domination of a Clausewitzian strategic doctrine that is inappropriate to combating or solving likely conflicts facing the West."[12] It would be difficult to compose a sentence that contained more serious errors, although John Keegan made a powerful entry into the competitive lists of the ignorant, when he wrote that "Clausewitz may ... be shown to have failed as a historian, as an analyst and as a philosopher."[13]

Nevertheless, this essay is far more interested in the robustness of Clausewitz's theory of war, given history's continuities and discontinuities, than it is in pursuing tiresome scholarly debate with those who do not seem to have bothered to read *On War*. By way of organization, therefore, the "story arc" of this essay proceeds initially by outlining an argument concerning the value of *On War* in interpreting history. The essay then moves on to discuss Clausewitz's theory of war in relation to "the future strategic world."

ASSUMPTIONS AND ARGUMENT

It seems strange that anyone would question the relevance of Clausewitz in the twenty-first century, but the evidence of such skepticism is all too easy to locate. In addition to skepticism, of course, there is the opinion that Clausewitz's theory of war, although really irrelevant, is both influential and harmful. Keegan, probably the most unrestrained of contemporary anti-Clausewitzians, accuses the theorist of promulgating "the most pernicious philosophy of warmaking yet conceived."[14] In Keegan's colourful view, "Clausewitz was polluting civilised thought about how wars could

---

[10] Bernard Brodie, *War and Politics* (New York, 1973), p. 452.

[11] Jan Willem Honig, "Strategy in a Post-Clausewitzian Setting," in Gert de Nooy, ed., *The Clausewitzian Dictum and the Future of Western Military Strategy* (The Hague, 1997), pp. 109–21.

[12] Ibid., p. 109.

[13] Keegan, "Peace by Other Means?", p. 3.

[14] John Keegan, *War and Our World: The Reith Lectures, 1998* (London, 1998), p. 41.

and should be fought...."[15] These are strong words. They require answer with comparable clarity, if not comparable eloquence. This section specifies an argument in five parts and the assumptions on which it rests.

First, to quote Robert Kaplan's stimulating book, *Warrior Politics*, "there is no 'modern' world."[16] This a shocking proposition to many, probably most, people. After all, is it not an article of liberal faith that history displays a march of progress, essentially arrowlike, rather than cyclical? For reasons of their optimistic national culture, even American conservative realists often seem to believe the future will improve over the present or past. In material respects, they are right. However, with regard to security, the politics of its provision and the organized violence for political ends known as war suggest a gloomier view. Ralph Peters suggests that in the West's search for guidance in the war against terrorism, it has more to learn from the Romans than from the counterterrorist campaigns of modern times. He notes

> *Do not look for answers in recent history, which is still unclear and subject to personal emotion.* Begin with the study of the classical world – specifically Rome, which is the nearest model to the present-day United States. Mild with subject peoples, to whom they brought the rule of ethical law, the Romans in their rise and at their apogee were implacable with their enemies. The utter destruction of Carthage brought centuries of local peace, while the later empire's attempts to appease barbarians consistently failed.[17]

For good or ill, centuries of evolution have much transformed the social context of war. Indeed, the social transformation of war is likely to be more significant than is the technology-focused transformation so actively pursued in the U.S. Department of Defense today. Peters's implicit approval of Rome's formula for lasting peace with Carthage reminds one of the bloody maxim of the ferocious Russian General Mikhail Skobelev. In 1881, explaining his approach to pacifying the troublesome Turcomans, Skobelev commented, "I hold it as a principle that the duration of peace is in direct proportion to the slaughter you inflict upon the enemy. The harder you hit them, the longer they remain quiet."[18] Russian methods in Chechnya over the past decade bear more than a faint trace of Skobelev attitudes.

The assertion that there is no modern world should be understood as a useful exaggeration. In their essential structure, nature, and purpose, war and strategy are unchanging. Recall the quotation with which this essay began: "[A]ll wars are things of the same nature." The author himself is guilty of

---

[15] Ibid., p. 43.

[16] Robert D. Kaplan, *Warrior Politics: Why Leadership Demands a Pagan Ethos* (New York, 2002), the title of chap. 1.

[17] Ralph Peters, *Beyond Terror: Strategy in a Changing World* (Mechanicsburg, PA, 2002), p. 65.

[18] Quoted in Peter Hopkirk, *The Great Game: On Secret Service in High Asia* (Oxford, 1991), p. 407.

writing a book with the arguably misleading title, *Modern Strategy*. Strategy is strategy, whether it be ancient, medieval, modern, or future. Naturally, the character of the military instrument, and the social, political, and even ethical contexts, are ever in flux. But, as we will see, that fact poses no real difficulty for Clausewitz's theory of war.

This essay's second thread has also been expressed with a convenient eloquence and economy by Kaplan: "The greater the disregard of history, the greater the delusions regarding the future."[19] Liberal and conservative optimists who believe deeply in progress resist the idea that history, especially strategic history, is broadly cyclical, notwithstanding technological and other changes. Clausewitz did not take a teleological view of history, but today most of his more severe critics and even many of his admirers do. In fact, a common ground for finding fault with Clausewitz, at least with his persisting influence, is that his ideas allegedly hinder the emergence of a new globalized world.

Some ten years ago, the author delivered an inaugural lecture bearing the unpopular message that the 1990s were an interwar period.[20] That unwelcome, distinctly cyclical, perspective on the course of history was notably out of step with the attractive notion that the post–Cold War world offered a unique opportunity for the right thinking to achieve lasting improvement in man's security condition. It is now unfashionable among historians to profess belief in the possibility of deriving lessons from history.[21] Fortunately, because the author is a social scientist, he can ignore that fashion. Far more dangerous is the disdain for history among defense professionals. This unhappy reality largely results from the fact that officials and analysts remain so focused on the distinctiveness of current and future issues that they cannot perceive that those concerns are only superficially novel. The other leading explanation for the disdain for history stems from nothing more complex than an ignorance of the past. One should not expect communities of soldiers or bureaucrats to place high value on a skill they by and large lack.

Whatever the deeper motives, other factors also combine to impede recognition of history's utility. Obvious changes in political, social, and technological contexts offer an easy excuse for those who assert that historical study is mere antiquarianism – interesting, fun perhaps, but not a serious contributor to current strategic thought or policy deliberation. Furthermore, even when political progressives grant the salience of historical experience, it tends to

[19] Kaplan, *Warrior Politics*, p. 39.
[20] Colin S. Gray, *Villains, Victims and Sheriffs: Strategic Studies for an Inter-War Period, An Inaugural Lecture* (Hull, 1994).
[21] For some judicious comments from the history profession, see Richard J. Evans, *In Defence of History* (London, 1997), p. 59; and Peter Mandler, *History and National Life* (London, 2002), pp. 5–6, 144–5.

be either as a record of the negative to be avoided or as steps already taken on the journey toward a world order of total security.

Moreover, it can be surprisingly difficult to convey the point that history, for all its imperfections, is the only confirmable evidence available. Simulations and other games may be valuable, even essential, but they cannot substitute for the real experience of conflict and war, accessible only through history. For better or worse, history is all we have. Futurology in its many guises is probably unavoidable and necessary, but if it does not rest on historical education, it is useless. Officials should find it reassuring, perhaps a little humbling, and just possibly helpful, to realize that there are no new strategic dilemmas. Others have been there. Of course, today's distinctive details matter, but those details pertain to issues themselves as old as the history of warfare. It is only the supremely self-confident, not to say arrogant, individual who intentionally declines to learn from two and a half millennia of recorded experience.

The third element in this essay's argument is the Clausewitzian belief that "all wars are things of the *same* nature". This eminently reasonable proposition is by no means widely understood. Michael Howard is thoroughly convincing when he restates this Clausewitzian postulate as follows:

> [A]fter all allowances have been made for historical differences, wars still resemble each other more than they resemble any other human activity. All are fought, as Clausewitz insisted, in a special element of danger and fear and confusion. In all, large bodies of men are trying to impose their will on one another by violence; and in all, events occur which are inconceivable in any other field of experience. Of course the differences brought about between one war and another by social or technological changes are immense, and an unintelligent study of military history which does not take adequate account of these changes may quite easily be more dangerous than no study at all.[22]

Some critics have seized upon the fallacy that there was a Clausewitzian era in warfare, an era supposedly coterminous with the Westphalian period of statecentric international politics. From such a perspective, while one might praise Clausewitz for his grasp of the experience of war from 1648 to either 1945, or possibly 1989, one could claim that Hiroshima and Nagasaki terminated the Clausewitzian era. Some have argued that the weaponization of atomic physics may have rendered his central dictum that "war is merely the continuation of policy by other means," obsolete, at least for all who possess a nuclear element in their security.[23] Alternatively, some might prefer to close the Clausewitzian era with what is often interpreted as the demise of interstate warfare. The end of the Cold War with its useful discipline over smaller states, and the unstoppable spread of information technology as the

---

[22] Michael Howard, *The Causes of Wars and Other Essays* (London, 1983), pp. 214–15.
[23] Clausewitz, *On War*, p. 87.

Schwerpunkt of globalization, has supposedly led to new, at least different, patterns of conflict. And so the argument continues that ethnic and cultural, including religious, motives, dominate the "new wars" of today – conflicts that tend overwhelmingly to be either civil or transnational in kind.[24]

However, it should not be necessary to add that war remains an instrument of policy, whatever the ideological or other urges that inspire it. The dates cited previously are challengeable. If 1648 is a little too neat a historical marker, so 1945 and 1989, or even 2001, are not beyond contention. What matters for this essay, though, is not the superior plausibility of one date over another, but the underlying postulate that there was a Clausewitzian era. It follows both that there could have been a pre-Clausewitzian period, and that now the world has entered a post-Clausewitzian era. This is simply wrong.

The error may have several causes, but the principal culprit is a misreading of Clausewitz's "remarkable trinity."[25] Many commentators have believed, indeed still believe, that Clausewitz's theory of war was a theory for an era of so-called 'trinitarian war,' when sovereign states raised and used armies as instruments of policy, while the people were a more or less potent source of emotion and support of their state's cause (obviously this was not the case prior to the nineteenth century). However, if Clausewitz's trinity is read not as a description of a recent era wherein recognisably modern states had armies, but rather as a description of the most fundamental ingredients of warfare, the idea of 'trinitarian war' dies an instant death. The better scholarship on Clausewitz has revealed beyond any room for argument that *On War* presents a primary and a secondary trinity.[26] Although the secondary, and subsidiary, trinity certainly makes qualified reference to the people, the commander and his army, and the government, that most definitely was not the dominant reality according to Clausewitz. In fact, Clausewitz himself clearly described the primary trinity in the following terms:

> War is more than a true chameleon that slightly adapts its characteristic to the given case. As a total phenomenon its dominant tendencies *always make war a remarkable trinity* – composed of primordial violence, hatred, and enmity, which are to be regarded as a blind natural force; of the play of chance and probability within which the creative spirit is free to roam; and of its element of subordination, as an instrument of policy, which makes it subject to reason alone.[27]

---

24 See Martin van Creveld, *The Transformation of War* (New York, 1991); and Mary Kaldor, *New and Old Wars: Organized Violence in a Global Era* (Cambridge, 1999).
25 Clausewitz, *On War*, p. 89.
26 See, especially, Edward J. Villacres and Christopher Bassford, "Reclaiming the Clause-witzian Trinity," *Parameters*, vol. 25, no. 3, 1995, pp. 9–19. Heuser, *Reading Clausewitz*, pp. 52–6, is also useful.
27 Clausewitz, *On War*, p. 89 [emphasis added].

In those words, Clausewitz unquestionably claimed a timeless and universal authority for his remarkable trinity of violence and hatred, chance and probability, and reason or policy. If he is persuasive, it would be ridiculous, certainly redundant, to refer to trinitarian war. In his theory, all war in all periods is trinitarian. Indeed, war cannot be other than trinitarian; it is war's very nature, and whatever critics ignorant of history might think, an enduring nature at that.

An important source of the erroneous belief that Clausewitz wrote for a distinctive era that has passed lies in the carelessness with which critics employ a key idea. The idea in question is the nature of war. Clausewitz conceived of war as having two natures: objective and subjective.[28] The former, war's objective nature, is the totality of the characteristics common to warfare in all periods. Indeed, those features, "the climate of war" and its primary trinity for just two examples, are what make war what it is, rather than something else.[29] One would think that Clausewitz could not easily be misunderstood when he explained as follows: "But war, though conditioned by the particular characteristics of states and their armed forces, must contain some more general – indeed, a universal element with which every theorist ought above all to be concerned."[30]

Clausewitz had just revealed the purpose behind the historical survey and analysis he was presenting in Book VIII, Ch. 3B:

> At this point our historical survey can end. Our purpose was not to assign in passing, a handful of principles of warfare to each period. We wanted to show how every age had its own kind of war, its own limiting conditions, and its own peculiar preconceptions. Each period, therefore, would have held to its own theory of war.[31]

It should be crystal clear that in his theory Clausewitz strives to identify the most vital parts of that "universal element" that comprises war's objective nature. His theory also recognizes that "every age had its own kind of war" and "[e]ach period...would have held to its own theory of war." The subjective nature of war is always evolving. If one rephrases Clausewitz for yet greater clarity, on the one hand he is arguing that war has a permanent nature in all periods. On the other hand, he makes the thoroughly unremarkable claim that the character of war is ever changing. It is something of an accomplishment to misunderstand an argument that simple. Nonetheless,

---

[28] For a particularly clear explanation of Clausewitz's notion of war having two natures, objective and subjective, see Antulio J. Echevarria II, *Globalization and the Nature of War* (Carlisle, PA, 2003), pp. 7–8.

[29] The climate of war is composed of four elements: "danger, exertion, uncertainty, and chance." Clausewitz, *On War*, p. 104.

[30] Ibid., p. 593.

[31] Ibid.

many have succeeded. Moreover, their misunderstandings have led to radically false conclusions about the future of war.

The contemporary defense literature contains profuse references to the alleged changing nature of war. With only rare exceptions, authors fail to reveal whether they refer to the changing objective or subjective nature of war. In other, more modern terms, are they envisaging change in war's very nature, in which case presumably war has to become something else, or are they merely discussing the changing character and conduct of war? As a general rule, they simply confuse the nature and character of war, two hugely different ideas. Whether they employ one word or the other appears simply to be a matter of stylistic preference rather than rigor. Because the thesis of a changing nature of war is vastly more exciting than the rather banal observation that war's character is always changing, the former tends to be the preferred formula. The fact that such a view is nonsense is not widely appreciated. Casual deployment of the notion that war's nature is changing when what is meant is only that its character is altering, inevitably has an encouraging impact on those who fail to realize they are being misled by conceptual incompetence or laziness. Liberal optimists and other progressives are soft targets for such attractive grand ideas as the demise of war itself, or at the least some systemic change in warfare in a benign direction. It is natural that when defense professionals, who should know better, make confident reference to the changing nature of war, they encourage large expectations.

At a less elevated level of misunderstanding, undisciplined advocacy of the alleged changing nature of war, when all that is meant, strictly, is its changing character, cannot help but fuel unsound analysis of a variety that unfortunately abounds globally. Such a fallacy inclines many to see new manifestations of politically motivated violence – new at least to them, that is – as examples of something different from what they really are. Terrorism and civil strife of all kinds have been phenomena of war through the ages. Clausewitz's theory of war applies to all. Above all, they are not activities of a nature quite distinctive from previous or other cases of war. Lt. Cdr. Ashcroft, RN, is entirely correct when he refers to "the perennial problems of war," as is Peter Paret with his reminder of "the timeless reality of war."[32] Clausewitz recognized that different features in war's "universal element" would function distinctively in each unique historical episode and that there must be a dynamic relationship between that "universal element" and the ephemeral circumstances of the day. Similarly, he specified that the relations

---

[32] A. C. Ashcroft, "As Britain Returns to an Expeditionary Strategy, Do We Have Anything to Learn from the Victorians?", *Defence Studies*, vol. 1, no. 1, 2001, p. 83; Carl von Clausewitz, *Historical and Political Writings*, ed. and trans. Peter Paret and Daniel Moran (Princeton, NJ, 1992), p. 3.

among the components of his primary (passion, chance, reason) and secondary (people, army, government) trinity are "variable" and cannot yield to a theory that "seeks to fix an arbitrary relationship between them."[33] If one judges Clausewitz persuasive when he insists that there is a "universal element" in war, and indeed that all wars, of all kinds and in all periods, are events of the same nature, the implications are irresistible.

The fourth element in this essay's argument follows necessarily from the third. Specifically, Clausewitz's theory of war is eternally relevant because his subject has an unchanging nature. In principle, a general theory of war superior to that of Clausewitz might yet be devised, although it would be sure to owe much to Clausewitz. Certainly, there are ways in which his theory could be improved. Clausewitz assuredly would have endorsed the latter point, and probably the former. After all, he informs us in an "Unfinished Note," probably written in 1830, that "[t]he first chapter of Book One alone I regard as finished."[34]

More often than not, criticism of Clausewitz tells one more about the critics than about the theory of war with which they find fault. The criticisms reflect the attitudes and opinions fashionable in the critics' time, and the identity as well as the character of the strategic problems to which those attitudes and opinions respond. *On War* was, of course, intended to be the author's definitive explanation of war's nature and working. If, as Raymond Aron observed, "[s]trategic thought draws its inspiration each century, or rather at each moment of history, from the problems which events themselves pose,"[35] there is no doubt that Clausewitz's first-hand experience of the new way of war enabled by the French Revolution, and practiced *à outrance* by Napoleon, was the basic fuel for this theory.

However, in at least two respects he managed to transcend the strategic problems of his day. First, he drafted a general theory of war that, whatever its origins in his bitter experience of humiliating national defeat at Jena-Auerstadt, was successfully nonspecific in its historical applicability.[36] Second, in his intellectual crisis of 1827, he succeeded in transcending the influence of the principal strategic experience of his active military career and began the process of reshaping his theory to accommodate wars of limited objective.[37] These were mighty achievements. No other theorist has been able to transcend in his or her writing the influence of the kind of traumatic strategic events that had dominated Clausewitz's life from the age of

---

33 Clausewitz, *On War*, p. 89.
34 Ibid., p. 70.
35 Raymond Aron, "The Evolution of Modern Strategic Thought," in Alastair Buchan, ed., *Problems of Modern Strategy* (London, 1970), p. 25.
36 See Peter Paret, *Clausewitz and the State* (New York, 1976), chap. 6.
37 See Azar Gat, *The Origins of Military Thought: From the Enlightenment to Clausewitz* (Oxford, 1989), esp. p. 199.

twelve, when he joined the Prussian Army in 1792, up to the Ligny-Waterloo campaign of 1815 twenty-three years later.

Clausewitz left much to be done on his general theory of war. His premature death in Poland in 1831 prevented him from doing much of what he knew needed to be done. Much of the manuscript of *On War*, Books II to VI in particular, still required revision at his death. Furthermore, as Beatrice Heuser has observed in her recent study, it is probable that some of the more intriguing and difficult political ideas that assumed prominence in Clausewitz's mind after 1827 were by no means fully explored, or necessarily even completely comprehended, by their author.[38] This is an observation, not a complaint.

Nevertheless, there has not been much to offer that improves on Clausewitz's theory of war in the past 172 years. It is thoroughly appropriate for us at the beginning of the twenty-first century to look for strategic inspiration to the finest general theory of war ever written. However, it is not appropriate to look to Clausewitz to resolve the deeper strategic quandaries of our century. The quality of *On War* is unparalleled, and its relevance, in keeping with the longevity of its subject, is prospectively permanent. Nonetheless, those plausible claims do not absolve us from thinking strategically for ourselves.

The fifth strand of argument is to the effect that the Clausewitzian theoretical legacy needs protection against ignorant, careless, or willful misrepresentation. Despite the importance of war to the course of history, there exist few first-rate efforts at building a general theory, and even that is probably an exaggeration. So rare is fundamental exploration and explanation of war, let alone a study as brilliant as *On War*, that mistaken and misleading criticisms are potentially too expensive to be tolerable. If the military and academic worlds were to retire Clausewitz on the grounds that his theory applied, allegedly, only to the period where the "master narrative" was the rise of total war, what strategic or antistrategic guru might replace him?[39] Philosophers of war worthy of the title, be they premodern, modern, or postmodern, are not exactly pressing hard and persuasively to seize Clausewitz's crown. Martin van Creveld and Edward Luttwak, for example, certainly have their virtues, but no one is likely to confuse them with Clausewitz.[40]

This final element in this essay's argument could hardly be more practical in its motivation. Because war remains so important, because there are so few studies that penetrate and explain its basic nature, and because *On War*

---

[38] Heuser, *Reading Clausewitz*, p. 180.

[39] Roger Chickering, "Total War: The Use and Abuse of a Concept," in Manfred F. Boemke, Chickering, and Stig Forster, eds., *Anticipating Total War: The German and American Experiences, 1871–1914* (Cambridge, 1999), pp. 13–28, claims that the "master narrative" of modern military history is the story of the intensification of war.

[40] From van Creveld's extensive canon, see *The Transformation of War*; from Edward N. Luttwak's, see *Strategy: The Logic of War and Peace*, rev. ed. (Cambridge, MA, 2001).

is the work of outstanding brilliance in an admittedly impoverished field, soldiers and theorists cannot afford to allow unsound criticism of Clausewitz to flourish unchallenged. Alas, it is also necessary to recognize that Clausewitz's theory of war can require protection not only from its detractors, but also from some of its more enthusiastic devotees. There is a long history of those who find in Clausewitz what suits them. This phenomenon is scarcely surprising when one considers the fact that Clausewitz died before he could revise much of his manuscript to reflect his post-1827 determination to theorize about real war – that is to say, war conducted for, and shaped by, political purpose. The pre-1827 nonpolitical Clausewitz is present in the text in good measure. *On War* allows for the waging of limited war for limited political goals, as well as for the conduct of Napoleonic-style operations intended to destroy the enemy's armed forces in decisive battle and thereby render him defenceless. There is a Clausewitz for everyone, so it seems. Adolf Hitler was fond of quoting Clausewitz, while Mao Tse-tung found his writings more inspirational than those of Sun-tzu.[41]

One cannot do much to reeducate those who willfully misread, if not actually misquote, *On War*, just as it is a sad reality that villains and heroes equally can make good use of Clausewitz's wisdom. However, much can and needs to be done to help those who inadvertently misuse some of the more potent ideas in *On War*. For leading examples, Clausewitz's "remarkable trinity" and his relatively few references to a belligerent's "center of gravity" have both fueled as much, if not more, honest misunderstanding as enlightenment. Recent scholarship should help address this problem, but it can take many years before light reaches those zones where it is most needed, let alone accepted there.[42] It may be no exaggeration to suggest that the American military has seized on the concept of the "center of gravity" and sought to apply it in a distinctly Jominian spirit. After all, here is a concept with direct practical use. Unlike friction, or the culminating point of victory, and other difficult concepts, center of gravity appears to be ready for the strategic primetime.

In addition, it is important to protect the Clausewitzian legacy from some of its more fanatical guardians, as well as from those who would misuse it either knowingly or in ignorance. Of course, it is essential to respect Clausewitz's theory of war on its own terms and comprehend it as its author intended as best one can. That can be difficult, given the vagaries of translation, the different cultural contexts between the 1820s and today, and the author's incomplete revision of his text. However, as a mildly blasphemous thought, one should not mistake Clausewitz for Moses. By his own

---

[41] Heuser, *Reading Clausewitz*, esp. pp. 138–42.
[42] See Antulio J. Echevarria II, *Clausewitz' Center of Gravity: Changing Our Warfighting Doctrine – Again!* (Carlisle, PA, 2002).

admission, as well as by the evidence of Clausewitz's arguments, its author regarded *On War* as a work in progress. One should embrace that reality. Clausewitz treats some of the most powerful ideas in *On War* in a quite cursory fashion. That is not surprising given the fact the author had barely three years in which to effect a systemic and near traumatic revision of his magnum opus.

Moreover, in those three years from 1827 to 1830, he was heavily engaged in historical writing, not to mention his admittedly light military administrative duties. In company with its author, one should regard *On War* as a living document, always provided that one begins by striving carefully and honestly to remain faithful to what one understands to have been Clausewitz's meaning. On the truly major issue of proper historical domain, it is scarcely possible to misunderstand Clausewitz, so direct is his argument. If this essay accomplishes little else, at least it should bury with ignominy the fallacy that Clausewitz theorized for an era now past. This error need not be an expression of liberal or conservative assumptions. Whether one is an optimistic liberal, a pessimistic conservative, or – confusingly – a different combination of noun and adjective, one might believe, honestly, yet mistakenly, that the strategic world about and for which Clausewitz theorized no longer exists. It is to this apparently contentious subject that the analysis now turns.

CLAUSEWITZ AND THE FUTURE

How does Clausewitz relate to the future strategic world? Some would want to rephrase the question to pose a ringing challenge: does Clausewitz relate to the future strategic world? The previous sections of this essay, devoted to assumptions and argument, should have answered that question to general, if not universal, satisfaction. Historians know much that can serve as a valuable education in preparation for what the future may bring. Nevertheless, they are not blessed with the kind of predictive wisdom that policy makers crave. If it is any consolation, social scientists are no better at prediction than are historians. At least historians rarely claim to be able to predict the future.

Fortunately, the precise character of the future strategic world is a subject of notable indifference to the argument of this text. As long as the future world remains a strategic world, Clausewitz's general theory of war will be as relevant as ever. By a strategic world, one means a world wherein states, groups, or individuals threaten or employ force for political ends. That force may be an instrument of policy for states, factions within states, or for movements and groups that lack any particular state affiliation. For as long as war or its possibility continues to scar history, for so long will humans inhabit a Clausewitzian world. Clausewitz was not much interested in predicting the future – an attitude the modern world would be wise to emulate – at least, that is, those whose duties do not require guesses and who pretend that their stabs into the dark rest on some useful knowledge. Trend analysis, for example, is notoriously apt to mislead. If history teaches anything, it is that trend-spotting is a relatively elementary matter, generally of little importance. What matters are the consequences of trends, particularly trends that appear in clusters, and those can be all but impossible to identify far in advance. Warfare and its vital social context evolve, but there is no prospect worth mentioning of conflict going out of style on a global basis. That fact suggests that nearly everything currently of interest in Clausewitz's theory of war will apply in the future. It simply does not matter what kinds of conflict dominate in the twenty-first century – as long as the world remains a strategic world, it will be a world addressed by Clausewitz.

The next point almost begs misunderstanding. Specifically, in preparing to cope with the future strategic world, the best guide is the past. But because history is played only once and in no sense can be a laboratory for the testing of theories, its inherent uniqueness limits its value as a guide to the future. However, although details of the future strategic world are currently unknown and unknowable, it so happens that man knows much about strategy, war, and warfare. What is the source of this knowledge? Scientific study of the future? Hardly. Guesswork, inspired and otherwise? Perhaps. In Clausewitz's view – and that of this author – understanding of the strategic future can derive only from the interpretation of strategic experience, which is to say, history.

Of course, critics may object that this deeply conservative perspective all but precludes antistrategic "constructivist" projects. There are those who believe history does not doom mankind to repeat its past errors in a cyclical process, but that one can construct a new world without a strategic dimension – an idle hope. Clausewitz did not build his theory on an architecture of hope, or even expectations, for the future. Instead, he was uncompromising in a commitment to achieving such objective historical knowledge as he could. He made plain his attitude in an early unpublished manuscript. Describing that manuscript on the theory of war, he confided that

> Its scientific character consists in an attempt to investigate the essence of the phenomenon of war and to indicate the links between these phenomena and the nature of their component parts. No logical conclusion has been avoided; *but whenever the thread became too thin I have preferred to break it off and go back to the relevant phenomenon of experience.* Just as some plants bear fruit only if they don't shoot up too high, so in the practical arts the leaves and flowers of theory must be pruned and the plant kept close to its proper soil – experience.[43]

43 Clausewitz, *On War*, p. 61 [emphasis added].

In a letter ten years later, dated December 22, 1827, Clausewitz reaffirmed unambiguously his view of the dependence of theory on historical experience. He wrote that "[i]f we want to deduce the art of war from the history of war, and that is indisputably the only way to get there, we must not dismiss as unimportant the manifestation of war in history."[44] Peter Paret explains that

> Clausewitz's theoretical writings on war were based on the experience of war – known experience and that of his generation, but also on another form of experience that only history can transmit. By opening up the past for us, history added to the fund of knowledge that we can acquire directly and also made possible universal concepts and generalisations across time.[45]

The twenty-first century presents mysterious aspects of the future strategic world, wholly impenetrable even to armed forces pursuing "information dominance" and "dominant battlespace knowledge." However, on the brighter side, that future strategic world must be obedient to "the timeless reality of war." If one reads Clausewitz and appreciates the theory of war that he derived empirically from historical study of war's objective nature, one will help mankind immeasurably to cope with the certain shocks and surprises of the future.

There is, of course, another possible approach to the creation of a general theory of war. One could proceed deductively from first principles and postulate "rational strategic persons" exercising culture-free rational choices. Much of the partial theory of war devised for the control of nuclear weapons was, perhaps had to be, of this character. After all, what did history have to say about nuclear strategy? The answer was a great deal, but it did not seem so to theorists in the 1950s, especially those innocent of history.[46]

Although one might consider *On War's* all but total silence on the subject of technology to be a weakness, that silence is in fact a virtue in that it serves as a healthy antidote to contemporary technophilia. Clausewitz's theory of war assumes belligerents will arm themselves competently and train in their weapons' effective use. Clausewitz's active service, off and on from 1792 to 1815, suggests that the absence of a technological dimension in his theory was anything but an oversight. Implicitly, at least, he accommodated the evolution of weapons technology, a slow evolution in his experience, by recognizing the ever-changing subjective nature of war. But the objective nature of war is in no fashion keyed to weapons technology. In words that might not find a friendly audience in the current Pentagon, Clausewitz advised that

---

[44] Quoted in Heuser, *Reading Clausewitz*, p. 31.
[45] Paret, "Introduction," to Clausewitz, *Historical and Political Writings*, p. 3.
[46] Writing in 1973, Brodie lamented the undue influence of scientists and economists in Washington. He noticed that "political scientists, including area specialists," had yet to achieve a comparable hearing among policy makers. *War and Politics*, p. 460 n. 35.

"[v]ery few of the new manifestations in war can be ascribed to new inventions or new departures in ideas. They result mainly from the transformation of society and new social conditions."[47] Communities do not fight because they are armed; they are armed because they want to fight. Understanding of this elementary political logic has not always been complete among those who have seen great value in arms control. Clausewitz's theory of war does not by any means dismiss technology as unimportant, but by implication he minimizes its importance. He wrote in the letter of December 22, 1827, quoted already, that

> War is nothing but a continuation of political endeavour with altered means. I base the whole of strategy on this tenet, and believe that he who refuses to recognise this necessity does not fully understand what matters. This principle explains the whole history of war, and without it, everything would appear quite absurd.[48]

A noteworthy fraction of the defense community treats the past, present, and future of strategic history as the story of machines. Studies of future warfare mostly represent reductionist efforts to forecast the impact of weapons and their supporting equipment. By implication, which in this case means by omission, Clausewitz suggests that technology is not a matter of primary significance. The great, or not so great, revolution-in-military-affairs debate of the 1990s, now revived under the banner of transformation, focused heavily indeed on the promises of an information-based way of war. Although the debate and the slow but inexorable momentum of policy by no means wholly fixated on hardware, in the end it was still a heavily technological story. In a period when no dominant threat was apparent to stimulate strategic thought, one could only expect the American defense community to devote itself to matters with which it felt most comfortable – namely, those with a preponderantly technological content.

However, many participants in the revolution-in-military-affairs transformation debate – who undoubtedly believed they were addressing cutting-edge issues for the future strategic world – undoubtedly missed, and may still be missing, the other strategic revolution of our time. Specifically, in addition to the narrowly military revolution-in-military-affairs transformation, the subject of seemingly countless conferences and studies, some have argued that there has been a transformation of war itself, regarded holistically.[49] More precisely, employing Marxist terminology, Mary Kaldor argues "that there has been a revolution in military affairs, but it is a revolution in the social relations of warfare, not in technology, even though the changes

---

[47] Clausewitz, *On War*, p. 515.
[48] Quoted in Heuser, *Reading Clausewitz*, p. 34.
[49] See Colin McInnes, *Spectator-Sport War: The West and Contemporary Conflict* (Boulder, CO, 2002), chap. 4; and "A Different Kind of War? September 11 and the United States' Afghan War," *Review of International Studies*, vol. 29, no. 2, 2003, pp. 165–84.

in social relations are influenced by and make use of new technology."⁵⁰ Later, she offers the pure Clausewitzian thought that "[e]very society has its own characteristic form of war."⁵¹ That characteristic form will show a distinctive subjective nature, in Clausewitzian terms, but it cannot reveal a unique objective nature because that nature is universal and timeless.

Those who are engaged in planning, executing, or commenting on the current military transformation, as announced by the U.S. Department of Defense, would be well advised to consider Clausewitz's theory of war and ask themselves why it lacks a technological element.⁵² They might profit from reflecting on these penetrating words by the British historian Jeremy Black:

> In its fundamentals, war changes far less frequently and significantly than most people appreciate. This is not simply because it involves a constant – the willingness of organised groups to kill and, in particular, to risk death – but also because the material culture of war, which tends to be the focus of attention, is less important than its social, cultural and political contexts and enablers.⁵³

Clausewitz's timeless theory of war also reminds the present that in the future strategic world, as in the past and present ones, "[w]ar is nothing but a duel on a larger scale."⁵⁴ This truth is as central to the fundamental and unchanging nature of war despite its consistent neglect by defense planners. *On War* insists, unarguably, that "[f]orce…is thus the *means* of war; to impose our will on the enemy is its object."⁵⁵ Proper respect for the enemy's culture, even in the narrow sense of a strategic culture likely to influence style in war, is the historical exception rather than the norm. Great powers, in particular, can have understandable, if unfortunate, difficulty taking lesser enemies as seriously as they often merit. Hubris is especially noticeable when a great power is both the rather aggressive bearer of a distinctive ideology and the beneficiary of clear technological superiority. Such a power is much in need of reminder by Clausewitz's theory of war of the potential strength of political will, as well as of the roles of chance and friction. The report of a recent conference at the U.S. Army War College on "The 'New' American Way of War," offered this revealing comment on America's future foes:

> Most of America's small wars have been successes, and recognizing that fact as the norm for future wars is more productive than the irrational mania surrounding the Vietnam War experience. The United States will not be fighting

---

⁵⁰ Kaldor, *New and Old Wars*, p. 3.
⁵¹ Ibid., p. 13.
⁵² For the official view, see Donald H. Rumsfeld: *Quadrennial Defense Review Report* (Washington, DC, 2001), chap. 5; *Annual Report to the President and the Congress* (Washington, DC, 2002), chap. 6; and *Transformation Planning Guidance* (Washington, DC, 2003).
⁵³ Jeremy Black, *War in the New Century* (London, 2001), p. 114.
⁵⁴ Clausewitz, *On War*, p. 75.
⁵⁵ Ibid. [emphasis in original].

peers, it will be fighting "indians". Thus, the past as prologue to the future is what Americans should expect.[56]

Almost any comment would be superfluous. However, a somewhat different view of the future strategic world has been offered by Steven Metz and Raymond Millen, both on the staff at the U.S. Army War College. Metz suggests that "[t]he era of the 'stupid' enemy is over."[57] Maintaining the spotlight on that institution, a former commandant, Robert Scales, an historian and professional soldier, has written a keen speculative essay on the all too pertinent subject of "adaptive enemies."[58] In recent years, the U.S. defense establishment has warmed to the fashionable concept of asymmetric threats and strategy. But asymmetry is a fundamentally vacuous concept, impossible to operationalize; all that it means is to be different. It can have no meaning save in contrast to its opposite, symmetry. The concept's only merit lies in its potential for underlining the fact that putative enemies possess independent wills. They will inevitably strive to find a way of war, perhaps a way of grand strategy short of war, that might compensate for their weakness.

Clausewitz's theory of war speaks to the future strategic world, as it does to the past, with its potent imagery of war as a duel or a wrestling match. His definition of war should make it difficult for us to ignore the enemy. He suggests that "[w]ar is thus an act of force to compel our enemy to do our will."[59] Further on, Clausewitz warns of the difficulty in assessing the enemy's strength accurately.

> If you want to overcome your enemy you must match your effort against his power of resistance, which can be expressed as the product of two inseparable factors, viz. *the total means at his disposal and the strength of his will.* The extent of the means at his disposal is a matter – though not exclusively – of figures, and should be measurable. But the strength of his will is much less easy to determine and can only be gauged approximately by the strength of the motive animating it.[60]

Not surprisingly, net assessment is a notoriously inexact business.

The crucial point on Clausewitz and the future strategic world is that his theory of war, driven and shaped by "a universal element," is eminently inclusive in the domain of strategic behavior. Those who would consign Clausewitz's theory to retirement for this period, when major interstate

---

[56] Raymond A. Millen, "The 'New' American Way of War," U.S. Army War College and Strategic Studies Institute, XIV Annual Strategy Conference, April 8–10, 2003, Conference Brief, p. 2.
[57] Steven Metz and Raymond Millen, *Future War/Future Battlespace: The Strategic Role of American Landpower* (Carlisle, PA, 2003), p. viii.
[58] Robert H. Scales, Jr., *Future Warfare: Anthology* (Carlisle, PA, 1999): "Adaptive Enemies: Dealing with the Strategic Threat after 2010," pp. 33–55.
[59] Clausewitz, *On War*, p. 75 [emphasis in original].
[60] Ibid., p. 77 [emphasis in original].

warfare has become a rarity, simply do not understand its reach. Lest the argument somehow be lost, *Clausewitz's theory of war applies to all cases of organized violence for political ends, regardless of the period, the identity of the belligerents, or the character of the warfare they conduct.* It is true that Clausewitz was writing with the organized strategic behavior of states in his mind. But that fact does not restrict the grasp of his theory. Certainly, he was open to new developments in warfare, witness his perceptive, if some- what ambivalent, chapter on "The People in Arms" in Book VI.[61] There is no room for doubt about Clausewitz's belief that his theory of war had a universal reach. The fact that he did not specify some of the forms of con- flict prevalent today is a point of little significance. He did not have much to say about the maritime dimension of war, about aerial warfare, or about nuclear, space, or cyberwar either. He was clear enough when he outlined the inclusivity of his perspective:

> Generally speaking, a military objective that matches the political object in scale will, if the latter is reduced, be reduced in proportion; this will be all the more so as the political object increases its predominance. Thus it follows that without any inconsistency wars can have all degrees of importance and intensity, ranging from a war of extermination down to simple armed observation.[62]

Elsewhere, Clausewitz makes the same point when he begins a most impor- tant chapter with these words: "The degree of force that must be used against the enemy depends on the scale of political demands on either side."[63] Again, he argues that "all wars are things of the *same* nature." Because "war is an instrument of policy.... [I]t must necessarily bear the character of policy and measure by its standards. The conduct of war, in its great outlines, is therefore policy itself."[64] This must be as true for the wars of the future as it was for those of the past. It is always possible for the policy logic of war to be undone by war's "grammar," especially "if statesmen look to cer- tain military moves and actions to produce effects that are foreign to their nature...."[65] There is nothing one can envisage about the future strategic world that would invalidate Clausewitzian theory.

Finally, while Clausewitz's theory of war is deeply philosophical and there- fore difficult, if not impossible, to operationalize, it also is crucial to helping us cope with the challenges of the future strategic world, as well as the temp- tations encouraged by our own apparent or anticipated prowess. A succes- sion of easy military victories against "indians" – to quote the U.S. Army War College again – may or may not provide a sound education for future

---

[61] Ibid., pp. 479–83.
[62] Ibid., p. 81.
[63] Ibid., p. 585.
[64] Ibid., p. 610.
[65] Ibid., pp. 605, 608.

strategic excellence. But even the wars that one could not lose, for example, the two Gulf Wars, Kosovo, and against the Afghan Taliban, should serve as reminders of the potency of Clausewitz's cardinal point concerning war as a political instrument. As he wrote in his letter of December 22, 1827, "[t]his principle explains the whole history of war, and without it, everything would appear quite absurd."[66]

Because war is so extreme an activity, so dramatic, so costly, and, depending on the period, so unusual, those who plan it and those who wage it have consistently given unduly short shrift to its political dimension. Because "*war is only a branch of political activity . . . in no sense autonomous*," its success or failure rests only on its political consequences, and not on the verdict of the battlespace.[67] The primacy of policy – of political purpose – is the most important of a host of concepts and perspectives that Clausewitz's theory of war bequeathed to the future, the better for future leaders – military as well as civilian – to deal with the challenges of the future strategic world. His inductive, timeless theory forearms us with ideas and caveats of priceless value. His study of the history of war and his personal experience produced such gems as friction, the primary trinity as a potentially master framework, the emphasis on war as the realm of chance, risk and uncertainty, the relationship between the policy logic and the grammar of war, center of gravity, the culminating point of victory, and, above all else, the primacy of the political. The aim here is not to suggest that these concepts should be extracted, or cherry picked, from a lengthy book for stand-alone utility. Rather, the point is simply that Clausewitz's theory of war is well armed with ideas that have the most profound implications for prudent political and strategic behavior.

CONCLUSION

Because this essay has been less an enquiry and more a sustained argument, the author has already flagged its conclusions. That granted, a handful of points of exceptional importance merit elevation to the status of conclusions.

First, Clausewitz's theory of war is as timeless as the phenomenon of war, notwithstanding war's rich cultural, political, social, and technological variety. *On War* recognizes that "every age had its own kind of war" and "would have held to its own theory of war."[68] Clausewitz's theory sought the universal elements in war; this is war's objective nature. In Clausewitzian terms, war's subjective nature is its ever-changing character.

Second, Clausewitz is probably doomed to attacks, both by those who misunderstand him and by those who do not. Many just do not warm to

---

[66] Quoted in Heuser, *Reading Clausewitz*, p. 34.
[67] Clausewitz, *On War*, p. 605 [emphasis in original].
[68] Ibid., p. 593.

a theory of war, least of all to one that enjoys the most elevated of reputations. The guiding light for Clausewitz's theory in his post-1827 revisions, the insistence that war must be an instrument of policy, is a descriptive and normative position that, again, many find distasteful, and possibly obsolescent. The unrevised or underrevised state of Books II to VI, and even Books VII to VIII in some measure, means there appears to be more than one Clausewitz, if one is seeking support for an assault on the man and his theory.

Third, to this author at least, it is clear that statecraft and strategy are always in need of education, not prescriptive advice, which Clausewitz's theory provides to those open to wisdom. In particular, his insistence on the supremacy of policy, indeed on the fusion of policy and the conduct of war at its higher levels, would be a banality, were it not so frequently ignored in practice. His discussion of friction, chance, and uncertainty is eternally essential as caveats to those who function in a "can do" mode and who have difficulty conceiving of bad luck or truly cunning enemies. One should not need constant reminders that war is "nothing but a duel on a larger scale," but enemy-independent planning is a perennial temptation to members of a profession who necessarily focus on what they intend to do to the enemy, rather than on what the enemy might do to thwart their plans.

Fourth, it is probably useful to repeat as a conclusion the point that the ever-changing character of future warfare is a matter of supreme indifference for the relevance of Clausewitz's theory of war. Whether the future strategic world resembles the present or is radically transformed is of course a subject of considerable significance for mankind at the time. Future strategists and military leaders will be fortunate in having on hand in *On War* an educational guide to war's permanent nature – one that is robust in the face of any and all historical developments, save one. That one would be the happy conclusion of strategic history per se. Because the threat and use of organized force for political purposes appears relevant for the long haul, the demand for the services of Clausewitz's theory of war should be all but permanent.

Fifth, although Clausewitz expressed his theory in philosophical terms, at times in an abstract fashion, it rests on the inductive reasoning of deep historical study. He believed that to be of any value, theory had to remain in close touch with historical experience, which is to say, with evidence. That belief may seem commonplace to historians, but social scientists of various persuasions are much given to deductive, abstract theorizing. The rational strategic person stalks the pages of modern strategic theory.[69] The tradition of strategic theory that owes much to the assumptions of rational choice and

---

[69] Rational choice is handled roughly in Hedley Bull, "Strategic Studies and Its Critics," *World Politics*, vol. 20, no. 4, 1968, pp. 593–605; Colin S. Gray, *Strategic Studies: A Critical Assessment* (Westport, CT, 1982), chap. 4; and Stephen M. Walt, "Rigor or Rigor Mortis: Rational Choice and Security Studies," *Security Studies*, vol. 23, no. 4, 1999, pp. 5–48.

next to nothing to cultural empathy, let alone historical knowledge, would benefit markedly from adopting a more Clausewitzian approach. War is a social enterprise in several senses, and one size in ideas does not fit all potential belligerents. In that regard, the interesting notion that the Clausewitzian domain may be culturally limited seems unsound to this author, but worthy of further investigation.[70] Jeremy Black, for example, argues that "war and success in war are cultural constructs."[71] Nevertheless, while that challenging proposition is an idea in need of careful consideration, it is not lethal for the timeless universality of Clausewitz's authority.

Sixth and last but not least, Clausewitz is not holy writ, only canon lore. Sensible claims for the excellence of his theory of war need to be carefully bounded. They amount to an insistence, not that *On War* provides the best theory of war that ever could be, but only that it is the best available. As Clausewitz himself admitted in some detail, the manuscript of *On War* was by no means the best that he could achieve, were he granted the time to complete the necessary revisions. Although one can criticize Clausewitz on many grounds for inconsistencies, omissions, and failures to develop key ideas, one would do well to be generous and recall the old motto that the best is the enemy of the good. In *On War*, underrevised though it may be, Clausewitz provided a theory of war good enough to explain the eternal nature of the phenomenon at issue. That was a heroic accomplishment. As Richard Betts has ventured: "One Clausewitz is still worth a busload of most other theorists."[72]

---

[70] Chris Brown speculates that "the Clausewitzian account of war … may be culturally specific." *Understanding International Relations* (London, 1997), p. 116.
[71] Black, *War in the New Century*, pp. vii–viii.
[72] Richard K. Betts, "Should Strategic Studies Survive?" *World Politics*, vol. 50, no. 1 (October 1997), p. 29.

9

History and the nature of strategy

JOHN GOOCH

To ask one question of an historian commonly elicits another by way of response. So it is with the question as to what we can learn from history about the nature of strategy, to which academic historians of the general sort will in most cases reply: "What can we learn from history about anything?" Many, perhaps most, of them maintain that there are no "lessons" that one can distil from the past. While this is not the most helpful of standpoints for those in search of practical guidance, it is worth spending a moment on the drawbacks of history as a suggestive discipline both to understand history's limitations and appreciate what it might do in providing enlightenment about the military dimensions of the past and their relationships with the present.

The discipline of history shares some of the characteristics of science, but not those that would obviously be of most value when crossing the border between understanding the past and offering advice or guidance on the future. For the most part, strategists have presented their subject as a science, and history does share some of the foundations of science in that it, too, is a body of knowledge based on the facts of experience, so strategy and history might appear to enjoy a close degree of kinship.[1]

At once, however, problems of which the scholar is all too well aware, but which some strategic writers of the past dismiss or disregard, begin to crowd in. The facts we possess are only those that are recoverable. This state of affairs has two corollaries which are of considerable importance. One is that our knowledge of the past, and therefore the extent of our understanding, is necessarily limited. The limitations from which they suffer may be neither obvious nor properly accommodated in the interpretations which form the body of our historical knowledge.

---

[1] J. J. Davies, *On Scientific Method* (London, 1968), p. 8; A. F. Chalmers, *What Is This Thing Called Science?* (Oxford, 1978), p. 9.

The other difficulty is that our historical knowledge is always increasing, albeit at varying speeds in different parts of the historical universe. The result of new knowledge, and of new interpretations of old knowledge, is that the shape of the past is continually changing. All written history is an interim report and can never be anything more than that. That reality is something that all those who sortie into the past on raiding parties to seize "useful" strategic knowledge would do well to remember.

Two brief examples from recent historical writing on strategic issues illustrate how wary we must be about assuming we have a correct understanding of the past, without which even heavily qualified historical inferences can only mislead. For more than forty years, the single most outstanding milestone of modern naval history has been the so-called "*Dreadnought* revolution" conceived and executed by Admiral "Jackie" Fisher during his time as First Sea Lord between 1904 and 1910 as a means of checkmating the Kaiser's naval programs. The strategic weapon of choice was seemingly the fast, all big-gun battleship, and the strategic event that navies sought in preference to any other was the Mahanian decisive battle.

Recent scholarship now suggests that this piece of historical "knowledge" is a fiction resting on a number of misapprehensions. In fact, Fisher favored cruisers, submarines, and flotilla craft over heavy battleships, and Russia was as prominent on his list of likely future opponents for the Royal Navy as Germany was.[2]

More arresting yet is the proposition that the Schlieffen Plan, the mainstay of so much strategic analysis of the origins of the First World War and the model for General Norman Schwarzkopf's ground offensive in the 1992 Gulf War, may never have existed at all as a plan for action, but may simply have served as a device in the internecine politics of the Reich's military budgeting.[3]

Strategic history, like other kinds of historical knowledge, comprises both the collection of facts and their interpretation. More facts therefore mean more knowledge, and insofar as volume improves interpretation, they can also mean better knowledge. But fewer facts do not inhibit interpretation to any discernible degree and so do not necessarily betoken less knowledge. Thus, the seeker after strategic wisdom can easily find himself or herself on unstable ground where uncertainty resides in the extent to which adequate factual knowledge can buttress interpretative knowledge.

---

[2] A. J. Marder, *From the Dreadnought to Scapa Flow*, vol. 1, *The Road to War, 1904–1914* (Oxford, 1961); Nicholas A. Lambert, *Sir John Fisher's Naval Revolution* (Columbia, SC, 1999).

[3] Terence Zuber, *Inventing the Schlieffen Plan: German War Planning 1871–1914* (Oxford, 2002).

An example from recent history would be the "Linebacker II" bombing offensive against North Vietnam in December 1972. In the face of a dearth of North Vietnamese, Soviet, or Chinese source materials, air power historians have argued that the bombing of Hanoi directly contributed to the signing of the Paris Peace Accords by the North Vietnamese that followed shortly thereafter.

In less highfalutin' terms, this time bombing clearly worked.[4] In fact, it seems at least as likely that the major audience for "Linebacker II" was not Hanoi but South Vietnam's President Thieu, and that bombing was rather less instrumental in bringing peace than Henry Kissinger's assurance to both Moscow and Beijing that what the United States wanted most was a "decent interval" between its departure from Vietnam and the reconstruction of the Thieu government in whatever form.[5]

Faced with health warnings about the imperfections of historical knowledge, whether resulting from incomplete inventories of relevant facts or imperfect interpretations of the facts available, the informed reader is likely to find that the most striking feature present in the lion's share of writings about strategy in modern history is the self-confidence with which its authors have tackled tasks, at which historians of other areas would most assuredly balk. The explanation for such a *deformation professionelle* is, of course, the philosophical positivism which emerged in the first half of the nineteenth century, and that, for entirely intelligible reasons related to the demands of pedagogy, survived and even flourished in the war colleges and service academies throughout the twentieth century. It was responsible not only for more or less the entirety of historical writing about strategy in the age between Napoleon and Hitler, but also for the creation of the general staffs that first consumed and then applied its products.[6]

Because the approach to the past of so many writers on strategy has been so determinedly utilitarian, the "lessons" that they have drawn from history can appear to the general body of historians as either bizarre or banal. One example of the former category of lessons can stand for many. In the surge of interest in contemporary history that animated so many Frenchmen after their disastrous defeats in the Franco-Prussian War, one of their leading military commentators, General Bonnal, claimed to have discovered the hitherto unknown "secret" of Napoleon's strategy. He argued that it lay in the general advance guard which provided the Emperor information on which to

---

[4] For example, Richard P. Hallion, *Storm over Iraq: Air Power and the Gulf War* (Washington, 1992), p. 21.

[5] Jussi Hanhimaki, "Selling the Decent Interval: Kissinger, Triangular Diplomacy, and the End of the Vietnam War," *Diplomacy & Statecraft*, vol. 14, no. 1, 2003, pp. 159–94.

[6] David Alan Rich, *The Tsar's Colonels: Professionalism, Strategy, and Subversion in Late Imperial Russia* (Cambridge, MA, 1998).

direct the battle most effectively. Later, Bonnal changed his mind and decided that Napoleon's practice of the strategic defensive and counterattack was the highest form of strategy.[7]

Questing of this sort still persists in the writing of strategic history, albeit at a more sophisticated level: Winston Churchill's wartime leadership is probably the single most frequent example.[8] This is not the kind of activity that is much in evidence elsewhere in the lists of history. Indeed, the notion that a political historian would ever go in search of the "secret" of, say, the foreign policy of the third Marquess of Salisbury or of Woodrow Wilson is inconceivable.

The idea that history provides evidence from which to adduce the operating principles of strategy exists even more firmly in the pantheon of strategic writing, reaching back at least as far as Baron Jomini's ten factors providing "The essential basis of the military policy to be adopted by a wise government" and "thirteen points that strategy embraces." The dangers of waging war by inventory that this approach encourages are both obvious and considerable: even in Jomini's own day, a state could fulfil the "Twelve essential conditions to make a perfect army" and still lose on the field of battle.[9] However, such inventories do not seem to go out of fashion. Fuller's eight principles of war – originally six in 1912, but expanded in 1915 with the "discovery" of two more – appeared in the *British Field Service Manual* of 1924 and do so still, more or less verbatim, in its modern successor, *Army Field Manual*, volume I – *The Fundamentals*, part I, *The Application of Force*.

Confronted with the longevity of such practices, the military historian must pause to acknowledge their utility. Evidence of the value of such precepts to soldiers and sailors – and doubtless to airmen, too – is readily available. To take one recent British campaign and two British force commanders: faced with the loss of the cruiser *Sheffield* on May 4, 1982, Admiral "Sandy" Woodward "reminded myself of the principles of war, in particular the one called 'maintaining the initiative.'" On land, Brigadier Julian Thompson pinned a copy of the list to the board above his desk as a reminder never to lose sight of the essentials.[10]

However, historians whose concerns are with the understanding and explication of military events can find such precepts banal. As John C. Cairns, an

[7] Eugene Carrias, *La pensee militaire francaise* (Paris, 1960), pp. 281–2.
[8] For one of the better examples of this kind of analysis, see Eliot A. Cohen, *Supreme Command* (New York, 2001), pp. 153–201.
[9] Baron Antoine Jomini, *Summary of the Art of War* (Westport, CT, 1971), pp. 49, 68, 43.
[10] Admiral Sandy Woodward and Patrick Robinson, *One Hundred Days* (London, 1992 [Fontana, ed.]), p. 21; Julian Thompson, *No Picnic: 3 Commando Brigade in the South Atlantic, 1982* (London, 1985). In earlier days, Admiral Woodward had made his own contribution to strategic thinking: J. F. Woodward, "Strategy by Matrix," *Journal of Strategic Studies*, vol. 4 no. 2, 1981, pp. 196–208.

authority on the collapse of France in 1940, has remarked with considerable justification as regards strategy and history, "[d]oubtless military literature, by returning always to first principles, is doomed to commit platitudes."[11]

Much historical writing about strategy, dwelling as it has on lessons, precepts, maxims, and guidelines, is not properly speaking history at all. It explains little or nothing because it operates according to a tautological logic. One succeeds, when one applies the "rules" that conduce to success. In the end, it can very well mislead.

A striking example of the pitfalls of mistaking conventional strategic analysis for historical explanation is Colonel Harry Summers's study of the Vietnam War, *On Strategy*. After identifying the principles governing battlefield operations – mass, the economy of force, and maneuver – Summers concluded that because U.S. military commanders failed to identify the Clausewitzian "centre of gravity," they could not apply these principles properly.[12]

The cause of America's failure in Vietnam is a good deal more complex than that, and indeed a reading of the current historical literature on Vietnam leaves one with the impression that, while at times commanders in the field employed strategies which did not work, and perhaps could never have worked, at the seat of government in Washington no strategic direction worthy of the name was being applied to the war at all.[13] This conclusion opens up a useful avenue for interrelating history and strategy to which we will return later.

The product of the approach to strategy so far described is not history, but at best historical discourse. It has value, without doubt, as a medium of instruction for young officers learning their trade. Whether such a study of the past produces great commanders is more problematic. General George S. Patton famously took Clausewitz's *On War* with him on his honeymoon – and subsequently complained to his wife that it was "as full of notes of equal abstruceness [*sic*] as a dog is full of fleas."[14] Patton's subsequent successes as a field commander in the Second World War may well have owed much to his study of the history of strategy. Marshal Alphonse Juin, in contrast, declared that the instructors at the *Ecole de Guerre* in the aftermath of the First World War had nothing to teach him.

Somewhere in between the two stands General Sir Richard O'Connor, progenitor of one of the most dazzling British victories of the Second World

[11] John C. Cairns, "Some Recent Historians and the 'Strange Defeat' of 1940," *Journal of Modern History*, vol. 46 no. 1, 1974, p. 80, fn. 18.

[12] Harry G. Summers, Jr., *On Strategy: A Critrical Analysis of the Vietnam War* (New York, 1984), p. 39.

[13] George C. Herring, *A Different Kind of War: LBJ and Vietnam* (Austin, TX, 1994), pp. 178–9.

[14] Christopher Bassford, *Clausewitz in English, The Reception of Clausewitz in Britain and America 1815–1945* (New York, 1994), p. 78.

War when he outmaneuvered and encircled Marshal Rodolpho Graziani's army in North Africa in 1940. O'Connor completed the second postwar course at the Staff College in 1920–1, alongside the future field marshal Bernard Law Montgomery. When asked for the sources of his methods, he responded:

> Well I think its what one's taught really I mean er – its the proper way to think of tactics, I mean the surprise is the base of all tactics and if you can produce a surprise on your enemy you're half way there, if not more.[15]

In fact, the source of O'Connor's success would seem to lie in his dismay at the heavy casualties of the First World War, his determination to reintroduce maneuver and surprise to the battlefield, and his particular comprehension of the capability for maneuver provided by motorization.

It is time to clear the decks and establish what exactly history can do in forwarding the study of strategy, before offering some suggestions as to what it might do. History is ideographic. That is to say, it studies the past by recovering and interpreting unrepeatable facts. It is not a science – or may be considered as such only in a circumscribed sense – and so has little predictability.

Historians of the general sort make poor predictors: As one example among many, Professor Richard Evans declared in December 1987 that "[German] re-unification is simply not a realistic possibility, and to... advance historical arguments in its favour is to indulge in political fantasising."[16] History shortly proved him wrong, as history will. The record of military historians is no better than their nonmilitary *confreres*.

However bad their record, it is more than matched by some strategic analysts. Many of the best-known strategic writers and commentators buried themselves beneath a mass of embarrassing and self-generated mistakes when offering opinions on the shape of the forthcoming Gulf War in 1991. One expert in quantitative modeling predicted that the coalition would suffer between 8,000 and 16,000 casualties and the Iraqis 60,000 casualties, figures that were wrong by several orders of magnitude.[17]

History should not take it as axiomatic that, when studying strategy, it is studying a science. Without getting into the deeper waters of debate venerated by age, we would perhaps do well to adopt something of Leon Trotsky's skepticism, when he remarked with characteristic trenchancy that "there is

---

[15] Interview with General Sir Richard O'Connor, Sound Records Department, Imperial War Museum 2912/02; quoted by Charles James Forrester, "Great Captains and the Challenge of Second Order Technology: Operational Strategy and the Motorisation of the British Army Before 1940," M.A. dissertation, University of South Africa, 2001, pp. 68–9.

[16] John Lukacs, "What Is History?," *Historically Speaking*, vol. 4, no. 3, 2003, p. 10.

[17] Michael J. Mazaar, Don M. Snider, and James A. Blackwell, Jr., *Desert Storm: The Gulf War and What We Learned* (Boulder, CO, 1993), p. 86.

no more a science of war than there is a science of locksmithing." Nevertheless, we should acknowledge that at certain times and as a result of particular sets of circumstances, primarily technological strategy can in practice take on some of the attributes of a science.[18]

The subject of our study is somewhat blurred, as the varying definitions of the term "strategy" demonstrate, so the sheer usefulness of the word can be misleading. However, to exclude any definition at all on the grounds that each possesses a host of exceptions, as one distinguished analyst does, invites the reasonable charge that if we do not know exactly what we are talking about, then we cannot talk about it with any degree of exactitude.[19]

The historian studying war and employing the kind of functional definition that the profession is willing to recognize and accept can best regard strategy as a method of solving problems by the application of military force. Like all historical subjects, its study requires the reconstruction of events and the re-creation of processes. It also requires that historians determine as accurately as possible the circumstances in which events happen and exert their influence to shape outcomes.

Events will never recur, but one can undoubtedly derive insights from understanding how they affected strategic circumstances and contributed to determining strategic outcomes in the past. However, the classic historical method of reasoning from cause to effect will only partially explain outcomes. Understanding the processes through which nations and political and military leaders have created and used strategies can illuminate a central historical issue of great importance that is still underexplored – namely how strategy is actually done.[20] In this way, the ideographic nature of history can be made to serve as a positive aid to thinking about strategy rather than as a justification for the accurate, but stultifying, observation that things are never the same twice.

To begin a positive consideration of what history can tell us about strategy by considering tactics might seem perverse and goes directly against the categorizing approach, which lays heavy stress on definitions and according to which tactics differs from strategy. Mahan certainly believed it beneath him: "I have neither time nor inclination for exhaustive study of tactics," he told a correspondent.[21] However, just as politicians ignore tactics at their peril, so too in different ways do both warriors and historians. For one

[18] Leon Trotsky, *Military Writings* (New York, 1971), p. 119. Trostky also remarked that "Military science does not belong among natural sciences, because it is neither 'natural' nor a 'science'": *Ibid.*, p. 110.

[19] Edward N. Luttwak, *Strategy: The Logic of War and Peace* (Harvard, 1987), pp. 69–70, 91.

[20] Eliot A. Cohen and John Gooch, *Military Misfortunes: The Anatomy of Failure in War* (New York, 1990).

[21] Robert Seager II and Doris D. Maguire, eds., *Letters and Papers of Alfred Thayer Mahan* (Annapolis, MD, 1975), vol. 3, p. 178.

thing, as the example of O'Connor suggests, an acute tactical awareness can translate into success on a conventionally strategic plane. Tactics may also represent a more conventionally "scientific" dimension of war in that it can be the subject of practical experimentation. One can recover the effects of advances in weapons technology, and therefore their impact on battlefield strategies, more easily than other kinds of historical "facts."

Much has been written about the tactical reforms effected by the British Expeditionary Force in 1917 and 1918. While historians may take a certain professional delight in debating whether or not tactics amount to a revolution in military affairs, no less interesting is the fact that they were the result of a series of work-a-day changes in methods of fire control, improved mapping, meticulous planning, and a recognition of the paramount importance of preparation through training.

Together, these improvements permitted British armies – and their French allies who underwent a similar experience under Marshal Phillipe Pétain's leadership – to undertake the campaign between August and November 1918 that brought German armies to the brink of absolute defeat.[22] The contrast between the successes of Allied armies in 1918 and their failures in 1915 and 1916 was largely the result of an initial mismatch between tactical conceptions that put their faith in time-tabled attacks and a strategy that aimed at breakthrough – a mismatch subsequently remedied by marrying a strategy of cumulative pressure with new tactical capabilities.[23] Professional soldiers will take note of this lesson. However, professional historians must stress the fact that this is an explanation for a particular victory and not a general recipe for success.

Although the exact interrelationships between tactics and strategy in the British field campaigns of the Second World War have yet to be subjected to as close a scrutiny as their First World War precursors, some striking dissonances are apparent. Montgomery's decision in electing on the eve of the Normandy landings to use the methods of tank-infantry cooperation he had perfected in the Western Desert in preference to those by which the home armies had trained threw a good part of British tactical doctrine into total disarray. The very structure and tactical conception behind British armored divisions meant that they were "neither trained nor organised for the kind of battles they would have to fight in Normandy."[24]

The result was not failure, but these facts may have delayed or impeded success. As an example of the difficulties attendant on putting history of this

---

[22] Peter Simkins, "Co-Stars or Supporting Cast? British Divisions in the 'Hundred Days,' 1918," in Paddy Griffith, ed., *British Fighting Methods in the Great War* (London, 1996), pp. 50–69.

[23] Simon Nicholas Robbins, "British Generalship on the Western Front in the First World War, 1914–1918," Ph.D. dissertation, University of London, 2001, pp. 335–49.

[24] Tim Harrison Place, *Military Training in the British Army, 1940–1944: From Dunkirk to D-Day* (London, 2000), p. 153.

kind at the service of the military profession, we may note in passing the absolute disagreement between experts as to whether or not Montgomery succeeded in imposing a common interpretation of doctrine on the units under his command.[25] Until historians resolve that question, it will be difficult to tell whether, and if so why, there was a serious mismatch between tactics and strategy in Twenty-First Army Group in the period 1944–5.

One of the epistemological problems of the "scientific" approach to strategy is that definitions are often blurred at the edges. Thus, tactics can blend into operations, which we can perhaps most usefully regard as the employment of substantial land, sea, and air forces, either singly or in combination, in a discrete and definable theatre of war over a finite period of time. In other words, theatres are the sites of campaigns. We are still very much in the realm of strategy if one considers strategy in the way earlier defined. We are also now dealing with one of the fundamental dimensions of war – and therefore, again, of strategy. No serious military historian, and no sentient military practitioner, needs to be persuaded of this, if only because, as Bernard Brodie wisely noted more than sixty years ago, "War is a question not of winning battles but of winning campaigns."[26]

Campaigns have a nature of their own, as General George C. Marshall acknowledged when, in 1943, he remarked that after having received an education based on roads, railways, and rivers during the First World War, he had during the previous two years "been acquiring an education based on oceans and I've had to learn all over again."[27] Implicit in Marshall's observation is a fact that is underremarked and insufficiently addressed: strategic geography actually changes over time. The primary cause has been technological change. The consequence has been that new strategic circumstances came into being that posed fresh strategic problems.

Two different examples will suffice to demonstrate that this is so. At the end of the nineteenth century, British strategists had to abandon any residual thoughts of resolving Anglo-Russian tension by repeating the Crimean War, when the completion of the trans-Caspian railway line placed the Russian supply route to Afghanistan beyond the reach of any British expedition to the Black Sea. One potential theatre of war was thereby removed from the map, to be replaced by another in the shape of India, a reality that greatly concerned the British government's machinery of decision making in defense until 1907.[28] Speaking to a different technological era, W.T.R. Fox noted in

25 David French, *Raising Churchill's Army: The British Army and the War against Germany 1919–1945* (Oxford, 2000) p. 261, adjudges that he did; Harrison Place, *From Dunkirk to D-Day*, p. 164, that he did not.

26 Bernard Brodie, *Sea Power in the Machine Age* (New York, 1969), p. 437.

27 Jeter A. Isely and Philip Crowl, *The U.S. Marines and Amphibious War* (Princeton, 1951), p. 3.

28 John Gooch, "The Weary Titan: Strategy and Policy in Great Britain, 1890–1918," in Williamson Murray, MacGregor Knox, and Alvin Bernstein, eds., *The Making of Strategy: Rulers, States, and War* (Cambridge, 1994), pp. 282–3.

1948 that "the atomic energy inventions have largely destroyed the military functions of the continent [of Europe] as a buffer," a judgment that turned out to be true only in part.[29]

For the historian, the central question must be whether – and if so to what degree – common and universal logic shapes theatre strategy, or whether the differences between theatres are not at least as significant as the similarities. The course of two key campaigns of the Second World War, the German offensives in North Africa and Russia, suggests that logistics are the primary consideration in theatre strategy. Those two campaigns underlined that beyond the calculable distance across which roadborne resupply is possible, the only possible outcome is starvation of supplies and consequent defeat.[30]

However, the historian can only demur at the proposition that "the logic of theatre strategy" – never clearly defined – seems to suggest that the farther you advance the more likely you are to be defeated.[31] The war in the Pacific undoubtedly presented the United States with enormous logistic challenges: as Louis Allen observed, defeating Japan necessitated "a siege on a continental scale, across a moat of unparalleled dimensions."[32] However, the fact that the Americans advanced triumphantly across a distance some six times as great as that separating Berlin from Moscow gives the lie to any such "universalist" and quasi-scientific notion of theatre strategy.

It is worth pausing briefly to discuss the Pacific theatre, because it illustrates the variety of strategic issues which can come into play at this level of war and the differing circumstances that can affect different theatres. Because of the variety of options open to the Japanese, forecasting the direction of their likely attacks was an extremely difficult and imprecise pastime before December 1941. Thus, it differed considerably from that obtaining on the Russo-German front before June 1941, where the issue was not where an attack would come but when. At first, imperial possessions such as Singapore and Borneo seemed the most probable targets, but after the German attack on Russia, the British commanders-in-chief in India and the Far East both doubted the likelihood of a Japanese attack southward. They believed the Soviet Union's straitened circumstances made her the more probable target.

After December 1941, devising a theatre strategy ceased to be a matter of enumerating the various strategic options open to Japan and assessing the implications of each one by reference to general principles of strategy. Instead, once Japan had committed itself to war, the constraints on

29 Quoted in Lawrence Freedman, *The Evolution of Nuclear Strategy* (New York, 1983), p. 49.
30 M. Van Creveld, *Supplying War: Logistics from Wallenstein to Patton* (Cambridge, 1977), pp. 142–201.
31 Luttwak, *Strategy*, p. 141.
32 Louis Allen, "The Campaigns in Asia and the Pacific," in John Gooch, ed., *Decisive Campaigns of the Second World War* (London, 1990), p. 165.

its freedom of choice and the limitations on its actions became easier to determine. Reach and lift, wastage and replacement, and attrition and staying power were matters planners could calculate, or on which they could at least offer more informed speculation. The new factors in play made it possible to enumerate orders of probability more securely – or, as the Joint Intelligence Committee's members put it in 1943, allowed them to offer "reasonable estimates of what we consider the Japanese might do in the various sets of circumstances."[33]

One can find further support for the notion that a degree of calculability enters into theatre strategy as an amalgam of established strategic premises and judgments about the range of options open to an enemy. In fact, the Japanese correctly forecast the planned location of an American landing on the island of Kyushu in 1945, and the Chinese forecast the American landing at Inchon and gave the North Koreans advanced warning of it, which the latter ignored.[34]

When we ascend to the highest rung of strategic activity, national or "grand" strategy, history comes into its own – but almost by default – absent any sizeable body of theoretical or normative literature written from a military point of view. Instead, encampments of political scientists occupy many of its open spaces. Michael Howard has best defined grand strategy as "the mobilisation and deployment of national resources of wealth, manpower and industrial capacity, together with the enlistment of those of allied and, when feasible, of neutral powers, for the purposes of achieving the goals of national policy in wartime."[35]

Because grand strategy is the pursuit of national political objectives by harnessing all the means at the disposal of the state, politics lies at its core. This fact alone accounts for the longevity of Clausewitz, whose timeless observations still command the respect and admiration of most students of strategy, and for the obvious fervor with which his adherents stress the political side of strategy over the technical and the technological.[36] But questions remain to be asked: in particular, what exactly is (or are) the "politics" of grand strategy? And how political has grand strategy actually been in the past?

The politics of grand strategy both decide the allocation of resources and define the ultimate purposes of their use. The outcomes, in terms of events,

---

[33] John Gooch, "The Politics of Strategy: Great Britain, Australia and the War Against Japan, 1939–1945," *War in History*, vol. 10, no. 4, 2003, pp. 424–47.

[34] John Ray Skates, *The Invasion of Japan: Alternative to the Bomb* (Columbia, SC, 1994), p. 102; Shu Guang Zhang, *Intelligence and Strategic Culture: Chinese-American Confrontations, 1949–1958* (Ithaca, NY, 1992), p. 93; Shu Guang Zhang, *Mao's Military Romanticism: China and the Korean War, 1950–1953* (Lawrence, KS, 1993), p. 72.

[35] Michael Howard, *Grand Strategy*, vol. 4, *August 1942–September 1943* (London, 1972), p. 1.

[36] Roman Kolkowicz, "The Rise and Decline of Deterrence Theory," *Journal of Strategic Studies*, vol. 9, no. 4, 1986, p. 5. Kolkowicz refers specifically to Bernard Brodie.

are the campaigns waged and the battles fought to defeat the enemy; but because grand strategy uses both nonmilitary and military means, victory is, as Gabriel Kolko observed of the Vietnam War, "not just the result of battles."[37] As a process, grand strategy is an activity whose outcomes are the result of the distribution of power among those taking part in its formulation. Large matters such as these give rise to big questions. The history of war through most of the twentieth century has produced two such questions that are preeminent: What is the best balance between the civilian "frocks" and the military "brasshats," and how far should the politics of the "endgame" shape the military strategy of any war?

The First World War is still the *locus classicus* for studies of the first of these two issues – although the Second World War is rapidly making up ground. Chance gave military commanders unparalleled authority during most of the First World War, something they would not enjoy in the next conflict. In France, the departure of the government from Paris before the battle of the Marne put power into the hands of General Joseph Joffre, and the politicians did not begin to recover their authority until the middle of the war.[38]

In Britain, the slow transition from "business as usual" to full national mobilization, and Prime Minister Herbert Asquith's considerable difficulties in holding his party and his coalition together while maintaining Liberal ideals meant that he exerted no intrusive political authority over the commanders of the British expeditionary forces on the Western Front, Field Marshals Sir John French or Sir Douglas Haig. And only when the miserable outcome of the Passchendaele campaign in 1917 propelled Asquith's successor, David Lloyd George, to take action did relations between civilians and military begin to change.[39] In Germany, where the authority of the military was in any case greater, the Kaiser directly and indirectly supported his generals in their pursuit of the wrong goals.[40]

Allied generals thus enjoyed an unprecedented degree of latitude, and debates continue as to the rights and wrongs of their strategic actions. From the point of view of the impact on the war of their political role, superficial similarities among them should not mask important differences. French, Haig, Joffre, Pétain, and Ferdinand Foch each brought his own conception of strategy into office with him and operated according to it.

---

[37] Gabriel Kolko, *Vietnam: Anatomy of a War 1940–1975* (London, 1985), p. 545.

[38] J. C. King, *Generals and Politicians: Conflict between France's High Command, Parliament and Government, 1914–1918* (Westport, CT, 1951).

[39] David French, *British Economic and Strategic Planning, 1905–1915* (London, 1982); John Turner, *British Politics and the Great War: Coalition and Conflict 1915–1918* (New Haven, CT, 1992), pp. 109–11; David French, *The Strategy of the Lloyd George Coalition, 1916–1918* (Oxford, 1995), pp. 148–70.

[40] Holger Afflerbach, "Wilhelm II as Supreme Warlord in the First World War," *War in History*, vol. 5, no. 4, 1998, pp. 427–49.

Haig adopted a narrow military approach, operating according to a pre-conceived and schematic conception of battle during 1916 and 1917. He only departed from that approach when forced to accept a major change in personnel at his headquarters, as a result of which he became both better informed and, to judge by the way in which he altered his style of command in the final months of the war, somewhat the wiser.[41]

Joffre adopted an equally aggressive and equally costly offensive strategy in 1914 and 1915. Pétain, while sharing Joffre's belief that France must conclude the war with an army which had demonstrably paid the price of victory if it were to secure its just reward, followed a strategy of survival in 1917 and advocated a general war of maneuver in 1918. Foch, concerned to keep casualty rates as low as possible, opted for the gradual enlargement of the battle front, forcing the Germans back through gradually increasing pressure along the whole line.[42]

The historical significance of these strategies – apart from their intrinsic interest and importance – is that each was different, each was in part a response to circumstance and in part a product of the man, and each gave the war a particular character that extended well beyond the field of battle to the counsels of governments and therefore shaped grand strategy. Frustratingly perhaps, as Guy Pedroncini points out, because history cannot replay events, we cannot put any of the three commanders in different circumstances and see how he and his strategy would then have fared.

Comparing the grand strategies of the First and Second World Wars, even in the most generalized and superficial way, two facts become apparent: first, that the nature of the activity of constructing grand strategies was broadly the same, but second, that the circumstances changed and as a consequence so too did the problems. On the one hand, waging a global war greatly increased the complexities of problem solving, whereas on the other hand, the particular state of international politics and the position of the Soviet Union as both a military ally and an ideological competitor introduced a new dimension into the conduct of war and the making of strategy.[43] An uncontested but still debated expression of the tensions this situation introduced was Eisenhower's "broad front" strategy of 1944–5. A contested and more hotly debated expression was the Americans' use of nuclear weapons against Japan, about the purposes of which dispute still

---

[41] Gerard J. De Groot, *Douglas Haig 1861–1928* (London, 1988), pp. 50–3; Tim Travers, *The Killing Ground: The British Army, the Western Front and the Emergence of Modern Warfare, 1900–1918* (London, 1987), pp. 85–100; Robbins, *British Generalship on the Western Front*, pp. 320–3.

[42] Guy Pedroncini, "Trois marechaux, trois strategies?," *Guerre mondiale et conflits contemporains* annee, vol. 37, no. 145, 1987, pp. 45–62.

[43] Of particular note among the vast plethora of books of this subject is Mark A. Stoler, *Allies and Adversaries: The Joint Chiefs of Staff, the Grand Alliance, and U.S. Strategy in World War II* (Chapel Hill, NC, 2000).

rages.[44] The history of the closing months of the Second World War suggests that the endgame came to occupy a position of greater importance in grand strategy than had been the case hitherto. Present-day events in Iraq tempt one to suggest that policy makers have rather lost sight of this in the intervening years.

Just as the problems of making grand strategy were more complicated in the Second World War than the First, so too the examples of how political direction was exerted and grand strategy actually done were more varied.[45] The range of models put into operation was extraordinarily wide, running the gamut from the Churchillian seminars that have received such widespread approbation from both historians and political scientists, through Stalin's undemocratic centralism, to Hitler's manic domination of a functional bureaucracy that, at intermediate levels, worked around the disjunctures and fissures characterizing the Nazi system of government.[46]

The inventory of such studies is, however, far from complete, because we lack an up-to-date work in any language on Mussolini's direction of Italy's war between 1940 and 1945. Nor is it uncontested: fundamental discord has broken out once more about Hirohito's role in leading Japan's war and directing its policies.[47] It is not for the historian to pronounce as to whether one of these examples could be considered the ideal type to which the wise polity should adhere. Nevertheless, he or she might reasonably endorse Mahan's observation that particular forms of government have exercised a marked influence on the development and use of military power, and even his elliptical hint that democracy is best.[48]

While bearing in mind the caveats against an overzealous and ill-informed use of history, it is still possible to give a more positive answer to the question "what can we learn from history about the nature of strategy?" than the one suggested at the outset. History suggests much by way of the examples

---

[44] J. Samuel Walker, *Prompt and Utter Destruction: Truman and the Use of Atomic Bombs against Japan* (Chapel Hill, NC, 1997); Richard B. Frank, *Downfall: The End of the Imperial Japanese Empire* (New York, 1999).

[45] Decision-making systems differed at the outbreak of the First World War, but not to the extent that they did during the course of the Second: Ernest J. May, "Cabinet, Tsar, Kaiser: Three Approaches to Assessment," in May, ed., *Knowing One's Enemies: Intelligence Assessment before the Two World Wars* (Harvard, 1984), pp. 11–36.

[46] Ronald Lewin, *Churchill as Warlord* (London, 1973); Richard Lamb, *Churchill as War Leader: Right or Wrong?* (London, 1991); Cohen, *Supreme Command*, pp. 153–201; Albert Seaton, *Stalin as Warlord* (London, 1976); Alan F. Wilt, *War from the Top: German and British Military Decision Making during World War II* (London, 1990); Geoffrey P. Megargee, *Inside Hitler's High Command* (Lawrence, KS, 2000).

[47] Herbert P. Bix, *Hirohito and the Making of Modern Japan* (London, 2000); for a precursor of this view, see David Bergamini, *Japan's Imperial Conspiracy* (New York, 1971).

[48] Mahan was of course speaking of one particular form of military power, and he also suggested that the maintenance and exercise of power could suffer from the fact that "popular governments" were not "generally favorable to military expenditure": A. T. Mahan, *The Influence of Sea Power upon History 1660–1783* (London, 1965), pp. 58–9, 67.

it offers of the different kinds of behaviors in differing circumstances that have led to different outcomes. Consuming history as a product feeds the strategist's mind with a rich and varied diet. Considering history as method educates that same mind by attuning it to ways in which thinking about the past can most safely inform thinking about the present or the future. In doing so, it can also sound warning bells about the propensity of some strategic writing to proceed from common horse-sense to fatuity.

One last example: one of Stalin's five "permanently operating factors" in strategy was "the organisational ability of commanders." In his hands, this amounted to not much more than the identification of a function coupled with an implicit requirement for quality. Overenthusiastic pursuit of this hare led one Australian officer to list as the first of his six principles of war "Brilliant, inspiring leadership at all levels."[49] This is no doubt as hard to come by in the ranks of the armed services as it is in the world of the universities, but an acquaintance with history is by no means the worst way to begin to foster it.

CONCLUSION

The professional historian is bound by the obligations of scholarship to sound warning about the difficulties entailed in using the past as an unproblematic repository from which to extract guides to the present and future, and to point, as many leading authorities in the field have done over the past half-century and more, to examples of historical work that can all too easily constrain the imagination rather than freeing it. The narrow campaign histories produced by such as G.F.R. Henderson – once beloved of staff colleges and by no means an extinct species even now – still offer a warning against straining for similarities in the past rather than recognizing their differences. More popular and more widely read historians, although writing in a quite different genre, can present the unwary and uncritical with similar pitfalls. Some at least of the writings of Sir Basil Liddell Hart serve to prompt the warning that there are no "hard lessons" in the past – not even that of the "indirect approach."[50]

However, once the health warnings have been uttered, the fundamental reasons for studying the past remain incontestable. It is all that we have in the way of concrete knowledge – rather than theoretical speculation – to give us help in facing the present and future. It is of such richness and

[49] John I. Alger, *The Quest for Victory: The History of the Principles of War* (Westport, CT, 1982), p. 162.
[50] Michael Howard, "What Is Military History?," *History Today*, vol. 34, 1984, p. 6; Jay Luvaas, "Military History: An Academic Historian's Point of View," in Russell F. Weigley, ed., *New Dimensions in Military History: An Anthology* (San Raphael, CA, 1975), pp. 24–7.

complexity, to say nothing of its compelling fascination, as to provide an almost endless range of moments, events, situations, and even cases from which to learn. This property is happily timeless; if it were ever true, as Walter Millis confidently asserted while the Cold War moved toward its height some forty years ago, that "[s]ince the development of nuclear arsenals, most of the materials [of military history] have become inapplicable," it is certainly not so today.[51] Everything, of course, depends on how those materials are approached, and narrowly mechanical conceptions of "utility" lead straight back to Henderson and his ilk. Last – and by no means least – there is a great deal more military (and naval) history available today than was ever the case, and very good much of it is, too.

Anything more than a cursory glance at the library shelves shows a pattern of movement and development which has introduced new perspectives on the past and refreshed old ones. The "war and society" model adopted by many historians thirty and more years ago, and absolutely derided by some of the more blinkered members of the historical profession then and since, has its own useful insights to impart. A long-established occupation with the history of strategic thought has widened over recent years to incorporate military doctrine and to marry both with the culture of military institutions and with "conventional" diplomatic history. The result has been particularly auspicious in deepening our understanding of the onset of the First World War. Military effectiveness and net assessment, both relative newcomers to the scene, have broadened the conventional perspectives of history and at the same time resonate with the present and the future. Combat effectiveness has thrown a new light on the tactical operations that formed the stuff of military analysis a century and more ago, and in so doing, has illuminated facts in the past, the significance and meaning of which would otherwise have remained partially or wholly obscure.

These and other types of military history – indeed, all history of whatever field or period – are important as much for how they are done as for what they contain. To be alert to how they work is as important as to absorb what it is they say. The reader of such works, whether uniformed or civilian, certainly does not first need to equip himself or herself with a capacity to dismember the intellectual systems of analysis that historians use, important and fascinating though they are to professional scholars, but simply to recognize such skills as contextualization and ponder on how they contribute to greater understanding. Reading to gain knowledge is as important to the military profession as to any other, and the past is the largest repository of such knowledge. It requires little more than time, a notebook, and a reasonably retentive memory. Reading to gain insights makes greater demands because

---

[51] Walter Millis, *Military History* (Washington, DC, 1961), p. 15.

it requires critical awareness both of what a book is seeking to do and where it fits in the body of existing literature, but brings greater rewards.[52]

Visiting the past is easy, and the variety of subjects and authors on the military history shelves combine to make it both entertaining and rewarding. Studying the past is a little harder but more enriching. It is, broadly, the difference between the tourist who samples another culture in limited form and the traveller who sets out to voyage through it and develop an understanding of what lies beneath and beyond the exterior it presents to the passerby. Both have their value, and both offer the opportunity to gain from military history without necessarily following George S. Patton's example and going to the length of taking a copy of Clausewitz on one's honeymoon.

---

[52] Jay Luvaas's observation that some books are written to learn and other to teach touches on this issue: Luvaas, "Military History," p. 31.

10

Military transformation in long periods of peace: the Victorian Royal Navy

ANDREW GORDON

The title of this essay suggests that what happened to the Royal Navy in the long Victorian peace is important because it may happen, or be happening, again. The author will not speculate on that. What he had to decide was to treat the state of internavy (or inter-great-power) war as the fundamental task for which navies exist, and that tasks lower down on the scale of violence, however beneficial, are what a serious warfighting navy does only when it has no serious wars to fight. In times of strategic change, although it is not terribly important how well a navy makes the transformation from warfighting to operations other than war, it is important how well and fast it makes the change back again when great power conflict reemerges. So this chapter focuses not only on how the Victorian Navy transformed itself into the peace support machine of *Pax Britannica*, but also on how those peaceful habits may have hindered its return to what one might call "main armament warfare."

If we are to regard interfleet warfare, or at least warfare to contest the use of the sea, as the fundamental task for which navies exist, then the Victorian Navy confronted during the long calm after Trafalgar a lapse of three generations before having to do it again. There must have been those in the service, anytime between, say, 1830 and 1880, who must have wondered if the era of great power confrontation at sea would ever return, even though the world's navies emphasized warships on the basis of their ship-killing guns. The pressures to keep the candle burning for fleet action were, therefore, not great.

The transformation of the Royal Navy after the revolutionary and Napoleonic wars into a force for peace and imperial policing was all the more accentuated because the service that began the period of peace was the product of nearly a century of transformation into a finely tuned warfighting machine. By the time of Nelson, the pressures of a century intense with maritime violence had revolutionized the centralizing, control-anxious methods of Torrington, Russell, Rooke, and Benbow that had marked the Wars of the English and Spanish Successions. Starting in 1738, the Navy was involved in major war for fifty of the next seventy-five years. Such continuity of active service, such empirical education, was unprecedented. Two and a half generations of naval officers tested the limits of their ships, their weapons, and their methods. They progressively reinterpreted the Fighting Instructions until sheer professional competence drove them more than theory. Through the War of Jenkins's Ear, the Seven Years War, the American War, and ultimately the French Revolutionary and Napoleonic Wars, the Navy's officers gradually discarded the old rules of strict uniformity and control. They came round to an unwritten doctrine of informed initiative and mutual support, virtually without signaling, while the French Navy – torn by revolution and blockaded – tried to compensate for its practical handicaps with complex, signals-intensive tactical theories.

It was perhaps inevitable that in a long era of only minor, incremental technological change, the prize would go to the navy that pushed the techniques of battle to the absolute limits – and there is a lesson there – but it is noteworthy that, in an era of Hanoverian regulation and draconian military discipline, the Royal Navy's action doctrine of the fleet actually moved in the other direction. The continuing accretion of action experience, the knowledge that any horizon might suddenly reveal an enemy, and the constant possible imminence of battle were all more eloquent and persuasive drivers of doctrine than the Signal Book, Standing Orders, or any number of untested theories.

Partly, it was John Jervis, Earl of St. Vincent, who distilled the progressive experiments of Anson, Hawke, Rodney, and Howe into the permissive command philosophy characterizing the officers of Nelson's era. Decentralization was the key: push the book aside and do not depend on signals. To do so, a meeting of minds was a fundamental precondition: trust your juniors with your aims and priorities, and then trust their seamanship and judgment to make it so. After much experiment, it seemed the only way to deal quickly enough with the emergencies of battle. This, combined with endless on-the-job training and sheer aggression, is what made the Royal Navy dominant on the world's oceans.

Six fleet victories (the Glorious First of June, St. Vincent, Camperdown, The Nile, Copenhagen, and Trafalgar) between 1794 and 1805 helped achieve that dominance. A distinguished American historian has calculated that the Royal Navy could not have retained command of the seas during the French Revolutionary and Napoleonic Wars had it relied only on the seventy-four-gun ships of the line produced by British dockyards. It did so by stealing other nation's ships, 121 of them in total (French, Spanish and Dutch), in exchange for four of its own – a kind of lend-lease without the consent of the donors.

Even so, the Victorians got it wrong. They deified Nelson as a saviour and a genius, and thereby avoided addressing the awkward, peacetime institutional foundations on which British victories in the period 1792–1815 had rested. Nelson was the very best of an outstanding generation of admirals and captains, but if one compares him with Napoleon, whom he passed in the fog one night in the Mediterranean in 1798, we can see what he, as an individual, did *not* do. He did *not* cause great organizational and administrative upheavals; he did *not* throw away his service's standard operating procedures and start anew; he did *not* really revolutionize the conduct of war. There was neither scope nor need for him to do so: he and his contemporaries operated within parameters that their predecessors had already explored and proved by the time he reached flag rank.

Had he chosen to become a parson like his father or been killed at Cape St. Vincent or Teneriffe, one cannot seriously suppose Britain would thereby have lost the war at sea against the French. The captains' and junior flag lists were jostling with competent and self-confident men, selected by the same empirical school of combat, men who were ready, able, and eager to take command and win. After Trafalgar, Villeneuve famously said (with ingratiation, no doubt, but only small exaggeration): "To any other nation the loss of Nelson would have been irreparable; but in the British Fleet off Cadiz, every captain was a Nelson."

Another distinguished American strategist asked this author recently what was the intellectual basis of the Royal Navy's officer corps' great age of success in the late eighteenth century. When I realized he was serious, I suggested he was asking a very un-English question and that he should not necessarily expect to find a coherent English answer. Had one asked the same question of an eighteenth-century admiral, he would probably have damned one for a fool. He and his colleagues did not sit around in smoke-filled cafes on Portsmouth waterfront earnestly discussing military theory or philosophy. They waged war.

Thus, they won and won again through a pragmatism born of an accumulation of experience that far outweighed, in immediacy and eloquence, anything that might exist in the realm of theory. Thereafter, however intervening trends so obscured the methods of Nelson's navy that his successors could remember them a hundred years later only with discomfort and reluctance.

The legacy of those long years of warfighting was that in the ensuing peace the Royal Navy's prestige was unassailable. The Navy did not have to sell itself to the world: the world had no choice in the matter. It had no doubts about its own credentials: until approximately 1880, many senior officers had served under senior officers who had served as young men in the Navy of Jervis, Duncan, Nelson, and Collingwood. In some cases, their fathers and uncles had won distinction or patronage under the famous names of legend or in the many frigate actions, celebrated at the time, if little remembered now. Their sense of inheritance and their professional chauvinism were extraordinarily strong.

However, the demands of continual peace are very different from those of continual war, and the cultural context within which the Navy had to exist and prosper was also greatly different. In the late nineteenth century, as the British became increasingly aware of their empire and sought to explain it to themselves and the world, there developed an unabashed sense of national and ethical chauvinism. The Indian Mutiny compelled a more hierarchical redefinition of rulers and ruled, but as important was the growing influence of neochivalry on English self-perception, with its complex, muscular-Christian mix of conceits and duties, along with the growth of religious evangelism. This served as a form of special pleading, as if to justify the vast empire and all its privileges by attaching to it a high moral mission – a God-given moral mission – that Kipling later termed the "white man's burden." This (by its own lights) most successful society believed in the rule of "civilized" laws, free trade, fair play, and cricket, and that its own enjoyment of their benefits brought a commensurate obligation to spread them around the world – if at times necessarily with the assistance of bayonets.

In the long view, one outcome was the beginning of the vaunted "clash of civilisations," a clash which the earlier years of commerce-driven empire had not seriously threatened. But this missionary sense of duty was also one of the motive forces behind most of the Royal Navy's main Victorian-era tasks. One has to be blinkered by a pathologically politically correct distaste for imperialism not to recognize that, for all its special pleading and racial chauvinism, British imperialism undertook some great and good endeavors. The Victorians would not readily have recognized how today's "New Labour's" Britain qualifies as a "force for good" in the world, while their own Britain somehow did not. On the contrary, the presumption of moral rectitude implicit in the concepts of an ethical foreign policy is perfectly consistent with Victorian ideas of what Britannia was all about.

Inevitably, therefore, the long Victorian era of *Pax Britannica* brought with it new trends and challenges that had a major influence on the outlook of naval officers and on the performance criteria on which the Navy based their promotion. Three trends were crucial, all interlinked.

First, there was no more war at sea in any great-power symmetric sense. Naval officers were increasingly the *inheritors* and *custodians* of the imperial status quo rather than the *winners* of empire or of decisive sea battles. Their sense of duty now focused on protecting, defending, and enforcing, a duty more concerned with the *exercise of authority* and with the *projection of power from the sea* than with the *application of force at sea*. Second, and following logically from this, the Navy and its officers now came to measure their perceptions of success and utility to the state, both institutional and personal, by criteria suited to the current demands of the new environment, rather than the anachronistic demands of the old. And third, of course, the arrival of industrialization prompted a massive revolution in military affairs that the Royal Navy had to assimilate and manage at an increasing rate over the course of the nineteenth century. We shall look at those three trends in turn.

The Navy would certainly have regarded itself, during that seemingly languid age of peace, as very busy, and – outside the main fleets – it often engaged in hazardous campaigns and operations, in which death from accidents, sickness, and poison arrows was a frequent occurence.

One of the first such campaigns, and an entirely self-assumed one, was the systematic surveying of the world's coastlines for the benefit of trade and the safety of all mariners. Another was the costly, thankless, and, in international terms, technically illegal sixty-year war against slavery in east and west African waters, an "out of the public eye" commitment that caused many remote, unglamorous casualties and many gaps in the Navy List. There were piracy-suppression campaigns – often violent – disaster-relief operations, and the many policing and punitive expeditions against warlords and tyrants.

In just the four years between 1857 and 1861, there were 105 requests from various civil authorities around the world for the dispatch and attendance somewhere of British warships to deter, terminate, or avenge disorder. Throughout this long era of what today would be called "peace enforcement" or "peace support," the Royal Navy's flag officers and captains became masters of operations other than war. They were less concerned with the application of heavy-duty naval force than with the maintenance of authority, and often shouldered heavy political responsibilities in distant parts of the world. Ships on the Canadian Pacific coast were 18,000 sea miles from Whitehall. "The prestige of the Royal Navy was tremendous, and the rumble of chain cable through the hawse-pipe as a cruiser or gun-boat wearing the White Ensign came to anchor was, time and again, enough to bring quiet to a troubled spot."[1] Just occasionally, it still is. When the rumble of chain cable was not enough, military projectiles – in the form of (in ascending order) Royal Marines, naval brigades, and then the British and Indian Armies – were fired ashore from the holy-stoned decks of the Royal Navy.

To quote from a research paper by a staff college student, "between 1820 and 1900 [which embraces Victoria's life, if not her reign] Britain carried out some 235 overseas military expeditions. From the very small to the very large, they ranged across the whole globe from the Red River expedition

---

[1]   Donald MacIntyre, *Jutland*, p. 27.

in Canada to the Maori Campaign in New Zealand. These operations covered the whole spectrum of military operations. There were multinational peace support operations such as that in Crete in 1896, and maritime interdiction and blockades such as operations off Zanzibar in the 1860s. The Navy rescued hostages and punished pariah states. Many of these operations were protracted and some were extremely violent."[2] All depended on the Royal Navy for sea power first of all, but also for transport, gunfire support, supplies, and (just occasionally) refuge.

In support of Sir Robert Napier's 1867–8 expedition to rescue hostages held in Magdala by King Theodosius of Abyssinia (following his unsuccessful efforts to romance Queen Victoria) and punish him for throwing his subjects off cliffs, the Royal Navy surveyed a prospective harbor on the Red Sea Coast of East Africa, constructed a series of lighthouses, and set up a naval pilot service, staffed by navigation lieutenants. Meanwhile, it transported the stones for two 700-foot deep-water piers (a prototype Mulberry Harbour) from India, along with the railway tracks to run along them, and laid them in place in just six weeks. Then, the Naval Transport Service organized a total of 621 voyages by 292 ships to deliver

- 14,000 troops, with artillery
- 26,000 native bearers
- 2,500 horses
- 22,000 mules and donkeys
- 6,000 camels
- 7,000 bullocks
- 44 elephants
- 8 girder bridges
- 12 miles of coastal railway
- 12 locomotives and a complex of engine sheds
- 20 sets of drilling machinery with pipes to line 100 wells
- 35,000 tons of food
- a major desalination plant

Thirty years later, the Navy mounted a punitive expedition to put an end to the atrocities (mass disembowlings, crucifixions, that sort of thing) practiced by King Ovonramwen of Benin City in what is now Nigeria. Within two days of the receipt in London of the telegraphed news of the murder of a British diplomat, an expedition was under way. Within a fortnight, ships and Royal Marines from Capetown, Malta, and Portsmouth had converged on the entrance to the Benin River, and within two and a half weeks of landing,

---

[2] Cdr. Charles Ashcroft, 1999 Defence Research Paper (JSCSC).

the force had marched 150 miles inland through dense jungle, accomplished its task, and reembarked.

By Queen Victoria's Diamond Jubilee in 1897, the Navy's peacetime reputation among the British public, its paymasters, and its would-be opponents had never stood higher. "The Fleet possessed [in the words of *The Times*] a significance which is directly and intimately connected with the welfare and prosperity of Empire. [It] is at once the most powerful and far-reaching weapon which the world has ever seen."[3]

We now know that even as *The Times*' pundit was penning those words, the era of *Pax Britannica* was already drawing to a close. As early as 1889, the Naval Defence Act had acknowledged a resurgence of competition from other naval powers. Several industrializing nations were already overtaking Britain in productivity. The U.S. Navy's Captain Alfred Mahan had drawn international attention to the strategic benefits of sea power. The Jubilee Review itself merely served to underline the link between naval power and imperial might. But these emerging trends and their imminent consequences were not apparent at the time. Theorizing about imperial decline was not a Victorian pastime. Even the *New York Times* could write: "We are a part, and a great part, of the Greater Britain which seems so plainly destined to dominate this planet and has made such enormous advances towards its conquest these last sixty years."[4]

In the early fifteenth century, Henry IV had created the Military Division of the Most Honourable Order of the Bath as an Arthurian reward for prowess on the battlefield. By the 1890s, the British government was scratching about to find individuals worthy to keep the order going. In 1893, it offered a KCB to the Commander in Chief Mediterranean, who modestly demurred on the grounds that to give one to an officer who had not fought a battle would be to "drive a coach and horses" through the regulations (he had a baronetcy already and wasn't easily impressed).[5] The First Lord of the Admiralty, Earl Spencer, told him that the Duke of Cambridge feared that the military division would die out if the rules were not bent and that the Prince of Wales wanted him to have a KCB.[6] In the end, they settled for a GCB (a Civil Division upgrade).

That cameo exchange of letters, though, illustrates the dearth of senior combat experience in the main naval fleets and army units toward the end of Victoria's reign, a happy circumstance, of course, but a symptom of the difficulties that officers were having in distinguishing themselves in a traditional warrior manner, and of the fact that the rules for professional advancement

---

[3] *The Times*, 25.6.97.
[4] *New York Times*, 24.6.97.
[5] 24.10.93, Althorp Papers, K437.
[6] 9.11.93, Ibid.

were no longer straightforward. In fact, a large fleet in peacetime can be so busy in the minutia of day-to-day training that the reasons for its existence keep getting pushed back in the pending tray. Then as now, there was plenty to keep Victorian senior officers focused on the immediate foregrounds and with which to judge their efficiency without an enemy in the offing.

But in the absence of maritime enemies against which to pit their skill and courage, many junior officers sought others means of standing out from their peers. Those born with silver spoons, or befriended by the service's aristocratic or royal members, gained advancement in the flagships of the main fleets and squadrons – if not actually in the Royal Yachts – where efficiency was measured in terms of showiness, swagger, and cleanliness: where spit and polish reigned, and where even gunnery practice was frowned on because it dirtied the paintwork. This was also a problem for the less-wealthy wardrooms because, although the Admiralty provided paint for three coats a year, a ship normally needed five or six, and the officers had to buy the extra paint out of their own pockets. A new coat would certainly be needed after target practice, and although dirty paintwork had consequences for a ship's reputation, bad shooting would probably never be discovered. Until the gunnery revival of the late 1890s, nobody much cared anyway. Sometimes ammunition was simply thrown overboard. It was spit-and-polish and set-piece evolutions at sea which defined efficiency. As for military effectiveness, that concept rarely, if ever, crossed the minds of admirals or ships' captains.

Even this requires a strategic context. Heavy guns were virtually irrelevant, not to the Navy's prestige, but to its habitual employment. For years and years, main-armament warfare with a symmetric competitor was extremely unlikely, although the Navy conducted regular Thursday drills, in which landing parties formed and maneuvered like soldiers. And naval companies and brigades were a regular feature of Victorian colonial expeditions.

The more ambitious officers despaired of ever finding action at sea and did everything they could to attach themselves to operations on land. Lieutenant Archibald Berkeley Milne, society dandy, was Lord Chelmsford's ADC during the Zulu War of 1879, later taking elegant refuge in Royal Yachting. Captain Arthur "Old Ard Art" Wilson found his way into the second battle of El Teb in 1884. He was present with the Yorks & Lancs when their square began to break. After his sword snapped, as he put it, "while having a cool prod at an Arab," he fought on with his fists and won the Victoria Cross. As a lieutenant, young Horace Hood, likewise, won the DSO in hand-to-hand combat with dervishes in 1904. Both Jellicoe and Beatty distinguished themselves with the naval brigade in the Boxer Rebellion, receiving both wounds and decorations.

Other officers sought distinction in polar exploration under the aegis of the Royal Geographical Society, which had two admirals on its council in the 1890s and thirty-five naval officers among its fellows. Every British expedition to the ends of the earth, from Sir John Franklin's in 1845 to Robert Scott's in 1911, was cosponsored by the Royal Navy, with participating officers selected by the Royal Geographical Society to comply with its rigorous standards of muscular-Christianity and social acceptability. That organization fiercely resisted any bid to democratize the polar regions. It considered Ernest Shackleton not quite a proper chap, being a merchant seaman and a Royal Naval Reservist.

A final, if slightly idiosyncratic, means to career recognition was through a command of the emerging technology of the industrial revolution. Because this is the subject of the next section, we do not discuss it here, beyond reflecting that the Navy's gentrified and increasingly aristocratic officer corps, with its affectation of amateurism, looked askance at technical specialists (equating them with "trade"), even while needing their expertise. It therefore failed to engage specialists in robust debate, and afforded them, in effect, a form of benefit of clergy – a sort of deference through fear of association.

We may consider some of these priorities to be quaint and inappropriate, or at best incomplete. But we are guilty of some of them today. They were merely responses to the real lack of opportunities for distinction at sea. Able and ambitious officers sought any piece of remotely combat-related experience, and that we must applaud.

They would thus have been outraged at the modern Navy's breathtaking edict in 1982 that combat performance in the South Atlantic must have no influence on an officer's promotion prospects because that would be unfair to those who had not participated.[7] Exactly whose precious weasel interests that policy served, one can only speculate. It meant that the service's main instruments of reward and punishment were, in effect, suspended for the duration of the Falkland's campaign, although nobody down south knew that at the time. Had it applied in 1898, young David Beatty would never have got his seniority boost for command of gunboats on the Nile, and one can think of many others. Thus, the modern Navy squandered a professional and national asset, however randomly gained – that of experience under fire. The Victorians had more robust common sense.

The Royal Navy's achievement in the long Victorian peace was all the more remarkable in light of the unprecedented revolution in military affairs resulting from the industrial revolution. Within one career span (approximately fifty years) the service successfully assimilated staggering material changes – changes that made obsolete and irrelevant virtually all former technologies of sea warfare. But instead of lapsing into decline as it might have done (and as some other navies did), it embraced these changes and

---

[7] Sandy Woodward, *One Hundred Days: The Memoirs of the Falklands Battle Group Commander*, 2nd ed. (Annapolis, 1997).

reaffirmed its supremacy. Compound engines, water tube boilers, electricity, Whitehead torpedoes, breach-loading guns – all were absorbed into the fleet and extended its power. By 1900, the Royal Navy was acknowledged as the world's benchmark in how to harness industrialization and how to embrace change.

The arrival of new technology was probably the most important factor in the erosion of Nelsonic doctrine because new technology appeared to eclipse historical lessons, however painfully learned. To some extent, and for obvious reasons, this is inevitable. In times of war, or recurring wars, the force of recent and continuing experience is too strong and too graphic to allow the mix of practice and theory to get out of kilter. But in long periods of peace, empirical experience fades, and rationalist – i.e., mainly technical – theory moves in to take its place. The moving in is fastest and most persuasive in times of rapid technological change, such as that which took place in the late nineteenth century and which has been taking place in the late twentieth. Furthermore, those on the cutting edge of technology, whose technical expertise is their career ticket, inevitably exaggerate the revolutionary nature of recent technological development. They claim that this or that new system has rendered previous experience obsolete, so there is no point in looking to the past for doctrinal guidance.

Then, having impressed the Navy, Army, or Air Force with the novelty of its predicament – assisted by a daunting lexicon of jargon – they proffer solutions of their own convenience, in return for promotion, power, and status. To all intents and purposes, the service may as well have been born yesterday – at least to them.

It was evident as early as the 1860s that ships powered by steam could act in precise unison, irrespective of wind direction or strength. A given number of engine revolutions would produce a known speed. Naval experts could measure, time, and tabulate turning circles. They could predict rates of acceleration and deceleration, and so on. The result was synchronized steaming; and over a period of perhaps twenty years, the technocrats, with their Victorian sense of order and tidiness, reasoned with Trenchardian logic and grandeur that technology had rendered the navy's increasingly distant warfighting experience spectacularly irrelevant. Only scientific, automated techniques of command and control, with their comforting processes of tabulation, automation, and *regulation*, could reasonably manage the new warfare of machinery and science. The attractions of this to an officer corps deprived of real war experience and armed with largely untested technology in a long period of peace were obvious. As an article in the *Saturday Review* on "The Over-Regulation of the Navy," suggested in 1894: "It is convenient for some men to have a nice book of arithmetic to save them the trouble of thinking and the responsibility of acting for themselves."

Under the sponsorship of officers like William Fanshawe Martin, commander-in-chief in the Mediterranean, 1860–3, and his former flag captain Geoffrey Phipps-Hornby, commander-in-chief in the Mediterranean, 1877–9, the mechanization of propulsion prompted development of "steam tactics," by which geometric fleet evolutions all but supplanted battle training. A major contributory factor in this regulation of tactics was the work of Commander – later Rear-Admiral – Philip Howard Colomb, a theorist on signaling and the leading proponent of what became known in the fleet as the "goose step." Colomb's seminal "Manoeuvring Book of 1874" actually contained the assertion that "To work a fleet at speed in the closest order is now admitted as the chief aim of the naval tactician."[8] One can argue that this conceit, if projected as far as 1916, sheds light on the management of the Grand Fleet at Jutland. Taking advantage of the enormous fallow capacity of the alphabetic signal book, Victorian tacticians tried to ritualize the fleet's concept of battle in the fashion that ballroom dancing was intended to ritualize courtship: they were trying to *regulate* the naturally erratic.

The fleet's preparedness to dispense with the inexact methods that had served it so well in the (now) distant past, the sophistication of its signaling, and its systemization of fleetwork and command and control were almost universally admired. It dove-tailed easily into Victorian social mores of deference, obedience, and tidiness; and, notwithstanding some dissent from within the Service, was advanced by Sir Michael Culme-Seymour, commander-in-chief Mediterranean, 1893–6, whose subordinates included most of the future trainers of the Edwardian Royal Navy. Therefore, a century after the Navy had accomplished so much by harnessing precisely opposite means, a fraternity of senior and greatly respected officers who measured efficiency and warrior skills by the devices of accountancy management had set its doctrinal framework in an entirely contrary direction. They immersed themselves in detail and control, at the expense of their clarity of view of principles. Their dominance lasted some twenty years, and Commander John Jellicoe, Culme-Seymour's flag commander and the commander of the Grand Fleet at Jutland, was a card-carrying member.

The return of great power competition at sea became the keynote of naval affairs in the years immediately after Victoria's death in 1901. Among the world's second-rank naval powers, the doctrines of coast defense and commerce raiding yielded to the regal, first-rank desideratum of "Command of the Sea." The world's leading navy was soon aware that the rest of the pack was steaming hard in its wake. The Royal Navy, joints stiffened and arteries clotted by the comfortable habits of unchallenged dominion, now confronted immense strategic, material, and organizational stresses. It would have been remarkable if the necessary new transformation – back to blue-water fleet

---

[8]   Milne Papers (NMM): MLN/198/4B 10.

competition – had occurred completely and swiftly. It was swift enough in material terms, as Sir John Fisher's famous *Dreadnought* revolution pushed the technological envelope far out into the new century, but it could not be swift in doctrinal terms as long as the materialists held sway. As Churchill was later sadly to comment, in 1914 "we had more captains of ships than captains of war."[9]

By about the time *Dreadnought* came into service in 1906, there was already a small but growing body of middle-ranking officers – not quite the same people as the anti-Fisher "Syndicate of Discontent," but there was certainly some overlap – that held that the Navy, dominated as it was by technologists, was "losing the plot" in terms of the realities of combat. A few of its members were probably frauds, men who were seeking to dignify their technical disorientation. Nevertheless, the group became known as the "Historical School." It broadly held that, notwithstanding technological changes, the Navy had too glibly discarded many empirical lessons of the past.

It may be that a service that owes everything to technology, as many thought the Navy did a century ago, is liable to fall into these habits. Today's Royal Air Force – both the product and the prisoner of twentieth-century technology – may offer a modern equivalent. In case there are light-blue hackles rising, let me hasten to justify the comparison. My source is a 2003 Staff College "Defence Research Paper" on leadership and management. The author electronically queried the entire advanced staff course for British officers in the United Kingdom about the most desirable attributes for future commanders and analyzed the returns.

Concerning the operational level of command, his respondents were asked to rate six skills in order of importance. There was broad similarity among the services, but refreshingly, each had, by a narrow margin, its own favorite. The Army's top skill was "organizing and staffing." The Royal Air Force's was "controlling and problem solving." The Royal Navy's was "motivating and inspiring."[10]

I would suggest, tentatively, that a century ago, the cutting-edge technocrats who dominated the senior ranks of the Royal Navy would probably have given the same answer as today's Air Force squadron leaders: "Controlling and problem solving" was what they were good at and felt comfortable with. Jellicoe certainly tried to lead the Grand Fleet with that command skill, and later, as First Sea Lord, almost lost the war through his obdurate quest for technical solutions to the U-boat problem.

In contrast, both the Historical School and the Syndicate of Discontent would probably have given answers similar to those given by today's staff

[9] Winston S. Churchill, *World Crisis*, vol. 1 (London, 1927), p. 97.
[10] Cdr. Alejandro R Ugarte, *Military Leaders and Managers...*, 2003 DRP (JSCSC).

college Navy lieutenant commanders, who put "controlling and problem solving" fourth out of six, after "motivating and inspiring," "organizing and staffing," and "aligning people." Only "establishing direction" and "planning and budgeting" were less important.

In terms of seniority, the Historical School's center of gravity was at captain and commander level, too junior to call the shots in 1914, although they had sufficient patronage to prompt the creation of the off-the-record journal *The Naval Review* in 1913. In one of its earliest editions, Captain William Boyle attacked the materialists with the following comment: "The fact that we know how to handle our ships and manipulate her armament does not indicate that we are ready to play our part in war."[11] Boyle and the new thinkers of the Navy enjoyed benign tolerance from Sir George Callaghan, commander-in-chief Home Fleets, 1912–14 (and the only prewar admiralissimo who had not trained under Culme-Seymour).

Rear Admiral David Beatty himself cannot really be described as an active member of the Historical School (a "country member" perhaps), and it is unclear how vigorous or profound his thought processes ever were. But whereas Jellicoe feared loose cannons, Beatty was stimulated by them and gathered them in his retinue. He did read history, and he gladly gave house room and staff jobs to thinkers and would-be reformers. One of his first actions in 1913, on hoisting his flag in HMS *Lion* as senior officer of the Battlecruiser Squadron in Callaghan's fleet, was to circulate a Battle Cruiser Squadron memorandum headed: "From a Study of Great Naval Wars."[12]

That memorandum argued: "It is impressed upon one that Cruiser captains – which includes Battlecruiser Captains – to be successful must possess, in a marked degree, initiative, resource, determination and no fear of accepting responsibility. To enable them to make best use of these sterling qualities, they should be given the clearest indication of the functions and duties of the unit to which they belong, as comprehended by the Commander of that unit. They should be completely comprehensive of his mind and intentions." This was an amazing statement for the Royal Navy of the time. Beatty had received command of the latest, largest, fastest, sexiest war machines in the world, and here he was looking back to the navy of scurvy and weevils and creaking timbers for doctrinal guidance.

Beatty was seeking enduring *principles* by which to lead his elite squadron without deferring to the common conceits of *process* – or rather his staff commander, Reginald Plunkett, was. But Beatty did attach his name to the paper and many others like it over the next five years. It is worth remembering that, when Beatty first took over the battle cruisers in 1913, he was free to sponsor such fundamentalism, enjoying as he did the indulgence of the

[11]   Ibid.
[12]   15.4.13, DRAX 4/1.

then commander-in-chief, George Callaghan; and that Beatty as a battle cruiser commander predated Jellicoe as commander-in-chief and thus gained enough of a head start in entrenching his doctrine to ring-fence it from outside interference after the change in high command.

That change in high command, in August 1914, when Sir John Jellicoe replaced Callaghan, instituted a doctrinal rift between the battle cruisers and the rest of the Grand Fleet that lasted until Beatty succeeded Jellicoe twenty-seven months later. On July 31, 1914, with the mobilized Home Fleets now combined in Scapa Flow under the new name Grand Fleet, Jellicoe arrived, fresh from the post of Second Sea Lord, ostensibly to become second in command to Callaghan. The newcomer had a fine reputation in the service.

Throughout his career, Jellicoe had cruised efficiently along, easily gaining the admiration of his bosses with his technical and organizational abilities. In the early years of the century, he was much a man of the future. As a junior officer, he gained the trust and admiration of the manic, driven Fisher, when the latter was captain of the Gunnery School, HMS *Excellent*. He proved technically gifted, a mathematician, with a mind described by Corelli Barnett as "a well ordered filing system of detail." His career progress was smooth and rapid: smooth, that is, until he was nearly killed in the Boxer Rebellion in China, where he received a bullet in his lung, a memento which he carried inside him for the rest of his life. On recovery, Jellicoe rejoined the Fishpond at the Admiralty, serving his patron as Director of Naval Ordnance and later as Third Sea Lord and Controller of the navy.

Jellicoe's talents exactly complemented Fisher's erratic, visionary methods. He had all the data at his fingertips. He had watched these ships, this magnificent fleet, take shape in memoranda and blue prints. Fisher, for his part, became convinced that he was building up the Navy for Jellicoe to lead it to victory in a North Sea Armageddon, an event which he long predicted would come in 1914. He actually wrote of the day when Jellicoe would return in triumph with one arm, etc. So, while Fisher "unrolled the carpet, Jellicoe stepped neatly along it."[13]

Three days after Jellicoe's arrival at Scapa Flow, a telegram arrived from the Admiralty ordering Callaghan to strike his flag and hand over command to the newcomer. Jellicoe was distraught, and the full reasoning behind the order may never be known. Callaghan was old and creaky, scheduled to strike his flag anyway in November. But the old boy was greatly respected, and having commanded the fleet now for three years, he was entirely at ease with it. Jellicoe, in contrast, had commanded dreadnoughts for only three weeks, in the 1913 annual maneuvers. It seemed disruptive, rude, unpopular, and

---

[13] Corelli Barnett, *The Swordbearers: Supreme Command in the First World War* (London, 2000), p. 26.

foolhardy to swap the well-proven chief for a novice when a new Trafalgar might occur as soon as war was declared, if not before.

Over the next two days, Jellicoe sent no fewer than six telegrams to Their Lordships, begging them to reconsider or postpone his appointment. A parallel which comes to mind is that of the Duke of Medina Sidonia's dismay at finding himself placed, at the eleventh hour, in command of the Spanish Armada. It is likely that Jellicoe was recoiling from the responsibilities now confronting him, recoiling, not, as Corelli Barnett spins it, because his long Admiralty service had given him privileged insight into the material flaws of the fleet, but because of self-doubts.

Above all, Jellicoe was unfamiliar with high command: he was in poor health, and he was long overdue for a rest. Now, suddenly, on the very cusp of war, he confronted the highest command of the largest assembly of naval power in the world, and on his slight, tired, anxious shoulders, awesome issues rested. There was a more specific problem. Callaghan had run an unusually permissive, countercultural regime in his relations with his juniors. He encouraged them to hone their initiative and to act on their own judgment. In that respect, Callaghan's supercession by Jellicoe was a doctrinal disaster for the Grand Fleet and its expectations of crushing victory.

But Callaghan's juniors were now Jellicoe's, and there were a number of loose cannons at the three-star rank who would somehow have to be secured to his neat and orderly deck or jettisoned. Sir Lewis Bayly (who would win the first Battle of the Atlantic in 1917) was the first to go in late 1914. Sir Frederick Sturdee, who joined the fleet after winning the Battle of the Falklands, was so independent of mind that Jellicoe considered him subversive and stationed him in the middle of the fleet's cruising formation. Thus, whichever way the fleet deployed into battle line, Sturdee would find himself astern of at least one other vice admiral. When the 24-knot *Queen Elizabeth* class of battleships formed up in autumn 1915, Jellicoe rejected both Bayly and Sturdee as possible commanders for the new Fast Battle Squadron on the grounds of their supposed unreliability.

Nothing better illustrates Churchill's distinction between captains of ships and captains of war than the officers with whom Jellicoe felt comfortable. That is an indictment not only of Jellicoe and of the rationalizing technocrats, whom he assumed to have the answers in the machine-age Navy, but also of the peacetime "regulating" mind-set. Jellicoe, the supreme materialist, heartily disliked and mistrusted the emergent Historical School and would hasten to suppress that organ of untrammeled professional discussion, *The Naval Review*, after he became First Sea Lord in November 1916.

Jellicoe's choice of staff officers and retainers reflected his obsession with control. There was some truth in Beatty's malicious remark that "Jellicoe is absolutely incapable of selecting good men because he dislikes men of character who have independent ideas of their own."[14] Jellicoe favored and trusted the sort of admiral Richard Hough has described as "dear blockheads" – efficient, decent, amiable, aged or prematurely aged Paddington Bear–like figures, whose actions or ideas posed no threat to the carefully constructed framework of Grand Fleet Battle Orders (GFBOs). Vice Admirals George Warrender, Cecil Burney, and Martin Jerram all were in this category. The first was "deaf and absent-minded," but remained on active duty for the incredible reason that he was "excellent as a squadron admiral in peace."[15] The second had "always been unwell," in Lady Beatty's waspish opinion. The third, Beatty later wanted to have court-martialed for failing to pursue the enemy at Jutland (how could he? – Jellicoe had not told him to). Jellicoe's chief of staff was his brother-in-law, and among his rear admirals one finds his old friend Hugh Evan Thomas, whose "professional attainments were highly regarded."[16] Thomas was steady and loyal, and completely lacking in imagination. Not surprisingly, Jellicoe gave him the Fast Battle Squadron. Finally, there was Herbert Heath, who was said to have had "a pumpkin on his shoulders" instead of a head.[17]

Jellicoe was simply, to borrow a marvelous phrase from George Bernard Shaw, "too military a man to be truly martial." The dynamics between Jellicoe and Beatty were like those between King Charles I and Prince Rupert, the leader of the royalist cavalry in the Civil War: the former, ponderous and slow, always trailing behind, the latter, impulsive, headstrong, and maneuverist, always seizing the main chance and courting danger.

It was Beatty's battlecruiser ethos of dash and risk-taking that inevitably found itself at odds with the laborious, centralized, control-intensive Battle Orders that the Grand Fleet's new and anxious commander-in-chief issued soon after the war's outbreak. The crux of the discrepancy between their methods was the role of signaling in battlefield command and control. Jellicoe, for reasons of both personality and career conditioning, believed in exercising control by means of detailed flag and radio signals. Beatty, in contrast, promoted doctrine and constantly warned that battle fleets could not rely on signals because of smoke, battle damage, or time. Indeed, he sought to liberate his semi-independent command from the unsafe tyranny of signals officers.

Jellicoe, heavily burdened by his strategical responsibilities, was an attritionalist in the way he led the fleet and in the way he visualized battle. GFBOs presumed that the German High Seas Fleet, if caught, would oblige the Grand Fleet by steaming in a straight line and on a parallel course until

---

[14] Letter to Lady Beatty, 13.5.17, *Beatty Papers*, vol. p. 430.
[15] Letter to Henry Jackson, 16.6.15, *Jellicoe Papers*, vol. I, p. 67.
[16] Arthud Marder, *From Dreadnought to Scapa Flow*, vol. II (Oxford, 1970), p. 441.
[17] Ibid., vol. IV, p. 223.

sunk. In fact, Jellicoe was seeking to control the very nature of warfare. He was by no means a stupid man, but this was wishful to the point of dishonesty to his sailors, the 60,000 men to whom the promise of crushing victory was an article of faith.

At the heart of the lasting animosity between the Beatty-ites and the Jellicoe-ites was of course the disappointment of Jutland on May 31, 1916. Owing to defects in both design and standing operating procedures, Beatty's ships suffered appalling losses, while drawing the German Fleet into the jaws of the battlefleet. And then Jellicoe did (seemingly) nothing. As well as needing German passivity, his elaborate battle plans needed time, several hours of good visibility and daylight, to bring his crushing force to bear. But it was late: visibility was clamping down and dusk was rapidly approaching. He resolved to wait until morning to finish the job, as Howe had done the evening before the Glorious First of June in 1794, and as Tovey would with *Bismarck* in 1941. By the time the First of June dawned, however, the enemy had gone.

One might think the German fleet's declining an attritional confrontation to have been entirely predictable. Why should it have been otherwise? If the arithmetic prevailed, the High Seas Fleet had no hope. It had perforce to train to maneuver, if need be without waiting for orders and without regard for parade ground station-keeping. Jellicoe, preoccupied with micromanaging his own unwieldy fleet, and despite (or because) of executive signals – one every sixty-seven seconds – never got inside his opponent's action–reaction cycle. So, despite monumental blunders by Reinhard Scheer, the German fleet escaped – not once, not twice, but (if one includes the events of the night) three times, and got back home to claim victory. Even Jellicoe supposedly commented despairingly on the way home: "I have missed one of the greatest opportunities a man ever had."[18]

Subsequently, Jellicoe tried unsuccessfully to block Beatty's being selected as his successor. He recommended instead his own chief of staff and brother-in-law, Charles Madden. But Beatty's succession as commander in chief in November 1916 signaled a change in the quality of officer in the flagship's orbit. When Beatty had a Christmas party in 1916 immediately after assuming command of the Grand Fleet, his flag lieutenant was struck by how different the group seemed from the last time he had seen the Grand Fleet admirals together: "None of them deaf or in any way aged or infirm."[19]

The new commander-in-chief evicted much of Jellicoe's office equipment from the admiral's quarters in *Iron Duke* (and replaced it with a strange sort of Turkish bath). Step by step, he prepared the subordinate admirals of the Grand Fleet for the replacement of his predecessor's voluminous battle orders

[18] Ibid., vol. III, p. 237n.
[19] 22.12.16, BTY 13/34.

with what was essentially Battle Cruiser Fleet doctrine by sending them out from Scapa to handle their respective formations without supervision. Then, in March 1917, he transplanted his battle cruiser standing orders into the wider Grand Fleet by subordinating Jellicoe's voluminous GFBOs to two brief pages of Grand Fleet Battle Instructions (GFBIs). Those two pages set out the guiding principles of decentralization and anticipation that he wished to govern the conduct of the fleet. In this, he was undoubtedly influenced by Captain Herbert Richmond, one of whose hobby horses was the ancient distinction between orders and instructions. Meanwhile, Beatty trained the fleet in the concentration of divisional gunfire by means of (first) flashing lamp and (later) short-range wireless.

Finally, in January 1918, Beatty abolished the GFBOs – or rather, he divided their contents into two separate publications. The more important, slimmer volume was an expanded version of the Grand Fleet Battle Instructions, already described. The less important, fatter volume was called Grand Fleet Manoeuvring Orders and contained all the practical minutiae, collated by Jellicoe, about the handling of squadrons and flotillas in various conditions and eventualities.

The successive modifications to the orders/instructions themselves, the change in their roles implicit in the new nomenclature, and the innovations in the training and practices of the Grand Fleet that took place between the Jutland postmortem and the beginning of 1918, amounted to a cumulative revolution. Steadily, Beatty made clear that whereas Jellicoe had expected a battle to conform to the script in his GFBOs, he, for his part, expected his squadron and division commanders to respond to the ebb and flow of the action: to take their orders from the enemy, and not, on any account, to let go of him. One can extrapolate everything in Beatty's Grand Fleet Battle Instructions from his early (1913–14) Battle Cruiser Squadron standing orders, but, equally, in almost everything his conviction had been greatly hardened by the mortifying memory of the Germans melting away into the twilight smog at Jutland, and the stately parade of Grand Fleet battleships declining his urgent, insubordinate invitation to support him in pursuit.

By early 1918, the fleet was thus a much more potent weapon than in 1916, for reasons as much doctrinal as material. It was certainly far too potent for the Germans to countenance symmetric warfare. The High Seas Fleet lapsed into disuse and disaffection, its best young officers syphoned off for the U-boat arm. In the end it was Beatty, not Jellicoe, who basked in the glory of its surrender in the Firth of Forth in November 1918.

By the war's end, most officers who served afloat in 1917–18 were to a greater or lesser degree Beatty admirers, and his acolytes came to set the tone of the interwar Royal Navy. Beatty and Ernle Chatfield, his flag captain, between them occupied the post of First Sea Lord for thirteen years, and six other future First Sea Lords had been present at Jutland. There is no doubt that 1939 Fighting Instructions (signed by two of Jellicoe's former battleship captains) were strongly redolent of the doctrine of the battle cruisers and of Beatty's originally select circle of thinkers.

If the Victorians had questioned the experts more closely in the years of peace, we might have been able to engage the enemy more closely in the real conditions of combat, most notably the High Seas Fleet in 1916. But Jellicoe, the brilliant cutting-edge technocrat, the man of the times in 1910, merely prolonged the doctrinal tunnel vision, reinstating it after Callaghan's tenure of command. He seems in retrospect to have been inflexible, pedantic, and out of date by 1916. It was certainly an unspoken commonplace by 1939 that that was *not* how one won a war, especially war against the odds Britain was then facing. From the mid-1930s onward, with Japan, Italy, and Germany polarizing together, Britain's admirals, even some of those who had been loyal battle fleet captains under Jellicoe, could see clearly that attritional methods were not likely to favor the Navy in a new world war: they would have to maneuver to win.

Beatty and his image loomed large over the post–Jutland Royal Navy, larger perhaps than any other single figure in the twentieth century. In big issues, he was mostly right. He and his flag captain held the post of First Sea Lord for thirteen years between them, and his philosophy (or the ideas which he endorsed) came to dominate the interwar fleet and permeated the 1939 Fighting Instructions.

In the long, successful maritime peace of the Victorian age, the Royal Navy had focused too little on the *use* of the material coming into service. Mahan remarked that first-rate men in second-rate ships are better than the other way round, and the British had put disproportionate thought into the ships. The admirals assumed they had sorted out the business of how to lead fleets in battle in the light of new technology, but they were wrong. The Navy was misled by the experts into supposing that technology had changed more than was really the case. They assumed that if the systemization of leadership and command matched the mechanization of the Navy, the Royal Navy could regulate battle and disarm its hazardous nature. As Mahan and certain Royal Navy dissidents kept trying to point out, systematization has its own hazards, and there must be maintained a balance between science and art: *a doctrinal safety net against systems failure.*

Beatty's role in relation to the rising groundswell of discontent with the overrationalized Edwardian Navy bears some comparison with that of John Jervis in relation to the Nelson generation. They both actively sponsored the philosophy of command by doctrine, delegation, and negation rather than by prescription, and sought to lift their juniors above the need of constant supervision. Jervis, needless to say, had much more promising and battle-tested raw material to start with, whereas as Cowan noted, Beatty's "rat catching" was mostly driven by instinct in the face of circumstances. Nevertheless, he was patron and client to officers like Plunkett, Brock, and Richmond (in whose age group he loosely belonged), who might otherwise not have achieved prominence and who did the serious headwork with which Beatty himself was too lazy or unfocused to bother.

After a century of peacetime sailoring, it took a major war and perceived failure (or at least massive disappointment) forcibly to complete the transformation of the British fleet back to a fully efficient fleet-fighting machine. That is a lesson we should not forget.

11

Military history and the pathology
of lessons learned: the Russo-Japanese
War, a case study

JONATHAN B. A. BAILEY

> On the day of battle naked truths may be picked up for the asking: by the
> following morning they have already begun to get into their uniforms.
>
> Sir Ian Hamilton (1908)

The Russo-Japanese War of 1904 was short but intense, leaving the world
shocked and enthralled by its drama. A large number of foreign military observers and journalists witnessed its conduct. Their findings were
widely publicized in popular books and official studies. Pundits immediately acknowledged that the war offered important insights into the nature
of future conflict at a time of seemingly revolutionary technological change
and social upheaval, as well as a novel strategic geography. The validation
of the lessons learned or forgotten in this Asian-Pacific "experiment" came
in the great conflict of 1914–18.

It is hard to identify any lesson of the war that was not appreciated or
documented at the time. Inevitably, many of these lessons were contradictory,
peculiar to the theatre, and more or less appropriate to different military
cultures. Moreover, observers viewed those lessons through the distorting
lenses of political intrigue, social attitude, military orthodoxy, and wishful
thinking. The result was that what historians at the beginning of the twenty-
first century now see as having been clear auguries of the future of warfare
(1914–18) generally went unheeded. The military organizations of the time
often ignored the lessons identified and, equally, those they did draw of the
future often proved lethally wide of the mark. Perhaps the greatest lesson of
the war was how human folly can arrive at lessons that in the end prove to
be self-destructive and delusional to a gargantuan degree.

Lessons often comprise an agreed historical perspective, the current
received wisdom, the addition of some recent experiences, predictions about
technological development, and an extrapolation about a possible future.

These contend with mandated lessons foretold, the prescribed view discussed previously, because military leaders often distort and contort new evidence to sustain their views of the future as they wish it to be.

Visionaries often have a point. The predictions of science fiction writers before 1904 often turned out to be astute, but also deeply uncomfortable. For that reason, military establishments generally ignored them. As the sign in the bookshop said, "In a biography it is permissible to make things up; but in a novel you have to tell the truth." Prior to 1904, many saw the potential of new technologies. In 1887, the Frenchman Albert Robida published *La Guerre au Vingtieme Siecle*, depicting submarines, tanks, planes, and poison gas; and in 1903, H. G. Wells produced his prophetic *The Land Ironclads*.[1] Nevertheless, the idea that the balance of power might be shifting from infantry to artillery, let alone to some fantastic armored force, was simply absent in mainstream military doctrine.

Military discourse did not remain limited to science fiction at the beginning of the twentieth century. There was plenty of recent combat experience prior to 1904 from which to construct a view of the future of war, and this proved decisive. The Russians took pride in the fact that at the siege of Plevna, their troops continued to attack despite suffering 40 percent casualties.[2] Despite the evidence of the Franco-Prussian War that underlined that infantry assaults inevitably resulted in heavier casualties, by 1884 French regulations were declaiming: "The principle of the decisive attack, head held high, unconcerned about casualties." The French Army's 1894 Regulation required the advance to be "[e]lbow to elbow, not breaking formation to take advantage of cover, but assaulting *en masse*."[3] Again, the Boer War demonstrated the increasing lethality of firepower in defensive positions. Nevertheless, in 1904, European armies regarded high morale rather than artillery fire as the primary means by which infantry could redress the physical effects of defensive firepower.

Some disagreed and drew more profound lessons about the future of warfare. In 1898, Jean de Bloch concluded that war between great states was now impossible, or rather suicidal. He argued that "[t]he dimensions of modern armaments and the organization of society have rendered its prosecution an economic impossibility."[4] He claimed support for this view from the memoirs of Field Marshal Graf von Moltke, the elder, who had argued that "when millions of men array themselves opposite each other, and engage

[1]   R. Hendrick, "Albert Robida's Imperfect Future," *History Today*, July 1998, p. 30.

[2]   C. van Dyke, *Russian Imperial Military Doctrine and Education, 1835–1914* (Westport, CT, 1990), p. 118.

[3]   Quoted in Michael Howard, "Men Against Fire: The Doctrine of the Offensive in 1914," in Peter Paret, *Makers of Modern Strategy* (Princeton, NJ, 1986), p. 514.

[4]   J. De Bloch, *Is War Possible? The Future of War in Its Technical, Economic, and Political Relations* (London and Boston, 1899), p. xi.

in a desperate struggle for their national existence, it is difficult to assume that the question will be settled by a few victories." Bloch predicted famine, bankruptcy, and social collapse, and cited civilian stamina and the propensity for revolution as decisive elements in modern war. His prescience is now clear, but at the time his ideas, while acknowledged, had little effect on military planning.

BACKGROUND TO THE WAR

Already before the Russo-Japanese War, there was a sense of the coming contest between East and West. Viscount Esher in Britain postulated the idea of an inevitable conflict between the civilizations. In the United States, Captain A. T. Mahan envisaged an unavoidable clash between his own "racial commonwealth" and the East.[5] The West might well have to use military means to prevent the Orient ruling the world.

Lord Wolsley maintained that all cultural vitality, empires, and civilization stemmed from war and that "war has often acted as a sharp corrective of sloth and luxury."[6] He added that "[w]hen the drill sergeant and gymnastics instructor are replaced by the ballet dancer and singer, not only does national power decline, but all healthy civilization seems to perish with it."[7] The painting *Gelbe Gefahr*, commissioned by Kaiser Wilhelm II in the 1890s, expressed the fears of many Europeans. In the Pacific, the Japanese noted how technology had enabled the European powers to advance rapidly around the world. They saw themselves as the likely victims of ever-growing imperial expansion. To add fuel to the fire, the Japanese read widely in the works of Darwin and Samuel Smiles. Yamagata Aritomo pondered on a "world-wide racial struggle between the white and coloured races" that would test the relative vitality of nations.[8]

It would, therefore, have been plausible in 1904 to foresee a titanic struggle between a rising Asian state and an established European one, in which both sides deployed fearsome new military technologies on such a scale and with such dire consequences that war might threaten the very existence of those states. In the face of this, the winner would likely be the nation with the highest sense of national commitment and the most disciplined and courageous army. In fact, this proved essentially to be the case. But European commentators failed to comprehend thoroughly such simple lessons. The conclusions they drew from the Russo-Japanese War proved in 1914 to be flawed and disastrous for their continent and eventually the rest of the world.

[5] Akira Iriye, *Across the Pacific* (New York, 1967), p. 61.
[6] Lord Wolsley, "War and Civilization," *The United Service Magazine*, no. 820, March 1897, p. 562. Ruskin observed that "All great nations...were born in war and expired in peace." Ibid., p. 561.
[7] Ibid., p. 577.
[8] Christopher Thorne, *The Issue of War* (London, 1985), p. 31.

Above all, the Russo-Japanese War offered tantalizing insights into the character of war in the coming decades of the twentieth century. Observers identified many factors and discounted many others. But by the blood-drenched year of 1918, the realities of the 1905 battlefield had eventually coalesced with those of the next war into a new style of warfare. Equally dramatic political/strategic lessons over the next thirty-six years would match the profound military developments of the Russo-Japanese War.

The war itself did not represent a fundamental discontinuity in the nature of war, but the experience should have resulted in revolutionary change. The failure to learn from that experience made change disastrously costly when it came ten years later. The war did have novelties: indirect artillery fire, hand grenades, machine guns, barbed wire, search lights, poison gas, wireless, and motor vehicles. Less obviously, the war spread to the streets of the Tsar's Empire and the world's financial markets. The characteristics of the war were scrutinized minutely – many believing that in them they were glimpsing the future, and others believing that, armed with this knowledge, they could shape something different.

THE LESSONS OF THE WAR

The Japanese took great pains to prepare for the coming war with accurate assessments of Russian strengths and weaknesses. They committed themselves to deep operations years before the outbreak of hostilities. Moreover, they began by undermining the Russian Empire itself before the war started. They courted revolutionaries and financed their insurrections and political activities. The Japanese even arranged the sequencing of battles with plans for the maturing of international loans. In comparison, Russian preparations were complacent. Their image of Japan was of a "fairyland" populated by artists and geishas – a conception that did not help the preparation of the Tsarist army for the coming struggle. At the same time, the Tsar encouraged contempt for the Japanese by referring to them as "makaki," a term eagerly taken up by the Russian press.[9] There was little rigor in Russian analysis. One official noted that: "The stagnation in the Foreign Office is indescribable. Everybody is asleep."[10]

The Russian Army produced two major informed reports in 1903 on the Japanese Army, but senior officers promptly dismissed them as alarmist and unreliable. On the eve of war, one of the Russian planning assumptions was that one Russian soldier was worth three Japanese. Although the Japanese Army required its officers to speak at least one foreign language, it appears that not a single Russian officer could speak Japanese. The Russians

---

[9] S. Wilson and D. Wells, *The Russo-Japanese War in Cultural Perspective, 1904–1905* (London, 1999), p. 3.
[10] Ian Nish, *The Origins of the Russo-Japanese War* (London, 1985), p. 6.

did assign a single general staff officer to its Japanese intelligence branch, but as even General Kuropatkin noted, "unfortunately, our selection was bad."

Historical models played a significant part in the way the two opposing sides fought the war, but these templates did not always serve them well. The Japanese modeled their army on that of the Prusso-Germans. They designed it for offensive action backed by high morale based on the European model. The Japanese craved a "Sedan" or a "Plevna" and identified Port Arthur as such a key to their campaign. From their point of view, early success was essential because they believed that the chances of triumph over an empire of vastly greater resources were no more than even, and that these would diminish the longer the war continued. Sedan eventually became the model for the Japanese offensive campaign in Manchuria, with General Oyama often attacking without knowing what the Russian dispositions were. For their naval operations, the Japanese had more recent experience to which to refer. Admiral Togo had used shock tactics against the Chinese in 1894. He repeated these in 1904 with a surprise attack by ten destroyers, armed with Whitehead torpedoes, on the Russian Second Pacific Squadron at Port Arthur.

In contrast, the Russian commander, Kuropatkin, looked to 1812 for his model, his aide Kharkevich lecturing the headquarters component for the coming conflict in Manchuria on this theme as their train headed east. Kuropatkin envisaged retreats, stretching enemy lines of communications, and weakening his opponent to the point of collapse. An equally damaging cultural passivity and aversion to risk-taking matched this irrelevant historical preference based on 1812.

Russian tactics of endless withdrawal, drawn from the irrelevant lessons of 1812, were in the end bad for morale. The Russian commander Alexeiev reported to the Tsar of "the exaggerated fear of envelopment of the flanks, thanks to which our successes are turned into defeats, terminated by retreats." A Russian company commander noted, "The conscious feeling that, whatever happened, the battle would terminate by a retreat, was demoralizing for both officers and men."

The Japanese learned the "Banzai" charge from their German instructors, and from the outset demonstrated their faith in the ability of mass and momentum to overcome firepower. After the Battle on the Yalu, the Japanese sent a telegram to their German mentor, von Meckel, thanking him for his teaching. Nevertheless, innumerable Japanese frontal assaults failed to dislodge the Russians from well-sited positions protected by wire and mines. Moreover, Russian infantry were often spectators as their indirect artillery fire shredded attacking Japanese infantry formations. The Japanese were only successful where the Russians suffered a moral rather than material collapse. This led some observers to note the power of defense, while others reported that the defense was doomed to succumb eventually to the will of the attacker. Here lay the seed of postwar controversies that set the offensive style in which European armies would go to war in 1914.

A Japanese officer remarked to a French attaché after the Battle of Liao-Yang:

> You are doubtless astonished at the difference between what you see here and anything you may have witnessed at home in times of peace. We were not less astonished ourselves. Our regulations, as you know, are identical with those of the European armies. We too began by manoeuvring according to the drill-books, and thus it was that we continued to carry the lines of Nan-Shan on 27th May in a single day. But at what terrible sacrifice!... We have profited by that lesson, and, thanks to the experience we have acquired, we have now learnt not only not to go ahead so fast, but also to keep under better cover.[11]

Colonel A. L. Haldane, attached to the Japanese Army, noted that "[i]n the attack, the Japanese infantry covered the ground with great rapidity, threw themselves down quickly after each rush, and as quickly rose again for the next rush."[12] This was more akin to German stormtroop tactics of 1917 than those of 1914. Even though the British Army had identified similar lessons from the Boer War, that was not how the armies of Europe planned to attack ten years later.

One French study concluded that "It is almost impossible for a front protected by really powerful weapons and field defences to be broken through even by troops of undaunted courage willing to sacrifice any number of lives." Yet, European armies still persisted in viewing moral cohesion as the primary lesson both for the offensive and the defensive, rather than reaching the less acceptable conclusion that the balance of technology and tactics had shifted firepower profoundly in favor of the defensive. The German General Friederich von Bernhardi even believed the unwieldy mass of armies would make it harder to adopt defensive positions than to attack, and thus the offensive would be decisive.

Not surprisingly, the German regulation of 1906 still emphasized the importance of the frontal assault in developing the infantry's offensive spirit: "Its actions must be guided by the single idea, 'Forward against the enemy, whatever the cost!... The defeat of the enemy is consummated by the assault with fixed bayonets.'"[13] There was also a strong cultural bias in most armies in favor of attack. Major General W. G. Knox, writing in 1914, observed

[11] De Negrier, "Some Lessons of the Russo-Japanese War," *Journal of the Royal United Services Institute*, 1906, p. 62.

[12] J. A. L. Haldane, "Lessons from the Russo-Japanese War," Minutes of the Aldershot Military Society, April 3, 1906, pp. 7–8.

[13] Quoted in M. Samuels, *Command and Control?: Command, Training, and Tactics in the British and German Armies, 1888–1918* (London, 1995), p. 76.

that "The defensive is never an acceptable role to the Briton, and he makes little or no study of it."[14] The Russian General Dragomirov maintained that the bayonet was "the exclusive embodiment of that will power which alone...facilitates the achievement of the objective."

The bulk of the evidence available in 1905, and not merely that of hindsight post-1918, should have led to the conclusion that, in the defense, well-sited machine guns and concealed artillery had little to fear from a purely infantry attack, however determined. Equally, a successful attack required a careful and possibly complex artillery fire plan that neutralized enemy artillery and machine guns so infantry could maneuver to close with the enemy. Virtually everyone ignored that evidence. Instead, European armies favored the "cult of the offensive," which discounted the tactical evidence of 1904–5 in the interests of maintaining high morale and an offensive spirit. "European leaders prepared poorly and took sloppy account of technological and historical evidence, armed with cults and myths instead of analytically derived, integrated and innovative systems for victory."[15] As a consequence, in 1914, stunning tactical defeats eventually resulted in static operational stalemates that were the antithesis of what all had intended.

The Defense and Infantry Weapons

The introduction of large numbers of high-velocity rifles and machine guns provided infantrymen even greater potency on the battlefield. One U.S. Army observer witnessed a Russian battalion fire from trenches in volleys, in the high angle, knocking out a Japanese battery 2,500 yards away.[16] Observers accepted that when advancing, the zone of effective infantry fire began at this range and became intolerable at 1,000 yards. At such ranges

> The reality of the field of battle today is that one has to deal with an invisible enemy....I placed myself on the summit of the hillock in order to discover with my glasses from where this hurricane of fire came. It was in vain that I sought for some traces of trenches, that I strove to discover someone. There was nothing and nobody. This created a painful feeling of uncertainty and distrust....A company begins to suffer from fire several thousand yards from (the enemy). Before the men can engage in the fighting, they are already materially and morally weakened.[17]

[14] W. Knox, *The Flaw in Our Armour* (London, 1913), p. 31.
[15] J. Shimshoni, "Technology, Military Advantage and World War I," in S. E. Miller, et al., *Military Strategy and the Origins of the First Word War* (Princeton, NJ, 1991), p. 149.
[16] M. M. Macomb, "The Russian Infantry Soldier," *Journal of the Royal United Services Institute*, 1906, pp. 1160–8.
[17] "Infantry Combat in the Russo-Japanese War, Reminiscences of the Commandant of a Russian Company Commander," *Journal of the Royal United Services Institute*, 1906, p. 1275.

The Defense and Artillery

As early as 1877–8, the Russian General Ouknov had said: "Artillery will become the scourge of mankind.... The day cannot be much longer delayed when artillery shall raise itself from being an auxiliary to the rank of principal arm." The key to this was the practice of indirect fire. Reformers in the British Army had widely suggested the need to adopt indirect fire before 1904. In 1897, Major J. L. Keir warned that through the practice of direct fire, "we may run the risk of suffering great losses at the outset of a campaign."[18] Captain C. D. Guiness predicted the outcome in a future war if British guns deployed in the open, firing directly against concealed German guns firing indirectly. He noted: "I make bold to assert that the odds are we shall get the worst of it in the first ten minutes of the artillery duel."[19]

Nevertheless, there was considerable opposition to the development of indirect firing techniques throughout the British Army, including in the artillery branch. Brigadier General C. H. Spragge, Colonel G. H. Marshall, Major J. Headlam, and Colonel E. S. May were all vociferous opponents of indirect fire. May, in particular, believed in the moral aspect of close engagement and that firing behind cover "will destroy the whole spirit of the arm." Headlam argued that the general employment of indirect fire in the field was "absolutely out of the question.... I only trust that the English field artillery will never consider their role is to sit behind a hill a mile and a half in the rear while the assault is taking place."[20]

Yet, the war in Manchuria told a different story. The common factor in the Russians' ability to hold off Japanese attacks was that Russian artillery outranged that of the Japanese and was able to fire indirectly from cover without coming under counterbattery fire. On some occasions, Russian infantry did not even man their trenches, achieving a successful defense by artillery fire alone.[21]

The use of indirect fire was fundamental to any discussion of the modern battlefield. Many writers widely advocated its use in the journals.[22]

---

[18] J. L. Keir, "Direct and Indirect Fire," *Proceedings of the Royal Artillery Institution*, no. 24, pp. 231–41.

[19] His article outlined the debate between advocates of forward and concealed deployments, and the ballistics and terminal effects of shells fired on indirect trajectories. C. D. Guiness, "Artillery Positions and Screening Guns," *Proceedings of the Royal Artillery Institutions*, no. 24, pp. 61–95.

[20] J. Headlam, "The German Method of Bringing Guns into Action," *Proceedings of the Royal Artillery Institution*, no. 24, p. 395.

[21] There were many examples of a relatively few guns effectively holding a front without significant infantry action. At Ta-Shih-Chiao on July 25, the I Russian Corps held its front all day with just six batteries, with its own infantry never engaged and Japanese attackers unable to approach closer than 3,000 meters.

[22] See, for example, B. Vincent, "Artillery in the Manchurian Campaign," *Journal of the Royal United Services Institute*, 1908, pp. 28–52.

However, despite pleas to adopt indirect fire, direct fire persisted, sacrificing the best characteristics of the weapon. Few senior officers in the other branches acknowledged the dominance of artillery or the power of the machine gun in the defense, especially when combined with wire, trenches, and obstacles, and the possible use of chemical weapons. Despite new evidence from the Russo-Japanese War, resistance to indirect fire persisted up until 1914. "There is absolutely no excuse for artillery remaining idle in face of the enemy; if they cannot see him, they must push forward until they do, even if this entails their being used as machine-guns."[23] In 1913, Major General Knox attacked the Secretary of State for War over the predicament of Britain's artillery: "Outranged by hostile gun and rifle, untrained to recognize friend from foe, innocent of the tactical requirement of a combined fire fight, does not the result spell murder?"[24]

Brigadier General J. P. Story of the U.S. Army attributed Japanese successes to superior organization and methods, even though their ordnance was inferior in many respects. However, even as late as 1916, there was concern that officers graduating from the U.S. Army's School of Fire could not conduct indirect fire missions effectively. That year the Army closed the School of Fire at Fort Sill to reinforce the border with Mexico, while the American Expeditionary Force of 1917 had to rely for equipment and training on the French and British.

Many commentators saw the value of shrapnel as of limited use, "hardly capable of inflicting damage on inanimate objects" and only of utility in rapid fire against personnel.[25] The importance of high explosive (HE) became clear: "The use of percussion shell filled with high explosive and giving out an easily discernible smoke greatly facilitates the ranging of artillery, and when firing at troops under cover or at villages it considerably increases the effect of the fire."[26]

Moreover, there was a serious shortage of heavy guns on both sides in the Russo-Japanese War, while the terrain imposed severe restrictions on the movement of those there were. By the end of September 1904, the siege of Port Arthur had become an artillery battle, employing 474 guns and mortars and a variety of 6-inch and 8-inch trench mortars. Yet, in 1914, most armies that went to war in Europe deployed with few heavy artillery pieces.

Fire discipline and ammunition conservation became intense problems throughout the fighting in Manchuria. As one report noted: "The men have a great tendency to open fire from the moment they lie down, even without waiting the order to fire, the determining of the object, the indication of the

---

[23] *Field Artillery Training 1914*, quoted in S. Marble, "Royal Artillery Doctrine, 1902–1914," *War Studies Journal*, Autumn 1996, p. 98.
[24] Knox, *The Flaw in Our Armour*, p. 41.
[25] Neznamov, *Lessons of the War*, translated by the general staff (London, 1906), p. 8.
[26] Ibid., p. 14.

range, and the nature of the fire."[27] Where ammunition was available, there seemed to be no limit to the demand. In all, the Japanese had to fire 1,500,000 shells into Port Arthur before the fortress fell. Observers attributed the high ammunition expenditures to indiscipline and poor training, but it was an ominous sign of what was to come.

Nevertheless, in 1914, the British field artillery entered the First World War supplied only with shrapnel at scales set by the 1901 Mowatt Committee. That committee based its recommendations on the experiences of the Boer War. The British Army made no attempt to amend these in the light of the Russo-Japanese experience, even after the introduction of quick-firing artillery in 1908. In that year, Colonel F. D. V. Wing noted, "The power of expenditure far exceeds the power of supply, the limit of the latter fixes that of our gun power."[28] In a report to the War Office in 1913, Lieutenant Colonel A. Forbes pointed out that existing plans for ammunition supply rested on experience in South Africa, with units making their own arrangements to collect stores from depots. He noted that "[s]uch a procedure seems to me inconceivable for a continental campaign." The convenient hope set against the experiences of Manchuria was that any war in Europe would necessarily be short.

All armies wrestled with the problem of how to generate high rates of fire while economizing on ammunition and resupplying the guns in mobile operations. The suggestion that improving accuracy could provide a solution was in practice mere rhetoric. Unfortunately, the apparent profligacy of inaccurate indirect fire became a widely accepted argument against the technique. By 1910, the French were turning against indirect fire. As a result, French artillery action in 1914 largely consisted of direct fire, with too little ammunition, generally in full view of the enemy, and accompanied by fearful attrition.

Combined Arms Firepower in Defense

Infantry and artillery firepower often resulted in combat becoming close and prolonged. Noted one observer, "[t]he real fact is, the last position today is no more than some dozen of paces from the enemy. On this position, one remains glued to the ground, often for long periods of time, because neither side ventures to risk an assault."[29] Firepower was changing the shape of the battlefield as well as the character of war itself. A Russian officer foresaw the nature of war on the Western Front ten years later. He described three

---

[27] "Infantry Combat in the Russo-Japanese War: Reminiscences of the Commandant of a Russian Company Commander," p. 1171.

[28] F. D. V. Wing, "Distribution and Supply of Ammunition on the Battlefield," *Journal of the Royal United Services Institute*, 1908, pp. 903–5.

[29] "Infantry Combat in the Russo-Japanese War," p. 1175.

days of combat in Manchuria in the following terms: "Lying down in our positions, mutually drenching each other with bullets and shrapnels, suffering considerable losses, and taking no repose, either by day or night.... In my opinion a similar situation could be prolonged for an indefinite time with the character of a war of position, and degenerate into immobility, without producing any decisive result."[30]

The most obvious tactical response to the increase in firepower was the construction of fortifications and entrenchments. The dominance of artillery fire encouraged both sides to increase the depth of no-man's land and made the attack even more difficult, thus prolonging the battle and increasing the digging on both sides. The spade replaced the shield as the infantryman's armour. Technical innovations such as wire obstacles carrying 4,000 volts added to the horror. The Japanese exacerbated the carnage by the use of arsenic fumes to clear the Russians out of their bunkers.[31] Port Arthur had become a symbol and focus for international attention, rather as Douaumont became in 1916. The lethality of artillery in static warfare was clear to those who chose to study the subject.

Changes in the Character of War

The battle at Port Arthur acquired characteristics grimly similar to the battlefields of a decade later. The participants vividly described scenes in Manchuria that are hauntingly familiar to anyone familiar with the fighting on the Western Front:

> Rifles cracked, machine-guns spluttered, guns boomed and boomed again and the air was turned into an inferno of shrieking missiles. The rays of the searchlights flashed up and down, rockets shot into the sky like enormous fiery snakes and burst, hundreds of large brilliant balls, eclipsing the light of the eternal stars and blinding the heroic little infantrymen who were attacking us.... It was hardly a fight between men that was taking place on this accursed spot; it was the struggle of human flesh against iron and steel, against blazing petroleum, lyddite, pyroxyline, and melinite, and the stench of rotting corpses.[32]

Ashmead Bartlett reported that "[t]here were practically no bodies intact; the hillside was carpeted with odd limbs, skulls, pieces of flesh, and the shapeless trunks of what had once been human beings, intermingled with pieces of shells, broken rifles, twisted bayonets, grenades, and masses of rock loosed from the surface by the explosions."[33]

---

[30] "Changes and Tendencies in the Russian Army Since the War against Japan," *Journal of the Royal United Services Institute*, 1910, p. 1176.
[31] "Infantry Combat in the Russo-Japanese War," p. 1052.
[32] E. K. Nojine, *The Truth about Port Arthur* (London, 1908), pp. 183–4, 252.
[33] E. A. Bartlett, *The Siege and Capitulation* (London, 1906), p. 330.

A recurrent theme in these accounts was the vulnerability and virtual isolation of individual soldiers beset by the technology of war. Not surprisingly, pre-1914 concerns for the maintenance of morale and sustaining *esprit de corps* assumed fresh urgency, with many stressing the moral and psychological qualities needed to win, while they criticized Bloch for ignoring the human spirit.

A Colonel Maude stressed that casualties and suffering were inevitable and that victory would go to whomever had the fortitude to bear them, a view endorsed by Major General Douglas Haig in 1907. By 1913, most accepted that casualties in the next war would be heavy and believed moral qualities would determine the outcome. Major General W. G. Knox predicted that a small British Expeditionary Force would lose 60,000 men in the first month.[34] In *The Principles of War* of 1914, Major General Altham spoke of "punishing losses," while Brigadier General Haking stressed willpower and the offensive spirit to overcome man's weak inner nature: "The little devil inside." But where were armies to find such stalwart human material?

The Russo-Japanese War had reinforced fears that the urban proletariat lacked the moral fiber for such a challenge. Demands grew for remedial action. There were calls for greater discipline and *esprit de corps*. Some took a broader view and stressed the need to "improve" the individual in a "Social-Darwinian" sense. In time, military pundits would apply this imperative to struggle and overcome as applicable to the whole of society as well as to the individual. Not only could the nation create a more advanced, better-trained, and enthusiastic soldier, but a new and invigorated society would result.

THE JAPANESE TRIUMPH: THE STRATEGIC LESSONS

If Bloch believed modern war would bring about the collapse of societies, the Russo-Japanese War convinced many that war was now an evolutionary struggle between cultures and races rather than merely an extension of policy. European ascendancy was not necessarily the "natural condition." Increasingly, strategic analysts regarded war as a normal, "natural," and in a sense necessary biological process that applied as much to the "organism" of human society as to man himself.[35] National morale and spirit were vital for success, and thus wars were contests of national and cultural vigor. This was to find its most overt and dark expression in the Third Reich.

The belief that the Russo-Japanese War had proved the martial spirit supreme caused expressions of concern in many nations over the quality

---

[34] Knox, *The Flaw in Our Armour*, p. 22.
[35] Shortly before the First World War, Bernhardi declared that war was "a necessity on which the further development of our people depends as a civilized nation ... we must rely on the sword." F. von Bernhardi, *On War Today*, vol. 1 (London, 1912), pp. 6–11.

of the human material available. President Theodore Roosevelt maintained that "[t]he nation which abandons itself to an existence of ease and looks upon war with horror, rots away without advancing. It is destined to decline and become a slave of other nations which have not lost the virile qualities."[36]

Evolutionary science and mysticism became entwined in attempts to describe the decline of Western societies. General de Negrier, Inspector General of the French Army and an observer of the war, spoke despairingly of France's apparent degeneracy. He urged the nation to work "towards our complete state of perfection," exerting itself

> so that our descendants may reach an intellectual and moral standard superior to our own. It is thus that races of warriors and brave men develop themselves. The Japanese are giving us at the present moment an example of this.... Life is an accident which death atones for.... To the force which this moral develops must be added that intense gratification, that under all trying conditions, no matter what a man's social condition may be, he will have no feeling of fear. It is for the man a sure source of consolation, of which decadent nations have deprived themselves, because the materialism in which they wallow necessarily destroys noble sentiments by the degradation of character.[37]

He maintained that races became pusillanimous when education destroyed patriotism and that nature ruthlessly punishes cowards: "Conquered and dismembered they disappear from the scenes of the world. It is the immutable justice of things." Decadent humanitarian theories purveyed by university professors and schoolmasters, imbued with notions of peace, humanity and fraternalism, would only result in Frenchmen becoming "timid poltroons."

A Russian General Staff Paper appearing in *Razviedchik* on August 3, 1909 maintained that

> War is no longer a duel between armies, but a life and death struggle between nations. Nothing short of paralysing the whole life of a country (to such an extent that any prolongation of it implies national death) constitutes final victory.... We have nothing to fear from an enemy – only our own lack of spirit. War is at hand....

Fear about the degeneracy of modern urban populations was widespread in Germany before 1914. Colonel Wilhelm Balck maintained that

> [t]he steadily improving standards of living tend to increase the instinct of self-preservation and to diminish the spirit of self-sacrifice.... The manner of fast

---

[36] De Negrier, "The Morale of Troops," *Journal of the Royal United Services Institute*, 1905, p. 1428.

[37] Ibid., p. 1429.

living at the present day undermines the nervous system...the physical powers of the human species are also partly diminishing.[38]

There was concern in some quarters in Britain about the fitness of the nation to bear its necessary martial burdens. In *The United Services Magazine* of June 1904, Captain Bellairs described the British nation as being "in a wild debauch of so-called freedom. It is time to call a halt...to inculcate discipline." Sir Alexander Bannerman noted in 1910 that "[w]ith all the old restraints removed, the nation must either have a new discipline or go to pieces. It is universal discipline which has brought Japan to her present pitch of efficiency."[39] A report of Sir Frederick Treves, who visited Japanese hospitals during the war, astonished many and worried some. He witnessed surgery performed without anesthetic on impassive patients. One Japanese surgeon told Treves that "[o]ur men do not always require chloroform or any anaesthetic; it is not necessary to use it with our men like it is with you whitemen."[40]

One practical method of producing a disciplined fighting force was to initiate youth training. Many in Britain saw General Baden-Powell's Boy Scout movement as a means for rebuilding national discipline and morale. In 1910, Colonel J. H. Rossiter, a retired officer working for a Schools Union, responded to Baden-Powell's call for volunteers to recruit for "the modern Bushido or Boy Scout movement....permeating itself over the whole country."[41]

LESSONS IDENTIFIED BUT NOT LEARNED

The direct lessons for a future war seemed clear: Infantry weapons and indirect artillery fire in defense would dominate the offense, especially when protected by trenches and wire. Frontal assaults by infantry in traditional phalanxes would lead to catastrophic losses for any army on the attack. There would probably be a stalemate between forces in field fortifications in close proximity to each other. Modern industrial war would be extremely gruesome. Why then did all armies in Europe plan for a quick war based on infantry maneuver, supported by artillery firing directly not indirectly, confident that victory was more the product of high morale than some new all-arms method supported by modern technology?

---

[38] Wilhelm Balck, *Tactics*, vol. 1 (Fort Leavenworth, KS, 1911), p. 194.
[39] Sir Alexander Bannerman, "The Creation of the Japanese National Spirit," *Journal of the Royal United Services Institute*, 1910, p. 709.
[40] W. Kirton, "With the Japanese on the Yalu," *Journal of the Royal United Services Institute*, 1905, p. 282.
[41] Bannerman, "The Creation of the Japanese National Spirit," p. 713.

The Russo-Japanese War became the most important subject of study in military institutions around the world, just as had the American Civil War forty years earlier. Most military experts recognized that its lessons would shape the future of warfare. The official histories of the major powers were translated into English, as were the reports of most foreign observers. More than twenty British officers observed the war from the Japanese side and four from the Russian.

Yet, within months, the First World War proved to be startlingly different from what the prevailing doctrines anticipated. Ironically, its conditions almost exactly mirrored what many observers of the Russo-Japanese War had foreseen. The power of defense dominated the battlefields of the first three years of the First World War, largely because little had been done to structure and equip forces and devise tactics to make it otherwise, despite the lessons of 1904–5 in Manchuria.

The weight of evidence had supported an approach emphasizing firepower and thorough all-arms planning in both the offensive and the defensive – what General Monash would later call "engineering." Instead, there prevailed a counterproductive belief in maneuver and élan in the attack with inadequate firepower and reliance in the final analysis on moral factors. What were the reasons for this failure to learn from recent experience (i.e., military history)?

"Bottom Up" Lessons Identified

Identifying lessons and teaching them is not enough. Authority and power are essential for learning and implementation. Despite the urging of many observers for radical reform, orthodox views prevailed and doctrinal regression almost immediately set in. By 1910, European armies were already fundamentally distorting the lessons of 1905, with predictable results in 1914. Advice to the War Office was plentiful, but acting on it was another matter. General Sir Aylmer Haldane later wrote bitterly of the unwillingness of the Army's hierarchy to take note of the suggestions that he and other observers of the war had put forward. The British Army Staff College Library contained shelves of such documents, but the British Army, like others, did not prove apt at learning from reports.

Armies need visions of how war will develop and how they can shape that development in the face of changing technological, strategic, and social factors. Speculations supported by unpopular evidence can face fearful and understandable inertia in the dead weight of existing structures and sunk-cost investments. Even in those cases where the intellectual case is won, actions taken in the field often bear little resemblance to what doctrine professes. This inaction owes more to human nature than culpable inefficiency, and for that reason there are inherent dangers when judging military failings, which one may not be able necessarily to remedy merely by more assiduous and competent staff work.

One lesson of 1904–5 was the frequency with which different observers could view an event and come to totally different conclusions. Partisans of particular doctrinal approaches tended to find what they wanted to suit their own arguments. Lessons were fragmented and often considered in isolation. Most of the military organizations refused to acknowledge consistent patterns that might challenge the prevailing orthodoxies of maneuver and élan.

Thus, European militaries were able to discard many substantive lessons for what seemed the necessary and greater good. Another problem was the fear of being too radical and the inclination to dilute conclusions with reassuring caveats such as "Too often are we told that some new invention 'will completely revolutionize warfare.'"[42] Sadly, on this occasion, radicals were proven correct. Although some, mainly gunners and sappers, saw the inevitability of trench warfare and the dominance of artillery in a future European war, others insisted that the Japanese had won because their moral qualities had overcome physical obstacles. By 1914, military organizations had carefully culled the lessons of the Russo-Japanese War to achieve the precise opposite of what they more obviously should have deduced.

The Real Lessons

After the Russo-Japanese War, many officers were eager to seize on new ideas and their consequences. The fora for debate on innovations were the military journals. The general view of the authors was that, in the new circumstances, there was a pressing need for more howitzers, machine guns, mortars, hand grenades, mines, and barbed wire. Unfortunately, such lessons generally remained no more than the ideas of those junior officers with the time to write articles.

In Britain, Captain C. E. P. Sankey, an officer of the Royal Engineers, wrote in 1907, "May we not expect that future sieges and battles will be reckoned in weeks and will in fact be indistinguishable?" He predicted that in a European war, unless one side blundered badly, both would entrench and all attacks would be frontal attacks. "[E]ach army will then practically become the garrison of an enormous extended fortress."[43]

The main concern of such "reformers" was how ground forces could reach and overrun enemy trenches, which would feature prominently in future combat, without overwhelming losses. Captain Rogers of the Royal

[42] K. Neilson, "'That Dangerous and Difficult Enterprise:' Thinking and the Russo-Japanese War," *War and Society*, vol. 9, no. 2, 1991, p. 27.

[43] C. E. P. Sankey, "The Campaign of the Future. A Possible Development," *Royal Engineers Journal*, no. 5, 1907, pp. 4–6.

Engineers believed engineers would have to take on the old role of artillery
in preparing a path for final assaults.[44] Major H. S. Jeudwine won the Royal
Artillery Institute's Duncan Prize of 1907 with his paper suggesting that long-
range heavy guns were essential for enfilading the lines of trenches that European armies would inevitably have to construct. He won again the following
year with his discussion of the problem, illustrated in the Russo-Japanese
War, of the casualties from friendly artillery fire that would be incurred, if
attacking infantry were to receive close support right up to enemy trenches.
Second place in the Duncan Competition went to Major C. C. Robertson,
who warned that, "[I]f we do not accept the lessons of the Russo-Japanese
War exactly as if it had been our own campaign we shall make mistakes in
the next war which it is most necessary to avoid."[45]

Captain E. D. Swinton, who was later to play a major role in the development of the tank, looked at the threat that artillery would pose to defended
trench lines and suggested the requirement to site the latter on secondary
crests or even reverse slopes.[46] Troops attacking an entrenched position
would themselves have to attack from protected trenches of their own, probably in three lines – a vision that would not become a reality for most of the
armies on the Western Front until after two years of killing. Another engineer, Captain J. E. E. Craster noted that, "The system of attack which has
been described will involve an appalling amount of spade work ... however,
it seems to be the only feasible method of carrying out the attack."[47]

Others were similarly prescient. Major J. M. Home observed:

> The great impression made on me by all I saw is that artillery is now the decisive
> arm and that all other arms are auxiliary to it. The importance of artillery
> cannot be too strongly insisted upon, for, other things being equal, the side
> which has the best artillery will always win.... It seems almost a question for
> deliberate consideration whether artillery should not be largely increased even
> at the expense of other arms. Infantry can, if necessary, be trained in about
> three months, whereas artillery cannot be so improvised ... Infantry fire cannot
> usefully be employed at ranges beyond 600 yards, as beyond that distance the
> hostile guns ought to be able to prevent infantry using their rifles.[48]

In a piece in the *Journal of the Royal United Services Institute* of November
1914, written at the beginning of that year, Captain J. F. C. Fuller discussed

[44] E. Rogers, "Siege Warfare," *Royal Engineers Journal*, no. 17, 1913, p. 283.
[45] P. A. Towle, "The Russo-Japanese War and British Military Thought," *Journal of the Royal United Services Institute*, 1971, p. 65.
[46] Between 1906 and 1914, Lieutenant Colonel Swinton wrote twenty stories in popular magazines on military developments. He was himself influenced by H.G. Wells's *Land Ironclads* of 1903.
[47] J. E. E. Craster, "Attack on Entrenched Positions," *Journal of the Royal United Servises Institute*, 1906, p. 342.
[48] *The Russo-Japanese War, Reports from British Officers*, vol. 3 (London, 1908), pp. 209–10.

the offensive penetration, citing artillery and machine guns as the decisive means to open up the defense for the assaulting infantry.

Lessons from the Top Down

The lessons identified by observers and discussed in the journals by junior officers did not match the strategic imperatives of the day mandated by their senior officers. This was true across Europe because there was a near consensus that a coming war would be short and won by rapid maneuver. Senior officers deemed the increasing firepower available to the infantry and particularly the artillery to make this more rather than less likely. In any event, they believed firepower would be less significant in the coming struggle than high morale. Moreover, to support such erroneous contentions, those in authority selectively pillaged the data gathered by observers. Where the reports of observers proved too awkward, senior officers declared the war of 1904–5 to be a special Asian case, not applicable to Europe.

Thus, the process of constructive analysis went disastrously astray. National politics and strategy, rather than unwelcome tactical "lessons learned" in Manchuria, proved decisive as 1914 approached. Armies obsessed with "*élan vital et pantalons rouges*," morale and shock, paid scant attention to the "firepower school." Their emphasis was less on how technology might change the next war, than on how new technology might permit a return to the old ways.[49]

Asserting the high cost of change was one method of avoiding military reform. Field Marshal Lord Roberts became commander in chief of the British Army after the Boer War and planned to reequip the army with new field and heavy guns, as well as a new infantry rifle to replace the cavalry lance. He also introduced the most progressive infantry tactics manual of the day. Unfortunately, he resigned before his reforms were complete. Rebuilding the Army along the lines advocated by the "firepower" enthusiasts would have proven prohibitively expensive, at least as far as the government of the day was concerned. A doctrine emphasizing lighter, more mobile forces and human qualities rather than costly technology was much more attractive.

But there were larger problems than simply cost in the way of reform. The practical, informed, and prescient thinking of many junior commentators was far removed from the reality of the debate in the corridors of power, where institutional obstruction and vested interest predominated. The failure to reform the cavalry was a case in point. In France, De Negrier believed the cavalry should use horses primarily for mobility – dismounting for action to sweep away the enemy with firearms, not sabres and lances. He argued

---

[49]   S. Marble, "Royal Artillery Doctrine, 1902–1914," *War Studies Journal*, Autumn 1996, pp. 89–106.

that "[f]or the old school, to place foot to the ground is to lose caste; it sees in equitation an object while it is only a means; and this accounts for its devotion to races, horse-shows, tournaments and its contempt for the fire-arm."[50]

The Germans were in no better shape. General von Bernhardi noted in 1912 that the rifle should be the cavalry's primary weapon. Nevertheless, "[t]he cavalry looks now... upon a charge in battle as its paramount duty; it has almost deliberately closed its eyes against the far-reaching changes in warfare. By this it has *itself* barred the way that leads to greater success."[51] There was also resistance to change in Japan even after the First World War. Major General Yoshibashi was so aghast at the cavalry training manual of 1920, which abandoned the massed cavalry charge, that he disemboweled himself.[52]

In Britain, the traditionalists soon reintroduced the lance, and the British Cavalry Manual of 1907 noted that "it must be accepted as a principle that the rifle, effective as it is, cannot replace the effect produced by the speed of the horse, the magnetism of the charge, and the terror of cold steel." Douglas Haig believed that the "moral(e) of cavalry will be injured by dismounted training" and would not accept that the sword and lance should be an adjunct of the rifle. In 1910, Erskine Childers called for the replacement of the cavalry by mounted infantry, but some suggested that cavalry was the arm best suited for driving infantry from entrenched positions.[53] Sir Ian Hamilton, a supporter of Robert's work, recalled that "the cavalry has been riding rough-shod over infantry who, with their spades and their rifles existed only on sufferance.... I felt so badly over the waste of men and horseflesh and money going into the Army that was being starved of big guns and machine-guns."[54]

Not surprisingly, cultural inertia in the field artillery was equally damaging. Indirect fire was still considered too technical, unsporting, bad for morale, and impractical in mobile warfare. Nor did the armies of Europe take any steps toward creating a powerful force of artillery at divisional or corps level, or to centralize the command of guns.

THE LOGIC DEFICITS: WHY?

A Short Account of the Russo-Japanese War for Examination Purposes of 1925 systematically addressed many aspects of the war. At the end of each

[50] De Negrier, "Some Lessons of the Russo-Japanese War," p. 916.
[51] Bernhardi, *On War Today*, p. 192.
[52] Nish, *The Origins of the Russo-Japanese War*, p. 243.
[53] Neilson, "'That Dangerous and Difficult Enterprise:' British Military Thinking and the Russo-Japanese War," pp. 23–4.
[54] Towle, "The Russo-Japanese War and British Military Thought," p. 67.

chapter, it measured these against the principles of war. Surprisingly, or per-haps sensitively, it made no comparisons with the First World War, of which all its students would have had personal experience; nor did it seek to learn from the failure prior to 1914 to apply so many of the lessons candidates were now required to study. It seems almost as if its aim was to wipe away the experience of the First World War with dry statements of principle. There seemed to be a gulf between the academic statement of lessons and the ability to change a style of waging war.

Perhaps a more cynical view might be that the lessons of firepower became as unwelcome to the emerging maneuver orthodoxy of 1925 as they had been prior to 1914. A similar volume for Staff College exam candidates was produced in 1926 with questions and notes for answers. It also dealt with the Russo-Japanese War in virtual detachment from the experience of the Great War.[55] The Official History of the Great War had yet to be written, and clearly no marks were to be awarded for risking interpretations of the searing experiences of the Western Front without official guidance, even eight years after the event. The Army had yet to publish the lessons learned from the First World War because none of its components had even addressed the lessons of that conflict. In fact, the *Kirke Report,* the first examination of the Great War, produced at the direction of the CIGS, Field Marshal Lord Milne, was promptly "buried."

In the decade prior to 1914, many believed that the answer to the mili-tary problems of the day lay in manipulating human nature, rather than in understanding and addressing the emerging technologies and tactical possi-bilities of war. By 1910, Sir Ian Hamilton had adopted a semimystical view of fighting spirit, despite his own experience of the Russo-Japanese War. He argued that human will could overcome wire and fireswept zones. He was to discover at Gallipoli that this theory was incomplete. Some believed one could communicate the spiritual through "thought waves." In a vision that seems less fantastic today than it probably did at the time, Colonel Maude predicted the day of the "automatic regiment," in which the commander would be the sender of "waves" and each private would be a "Marconi receiver," with an *esprit de corps* impervious to suffering.[56]

Ironically, it was the recognition of the technological realities of modern war, described by Bloch and manifested in the Russo-Japanese War, that caused armies to seek desperate, alternative, nontechnological remedies in the form of discipline, fortitude, moral strength, and *esprit de corps.* The consequences of this proved disastrous in 1914, and it would take three

---

[55] P. W., *Outline History of the Russo-Japanese War, 1904 up to the Battle of Liao-Yang* (London, 1924).

[56] T. H. E. Travers, "Technology, Tactics, and Morale: Jean de Bloch, the Boer War, and British Military Theory, 1900–1914," *Journal of Modern History,* no. 51, June 1979, p. 283.

years for armies to catch up with the harsh tactical and technological realities. But they would do so only after soldiers had demonstrated at enormous cost the very qualities of fortitude of which many had believed them
incapable.

Once the enormity of the failure to learn the lessons of the Russo-Japanese
War became clear, many looked to shore up their reputations by rewriting
their own versions of events with unashamedly self-serving delusion. On
April 3, 1906, Lieutenant General Sir John French, a student of the 1904–5
conflict, declared wisely enough that "[w]e shall have battles lasting for several days, troops probably perfectly stationary, and firing at one another in
the hours of daylight, whilst all movements in the attack, whether infantry,
or artillery, and all entrenching, whether in attack or defence, will have to be
done under cover of darkness." In this at least, French was essentially correct. Despite these comments, writing on December 10, 1914, he expressed
surprise "that modern weapons and conditions have completely revolutionized war. It is quite different to anything which you and I have known. A
battle is a siege on one side and a fortress on the other, but on a gigantic
scale."[57]

Any officer with his extensive knowledge of the Russo-Japanese War
should have believed his views confirmed rather than voiced surprise.
French's disingenuous and convenient change of opinion from that expressed
in 1906 included the assertion that, "[n]o previous experience, no conclusion . . . or study of the new conditions of war . . . had led me to anticipate a
war of positions."[58] He then expressed apparent bemusement at the effects of
modern weapons: "had we realized the true effects of the modern appliances
of war in August 1914, there would have been no retreat from Mons."[59]

In his introduction to *A Short Account of the Russo-Japanese War for
Examination Purposes* of 1925, General Sir Horace Smith-Dorrien wrote: "It
was a great war, and bristled with lessons. . . . So valuable did I consider them
that, from the conclusion of the War to the date I gave up command of the
4th (Quetta) Division in 1907, I based much of my training on them."[60] He
noted that the Russo-Japanese War had taught the lessons of trench warfare,
the power of the rifle, and the value of hand grenades and concealment. He
made no mention of the lessons learned about machine guns, the perils of
frontal assaults on prepared positions, the decisive power of artillery, or why
the army had not fully incorporated these lessons into its doctrine before
1914. Sir Ian Hamilton proved to be one of the most astute observers of the

---

[57] Towle, "The Russo-Japanese War and British Military Thought," p. 64.
[58] Field Marshal Sir John French, *1914* (London, 1919), p. 11.
[59] Ibid., p. 12.
[60] Footslogger, *A Short History of the Russo–Japanese War for Examination Purposes* (London, 1925), p. v.

Russo-Japanese War, but this did not equip him for success when his turn came to command at Gallipoli in 1915.

The Long-Term Strategic Implications

Ironically, observers, military as well as civilian, saw the long-term strategic implications of the war more clearly than they did either the short- or midterm possibilities. Much of the debate about the Russo-Japanese War being essentially a clash of civilizations seems remarkably modern. If 1905 marked the waning of the West in Asia, it also marked the waxing of the Asians themselves. Fuller regarded the Russo-Japanese War as one of the great turning points in Western history because "[i]t was not merely a trial of strength between an Asiatic and a semi-European power, but above all it was a challenge to Western supremacy in Asia.... The fall of Port Arthur in 1905, like the fall of Constantinople in 1453, rightly may be numbered among the few really great events of history."[61]

The Times of London of February 6, 1904 noted of the war that "[i]t is really the contest of two civilisations, and in this lies, perhaps, its profoundest interest to the observer." The German *National Zeitung* of May 31, 1905 warned that the Russian defeat "must cause grave anxiety to all those who believe in the great commercial and civilizing mission of the white race throughout the world."[62] T. Miller Maguire foresaw that Japan's victory, like Britain's after Trafalgar, was more the beginning of a process than the end of one: "The ambitions of the Japanese are not yet satisfied. But by the shores of the Pacific they find enormous fields for commercial expansion, and to the unoccupied lands of South America and Australia, panting for want of development and labour, they turn their longing eyes." Miller Maguire had correctly identified the strategic dynamics of the next forty years, while many others were contemplating merely the tactics of the next ten.

The Japanese victory in 1905 served to exacerbate fears not only of Asia in general, but also of China in particular. General Alexei Kuropatkin, who became administrator of Central Asia after the Russo-Japanese War, warned in 1916 of the emergence of China as the real threat to Russia: "As for China, the danger menacing Russia in the future from that empire of 400,000,000 people is not to be doubted." In 1910, Jack London's *The Unparalleled Invasion* speculated that the new power of Japan would fade, but not before China, "a kindred race," had learned from it the skills of the West. By 1976, China would rise to economic dominance and threaten the West in a

---

[61] J. F. C. Fuller, *The Decisive Battles of the Western World*, vol. 3 (London, 1963), pp. 142 and 170.
[62] Wilson and Wells, *The Russo-Japanese War in Cultural Perspective*, p. 14.

challenge that could only be met by a united assault by Western nations, led by the United States. His tale posited Western victory through the use of air-delivered biological weapons, in an "ultra-modern war" – "the war of the scientist and the laboratory," in the aftermath of which "[a]ll (Chinese) survivors were put to death."[63]

The Corrupting Influence of Emotion

Emotion often corrupts thought. It can cause analysis to veer from one extreme to another. In the 1904 case, erroneous cultural and racial stereotyping distorted lessons that should have been learned and prevented serious balanced assessments. For example, when Britain's ally, Japan, defeated Russia in 1905, many regarded the Japanese as "plucky" and examples of Darwinian forces at work in a dynamic society, the secrets of which should be discovered and applied. President Theodore Roosevelt called the Japanese surprise torpedo attack on the Russian Pacific fleet "a bold initiative" and referred to "gallant little Japs."[64] Of the Japanese victory at Tsushima, he enthused "[t]his is the greatest phenomenon the world has ever seen...I could not believe it...as reports came, I grew so excited that I myself became almost like a Japanese, and I could not attend to official duties."[65]

From overestimating the "racial" and cultural characteristics of the Japanese after 1905, Westerners suffered from underestimating the qualities of the Japanese once they became potential enemies in the 1930s. The complacency and scorn with which British commanders described the Japanese had the ominous ring of Russian attitudes in 1904.[66] They portrayed the Japanese as myopic, racial delinquents, whom Western forces could readily defeat. When General Percival awakened Sir Shelton Thomas, Governor of Singapore, and told him that the Japanese had landed in Malaya, Thomas replied "I trust that you'll chase the little men off." In April 1941, the British military attaché in Tokyo, Colonel G. T. Wards, lectured the Singapore garrison on the outstanding military qualities of the Japanese. The commander in Singapore, General Bond, countered the lecturer with the reassurance to his men that "What the lecturer has told you is his own opinion and is in no way a correct appreciation of the situation....I do not think much

---

[63] Quoted in I. F. Clarke, *The Tale of the Next Great War, 1871–1914* (Syracuse, NY, 1995), pp. 269–70.

[64] Storry, *Japan and the Decline of the West in Asia*, p. 63.

[65] Quoted in Wilson and Wells, *The Russo-Japanese War in Cultural Perspective*, p. 23.

[66] In 1935, the British naval attaché in Tokyo informed the Admiralty that the Japanese "have peculiarly slow brains." Thorne, *The Issue of War*, p. 4. The British commander in the Far East, visiting Hong Kong in 1940, described the Japanese across the border as "various sub-human species dressed in dirty grey uniform." Queen Wilhelmina of the Netherlands looked for the defeat of Germany before turning to the Japanese who should then be "drowned like rats." Also quoted in Thorne, *The Issue of War*, pp. 18–19.

of them and you can take it from me that we have nothing to fear from them."

In the event, the Japanese proved formidable soldiers, just as they had thirty-six years earlier. After the fall of Singapore, British commanders regarded the Japanese as "jungle super-men," an image that did much to undermine the morale of Allied soldiers. Stunning Japanese victories in 1941 and 1942 resulted in another radical and unbalanced shift in Western perceptions. There were expressions of admiration for the Japanese, empha- sizing the "spiritual" element. John Masters noted that, "They believed in something, and were willing to die for it, for any smallest detail that would help them achieve it. What else is bravery? ... They came on using their skill and rage, until they were stopped by death."[67] Such positive Western per- ceptions mirrored those of 1905, and caused alarm in Allied governments, which countered vigorously with their own propaganda.

CONCLUSION

The Austro-Hungarian Chief of Staff in the First World War, Conrad von Hoetzendorf, noted that "[a] general is always right, especially when he is wrong." Those concerned about the judgment of history should take care to write the lessons themselves. Hitler observed that "[h]istory shall be kind to us, for we shall write the history." He was wrong, of course, because his enemies wrote the history.

The Royal Artillery failed to adopt indirect fire as its preferred method of fire prior to 1914, despite overwhelming evidence before and during the Russo-Japanese War that it was essential. Colonel John Headlam played a key role in preventing its adoption. On August 26, 1914, Brigadier General Headlam, commanding the artillery of 5th Division, deployed five brigades of guns in exposed positions at Le Cateau, between 50 and 200 meters from the infantry's front line. Two battery commanders who believed their posi- tions untenable moved their guns to covered positions. Headlam immediately ordered them to return to their forward position. When the battle began, British artillery was unable to engage German artillery, much of which lay in concealed positions 3,500 to 5,000 meters away. After eight hours of bom- bardment, the British had lost the battle and Headham had seen twenty-seven of his forty-two guns captured. The *History of the Royal Artillery* covering the period 1860–1914 does not examine the reasons for the failure to adopt indirect fire before 1914. It merely notes that prior to 1914, indirect fire was impractical. The author of the history was Major General John Headlam.

Liddell Hart noted that, "If the study of war in the past has so often proved fallible as a guide to the course of the next war, it implies not

[67] J. Masters, *The Road Past* (London, 2002), p. 163.

that war is unsuited to scientific study but the study has not been scientific enough in spirit and method."[68] Those who pass judgment today on the flawed attempts of the belligerents and contemporary students of the Russo-Japanese War to understand the significance of what had happened should exercise cautious humility. It falls to them to make equally important assessments about the significance of major advances in military technology and its strategic implications for their own time.

What did the military analysts of 1905 need, just as we today need? Objective data, visionaries with imagination to project ideas into the future, the ownership not the corruption of lessons by those in power, the will and resources to implement change, to recognize evidence as ephemeral and not the basis of dogma and to resist templates, but to use lessons to develop a Clausewitzian "educated judgment," to make better decisions subsequently in novel circumstances. That after all is the true value of military history to the military profession.

---

[68] Quoted in R. M. Connaughton, *The War of the Rising Sun and Tumbling Bear: A History of the Russo-Japanese War, 1904–5* (London, 1988), p. 275.

12

Obstacles to innovation and readiness: the British Army's experience 1918–1939

J. PAUL HARRIS

Less than twenty-one years separated the Armistice of November 1918 from the British Army's renewed commitment to a continental war in September 1939. Until 1931, the British Army could reasonably claim leadership in crucial areas of military theory and practice – most notably, in mechanization and in the development, organization, and employment of armored forces.[1] After 1933, however, the British General Staff looked with an increasing fascination at the burgeoning power and skill of the German Army. For reasons to a certain extent beyond its control, it was unable to make an adequate response. By 1935, Britain's lead in the development of armored forces had clearly been lost.[2] Desperately weak and unready in 1939, the British Army's performance for much of the Second World War was distinctly poor.[3]

For much of the First World War, too, the British Army had struggled to bring itself up to the standards of competence of the French, much less the Germans.[4] (The latter were undoubtedly the most efficient in the world until near the end of that conflict.) But British difficulties in achieving such standards are hardly surprising. The little army fielded in August 1914 was by no means a "contemptible force." It was at least the qualitative equal of its

---

[1] Robert Larson, *The British Army and the Theory of Armored Warfare, 1918–1940* (Newark, 1984), p. 132.

[2] The first three German panzer divisions were established in 1935. At that time, the British still did not have a single armored division. Richard Ogorkiewicz, *Armour: The Development of Mechanized Forces and Their Equipment* (London, 1960), pp. 159 and 211.

[3] David French, *Raising Churchill's Army: The British Army and the War Against Germany 1919–1945* (Oxford, 2000), p. 1. French goes on to give the most balanced and scholarly appraisal currently available of the British Army during the war against Hitler.

[4] As late as December 1917, the balance of opinion in the German high command was that the French Army was a far more skillful and effective opponent than the British. Martin Kitchen, *The German Offensives of 1918* (Stroud, 2001), p. 28.

vastly larger continental contemporaries. By year's end, however, the intense fighting had destroyed much of it. Lacking a system of peacetime short-service conscription that was general among the Continental great powers, the British had to improvise a mass army in the middle of major war from autumn 1914 onward.[5]

The British Expeditionary Force undoubtedly proved the German Army's most dangerous and destructive opponent in the last hundred days of the war.[6] But attaining that level of competence took years and enormous cost. While the British were improvising their own mass army, the burden of the land fighting for the Allies fell massively and devastatingly on the French. The latter came close to breaking under the strain.[7] Perhaps the most obvious lesson learned from this was that if Great Britain wished ever again to participate fully in warfare on the Continent, it required peacetime, short-service conscription on the Continental model. Yet this issue, very much a live one before 1914 and again after 1945, scarcely raised its head in the period immediately after World War I.[8] National mood obviously had much to do with the rejection of compulsory military service. Most could not get out of uniform fast enough, and there was a deep desire to return to a prewar normality that had not included military service for the bulk of the population.[9] The government had sold the war as one to end all wars, and with the defeat and disarmament of Germany, there was no obvious military threat. Massively in debt and financially fragile, moreover, Britain had an urgent need for retrenchment in defense spending. A larger peacetime army, however organized, simply was not on the national agenda. In the postwar period, massive economies were the order of the day. The Treasury's notorious Ten-Year Rule eventually formalized a policy of financial stringency for the armed forces. Stipulating for the purposes of defense estimates that there would be no major war for ten years, the government abandoned the policy only in 1932 after the Japanese invasion of Manchuria.[10]

Over considerable tracts of the globe, the war to end all wars led to increased chaos, confusion, and violence. In addition to the continuing civil

---

[5]   Peter Simkins, "The Four Armies 1914–18," in David Chandler and Ian Beckett, eds., *The Oxford History of the British Army* (Oxford, 1994), pp. 240–55.

[6]   J. P. Harris, *Amiens to the Armistice: The BEF in the Hundred Days Campaign, 8 August–11 November 1918* (London, 1998), pp. 291, 202, and passim.

[7]   Anthony Clayton, *Paths of Glory: The French Army 1914–18* (London, 2003), pp. 124–64.

[8]   A National Service League led by Lord Roberts had vociferously, although unsuccessfully, campaigned for conscription before 1914. Edward Spiers, "The Late Victorian Army 1868–1914," in Chandler and Beckett, eds., *The Oxford History of the British Army*, p. 225.

[9]   There were some mutinies by troops who believed they were not being demobilized quickly enough. For details of some such troubles, see Julian Putkowski, *British Army Mutineers 1914–1922* (London, 1998), pp. 31–9.

[10] G. C. Peden, *British Rearmament and the Treasury 1932–1939* (Edinburgh, 1979), pp. 6–8.

war in Russia, which involved considerable numbers of British, 1919 saw small wars in Afghanistan and Ireland, serious disturbances in India, and dissident violence in recently conquered Iraq followed by full-scale rebellion the following year.[11] Nor was stability quickly restored. The drastically downsized British Army remained exceptionally busy during the 1920s. A General Staff paper of 1927 on the Army's strength in relation to its role described it as stretched to breaking point.[12] Doubtless there was some dramatization for the Treasury's benefit, but the sense of crisis seems to have been real enough. In these years, the Army remained occupied with a type of soldiering (essentially small wars and imperial policing) familiar to its Victorian and Edwardian predecessors. Nevertheless, such tasks had little or no connection with the mass Continental warfare of 1914–18. It is perhaps hardly surprising, in these circumstances, that even some highly intelligent officers regarded the whole Western Front experience as an aberration of dubious relevance to the Army's present and future tasks.[13]

Such an attitude was by no means universal and, except in the brief period of optimism following the 1925 Locarno treaty (roughly 1926–32), it was not endorsed at the top. General Staff policy was that the Army should train and equip, as far as budgets permitted, to fight a first class enemy – the army of a European great power. Throughout the interwar period, the General Staff remained deeply suspicious of Germany. In early 1925, Lord Cavan, then Chief of the Imperial General Staff (CIGS), told the Committee of Imperial Defence that his organization regarded the Germans as a "primitive people, scientifically equipped, combining the height of modern efficiency with the mentality and brutality of the Middle Ages." In the mid-1920s, the General Staff insisted that Britain's real frontier was no longer at the Channel but on the Rhine, its national security inextricably linked to that of Belgium and France. It favored a defense pact with those countries and did not believe that Britain could limit its liability to fight in their defence. The General Staff welcomed the climate of reconciliation that led to Locarno and hoped the Germans would become civilized members of the international community. But it still believed they needed careful watching. "Germany's conversion must be begun under discipline and in the knowledge that the

---

[11] For Afghanistan, see T. A. Heathcote, *The British Military in India: The Development of British Land Forces in South Asia 1600–1947* (Manchester, 1995), p. 233; for Ireland, see R. F. Foster, *Modern Ireland 1600–1972* (London, 1988), pp. 494–502; for India, see Heathcote, *The British Military in India*, pp. 232–233, and Percy Sykes, *A History of Afghanistan*, vol. 2 (London, 1940), pp. 271–282; and for Iraq, see Lt. Col. Sir Arnold T. Wilson, *Mesopotamia 1917–1920: A Clash of Loyalties* (Oxford, 1931), pp. 123–233. Philip W. Ireland, *Iraq, A Study in Political Development* (London, 1937), pp. 266–76.

[12] PRO WO 32/2823, "The Present Distribution and Strength of the British Army in Relation to Its Duties."

[13] Brian Bond, "The Army Between the Two World Wars 1918–1939," in Chandler and Beckett eds., *The Oxford History of the British Army*, p. 257.

first class Powers can and will prevent her trying to reassert herself by resort to war."[14]

Far from dismissing the 1914–18 experiences, the General Staff tried hard to learn from them. It initiated a serious investigation of its lessons, the Kirke Committee's report eventually appearing in 1932.[15] Field Marshal Sir Archibald Montgomery-Massingberd (CIGS 1933–6), who had been the chief of staff of the most successful of the British armies in the Hundred Days, initiated a series of staff tours of these 1918 battlefields.[16] Yet, the fact remains that whereas French and Russian military thinking of the interwar period took the military circumstances of 1918 as a starting point, the same was not true of the most interesting, original, and influential British thought.[17]

The ideas of the people the author has elsewhere termed the "RTC (Royal Tank Corps) *avant garde*" (which dealt with mechanisation and armored warfare) largely bypassed or set aside the Western Front experience of 1914–18. Most of the leading advocates of armored warfare – George Lindsay, Charles Broad, and Percy Hobart among others – had not served with tanks during the war.[18] Whereas French and Russian military thought in the 1920s started from the premise of mass armies and continuous fronts, the RTC *avant garde* assumed smaller forces, a lower force-to-space ratio, and thus greater room for maneuver. They assumed, as they later put it in a 1931 General Staff pamphlet, that the conception of the nation in arms was declining and that armies would become smaller.[19] From our perspective, these appear breathtaking assumptions, at least concerning the warfare of the next decade or two. In their minds, however, it was a truth so self-evident they did not bother to argue it. Nevertheless, although quite wrong, it was in some ways a useful assumption, allowing them to conceive of a theatre of war in which room for maneuver existed and in which it would not be

---

[14] French, *Raising Churchill's Army*, p. 13, and Brian Bond, *British Military Policy between the Two World Wars* (Oxford, 1980), pp. 76–8, 81, 93–5.

[15] On General Staff efforts to learn from the 1914–18 experience, see French, *Raising Churchill's Army*, pp. 13–19, and PRO WO 33/1297, "Report of the Committee on the Lessons of the Great War," published in a special edition of the *British Army Review* (2001).

[16] Major-General Sir Archibald Montgomery-Massingberd, *The Fourth Army in the Battles of the Hundred Days, August 8th – November 11th 1918* (London, 1919), passim. "Handing Over Notes by Field Marshal Sir A. A. Montgomery-Massingberd," section 8, "Battlefield Tours," Liddell Hart Centre for Military Archives (LHCMA), King's College London.

[17] Williamson Murray, "Armored Warfare," in Williamson Murray and Alan R. Millett, eds., *Military Innovation in the Interwar Period* (Cambridge, 1996), p. 32. Robert Doughty, *The Seeds of Disaster: The Development of French Army Doctrine 1919–1939* (Hamden, CT, 1985), pp. 118–20 and passim. V. K. Triandafillov, *The Nature of the Operations of Modern Armies* (Ilford, Essex, 1994), pp. 62–5 and passim.

[18] J. P. Harris, *Men, Ideas and Tanks: British Military Thought and Armoured Forces* (Manchester, 1995), pp. 197–200.

[19] *Modern Formations* (London, 1931), Tank Museum.

necessary to break through a continuous front defended by massive field fortifications.

Lindsay had transferred to the Tank Corps after the war; he had held a pioneering role in the development of machine gun tactics in the Machine Gun Corps during that conflict. Beginning in 1923, he began to advocate the establishment of an Experimental Mechanical Force of brigade strength that would combine various elements, including armored cars or tankettes for reconnaissance, medium tanks, motorized artillery, machine gunners, and sapper support, the whole to work closely with the Royal Air Force (RAF).[20] After Field Marshal Sir George Milne became CIGS, the Army assembled such a force on Salisbury Plain in the 1927 training season. Milne appears to have been influenced in favor of the Experimental Mechanical Force by his Military Assistant, Colonel J. F. C. Fuller. Fuller, who had been the Tank Corps' chief of staff for much of the war, was Britain's best-known writer on mechanization, and is sometimes (wrongly) believed to have originated the idea of the Experimental Mechanical Force.[21]

With greater boldness than judgment, Milne offered Fuller command of the force. In one of the more bizarre episodes of his distinctly strange life, Fuller effectively turned the assignment down.[22] In the process he publicly cast doubt, through his press contact, Basil Liddell Hart, on whether the General Staff was really serious about the mechanized force. Liddell Hart's articles on the subject accused the War Office of lying to Parliament and the public. Nevertheless, the notion that Liddell Hart's journalism saved the force from emasculation by a reactionary War Office plot is still given credence by some historians.[23] This is indeed doubtful. Fuller was an eccentric, highly strung officer who had not held command for years. He had never in fact commanded anything of any size; and he now seems to have doubted his ability to do so. His demands and preconditions for acceptance of the appointment represented the behavior of a *prima donna*.[24] Liddell Hart's journalistic intervention seems to have been grossly unfair to a General Staff running an Army with global responsibilities on a shoestring budget – yet still trying to initiate an imaginative experiment of the greatest importance for the Army's future.

During the training seasons of 1927 and 1928, the force did carry out a series of exercises on Salisbury Plain. These efforts were not an unqualified success – at least in part because they were ahead of their time. Wireless

---

[20] Harris, *Men, Ideas and Tanks*, pp. 210–11.
[21] Ibid., pp. 211–16.
[22] A. J. Trythall, *'Boney' Fuller: The Intellectual General* (London, 1977), pp. 40–74 and 120–44.
[23] Harold Winton, *To Change an Army: General Sir John Burnett-Stuart and British Armoured Doctrine* (London, 1988), p. 79.
[24] Trythall, *'Boney' Fuller*, pp. 215–17.

telephony – so crucial to command and control in high-tempo mechanized warfare – was not yet reliable. Thus, the force was heavily dependent on motorcycle dispatch riders and sometimes on the semaphore.[25] Despite such limitations, the experiments, written up at length by Liddell Hart in the pages of the *Daily Telegraph*, created international interest. The Americans were sufficiently impressed to set up their own experiments.[26] But the foreign army most excited and influenced by the "great experiment," as Liddell Hart christened it, was the German Army.[27]

The precise extent of British influence on the Germans is a matter of some controversy.[28] Although German thought about and organization of armored forces had generally overtaken and deviated from that of the Royal Tank Corps *avant garde* by 1935, the evidence that British influence was important before then is overwhelming. The Germans obtained and translated British General Staff pamphlets on armored forces and assiduously read and commented on the published writings of Fuller, Martel, and Liddell Hart. It is true that Liddell Hart manipulated the evidence to magnify his own role, but Guderian, for one, was happy to acknowledge a strong British influence without any postwar prompting from Liddell Hart.[29]

The Army wound up the Experimental Mechanical Force at the end of the 1928 training season, but a variety of other experiments continued. An experimental tank brigade, for example, was tested in 1931 under the command of Charles Broad, who also conducted early experiments in command and control by wireless telephony.[30] Yet, 1931 also marks the point at which British began to lose their lead. In that year, the Great Depression resulting from the Wall Street Crash of 1929 hit Britain. The government reacted with swinging cuts in public expenditure, which fell particularly heavily on the Army. The design and development of new weapons and equipment suffered particularly. The Army had to abandon development of an experimental medium tank, known as the "Sixteen Tonner," that the Royal Tank Corps thought especially promising, because it was too expensive to put into production. British tank development was thrown into disarray – a state of

---

[25] Harris, *Men Ideas and Tanks*, pp. 217–22.

[26] Azar Gat, *A History of Military Thought from the Enlightenment to the Cold War* (Oxford, 2001), p. 635.

[27] Heinz Guderian, *Achtung Panzer!*, trans. Christopher Duffy (London, 1992), pp. 141–2.

[28] James Corum, *The Roots of Blitzkrieg: Hans von Seeckt and German Military Reform* (Lawrence, KS, 1994) pp. 136–43, tends to play down British influence on German armor. In this he, in part, echoes Major-General F. W. von Mellenthin who indicates in *Panzer Battles* (London, 1977), pp. xiv, xv, that the Germans, while owing something to British influence, had outgrown it by the end of the 1920s. Yet, evidence that a degree of British influence persisted into the mid-1930s is strong. See Murray, "Armored Warfare," p. 41, n. 130.

[29] A large part of Guderian's 1937 text, *Achtung Panzer!*, is about the British. See also Azar Gat, *British Armour Theory and the Rise of the Panzer Arm* (London, 2000), passim.

[30] Harris, *Men, Ideas and Tanks*, p. 225. French, *Raising Churchill's Army*, p. 165.

affairs from which, for complex reasons, it did not recover until well into World War II.[31]

Even its most stringent critics admit the British Army was in the forefront of development of mechanization and armor through the early 1930s. However, in his version of British military history, Basil Liddell Hart depicted the positive developments of the 1920s and early 1930s as the work of small numbers of visionaries and progressives – mostly, his friends in the Royal Tank Corps, men who had to struggle against a hidebound "military establishment."[32] Liddell Hart had to admit that some individual members of the Army's senior hierarchy had acquiesced in a degree of reform. He did give some grudging praise to Field Marshal Sir George Milne for his first few years as CIGS. But (in Liddell Hart's view) by the early 1930s, Milne had succumbed to a War Office culture of obscurantism and inertia. Things, Liddle Hart argued, only became worse under Milne's successor, Sir Archibald Amar Montgomery-Massingberd (CIGS 1933–6).[33]

During the 1920s, Montgomery-Massingberd had, indeed, displayed some strongly conservative attitudes and suspicion of the ambitions of the Royal Tank Corps. Yet, he became a progressive CIGS, whose most crucial decisions aided the cause of the RTC and mechanization in general. He established the Tank Brigade as a permanent formation in late 1933. He encouraged its work and gained the admiration of its commander, Brigadier P.C.S. Hobart. Hobart described Montgomery-Massingberd in a letter to Liddell Hart (of all people) as "a far seeing, resolute and open-minded CIGS who is giving us a chance to try and is so remarkably understanding."[34] In 1934, Montgomery-Massingberd ordered the formation of the first mechanized mobile division, which eventually became the 1st Armoured Division. In succeeding years, he moved relentlessly toward the abolition of horsed cavalry in the British Army.[35]

Admittedly, a number of things went wrong with the development of British armored forces in the early and mid-1930s. The savage cuts in expenditures in the early 1930s fell on a narrow base of research and development, and massively disrupted the fielding of modern armored fighting vehicles. A further problem was the decline in the personal and professional fortunes of George Lindsay, the most outstanding of the officers who constituted the Royal Tank Corps' *avant garde*. Lindsay had the most balanced and sensible ideas on the structure of future armored formations and by far the most pleasing personality. Tragically Lindsay's wife, to whom he was

31 Richard Ogorkiewicz, *Armour: The Development of Mechanised Forces and Their Equipment* (London, 1960), pp. 153–67. Harris, *Men, Ideas and Tanks*, pp. 237–8.
32 B. H. Liddell Hart, *Memoirs* (London, 1965), pp. 211–55.
33 Ibid., pp. 227–8, 303–4, 261–5.
34 Larson, *The British Army and the Theory of Armoured Warfare*, p. 162.
35 Ibid., pp. 171–96.

devoted, was, by 1934, suffering quite seriously from some form of mental illness. Lindsay himself became anxious and depressed and could not concentrate. This affected him badly when, in 1934, he commanded an improvised armored division, known as the "Mobile Force," in exercises on Salisbury Plain.[36]

The task set for the Mobile Force was made exceptionally difficult by the exercise director, the enigmatic "Jock" Burnett-Stuart, while the umpiring was undoubtedly unfair. Lindsay's lot was made even harder by the uncooperative behavior of his principal subordinate, Brigadier Percy Hobart. Hobart, commanding the Tank Brigade, did not, at this stage in his career, really believe in the concept of an armored division. In the debriefing session at the end of the exercise, Burnett-Stuart humiliated Lindsay. Lindsay's personal morale and position in the Army never recovered.[37] His position as leader of the RTC's radicals was to a large extent assumed by Hobart. This was most unfortunate. Hobart's views on armored formations were much more narrowly tank centered than were Lindsay's. The former had a scarcely concealed contempt for the older arms and, a sufferer from manic depression, his mental balance was open to question.[38] The whole episode of Lindsay's loss of influence is indicative of the problems of a small officer corps. Here, personal misfortune afflicting a single individual had a quite disproportionate influence on the eventual course of events.

Liddell Hart implied that the "Mobile Force" exercises of 1934 represented a War Office conspiracy against the development of armor in the British Army. This line of argument is sheer nonsense. As Hobart testified, it had no discernible effect on official policy toward armor. The CIGS continued to favor the vigorous development of armored forces. Lindsay's loss of influence seems to have been primarily owing to domestic problems affecting his professional effectiveness. It was most definitely not owing to the hostility of Montgomery-Massingberd or the General Staff in the War Office. If Lindsay suffered unfairly at the hands of a senior officer, it was at those of Burnett-Stuart. Ironically, not only was Burnett-Stuart on poor terms with the CIGS, but he was one of the senior Army officers outside the Royal Tank Corps most friendly with Liddell Hart.[39]

The development of the armored forces was, of course, just one aspect of the General Staff's duties. The context in which it took place occurred in the face of a rapidly deteriorating international situation of the mid-1930s. Even before Hitler came to power (indeed even at the most favorable time between the wars), the War Office retained considerable suspicion of the

[36] Harris, *Men, Ideas and Tanks*, pp. 249–54.
[37] Winton, *To Change an Army*, pp 177–83.
[38] J. P. Harris, "Sir Percy Hobart," in Brian Bond, ed., *Fallen Stars: Eleven Studies of Twentieth Century Military Disasters* (London, 1991), pp. 86–106.
[39] Harris, *Men, Ideas, and Tanks*, pp. 246–53; and Winton, *To Change an Army*, pp. 177–83.

Germans. MI3, the intelligence branch concerned with Germany, was aware throughout the 1920s that the Germans were trying to evade some of the major military clauses of the Versailles Treaty and had by the early 1930s carried out a degree of covert rearmament. After Hitler became chancellor of Germany in January 1933, it took most people in government and defense circles in Britain only a few months to recognize that the whole European security situation had considerably worsened.[40]

Recognizing the problem was, of course, the easy bit. Knowing what to do about it was more difficult. A Defence Requirements Committee of all three armed services, established in late 1933, submitted a major report to the Cabinet early in February 1934. Montgomery-Massingberd, representing the General Staff point of view, was a skillful and effective negotiator. Although there were significant differences in outlook between the services, the General Staff was able to obtain a considerable degree of endorsement for all its most crucial positions.

The chiefs of staff of all three services recognized a triple threat, from Germany, Italy, and Japan. All three chiefs were prepared to designate Germany as the "ultimate enemy" against which Britain should primarily direct its attention. All agreed that, in the event of war with Germany, Britain would have to send an expeditionary force to the continent to cooperate with the French and keep as much of the Low Countries out of German hands as possible. If the Germans seized the Low Countries, the British chiefs agreed, they would be in a much improved position to undertake the bombing of southern England and mount a U-boat offensive against British shipping. An indication of the horse trading that had occurred to enable the three armed services to reach this consensus was that each service demanded a virtually identical amount of money to redeem its worst deficiencies – 40 million pounds in each case. These proposals were in fact modest in relation to the state of Britain's defenses after twelve years or so of neglect. The Chiefs of Staff were trying to be realistic about what they could get past the Treasury. For the Army, however, it did not work.[41]

When reviewed by ministers, the Defence Requirements Committee's report came under attack from Neville Chamberlain, the Chancellor of the Exchequer, and one the most powerful figures in the government at that time. Chamberlain flatly stated that the Treasury now confronted proposals "impossible to carry out." Such vast military expenditure would wreck the government's economic plans for recovery from the Depression. Chamberlain singled out the Army's proposals for attack. The preparation of

---

[40] Bond, *British Military Policy between the Wars*, pp. 93–4 and 101.
[41] J. P. Harris, "The General Staff and the Coming of War 1933–39," in David French and Brian Holden Reid, eds., *The British General Staff: Reform and Innovation, 1890–1939* (London, 2003), pp. 179–80.

another expeditionary force for the continent was, he felt, politically inexpedient. It would raise the terrible spectre of the Western Front 1914–18 and, he implied, damage the government's electoral chances. He preferred to concentrate expenditure on the RAF and believed the construction of a powerful bomber force might deter war altogether.

Chamberlain's proposed deterrence strategy was amateurish nonsense. The RAF at this period could not even reach most targets in Germany from bases in Britain. When ministers referred the matter back to the chiefs, the latter remained firm that dispatching an expeditionary force to the Continent and being prepared to fight the Germans for control of the Low Countries was crucial to Great Britain's strategic interests. Despite this, Chamberlain insisted that the budget the War Office had proposed to repair the Army's worst deficiencies over the next five years should be slashed to 20 million pounds from 40 million pounds. The RAF's budget, in contrast, was significantly increased. Half a loaf was better than none, of course, but this ministerial decision effectively delayed the commencement of a serious rearmament effort for the Army for another two years.[42]

The General Staff, however, was by no means inactive in the interval. It made important decisions about the form it wanted rearmament to take, even though the means to carry these out remained extremely limited. The most comprehensive General Staff paper of the period, entitled "The Future Reorganisation of the British Army," was drawn up on Montgomery-Massingberd's instructions and signed by him in September 1935. Sweeping in its scope and penetrating in some of its insights, it contained exactly the sort of thinking for which general staffs exist. A broad overall view of Britain's strategic position in relation to the international situation introduced a review of the circumstance likely to lead to the nation's involvement in the next major European war. There followed a fairly detailed scenario for the opening stages of such a war and the part that a British field force might play. Finally, there was an assessment of the changes needed in the Army's organization and equipment.

Given that the paper was completed before the Germans had yet created a substantial panzer arm, the General Staff's level of understanding of the likely German operational approach was impressive. The Germans, it believed, would seek a quick victory. They would probably bypass the major French fortifications on the Franco-German border by passing through Belgium and probably Holland as well. German hopes would center on the combined use of airpower with mechanized spearheads on the ground. The targets the Germans would select for air attack in the early stages of a war would conform to the objectives of the field armies, "air action being directed at enemy

---

[42] Peden, *British Rearmament and the Treasury*, pp. 123–5. Harris, "The General Staff and the Coming of the War," p. 181.

air bases, railway nodal points and concentration areas." The German objective would probably be "to paralyse the enemy's movements, concentration and administration systems" and to make possible "a breakthrough by highly mobile land forces." Given its accurate understanding of the importance of airpower in a future land campaign, the General Staff wanted the RAF to devote more effort to helping the Army, although it rather suspected that such pleas would fall on deaf ears. The General Staff, therefore, wondered aloud whether a system analogous to that of the Fleet Air Arm might not offer better results for the Army.

The role of a British Field Force on the continent was quite clear – to offer sufficient moral and material support to France to prevent its collapse early in the war, and if possible, to keep a good part of the Low Countries out of German hands. To this end, at the outset of hostilities, the Army hoped to dispatch a first contingent consisting of four infantry divisions and a mechanized division. For the field force, mechanization would be the key note for future development. The first contingent was to include enough motor transport to lift a complete division, if required, and there was to be a substantial proportion of armor. In addition to the mechanized division, there was to be an Army Tank Brigade, consisting of four battalions of heavily armored tanks for close support to the infantry in the assault. There would also be light tank regiments attached to the infantry divisions for reconnaissance. In the early stages of the war, the Allies would assume a defensive posture. If they survived the opening stages, further British contingents, based on a rearmed Territorial Army, would reinforce the regulars of the first contingent. In the fullness of time, the General Staff believed, the Allies would be able to take the offensive, although there was no attempt to specify how long this might take.[43]

One can criticize the British General Staff's approach in 1935 in matters of detail. Some weaknesses are apparent, for example, in its plans for the future of British armored forces. The idea that every infantry division needed a light tank regiment for reconnaissance was certainly wrong and was to be a factor leading to a gross overproduction of rather useless light tanks. The General Staff was clearly not yet sure about how it should organize the one mobile division it envisaged in 1935. Already adumbrated in this September 1935 paper was a splitting of British armored forces (other than the reconnaissance regiments attached to the infantry divisions) into two main branches – so-called Army tank battalions and brigades, on the one hand, and the mobile (later armored) divisions, on the other. The Army tank units, with heavily armored but slow-moving infantry tanks, were to offer close cooperation to nonmechanized infantry in the assault. Mobile or armored divisions, mainly equipped with less heavily armored, faster tanks (later

[43] PRO WO 32/4612, "The Future Reorganisation of the British Army."

classified as Cruiser tanks), were to operate ahead of the infantry divisions and against the enemy's flanks, if opportunity presented itself.

The distinction came about, at least in part, as a result of the underpowered commercial engines that British tank designers had to use in the early and mid-1930s. Thus, designers found that they could make a tank either heavily armored or highly mobile. But they could not combine both properties in the same machine. Hence, two basic types of fighting tanks and two distinct kinds of armored units and formations emerged. This was, however, an unfortunate conceptual dichotomy and its development arguably impeded development of British armored forces in World War II.[44]

In general, however, the British General Staff's thinking in September 1935 is remarkable for its broad scope, clarity, and logic. The General Staff's 1935 analysis of how the Germans would attempt to combine airpower and mechanized spearheads to bring about the swift defeat of France is clearer and more definite than anything that Liddell Hart or Fuller wrote at the time. As German rearmament progressed and the international situation deteriorated, the General Staff went on to propose, as part of a further Defence Requirements report, a balanced and sensible program of rearmament. Once again, however, the government treated the Army as "the Cinderella of the services." It approved the proposals made by the other two services, but while it sanctioned preparation of a regular field force of five divisions for the Continent, it ruled out the rearmament of the Territorial Army, without which the Army could not reinforce the first contingent for the immediate future.[45]

Nor did the General Staff's difficulties end there. Rearmament remained under the Treasury's tight control – a Treasury where a distinctly unsympathetic Neville Chamberlain was still the departmental head. It would also occur within a framework of industrial policy known as "business as usual." The Treasury entirely focused on worries about damaging the country's financial viability and balance of trade. The War Office, the government department controlling the Army, was forbidden from diverting industrial capacity from normal commercial production and only allowed to use capacity that would otherwise lie idle or, in some cases, to develop new capacity. In the end, the Army was the least favored service when it came to access to industrial capacity. Even when the War Office gained sanction from the Treasury Inter-Service Committee for a particular item of expenditure, its officials often had considerable difficulty in finding firms able to accept its contracts.[46]

---

[44] Harris, *Men, Ideas and Tanks*, pp. 238–42 and 278–9. Richard Ogorkiewicz, *Armour*, pp. 155–9.
[45] Harris, "The General Staff and the Coming of the War," pp. 185–6.
[46] Peden, *British Rearmament and the Treasury*, pp. 171–5.

It did not bode well for the rearmament of the British Army that in May 1937 Neville Chamberlain succeeded Stanley Baldwin as the prime minister. One of his first acts was to remove Alfred Duff Cooper, Secretary of State for War 1935-7, from the War Office. Duff Cooper, who had served with distinction on the Western Front in 1918, had, as Secretary of State, been a firm supporter of General Staff in its efforts to prepare the British Army for a Continental commitment. He had dared to raise again – greatly to Chamberlain's irritation – the issue of the Territorial Army's rearmament. In his place, Chamberlain put Leslie Hore-Belisha.[47] A rather isolated member of a small political party, the latter's whole political future was entirely in Chamberlain's hands.

Liddell Hart was to acclaim Hore-Belisha the greatest Army reformer since Richard Haldane (before the First World War). Unfortunately, many historians have endorsed this opinion. Hore-Belisha was indeed to bring about a series of reforms in the Army's personnel policies – most of them in themselves creditable. Liddell Hart heavily publicized these reforms and formed with Hore-Belisha for several months a close partnership. But it seems clear that Chamberlain sent Hore-Belisha to the War Office with one purpose in mind – to cut down the scale of expenditure on the Army's rearmament. From an early stage, Chamberlain made clear to Hore-Belisha that he was expected to do this by reorienting the War Office's strategic policies away from the Continent.[48]

At the end of 1937 Hore-Belisha, with Liddell Hart's active encouragement, sacked most of the Army Council, including Field Marshal Sir Cyril Deverell, Montgomery-Massingberd's successor as CIGS. The whole matter was handled in a shabby and dishonest way, even by political standards. Hore-Belisha made it clear in a letter to Chamberlain that Deverell was being sacked because Hore-Belisha was in the process of changing the Army's strategic priorities. The Army was now to concentrate on home and imperial defense, effectively dropping efforts at preparing a field force for service on the Continent. Although Deverell said he was prepared to go along with what became known as the "New Army Policy," he clearly did not believe in it. Therefore, he had to go. However, Hore-Belisha's letter to Deverell, giving reasons for the dismissal, made no reference to differences of strategic principle. The government was sacking Deverell, he said, because of the slow pace of the Army's rearmament, a matter of grave concern "in these anxious times when action brooks no delay."[49]

---

[47] John Charmley, *Duff Cooper: The Authorised Biography* (London, 1986), pp. 22-7 and 92-102; and R. J. Minney, *The Private Papers of Hore-Belisha* (London, 1960), pp. 23-30.

[48] J. P. Harris, "Two War Ministers: A Reassessment of Duff Cooper and Hore-Belisha," *War and Society*, vol. 6, no. 1, 1988, pp. 67-72.

[49] Ibid., pp. 67-72.

This was the grossest hypocrisy. It was the National Government itself –
Chamberlain in particular – which had taken the decision to delay, for
two years (1934–6), the Army's rearmament. The government was to fol-
low Deverell's dismissal not by expanding or accelerating rearmament,
but by severely cutting back on its planned scale. Hore-Belisha wrote to
Chamberlain indicating the savings he intended to make, especially on the
Army's tank program.[50] It is hardly surprising in these circumstances that
Deverell, rather than taking his dismissal in good part, reacted with outrage.
"My conscience is clear," he wrote to the Secretary of State, "as to my duty to
the army and as to its rearmament." He regarded Hore-Belisha's comments
about on his own performance as being "as unjust as they [were] cruel."[51]

Although the introduction of the New Army Policy resulted largely from
financial considerations, Liddell Hart offered intellectual justification on military grounds. He argued that under current conditions the defense was vastly
stronger than the attack. The French should have no difficulty holding their
own without British help, provided they made full use of their fortifications and did not weaken themselves in fruitless offensives.[52] The taproot of
Liddell Hart's opposition to a Continental commitment, however, probably
went to a deeper emotional rather than cerebral level. He had, as his official
biographer has suggested, been somewhat traumatized by his own experience
in World War I. Commanding a platoon on the Somme, he disappeared for
four days in Mametz Wood, after having been gassed and probably having
suffered some sort of breakdown. He was not employed on front line duty
again. The horrors of the Western Front 1914–18 made the British Army's
large-scale involvement in another continental war almost unthinkable
for him.[53]

Although commentators generally associate Liddell Hart with mechanization and armored warfare, during the period that he was most influential
on British military policy, in effect he did much to restrict the growth and
rearmament of British armored forces. By the second half of the 1930s, he
had to a great extent lost his belief in the power of armored formations to
transform land warfare. Although he was still willing to intervene in military
appointments to secure favorable appointments for his friends in the RTC,
his real interest had switched from armor to air defense. Like many others in
Britain at the time, he was becoming increasingly mesmerized by the threat
of the aerial bombardment. By the late 1930s, he seems to have believed
strategic bombing was more likely to prove decisive in the next war than
military operations on land.[54]

---

[50] Harris, *Men, Ideas and Tanks*, p. 293.
[51] Quoted in Minney, *The Private Papers of Hore Belisha*, p. 72.
[52] Harris, *Men, Ideas and Tanks*, p. 262.
[53] Alex Danchev, *Alchemist of War: The Life of Basil Liddell Hart* (London, 1998), pp. 59–68.
[54] Harris, *Men, Ideas and Tanks*, pp. 291–2. "Outline of the Opposition to the Development
      of the Air Defence of Great Britain," 11/1938/89, Liddell Hart Papers, LHCMA.

The New Army Policy remained in force from January 1938 until February 1939. During this period, the government effectively banned the General Staff from using public money or industrial capacity for any effort designed to prepare the British Army to fight the Germans on the continent. The CIGS selected by Hore-Belisha to replace Deverell, General the Viscount John Standish Gort, and his Director of Military Operations, Major-General Henry Pownall, were no more convinced of the wisdom of this policy than their predecessors.[55] The General Staff continued its efforts at building a Field Force of some strength. But this became increasingly difficult. As soon as the New Army Policy was introduced, the Treasury positively pounced on one of the most expensive element in the Army's rearmament efforts, the tank program. It immediately demanded massive cuts. The General Staff, and the War Office as a whole, fought a skillful rear-guard action on this issue.

Although the government had ordered the General Staff to desist in its efforts to prepare a field force for the Continent, it still had the duty of defending the Empire. General Staff officers could and did argue that they needed a substantial field force for this purpose. In particular, they emphasized the Italian threat to Egypt and the need for a number of tanks for Egypt's defense. In fact, the General Staff was actually rather contemptuous of the Italians, and this emphasis on the Italian threat represented to a considerable extent, as the Treasury realized, a ploy to enable it to continue efforts to prepare a field force for the continent. The Treasury was most annoyed: one senior official privately dismissed the "whole idea of a desert war" as "merely silly." But Treasury bureaucrats were not altogether able to refute the General Staff's arguments and thus could not make quite such massive savings in the tank program as they originally had hoped.[56]

Hore-Belisha had, however, shown himself most willing to cooperate with the Treasury in substantially reducing the scale of the Army's rearmament. The Treasury helped him (in what was probably an informal quid pro quo) in offering up the much smaller sums necessary to improve terms and conditions of service for both officers and soldiers in the Army. Hore-Belisha's predecessor, Alfred Duff Cooper, had lobbied the Treasury unsuccessfully for money to replace the grim, prisonlike Victorian barracks, which still accommodated many soldiers. But the money to build modern, open-plan, lighter, and healthier barracks only became available under the more cooperative Hore-Belisha. New barracks at Borden and Tidworth thus became known as Belisha barracks. In other words, it is a reasonable hypothesis that a good deal of the much-vaunted Hore-Belisha reform on the personnel side of the

[55] Brian Bond, ed., *Chief of Staff: The Diaries of Lt. General Sir Henry Pownall*, vol. 1 (London, 1972), pp. 126–43.
[56] Harris, *Men, Ideas and Tanks*, pp. 293–4. J. P. Harris, "Egypt, Defence Plans," in Michael J. Cohen and Martin Kolinsky, eds., *Britain and the Middle East in the 1930s: Security Problems, 1935–39* (London, 1992), pp. 62–3.

Army came at the expense of its rearmament for the impending European war.[57] The whole question of military reform is indeed a complex one!

Yet, Hore-Belisha's own belief in the wisdom of the New Army Policy, by which he saved the Treasury money on the Army's rearmament and (probably) gained lesser sums for personnel reform in exchange, was relatively short lived. The Munich war scare of September 1938 led to some acceleration in the rearmament process. By that time, Hore-Belisha seems to have been worried that, if war came, he would carry a good deal of the blame for the country's inability to put an army in the field. Others in the government came to share his anxiety. By February 1939, the virtual Cabinet/Treasury ban on preparing the Army for war on the Continent had dissolved under the looming German threat. Hore-Belisha himself was instrumental in introducing a doubling of the Territorial Army in March 1939 and a limited form of conscription in April. These were measures to grab headlines. They were also necessary in the long run. They did little, however, to increase the Army's readiness for war in the immediate future.[58] When war came, the government did in fact send the Army to the continent, as the General Staff had always believed it would.

THE RECKONING

The British General Staff certainly made a number of critical mistakes in the interwar period, and the British Army had faults that might have been corrected even without massive additional funding. Yet, the belief that the British General Staff or the Army as a whole were essentially reactionary institutions, mindlessly clinging to the past, is quite untenable. World leaders in armor until the early 1930s, the British were also pioneers of the military use of wireless telephony. The myth that an obsession with the horse seriously impeded modernization between the wars is largely nonsense. The British remained leaders in general mechanization even when large-scale German rearmament was underway. In 1939, the Army was less dependent on animal power than any other major army in 1939 in Europe. Many British officers retained a devotion to equestrian pursuits (and to think some such pursuits had military value).[59] But the evidence that this seriously warped the understanding of the Army's leadership about the future of war or needs for organization and equipment appears slight.

The major obstacles to the development and war readiness of the British Army were external rather than internal. Most of these resulted from Britain's

---

57 On Hore-Belisha's reforms, see Bond, "1918–1939," in Chandler and Beckett eds., *The Oxford History of the British Army*, pp. 268–9; and Harris, "Two War Ministers," pp. 75–6.
58 Bond, *Chief of Staff*, vol. 1, pp. 177, 200–2.
59 Bond, *British Military Policy Between the Wars*, pp. 63–7.

weakened position in the world following the First World War. The Empire and Commonwealth achieved their maximum territorial extent in 1919. The range and complexity of defense commitments that this entailed were, however, out of proportion to the country's real economic strength. During the 1930s, with the emergence of a triple threat from Germany, Italy, and Japan, Britain faced defense problems arguably beyond its resources, no matter how well managed. Imperial internal security problems did not diminish as the threats from the dictatorial great powers increased. In 1936–8, the British had to use up to two divisions' worth of troops to suppress a revolt by Palestinian Arabs.[60] It was easy to conclude, as some did, that the only solution was to come to terms (however distasteful) with at least one of the more powerful of these expansionist powers – either Germany or Japan.[61]

The 1914–18 conflict had consumed vast amounts of the nation's wealth, and Britain could not have fought through to victory without massive loans from the United States. In addition to the burden of national debt carried in the interwar period, Britain possessed a much weakened trading position. British industrialists had often been unable to keep their usual customers supplied throughout the war and lost markets to competitors, sometimes permanently. In the First World War, the involvement of the New World had redressed the balance of the Old. But so uncomfortable were Americans with this role that Congress had passed neutrality legislation to ensure the United States would never again participate in a European war. With the British government now banned from wartime borrowing in America, the Treasury feared Britain might run out of foreign exchange within weeks of another major conflict. Unable to pay for vital imports, the nation would face inevitable defeat. Its profound consciousness of national economic weakness led the Treasury to insist that the government consider finance the "Fourth Arm of Defence."[62]

This meant (in the Treasury's view) that it was necessary to limit expenditures on rearmament and to ensure those expenditures made did not substantially detract from normal economic activity, thereby further eroding the nation's fundamental strength. British governments had, moreover, traditionally recognized that defense of Britain and its empire depended crucially on the Royal Navy. The Cabinet and Treasury also shared the widespread popular preoccupation with the potential of strategic airpower. Moreover, the RAF had the advantage of appearing more modern, glamorous, and "hi-tech." The General Staff presented valid, cogent arguments in favor of rearming the Army for a Continental commitment. But for leading politicians, such

---

[60] Paul Kennedy, *The Rise and Fall of the Great Powers* (London, 1988), pp. 407–10; and Bond, "1918–1939" in Chandler and Beckett, eds., *The Oxford History of the British Army*, p. 265.

[61] Bond, *British Military Policy Between the Wars*, p. 235.

[62] Peden, *British Rearmament and the Treasury*, pp. 65, 82, 85, 91.

arguments only conjured up depressing images of the trenches of 1914–18. The British Army in the 1930s became the "Cinderella of the services."[63] Ultimately, nations only get the armies for which they (or their allies) are able and willing to pay.

The problems of the British government in relation to its Army, however, seem to have gone beyond a simple inability to provide the funding and industrial capacity needed for serious rearmament. From 1933, the Nazi government relentlessly prepared its army for war. It gave the Army the highest industrial priority and took extreme risks with the nation's financial stability in pursuit of rearmament.[64] It inculcated quasimilitary values through the Hitler Youth into German boys long before they joined the Army. The contrast with Britain could hardly have been more graphic. A certain disdain for the military, at any rate in peacetime, was a tradition in Britain. The reaction that had set in by the 1930s to the horrors of the First World War only served to exacerbate such attitudes.[65] In that decade, British governments, for the most part, treated their General Staff with scarcely concealed contempt. This was undeserved. A high proportion of the General Staff's advice was sound. However, for much of the 1930s, it was in a less favorable position than the Biblical Joseph, asked to make bricks without straw. The British government seemed to indicate that it did not even want the bricks. The overriding lesson of the British military experience between the two world wars (especially in the 1930s) is that no government can treat its military in such a fashion for years and then send it, at short notice, against the most powerful opponent in the world and expect it to perform effectively.

Obstacles coming from within the Army itself to modernization and preparation for war were minor in comparison. Yet, they did exist. One of these was what the British Army today calls "cap-badge" rivalry – jealousies between the different regiments and arms. The Royal Tank Corps' radicals created anxiety and resentment by seeming determined to dominate the Army in the future, leaving little room for other arms. In the famous exercise of 1934, this apparently contributed to umpiring biased against Lindsay's Mobile Force. But prejudice was not all on one side. Whereas, by 1934, Lindsay had realized the need to create armored divisions that included all arms in a balanced combination, Hobart, who became the leading RTC personality after the collapse of Lindsay's influence, did not. His excessively

---

[63]   Bond, *Chief of Staff*, vol. 1, p. 48.

[64]   Wilhelm Deist, *The Wehrmacht and German Rearmament* (London, 1981), pp. 36–53, 105–6.

[65]   On the Hitler Youth, see Karl Dietrich Bracher, *The German Dictatorship: The Origins, Structure and Consequences of National Socialism* (Harmondsworth, 1973), pp. 326–9. Of the culture of disdain for the military in the Britain of the interwar period, one of the most notable symptoms was the popularity of David Low's cartoon character "Colonel Blimp." See Chandler and Beckett, eds., *The Oxford History of the British Army*, pp. 260, 312–14.

tank-centered ideas were associated with contempt for the older arms and a reluctance to work closely with them.[66]

Interarm jealousies, as well as shortages of money and equipment, seem to have impeded the development of British armored divisions in the late 1930s.[67] The weak performance during much of the campaign in the Western Desert of British armored divisions against the Germans, was, in large measure, the result of poor interarms coordination.[68] In some cases, this seems to have been primarily owing to hurriedly raised divisions pitched into battle with inadequate time for training. But a more fundamental lack of interarms trust and understanding was also a factor.[69] The importance of controlling petty jealousies and destructive rivalries between different branches of an army must also be a crucial lesson of this period. Some central authority, with sufficient institutional control, must be able to knock heads together, overcome frictions, and establish effective cooperation and common doctrine and purpose. This is an area in which, with regard to its embryonic armored divisions, the British General Staff of the 1930s was certainly found wanting.

Although the Army's access to money and industrial capacity remained limited, it might have made better use of what was available. This seems to have been true with the Royal Tank Corps and medium tank development. Following the cancellation of the "Sixteen Tonner" tanks, designed to meet particular requirements, the Royal Tank Corps was offered a machine known as the six-ton tank that Vickers was producing as a commercial venture, for export. The six-ton tank was never given serious consideration, despite its being a sound machine for the time with considerable potential. Arguably, the RTC was overfussy in its requirements, insufficiently willing to cut its coat to suit its cloth or to buy "off the shelf."[70] One of the most reliable and (within limits) effective tanks in the British Army until the middle of the Second World War was the Valentine, another machine designed by Vickers without user input and accepted with some reluctance in 1939.[71] There is a well-known saying that in procurement, "the best is the enemy of the good." Excessive perfectionism can become a menace, depriving the Army of usable equipment in pursuit of that which is unattainable in reasonable time at reasonable cost. That was certainly the case with the British Army in the late 1930s.

---

[66] Harris, "Sir Percy Hobart," pp. 96–100.

[67] "Notes on my Life," pp. 86–8, ALANBROOKE, 3/A/2, Alanbrooke Papers, LHCMA.

[68] Shelford Bidwell and Dominic Graham, *Fire-Power: British Army Weapons and Theories of War 1904–1945* (London, 1982), p. 225.

[69] French, *Raising Churchill's Army*, pp. 217–23.

[70] Ogorkiewicz, *Armour*, p. 154.

[71] David Fletcher, *The Great Tank Scandal: British Armour in the Second World War*, Part I (London, 1989), p. 45.

Individuals with vision *and* the ability to implement their vision through organizational change are a crucial resource. They are usually scarce, especially in small armies. It is critical that the highest military authorities accurately evaluate officer potential. This was not always the case in the British Army in this period. Liddell Hart blamed Montgomery-Massingberd, on these grounds, for the (allegedly) premature retirement of Fuller in 1934.[72] This is dubious. Fuller was a stimulating, provocative thinker and writer. But he could think and write just as well in retirement. Too eccentric and erratic to be a good organizer or practical pioneer, he had neither the experience nor temperament for a substantial field command. In fact, it was probably Milne who erred in offering Fuller command of the Experimental Mechanical Force in 1927, an offer that produced only embarrassment for Fuller personally and for the Army as a whole.

A more serious case of an individual's potential being largely wasted in the approach to the Second World War, was that of George Lindsay. Lindsay's mind was much more practical than Fuller's. By the mid-1930s, he had the most sophisticated, balanced, and sensible ideas on the future development of British armored forces. Lindsay's loss of influence resulted from his poor performance on exercise in 1934. Yet, however weak he had shown himself in a command appointment, his advice on the further development of British armored forces was desperately needed at War Office level. It now seems clear that allowing the British Army's most perceptive thinker on armored forces to be shunted off to a routine administrative appointment in India in the mid-1930s, never to be employed again in his principal area of expertise, was a mistake.[73] Armies must make the best use of the expertise they have available, even when, for whatever reason, it is not allied to command ability.

With the benefit of hindsight, it is possible to suggest ways in which the British General Staff in the interwar period, despite its limited resources, might have done better. Yet, given the difficulties under which that leadership worked and the sheer scale of the problems it faced, it is perhaps surprising that it did not do worse. The upshot was that the British in the Second World War, as in the First, found themselves trying to improvise a large army, on an inadequate foundation, in the course of an enormous war. For the second time within a quarter of a century, the Americans essentially followed the British example. In a sense, on both occasions, both got away with it. They ended up on the winning side. But they did so only because other armies bore the brunt of the fighting until they got their respective acts together. In World War I, this role was played principally by the French, and in the Second, principally by the Soviets.

[72] Liddell Hart, *Memoirs*, vol. 1, pp. 230–1.
[73] Winton, *To Change an Army*, pp. 183 and 222.

The world has changed since the Second World War, indeed since the Cold War. At the time of writing, the Western democracies seem to face no immediate threat from a first-class power with a mass army like that of Nazi Germany or the Soviet Union. Indeed, for the British and Americans, really large-scale "conventional" war against a proficient enemy seems, although by no means inconceivable, much less likely than other forms of armed conflict.[74] Lessons from the British experience 1918–39 with regard to interarms friction, procurement, and the handling of officer careers may still, however, have some considerable validity.

CONCLUSION

Britain between the two world wars is an example of a world power with extraordinarily complex global commitments, yet finite and diminished resources. It had become by 1918 a full-fledged democracy. Its population, which generally had no great relish for military expenditure or military service in the best of times, was tired of war. After the onset of the Great Depression in the early 1930s, much of the population became thoroughly disillusioned with the last war and increasingly reluctant to face another.

The British Army during this period, with tightly restricted money and manpower, had to meet challenges as various as intercommunal and nationalist rioting in Indian cities, the depredations of marauding tribesmen on the Northwest Frontier, and guerrilla warfare in places as different as Ireland and Palestine. From the early 1930s, it also had to face – even if the politicians it served found it difficult to do so – the real threat of large-scale warfare against three hostile powers: Germany, Japan, and Italy. A war against all three simultaneously, while ferment and disorder increased within the Empire, was, of course, the ultimate nightmare scenario, and one that had by the end of 1941 become reality. These challenges had to be faced during a period when technology was developing rapidly and when the art of war was also in a state of considerable flux.

It is probable that no army has ever faced more complex or greater challenges than the British Army did between the two world wars. It did not help that most of the population it defended and most of the politicians it served held attitudes concerning its relevance that were, at best, ambivalent and which sometimes smacked of contempt, at times even hostility. Given its low prestige and poor pay, the Army could, in reality, hardly claim to embody the best and brightest of British society. Despite this reality, it was a world leader in military thought and even technical innovation for much of the period.

---

[74] One conceivable scenario would be the renewal of the Korean War after a fifty-year truce.

With the resources at its disposal, it could not ultimately meet all the challenges that it confronted – and it was at times ordered not to try and meet some of them by British governments that simply refused to recognize the looming threat that Nazi Germany, for example, posed. Nevertheless, its leaders struggled manfully to meet what they believed were the foremost challenges to Britain's security and interests. Although the Army suffered heavy defeats in the early stages of the Second World War, it was able to soldier on and, ultimately, with the help of allies, to win through. For all these reasons, this army at this period, the problems it faced, and the way it dealt with them, are worthy of study by the military officers of today's democratic states, including those of the United States.

13

What history suggests about terrorism and its future

CHRISTOPHER C. HARMON

In late October 1954, an Algerian rebel military leader who helped initiate the coming revolution against French rule, Mostepha Ben Boulaid, gave detailed orders to a subordinate commander, Bachir Chihani. These included the usual tactics so commonly seen when guerrilla wars begin: sabotage phone lines, attack small military garrisons, and invade police depots to take weapons. But there was something else in those orders: ambush passing vehicles on the highways and kill any Moslem collaborator types found in them. The name for such Algerian persons, in this total war, was "Beni Oui Oui" – "yes men." They were to die, not for taking action against the revolutionaries – because as yet there was no revolution – but merely for what they represented: comity among the mix of races, association with Europeans, and willingness to hold positions in the mixed political order controlled from Paris.

That directive was a first step in a war that would come to include many wrenching forms of "terrorism." That word has been most usefully defined as "the deliberate and systematic murder, maiming, and menacing of the innocent to inspire fear for political ends."[1] What the *Front de Libération Nationale* (FLN) wanted, and used terrorism to advance, was polarization – social, political, and psychological. Few tools achieve it as readily as terrorism. The commander who wrote the orders of October 1954 understood that reality, although initially his victims might not have.

A year later, when Chihani himself wrote orders to subordinates, they included these lines: "Kill the caids [local Arab governors]. Take their children and kill them. Kill all those who pay taxes and those who collect them. Burn the houses of Muslim NCOs [noncommissioned officers] away on

---

[1] Definition by The Jonathan Institute in 1979, *Terrorism: How the West Can Win*, ed. Benjamin Netanyahu (New York, 1986), p. 9.

217

active service." By mid-1956, this brutish approach triumphed at the strategic level, when it was debated and approved in conference in the mountains at Soummam. The man most responsible for assembling FLN political and military leaders there, Ramdane Abane, was known for his calculus that "one corpse in a [suit] jacket is always worth more than twenty in uniform." Soon after Soummam came the first horrific bombings in the capital, Algiers, where the targets were public gathering places, not exclusively French attractions, and certainly not security related. They had place names like Le Milk Bar and Lucky Starway dance hall. The carnage was shocking. That was precisely the point.[2]

The first and most powerful lesson about terrorism from this nationalist revolution of a half-century ago in Algeria is the one Alistair Horne illuminates and some other historians of that conflict have missed: terrorism is a deliberate choice – not merely the product of passion, nor of the environment of war, nor of the strength of feeling behind a cause. It is a method, not just a description.[3] That is central to the first of the four parts of this chapter.

WHY TERRORISM OCCURS

Terrorism is about power. It is, indeed, a complex phenomenon, challenging to understand, whether one is a social scientist, military commander, or political leader. There are indeed many tangled roots of the phenomenon in economic, social, and political conditions. In more cases than not, there is indirect or direct involvement of a sovereign state.[4] What is most evident,

---

[2] Jacques C. Duchemin, *Histoire du F.L.N.* (Paris, 1962), pp. 218–19. Yves Courriere, *La Guerre d'Algerie*, vol. II, *Le Temps des Leopards* (Paris, 1969), pp. 130–1, 195, 226–8, 427. Alistair Horne, *A Savage War of Peace* (New York, 1977), pp. 89, 135. The platform adopted at the Congress of Soummam described armed action as "a psychological shock that has freed the people from its torpor . . ." (trans. CCH, after Duchemin's text, p. 181). Also useful on that political/psychological phenomenon are Richard and Joan Brace, *Ordeal in Algeria* (Princeton, 1960), e.g., pp. 86–90.

[3] This is also a theme of Martha Crenshaw's impressive essay "The Effectiveness of Terrorism in the Algerian War," in *Terrorism in Context*, ed. Martha Crenshaw (University Park, PA, 1995).

[4] The documentation of state support of given terrorists is vast. Two commendable titles of the mid-1980s were Yonah Alexander and Ray Cline, "State-Sponsored Terrorism," a report for the Subcommittee on Security and Terrorism, Committee on the Judiciary, U.S. Senate, June 1985, and Uri Ra'anan, Robert L. Pfaltzgraff, Jr., Richard H. Shultz, et al., *Hydra of Carnage: The Witnesses Speak* (Lexington, MA, 1985). Dr. Harold W. Rood, reviewing my manuscript, pointed to a dozen relevant past examples of states' involvement; e.g., there was an announcement by the Mexican government in March 1971 that many Soviet diplomats were being ejected because of the direct aid Moscow and North Korea gave to the "Movimento de Accion Revolucionaria" (MAR); letter to author of July 19, 2003 (6 pp.). After the fall of the USSR, admissions and new documentation flowing from the region's archives literally ended years of public debate about whether communist states had been fostering international terrorism.

however, is that terrorism is about power. One might first explore that premise in the dual dimensions of psychological and political power.

It has become commonplace to read that violence by Moslem fanatics is rooted in the deep resentment and humiliation they feel. Some observers emphasize that in the rise and fall of great powers, Moslem and Arab peoples have done relatively poorly in modern times. Some argue that globalization has maximized the cultural influence of the West at the expense of the cultures of North Africa and the Middle East. Others allege that the United States pays too much attention to Israel (although it was Arab countries that were liberated in 1991 and 2003). The resentment is tangibly real: polling data published in 2002 drove home the point that even in countries with mixed or friendly relations with the West, anti-Americanism is deep. Such sentiment may inspire al Qaeda. Surely its supporters are buttressed by such feelings.[5]

There are numerous other historical examples of similar inspiration for terrorism. One may examine Palestinian resentment of second-class political status among the Jews, as well as Palestinian resentment of the Arabs. There was the Palestine Liberation Organization's (PLO's) expulsion from Lebanon in 1983, and before that the PLO's expulsion from Jordan in the Black September of 1970. The team that killed the Israeli athletes in Munich in 1972 was called Black September out of defiance, resentment, and humiliation, as much as hatred of Israel.

Resentment and humiliation are visible in the histories of what often are called "the first terrorists," known as the Assassins, Ismaili moslems of the eleventh, twelfth, and thirteenth centuries. Their resentment was against the dominant Sunni faith. Their aim was physical and religious independence. Their strategy was a mix of manipulation of regional forces, alliance making, a network of strong castles, and audacious assassinations. They killed area rivals, irritants, conquerors, or leaders too proud to submit to Assassin requests or demands. For more than a century, they killed no westerners. Rather, their enemies were local and regional rivals for the moslem soul.[6] It

---

[5] See, for example, "Poll: Muslims Call U.S. 'Ruthless, Arrogant,'" CNN, Feb. 26, 2002, as well as "This Week," ABC TV, March 3, 2002. Of those questioned in nine Muslim countries, 53 percent had unfavorable opinions of the United States; most were "resentful" of the superpower. For suggestions of direct linkage between such muslim resentment and al Qaeda, see the articles on Kenya in the *New York Times* of Dec. 1, 2002.

"Humiliation" is now commonly referenced regarding causes of terrorism. For example, M. L. Cook's review in the Summer 2003 issue of *Parameters* directs us to this topic in Mark Juergensmeyer's book *Terror in the Mind of God: The Global Rise of Religious Violence* (Berkeley, CA, 2000).

[6] This pattern whereby the Assassins' victims were nearly always other moslems is important and its corollary in terrorism today has been ignored. Yet, innumerable victims of the new moslem militants are other moslems – accused of apostasy, cultural infidelities, political despotism, submissiveness to the West, etc. In recent years, I suggested to

(continued)

was always the powerful who fell before their daggers – a notable distinction between the Assassins and their modern descendants who often inflict promiscuous human wreckage.

After resentment or humiliation, a second powerful psychological spur to terrorism through the ages has been revenge. One authority builds the word "revenge" into her definition of terrorism, so convinced is she of its significance.[7] The Levant since World War II has been a case study in this motive. Northern Ireland is another manifestation, requiring no footnotes for proof. Revenge is one of the most visceral of all human feelings, and when it becomes a motive for action, by terrorists, Sicilian mafia rivals, or antagonistic gangs in a U.S. city, it is supremely difficult to eradicate.

Any statesman or negotiator who can make substantial progress against a deepening cycle of revenge deserves generous understanding and support. One thinks of Irish Prime Minister Bertie Ahern, laboring to make lasting peace between professional "retaliants," in unending hours in council rooms, hallways, and the homes of new widows. Before him came others such as Winston Churchill, praised by historian Paul Addison for his "Search for Peace in Ireland" in 1920–22.[8] Despite being the son of a famous advocate for British Ulster, he won the overt admiration of Irish Republican Army (IRA) chieftain Michael Collins for his efforts to end Irish strife.[9] After principals and mediators, there are also war leaders, commanders who *could* have directed their fight into terrorist byways but chose not to do so. Robert E. Lee explicitly declined this option when implored by subordinates to undertake guerrilla warfare rather than surrender – thinking terrorism worse for his country than defeat.[10]

(continued)
some State Department officers, colleagues, and students that we should quantify and study this reality, especially evident in the Algeria of the 1990s and the Taliban's Afghanistan. The long silence on this matter in American commentaries may have finally been broken by Zahir Janmohamed: "Radical Muslims Killing Muslims," a *Washington Post* editorial, June 25, 2003. That paper's Jim Hoagland made another cut at the problem July 13, 2003 in "Fighting for the Soul of Islam," asking "Why do they hate *them?*" France's Bernard Henri Levy has also addressed the subject in a Sept. 2003 interview about his book *Who Killed Daniel Pearl?*

7   Jessica Stern, *The Ultimate Terrorists* (Cambridge MA, 1999), p. 11. Dr. Crenshaw's article on the FLN, op. cit., describes revenge as central to the Algerian war; see pp. 482–3. There are examples of Palestinian terrorism attributed to revenge in chap. 4 of Paul Pillar's *Terrorism and U.S. Foreign Policy* (Washington, DC, 2001).

8   See chap. 7 of *Churchill as Peacemaker*, ed. James Muller (Cambridge, 1997).

9   Similarly, Winston S. Churchill in 1918 and 1919 was speaking out against revenge and for appeasing differences with the Germans, and again, seeking to do the same for French–German relations from 1945 onward.

10 As the definition of terrorism offered at the outset indicates, it is different from "guerrilla war," which is usually directed against military targets during a state of war. There is no record of Robert E. Lee contemplating the use of terrorism, as would some losing belligerents today.

From psychological motives such as resentment and revenge, one may turn to political sources of terrorism. History reveals something as important as it is obvious: disorder and the absence of good governance are a prime source of deliberate violence against the innocent. Some social scientists in the 1990s called this the "gray area phenomenon," assigning it a descriptive acronym, GAP,[11] indicating a region of indefinite size or shape in which the absence of governance, more than malgovernance, leaves a population despairing for peace and civil order. In such an environment, the most brutal or ambitious or energetic may assume the powers of the absent governors. This can yield anarchy, despotism, or a dozen conditions in between. Any of these might lead to terrorism.

That was certainly much of the story of Lebanon in the 1980s, and the repercussions for France, the United Kingdom, and the United States were stinging. It was in part the story of the Sudan in the 1990s and of Afghanistan in that decade through 2001. Osama Bin Laden sought out both those states for their relative incohesion, as well as for the radical moslem authorities in their capitals.[12] There are other examples, such as the "tri border" area between Argentina, Paraguay, and Brazil, a zone where legitimate authority seems to have collapsed in favor of blackmarketeers and violent political subcultures.[13] According to Argentine prosecutors, this area is where the Iranians found the terrorists they employed against two major civilian targets in Buenos Aires, attacks that left hundreds injured or dead.

The art and science of governance are almost beyond the Democratic Republic of the Congo at this writing in mid-2003, with news of fresh horrors emerging steadily, another case of what journalist Robert Kaplan called "the coming anarchy."[14] Two rival ethnic groups are striving for power, and tens of thousands of citizens have paid a devastating price for the absence of consensus and of legal and political authority. Shootings, beatings, and rape are the coin of the day – all aimed at gaining political power and security, or reflecting a fear of losing security and political power.[15] Today's situation somewhat recalls the Congo in 1964. Then, too,

---

[11] Among the most productive working in this area were Peter Lupsha, Max Manwaring, and, at the National Strategy Information Center, Dr. Roy Godson.

[12] This useful observation about Bin Laden and GAP is owed to Col. Carl Shelton, USMC.

[13] This area including Brazil's Foz do Iguacu and Cuidad Del Este of Paraguay drew attention in the mid-1990s, so I noted it in my book *Terrorism Today* (London, 2000), pp. 90, 127. For the latest evidence of terrorists basing there, especially Middle Easterners, see "Tres Fronteras" by Lawrence J. Martinez, *Journal of Counterterrorism and Homeland Security*, vol. 9, no. 1, 2003, pp. 35–6.

[14] His article appeared in *The Atlantic Monthly* in Feb. 1994 and later grew into book form.

[15] The idea that rape, used deliberately and systematically, can be accurately considered a form of terrorism has been explored in several articles in the Frank Cass journal *Terrorism and Political Violence*.

the country possessed little or no real government. Belgian withdrawal had left a political vacuum. In August 1964, it produced insurrection: the provincial capital Stanleyville fell and 1,500 foreigners from two dozen countries became hostages, some of whom were murdered. Year's end brought the first great airborne counterterrorism mission. Belgian troops on the ground liberated hostages and gathered in other terrified victims of violence, and a combined Belgian-American air evacuation – the all-but forgotten "Dragon Rouge" – removed them to safety abroad.[16] Today's intervention by France is just as necessary, for many of the same human reasons. For half a century, this equatorial country has lingered in the GAP.

From ungoverned areas, one may turn to a more common political source of terrorism. Countries in which strife and division are daily factors may also yield terrorism or terrorist groups. To paraphrase an admirable recent British Army field manual on counterinsurgency operations, it is not unusual for a soldier to find him- or herself serving in a nation or state where inherent social divisions based on racial, cultural, religious, or other differences drain away national cohesion.

Foreign commentators on Sri Lanka often seek the roots of that island nation's turmoil in British colonialism, but in reality British colonials had been gone for a generation when insurrection began in 1971. Its power-hungry sponsor was a man named Rohan Wijeweera; his organization was the JVP [Janatha Vimukthi Peramuna, or People's Liberation Front], founded to enhance the majority status of the Sinhalese Sri Lankans and to maximize their advantages in the legal and political order of the country. Wijeweera himself reflected Chinese and Soviet influences, as well as a volatile combination of the left and right – a Patrice Lumumba University graduate who successfully exploited majoritarian nationalism. His JVP shredded the lovely island in the latter 1970s, and its decline facilitated the next phase of political violence by the Leninist "Liberation Tigers of Tamil Eelam," now one of the world's most significant terrorist groups as well as a capable guerrilla army.

The form of national separatism demonstrated by Tamil activists is similar to that of Basques within Spain, Irish Catholics within Ulster, and Palestinians within Israel. Despite the generous nature of the modern democratic state – against the backdrop of history, it is no overstatement to call the modern democratic state "generous" – there remain incentives for rebellion, deeply encoded and sometimes impermeably reflected in the traditions of certain families or the minds of certain leaders. National separatism has been and will remain a leading cause of terrorism, both domestic and international. When the Cold War ended, experts disagreed about whether the

---

[16] Fred E. Wagoner, *Dragon Rouge: The Rescue of Hostages in the Congo* (Washington, DC, 1980).

picture would improve because of the end of Soviet sponsorship of terrorism or worsen because of emergent nationalist strife. In fact, terrorism has *not* become more common. Many national groups have rejected violence. But nationalist terrorism is unlikely ever to disappear from the globe.[17]

Religion has become a greater concern. That trend in the last decade has been documented in the journal *Terrorism & Political Violence*: fewer new terror groups formed in the last decade than in the 1980s or the 1970s, but of the seven groups created in the 1990s, five had a religious cast.[18] Among transnational terrorist groups active on the world stage today, the religiously based compete seriously with those based on ethnicity, ideology, or crime. New strands of militancy with origins in eccentric visions of religious truth include the Christian Identity faith, which denounces jews while exalting white christians. Originating in England in the mid-nineteenth century, it crossed the Atlantic in the latter twentieth to inspire American "Patriot," militias, and white supremacy groups. Those with this religious background and records of lethal violence include Posse Comitatus, Aryan Nations, and Eric Rudolph, the suspect in the Atlanta Olympics attack and other bombings, a fugitive who evaded capture until 2003.[19]

Observers today tend to shun the question whether the term "terrorism" applies to religious violence. Of course it does. One need only examine the deeds, statements, and writings of the relevant groups themselves. The 1994 American documentary film "Jihad in America" opened and closed with pictures of the New York Trade Towers, truck-bombed the year before, and included extensive footage from American cities of clandestine pep rallies for violence. The mass media ignored the film and so did commercial chains. Statements by Osama Bin Laden before 1998 were also largely disregarded. Now, of course, we have the remarkable video interviews, the Manchester safe-house training manual, and the recovered documents from computer hard drives found in terrorist headquarters in Afghanistan in late 2001.[20] These documents reflect the choices and reasons made to employ terror: power, hatred, politics, and religion. Actions are confirming years of words from self-declared warriors who are lethal enemies of those they consider to

---

17   Among the new books on nationalism is Vamik Volkan, *Blood Lines: From Ethnic Pride to Ethnic Terrorism* (Boulder, CO, 1997).
18   Ami Pedahzur, William Eubank, and Leonard Weinberg, "The War on Terrorism and the Decline of Terrorist Group Formation: A Research Note," *Terrorism and Political Violence*, vol. 14, no. 3, 2002, pp. 145–6.
19   Gregory A. Walker, "Service to Other Christians: Christian Identity's Underground Railroad...," *Journal of Counterterrorism and Security International*, vol. 6, no. 3, 2000.
20   The manual is entitled "Military Studies in the Jihad Against the Tyrants" [undated; 180 pp.]. The most remarkable of the *Wall Street Journal*'s articles was by Alan Cullison and Andrew Higgins, "Files Found: A Computer in Kabul Yields a Chilling Array of al Qaeda Memos," Dec. 31, 2001. Later, the *New York Times* also acquired terrorists' documents in Afghanistan.

be apostates who left the true path, most existing Arab or Middle Eastern regimes, jews and Israel, and the West.

The violent spectacles recorded in the daily newspapers of the world underline that diverse causes ignite terrorist thoughts and terrorist acts. For Americans, the most significant causes have changed over time. Americans were most concerned from 1958 to 1961 about communist-inspired terrorist and guerrilla attacks against their citizens in Central and Latin America.[21] This problem intensified during the 1960s and 1970s. It was followed in the 1980s by racial attacks that shifted U.S. attention to domestic White Power groups and religious anticommunists. Then, in the 1990s, U.S. concern shifted again, to two different and rather new problems: militant Islam and "single-issue" terrorist groups concerned with such diverse issues as animal rights, protecting the environment, and antiabortion. Other nations have wrestled with similar challenges. Canada must watch the militant Tamil immigrants and their allies who raise millions of dollars to support the communist and separatist fight in Sri Lanka. In other countries, immigrants are often the victims, as with skinhead violence in such tolerant countries as Norway, Denmark, Sweden, and the Czech Republic. Colombia confronts terrorism from old Marxist-Leninist groups whose political insurgency has melded with organized crime and narcotics trafficking. Peasant militias which arose to combat militant leftists are now a similar source of problems.[22]

HOW TERRORISM WORKS

In April 2000, there began a strange drama in the Republic of the Philippines. It was staged by the separatist Muslim militants of Abu Sayyaf, the latest in a long line of indigenous Filipino insurgents in non-Catholic southern areas. Abu Sayyaf terrorists took foreigners hostage. Naturally that created a crisis – for the Filipino government, for the countries whose nationals were kidnapped, and, it goes without saying, for the victims. Tension and waiting ensued. Armed forces hunted and maneuvered. Strain showed in some political forums. Tourist receipts for the region fell. Some hostages were released, but others were not.

All this was archtypical. It had replayed in many climes and places. Then, about six months later, in October 2000, the crisis abated. Why? Apparently, the Libyan government – a past supporter of muslim militants in the Republic of the Philippines – managed negotiations, which included millions of dollars

---

[21]   David Tucker, *Skirmishes at the Edge of Empire: The United States and International Terrorism* (Westport, CT, 1997), pp. 1–2.

[22]   On the militia called AUC, see the confidential report for the new president of Colombia as described in the *Washington Post*, June 26, 2003. In his published autobiography, the group's leader apparently admits the widespread drug trafficking.

in Libyan funds going to Abu Sayyaf. This money, it was suggested, helped "solve the crisis." Indeed, it probably did.

No one can be against "solving a crisis." For the most part, international silence settled over the case, a vague indicator of tacit approval of the settlement. The Abu Sayyaf group, predictably, bought more guns and speedboats and took more hostages. The Philippines' armed forces continued their hunt and did catch several terrorists. Most hostages remained captives; yet, the news story sank from sight. Only two years later did the Filipinos capture most of the other terrorists.

Throughout, no one publicly asked certain questions: What would international reaction have been if, before April 2000 and without a hostage crisis, Libya had given this known terror group millions of dollars? What if millions in cash had been tendered, and after that, Abu Sayyaf had kidnapped the hostages? In both cases, the reply could only be international scandal and widespread denunciations of Tripoli. Yet, what has in fact happened? Hardly one adult in a thousand remembers the money paid by Libya. The main public discussion in Washington, DC, about Libya concerns Tripoli's efforts to be removed from Washington's list of state sponsors of terrorism.[23]

That example is instructive concerning how terrorism works its effects. Tactics are often simple and indifferent to state or national borders. In an open society such as India's, a semiopen society such as Pakistan's, or even an authoritarian one such as Burma's, it is not difficult to attack a person with a knife or a pistol. The world is awash in small arms, and most who seek underworld dealers can find them. A claim of credit need not accompany each attack. Escape is not even regarded as necessary by some kinds of killers. For the more pragmatic, escape through urban traffic on foot or a motorcycle is likely, if planning is competent. Luck, or having no past criminal record, may enhance one's chance of escape. Perhaps twice a month an innocent Asian dies for some political or religious reason at the hands of assassins who have tracked him through the streets, attacked suddenly, then vanished into the seams of urban life. Later arrest of the perpetrator is the best hope of lawful society because preventing such attacks is on most occasions too difficult.

At the strategic level, terrorism works in diverse ways. The oldest form is the killing of a foreign leader for reasons of state. Bulgaria used Mehmet Ali Agca, a Turk, to try to kill a pontiff (John Paul II) whose charisma

---

23 Paraphrase of a part of the author's speech at the Secretary's Open Forum, U.S. Dept. of State, Oct. 22, 2001, and reprinted in *Vital Speeches*, Dec. 15, 2001, pp. 135–41; see p. 136.
   Officials in the second Clinton Administration often publicly discussed how Libya might be removed from the State Dept. list of state sponsors of terror. This was enhanced when Tripoli pledged to pay compensation for the dead on Pan Am flight 103. The crisis of September 11 perpetuated the bilateral conversations due to hopes of gaining intelligence and other Libyan aid against religious zealots disturbing even to Col. Quaddafi.

was disturbing the totalitarian regimes of Eastern Europe. Another example occurred when the Hasan al Turabi/General Bashir regime in the Sudan turned trained assassins loose in neighboring Ethiopia in anticipation of a state visit by Hosni Mubarak. The Egyptian president was nearly shot in the route taken by his motorcade.[24]

Decades of modern terrorism reveal numerous examples of the use of assassins to attack domestic rivals, at home or abroad, to silence their political activity or to remove them from the list of prospective future rulers. Thus, Bulgaria's communist authorities used assassins to hunt émigrés in London. The Ceaucescu regime reportedly hired "Carlos the Jackal" – Ilich Ramirez Sanchez – to kill a number of Romanian dissidents and exiles living in Paris. Paris was also the scene of several stealthy murders of Iranians, hunted down by the Khomeini regime, suggesting that religious totalitarians are no more troubled by the use of assassins than are communist totalitarians.

A related form of assassination are those acts aimed at removing a pretender to the throne. Such actions are often done by "substate actors." The genre includes Gavrilo Princip, a Serbian nationalist of the group "Union or Death" (often called Black Hand). On Serbian National Day, he attacked the car of Archduke Franz Ferdinand in the streets of Sarajevo, his pistol shots igniting the second bloodiest war in history.[25] Another recent instance of a fateful killing on the verge of international war has already been nearly forgotten: the murder of a great guerrilla warlord and anti-Taliban figure, Ahmad Massoud, "The Lion of the Panshir Valley," blown up by explosives cleverly hidden within a camera, two days before the attacks on America on September 11, 2001. Both aimed at removing a potential ruler, and both did so. In the first case, war was an intended consequence. In the second case, it was already in progress.

A growing literature in the last decades of the twentieth century describes other strategic uses of terrorism. For example, terrorism has assumed a central role in certain insurgencies and has served as an adjunct to conventional war, as Saddam Hussein attempted to do worldwide as the coalition moved to liberate Kuwait. Psychologically, terror can be far more subtle and far reaching than the sounds of the bombs on which it depends.[26] It often makes use of the inevitabilities in human nature. As the Algerian FLN story of 1954

---

[24] One collection of details on Sudan and international terrorism is the author's "Sudan's Neighbors Accuse It of Training Terrorists," *Christian Science Monitor*, Dec. 19, 1995. Five years later, the head of state demoted al Turabi and his followers, some of whom were placed under house arrest.

[25] The Princip case is covered in James Joll, *The Anarchists* (New York, 1966), pp. 73–5, and Martin Gilbert, *The First World War: A Complete History* (New York, 1994), pp. 16–18.

[26] See, for example, the U.S. Navy's Randall G. Bowdish, "Global Terrorism, Strategy, and Naval Forces," in *Globalization and Maritime Power*, ed. Sam J. Tangredi (Washington, DC, 2002), pp. 79–99. I also wish to thank Captain Bowdish for reviewing a draft of this chapter.

suggests, terror can polarize a community along racial, religious, or other lines. Osama Bin Laden understood this when crowing about his success in the first days after September 11: he boasted that al Qaeda actions were forcing the world's moslem community to make a choice – would it be with the militant purists or the degenerate West?

Violence is of course, quite overtly, a recruiting tool. Terror represents a flag, to signify movement and action, announce an offensive, and seek comrades for further actions. It remains unclear whether Bin Laden's claim after the attacks on the eastern United States that recruiting for his organization had never been stronger was accurate. Normally, that is one result of well-executed strikes. But there are exceptions, as when the human damage repels enough of the target audience sufficiently to cause the radicals to lose heart or at least set aside such methods. U.S. "Patriots" became quiet after the bombing of the federal building in Oklahoma City caused such loss of innocent life in 1995.

Terror also has important roles *within* a militant movement. Landmark studies of terrorism's role in fascist and communist organizations of the 1930s and 1940s as yet have no counterpart in academic work on modern international terror groups. But the threat and practice of internecine violence against militants themselves for deviation or tendencies toward capitulation is common. In the fifteen months after the "Good Friday" accord, the IRA carried out both killings and some 150 "punishment beatings," many against its own, not its enemies.[27] Capital punishments following one mass self-criticism session cut deep into the ranks of the tiny Japanese Red Army. The death penalty was regularly used by the Abu Nidal Organization. Such internal terrorism communicates a spirit of insuperable force within the group and simultaneously rids it of troublesome potential rivals or nascent opposition. Killing can suppress the moderation that tends to appear in all human organizations. The FLN shoved aside some earnest and conscience-filled moderates in its drive to ignite violent revolution in Algeria. Ferhat Abbas, a long-known leader of the moderate movement toward Algerian independence, was in one sense a rival to the FLN as it initiated its revolution. His nephew was soon murdered, explicitly because of the younger man's criticism of FLN bloody excesses, but also perhaps as a warning to his famed uncle.[28]

---

[27] Punishment beatings as a reality in such illegal groups are mentioned by Andrew R. Molnar et al., *Human Factors Considerations of Undergrounds in Insurgencies* (Washington, DC, 1965), p. 172.

[28] Horn, pp. 119–20. Two years later, Ferhat Abbas himself joined, or was allowed to join, the FLN, all but abandoning his own brand of gentle political pressure on France. There followed a Machiavellian use of the gentleman's profile: he was elevated as head of the FLN Provisional Government, a handsome face for outside eyes. But after the successful parade into Algiers amidst victory in 1962, Abbas could be shunted aside three years later.

That is also often the pattern in successful revolutions. Moderates critical to revolutionary success are removed once the revolution has succeeded. The French Revolution began with great idealism, but soon degenerated into what analysts often describe as the modern world's first explicit state terror, dominated by men ostensibly devoted to "liberty, equality, and fraternity." Similar actions by the Bolsheviks led to Churchill's description in *The Aftermath* of how communists in Russia worked with liberals and socialists to make revolution, using them as "well-meaning and unwitting decoy ducks," only to destroy them immediately when their usefulness had passed.[29]

Terrorism is sometimes used to undermine public support for an ally. In the mid-1980s, Abu Nidal set a new standard for publicized mass murder of civilians at targets in Asia, the Middle East, and especially Europe. To this was added Hezbollah's hijacking of TWA 847 and a long drama in Beirut, complete with an execution, beatings, and press conferences. As the summer horrors by these two enemies of Tel Aviv mounted, pollsters reported no rise in sympathy for Israel; instead, their polls showed a decline in American public support for Israel. More than half of America believed Israel should do more to resolve the crisis. Private citizens queried each other on their views, sometimes with suspicion and resentment. Military officers quietly spoke of an "imbalance" in U.S. policy in the region. Public press organs and their commentators called for adjustments in Israeli policy. Although none of these speakers ever described themselves as "yielding to terrorism," their behavior illustrated its psychological and political effects.[30]

Terrorism by West European communists has often aimed at weakening NATO by driving wedges between its European and American partners.[31] Examples include the troubles in Germany during the 1990s. Frequently attacked in Germany by the PKK "Kurdish Workers Party," Bonn found itself further troubled when several long-standing international allies became unwilling to sell arms to the *Bundeswehr*. Consider the meaning of that quiet erosion of support for a NATO ally. Few states in recent decades have been less aggressive than Germany. Yet, a modest propaganda campaign by the PKK and neutral human rights activists focused on Ankara's use of German weapons against armed Kurds within Turkey caused serious problems for Berlin.

---

[29] Winston S. Churchill, *The World Crisis*, vol. 6, *The Aftermath* (Boston, 1928), pp. 76–7.
[30] Rep. James A. Courter explained, and sought to correct, this drift in public opinion in two brief floor speeches in the U.S. House of Representatives, June 18 and July 23, 1985.
[31] Harold W. Rood's lectures at Claremont Graduate School alerted me to this, and I then profited greatly from studying Paul B. Henze's work on the matter, including his book on the plot to kill Pope John Paul II and his essay "Goal: Destabilization: Soviet Agitational Propaganda, Instability, and Terrorism in NATO South," a Dec. 1981 report for the European American Institute for Security Research, Marina del Rey, CA.

This phenomenon occurs despite historical evidence that yielding rarely appeases terrorists.[32] The attacks in 2003 on Saudi Arabians and foreigners working in Riyadh occurred two weeks *after* the American Secretary of Defense made headlines on April 29 announcing that U.S. troops would be withdrawn from the kingdom. Supposedly, such a withdrawal was the leading political objective of al Qaeda, but the group, nevertheless, proceeded with synchronized attacks that killed dozens of people. Saudi Arabia once was one of the half-dozen safest places in the world for a U.S. soldier – notably safer, for example, than Detroit at night. But since terrorist attacks began in 1995, Saudi Arabia has become much less friendly. A decade ago, Americans were standing with Saudis as brethren in arms to face down Iraq. By mid-2003, some Saudis were breathing relief with Americans' departure. Terrorism directed by non-Saudis has driven a wedge into a century-old friendship.

Politically, terrorism has many other strategic effects. The most apparent to an interknit world is international publicity. Time and time again, the media elevates obscure causes into the public view as a result of terror inflicted by activists willing to target the innocent to attract attention. The Algerian FLN was media savvy. It self-consciously and explicitly sought world attention and United Nations support when it opened its campaigns of publicity, organization, guerrilla war, and terror.[33] It undertook armed activity and founded the revolutionary newspaper *El Moudjahid* to report on it. FLN emissaries appeared at the UN in New York and also staffed seven regional bureaus in Cairo, Damascus, Tunis, Beirut, Baghdad, Karachi, and Djakarta. They were supplemented by "mobile delegations" of roving diplomats.[34] Dr. Frantz Fanon was not only an editor of *El Moudjahid* in Tunis, but later a diplomat of the provisional government. A world sensitive to self-determination apparently accepted FLN terrorism. It looked at the blood and then beyond, just as the perpetrators hoped. Some accepted the human damage as resulting from a natural excess of nationalist passion. Others accepted it as the inevitable response to a century of French repression. Optimists believed that, whatever the cause of the terrorism, victory for the perpetrators would end the violence. It did not. Thus, long before the PLO existed, this North African insurgency made itself, in the world eyes, "the sole legitimate representative of the [Algerian] people."

---

[32] See Henze, "Goal: Destabilization," p. 61, for one example. President Ronald Reagan, Prime Minister Margaret Thatcher, and certain of their subordinates also enunciated the view that appeasement of terrorists would fail.

[33] Duchemin, *Histoire du F.L.N.*, p. 222, quoting Yacef. See also the detailed work by Matthew Connelly, *A Diplomatic Revolution: Algeria's Fight for Independence and the Origins of the Post-Cold War Era* (Oxford, 2002). This book does not explore the FLN's terrorism.

[34] Connelly, *A Diplomatic Revolution*, p. 110.

The FLN's print-press offensive anticipated the media efforts of contemporary violent groups. Hezbollah runs a TV station. The Tamil Tigers have an endearing Web site. Support letters for the Iraqi-based terrorists of "People's Mujahideen" circulate annually in the halls of the U.S. Congress and win many signatures. A famous front group for the IRA Provos collects bag loads of money in New York and Boston, and has sent representatives to dine in the White House.

Terrorism also has an economic component. The economic dimensions of terrorism have been little studied. Social science and news journals – even those devoted to terrorism – rarely dwell on the economic impact of bombs, shootings, and threats. Private corporations have been left to their private concerns. Public citizens' groups seem not to notice. In the later 1990s, discussion emerged about what is variously called infoterror or cyberterrorism, which would not be "violent," but could be destructive in ways that are economic, bureaucratic, and psychological. September 11 brought instantaneous change. Now there is immense attention to economic losses, changes in stock prices, the bill for recovery in New York, the price of Homeland Security, the great costs of private security, and so on.[35] Whatever one thinks of the terrorists' objective, all these losses are an irretrievable wastage of the fruits of human labor.

Oil pipeline attacks by the ELN (National Liberation Army) in Colombia have severely injured state revenues from exports. But for the terrorists such attacks are effective in flying the ELN flag, in injuring Columbia's financial ability to defend itself, and in garnering money because some corporate victims will pay "revolutionary taxes" to avoid the damage. Through such extortion, terrorists drain the state's financial resources into their own purses. ELN is economically more powerful than most businesses in Colombia, and yet it is a weak rival to the larger FARC (the Revolutionary Armed Forces of Colombia), another terrorism-dependent insurgent group.

The economic strategies of terror groups also include damaging the tourism industry. Fanatical adherents to Islam have done this in Egypt. Gama'at and Jihad made many such attacks in the 1990s. The shooting of fifty-eight foreign visitors to Luxor Temple in November 1997 was their most deadly success. This tiny Egyptian minority sacrificed millions in future tourist dollars and ironically deterred visitors and students from learning about places and cultures which Islamic militants invariably claim outsiders ill understand.

---

[35] The first such book in the United States – doubtless the tip of an approaching mass – is *Terrorism and Business: The Impact of September 11, 2001*, edited by Yonah Alexander, perhaps the most published author on terrorism studies in the English language. It was appropriate that he move first because his 1979 work *Political Terrorism and Business: The Threat and Response* is one of a very few books on this line during the quarter-century before 2000.

History's overriding lesson is that terrorism does work, at least well enough to keep terrorists and their imitators attempting it. Such a conclusion is contentious.[36] But terrorism often does attain its tactical objectives. Moreover, it can survive at the operational or strategic levels for a long time even without apparent results, and that low standard for success is all many terrorists and guerrillas require. Some terrorists have indeed succeeded, such as Lenin, Mao, the Khmer Rouge, and the Ortega brothers in Nicaragua.[37] They used terror in calculated conjunction with other means to gain power and then used it again to hold power.[38] That is probably their own highest standard for success, and they achieved it. Finally, in other places and circumstances, groups could not win power, but did use all they had to batter the existing social structure or state, or obtain limited changes to the status quo. These are interim objectives obtained. Governments fell in Turkey and in Uruguay because of terrorist violence, clear defeats for democracy.

HOW TERRORIST GROUPS END

The Assassins – sometimes called Isma'ilis, sometimes Nizaris, were an off-shoot of Shia Islam. They arose in Iraq and Persia near the end of the eleventh century. Although never powerful in Iraq, the sect was immensely so in Persia, and it spread to Egypt and Syria for shorter periods. Not until the latter thirteenth century was the Assassins' power destroyed. The causes of this end were mixed.

In Egypt, violent Shia had a fair run – one branch even established its own caliphate. But Sunni Turkish authorities broke the strength of these "deviants" from mainstream Sunni faith – especially under the accomplished military leader Saladin (Salah al-Din Yusuf ibn Ayyub). From 1171, he ruled his opponents in Egypt, and even found time to turn his attention to Syria.

In Syria, local strongmen let the Assassins (Nizaris) spread, either from tolerance or from hopes of using them to their own ends. But gradually the authorities' successors perceived the threat, and opposed it, often with

---

[36] My view on this problem is probably not shared by the admirable Georgetown University authority Walter Laqueur. It is loudly disputed by a slender new book in print in the wake of September: Caleb Carr's *The Lessons of Terrorism: A History of Warfare Against Civilians: Why it Has Always Failed and Why it Will Fail Again*. Both authors deny terrorism's success; one hopes they are correct.

[37] A relevant source, describing all these revolutionary movements in a single large volume, is that prepared by a team of scholars including Stephane Courtois, *The Black Book of Communism: Crimes, Terror, Repression*, trans. Jonathan Murphy and Mark Kramer (Cambridge, MA, 1999).

[38] Terrorism is a psychological and political tool and a method, and one who uses it can legitimately be called "a terrorist" – even if he is also a revolutionary, a self-described humanist, an insurgent, a militia leader, a father of his country, etc. Examination of terrorists' writings and utterances yields cases, in which they call *themselves* terrorists – despite others hastening to their defense. These admissions are among the many indicators that, despite the difficulties, terrorism can be defined and described.

force, sometimes with massacres. Sunni rulers were the most devastating opponents of these Shia, and the latter's clever deals with Crusaders and Frankish authorities brought as many troubles as benefits. The sect in Syria suffered badly when Mongols battered the Assassins' human and ideological centers of gravity in Persia. Early in the fourteenth century, the line of Nizari Imams divided, and this schism doomed them in Syria.

In Persia, their stronghold, the cause of the sect's demise was the Mongols. Being ruthless, these Eastern horsemen and conquerors recognized total ruthlessness in their enemy, and from 1256 to 1270 systematically destroyed or defeated the Assassins' castle strongholds along the Caspian Sea and at points south. When the most celebrated and inaccessible fortress, Alamut, fell, a chronicler of the time gloated: "All the inmates of that seminary of iniquity and nest of Satan came down with all their goods and belongings."[39]

Twenty years ago, Britain's Peter Janke compiled a large and reliable volume of *Guerrilla and Terrorist Organizations: A World Directory and Bibliography*.[40] Most of the groups named in his volume have since departed the world stage. How that happens, however – how terrorist movements end – has received little attention. The following six ways in which groups have expired may be considered an introduction to this important phenomenon.

Perhaps the most historically common way that a terror group ends is that, confronting such a lethal threat, the regime strikes back with force, overwhelming or crushing the group or movement. That is what happened to the Assassins: deviousness and savagery were defeated by greater organization and greater savagery. That resolution anticipated the early twentieth-century demise of certain rivals to the Bolsheviks. Vladimir Lenin defeated other active revolutionary movements – some larger than his own – by being better organized and equally ruthless. In Churchill's words from *The World Crisis*, Social Revolutionaries, Mensheviks, and other leftist rivals:

> crumpled up almost simultaneously. One sect alone made a momentary stand. The Anarchists, strong in the traditions of Bakunin, conceived themselves unapproachable in extremism. If the Bolsheviks would turn the world upside down, they would turn it inside out; if the Bolsheviks abolished right and wrong, they would abolish right and left. They therefore spoke with confidence and held their heads high. But their case had been carefully studied in advance by the new authorities. No time was wasted in argument. Both in Petrograd and in Moscow they were bombed in their headquarters and hunted down and shot with the utmost expedition.[41]

---

[39] Bernard Lewis, *The Assassins: A Radical Sect in Islam* (New York, 2003). W. B. Bartlett, *The Assassins: The Story of Medieval Islam's Secret Sect* (Phoenix Mill, UK, 2001). The quotation at the end of my paragraphs is from Bartlett, *The Assassins*, p. 180.

[40] Peter Janke with Richard Sim, *Guerrilla and Terrorist Organizations: A World Directory and Bibliography* (New York, 1983).

[41] Churchill, *The World Crisis* (London, 1929), p. 80.

A second way in which terrorism ends is through suppression by a moderate regime, roused into taking comprehensive and hard measures against the threat. It employs its local and national police, other law-related measures such as wire taps and prolonged detention, policies such as immigration controls, administrative powers such as regulating bank transactions, public information or propaganda campaigns against the terrorists, and perhaps corrective measures promoting public welfare. Sometimes, it also uses dramatic force; it may even use its army on its own citizens.

This is the approach modern democracies have at times taken since World War II. Two of the successes were against terrorist movements within larger insurgencies: the Malayan Emergency and the Huk movement in the Philippines. In both cases, indigenous leadership was important, for credibility as well as for efficiency. Tunku Abdul Rahman in Malaya had appeal to all parties and major social groups.[42] In the Philippines, Ramon Magsaysay was surely one of the most impressive Third World leaders of this past century, however short his tenure as Defense Minister and President.[43] These leaders also had the advantage of aid from outside powers, Britain and the United States, respectively, but neither power overwhelmed its indigenous ally. Moreover, the insurgents in both countries lacked strong outside help. Both countries were moving rapidly to formal independence so the rhetoric of anticolonialism was blunted. And the two governments adopted comprehensive antiterror strategies. Making defeat of terrorism and insurgency their number one priority, they used all manner of political, psychological, economic, and military powers. They emphasized good human intelligence. Smart individual policemen were as important as high-ranking generals. A doctrine of minimal and responsible use of force was successful because the guerrillas were not substantially reinforced or armed from outside. In both countries, the governments moved belatedly, but they moved decisively, suppressing terrorism by arrests and small unit military action, which produced waves of defections from the communist side. Insurgency, and its components of guerrilla war and terrorism, ended together.[44]

---

[42] Dr. Ian Beckett, lecture on the Malayan Emergency, U.S. Marine Corps Command & Staff College, Quantico, VA, April 28, 2003. And see the classic by Robert Thompson, *Defeating Communist Insurgency: Experiences from Malaya and Vietnam* (London, repr. 1987).

[43] On counterinsurgency against the Huks at the level of grand strategy, see Edward Geary Lansdale, *In the Midst of Wars: An American's Mission to Southeast Asia* (New York, 1972).

[44] Although Malaysia has in fact remained at peace, the same cannot be said of the Philippines. Before the Huk crisis, there had been a major war of independence waged by Aguinaldo at the end of the nineteenth century; after the mid–twentieth-century Huk crisis, there followed the (communist) New People's Army, which has waxed and waned but remains strong in some areas. There have always been muslim movements against the authorities, especially in the southern islands; Abu Sayyaf is one of these regularly employing terror. Terrorism, whether by NPA or moslem groups, has thus been a low-level perennial in the lives of this generation of Filipinos.

A third way terrorism ends is by the arrest of the individual who is its center of gravity. In the Algerian FLN, there was no such individual. The arrest
of Ben Bella and several other revolutionary leaders, when the French forced
down their Moroccan aircraft in 1956, merely injured the FLN without in
any way crippling it. But the last decade has supplied two illustrations of
how "decapitating" a group may render it helpless. The arrest of Abimael
Guzman in September 1992 and the arrest of Abdullah Ocalan in February
1999 all but ended the considerable power of Sendero Luminoso and the
Kurdish Worker's Party. The former wound down immediately and steeply.
A follow-on leader emerged but was soon arrested. For a decade, the group
has been almost completely silent.[45] The Kurds of PKK have changed their
group name and pledged themselves to peaceful activism.[46] PKK attacks,
once commonplace in Europe, especially Turkey and Germany, are now
uncommon.

This raises the question of assessing al Qaeda, a new organization, for
none is precisely like another. If Bin Laden's personal authority is not assum-
able by another, if his purse strings are nontransferable, or if his lieutenants do not share his global vision, but desire to focus only on their
different homelands, then capturing or killing Bin Laden would probably
send the organization into precipitous decline, leaving more manageable
splinter groups, each in its own locality or region. However, if al Qaeda
is a kind of global religious insurgency, based on broad popular resentment, the death or capture of Bin Laden would be significant but not decisive.[47] It might simply shift the group's control to Egyptian medical doctor
Aiman al Zawahiri, currently the number two in the organization, a terrorist leader in his own right a decade ago, just as prolix as Bin Laden,
and perhaps as good an organizer. He could assume rule; so could a committee. Successful defeat of al Qaeda then would require defeating and
discrediting the militancy of Islamic radicals. Cultivation of sober Islamic
leaders; good bilateral relations with Arab states; psychological operations
against terrorism; targeted economic aid programs for poor "gray areas" in
moslem sections of the Philippines, Sudan, and similar countries; and other

---

[45] In the new millennium, Sendero has shown limited signs of revival; see, for example, the
     New York Times, July 23, 2003.
[46] The name change to "Democratic Republic Party" was reported by the *Washington Times*,
     Feb. 20, 2002; a later State Department report indicates a change to KADEK, the "Kurdistan
     Freedom and Democracy Congress" and notes the group still maintains some 8,000 trained
     fighters. Attacks have all but ceased. A recent exception was casualties from an engagement
     with Turkish forces as some members reinfiltrate into Turkey following the coalition success
     against Saddam Hussein.
[47] The view of al Qaeda as a global insurgency – probably not subject to strictly military or
     "decapitation" strategies – is one propounded by Dr. Tucker, lecturing in Spring 2002 at
     the Institute of World Politics, Washington, DC.

measures would be as appropriate as was terminating Taliban influence in Afghanistan.[48]

A fourth way terror groups have met their end is through sheer fatigue. Some just wear out. Chin Peng fought and held out hope for even longer than Mao Tse Tung, yet never prevailed, and eventually surrendered to Malaysian authorities, which ended his meager violent operations. His will was remarkable, yet even that could break. The other target of a well-directed 1950s counterinsurgency campaign mentioned previously, Luis Taruc of the Filipino Huks, ended his fight the same way: by surrender.

Many terrorists give up much faster. In a revealing memoir, *The Reckoning: A Neo-Nazi Drops Out*, Ingo Hasselbach recounts his swift rise to high rank on the right wing extremes of a reunited Germany. His descent was as swift. After only five years, he quit because of growing self-loathing and weariness. Hatred had been hot and fueled street action, but it ran short, and diffidence, self-contempt, and longing for civilized friendships crept in. He was a mere twenty-five years old when he left the movement, which he now condemns.[49]

Failure of will is one of the reasons many former terrorists have disappeared from the public eye. Ulrike Meinhof, the gifted German propagandist and leader of Baader-Meinhof, might now be a contented grandmother several times over, but that was never her aspiration. Serving a mere eight-year sentence for her crimes, Meinhof must have despaired, for she committed suicide in jail. The other two principals, Andreas Baader and Gudrun Ensslin, also jailed, staked their hopes on being freed by comrades hijacking a Lufthansa jet in 1977. When that plan was ruined by a brilliant German commando operation, which retook the airliner in Mogadishu and rescued eighty-seven passengers, the two terrorists hanged themselves in jail, a year after Meinhof.[50] Clearly, this fourth termination mechanism, terrorist fatigue, owes something to the resistance by the state enemy.

A fifth way terrorism ends is that the perpetrators fold themselves into normal politics or civilized life. This was the approach taken by individuals such as Danny Cohen-Bendit, now a German official, and Mark Rudd, the American "Weatherman" leader, who by the mid-1980s was a school teacher in the American southwest. On occasion, an entire terror group has taken this path. Colombia's M-19 was a Castroite organization, small but with a high

---

[48] Another way to study al Qaeda would be as a complex adaptive system, in accordance with the Complexity Theory in use at the Santa Fe Institute and other locales. At Sandhurst in July 2003, conference speaker Lieutenant General P. K. Van Riper, USMC retired, recommended this to the author as a promising line of inquiry.

[49] The U.S. title by Ingo Hasselbach (with Tom Reiss) is *Fuhrer-Ex: Memoirs of a Former Neo-Nazi* (New York, 1996).

[50] Although there was a second generation RAF, it also lapsed. Today, in Germany, there is great contention over plans for a late 2004 exhibit on the RAF and its meanings.

profile in the late 1970s and early 1980s. It enjoyed state support from Cuba, Nicaragua, and even Libya. In 1985, this "19th of April" organization took five hundred hostages while occupying the Palace of Justice in Bogotá. When the day ended, Colombia's security forces stormed the building. Eleven high court justices died; the building was burned, and with it burned the records of M-19s narcotrafficking partners. M-19 lost many leaders that day and could no longer prevail against Colombian authorities. It accepted the offer of an amnesty and engaged in overt politics. A few members were successfully elected to politics and lived, but political enemies also assassinated many M-19 leaders once they set aside their guns and their precautions.

El Salvador's one-time revolutionary Joachim Villalobos has done well folding into postwar democratic life. This talented extremist maneuvered and shot his way into leadership of the ERP (Revolutionary People's Army).[51] When five such Salvadoran groups melded, he became a top field commander. Today, Villalobos is married to a millionaire, lives in a walled compound in a rich area of San Salvador, and is modestly active in politics. He often speaks abroad at conferences on conflict resolution, including the U.S. Army's War College and Oxford, where he earned a doctorate. Several other Salvadoreans famous for terrorism and/or guerrilla war are now members of parliament in El Salvador.[52]

The Nicaraguan Sandinistas represent a similar case of a group that combined the practice of terrorism with clandestine organization and guerrilla war to attain power. But then they submitted to different rigors: electoral politics. Many observers were amazed when, after a decade in power, the Daniel and Humberto Ortega regime allowed popular elections. Perhaps the Ortega brothers and their comrades were themselves astonished when they lost. Since that time, 1990, they have kept the Sandinista Party alive.[53]

The Sandinistas' decade in power suggests a sixth and final end: terrorism may win. This is not to argue that it always succeeds, much less that it succeeds by itself. But terrorism's methods and calculations, when combined with persistence and fortune and some forms of public appeal, may triumph. Revolutionary parties, using terrorism in a calculated mix with guerrilla war and covert organization and other forms of politics that have

[51] Michael Radu and Vladimir Tismaneanu, *Latin American Revolutionaries: Groups, Goals, Methods* (Washington, DC, 1990), p. 210. Now dated, this superb volume has been the best English-language encyclopedia on militant leftists in the lower Western Hemisphere. Given the decline of most subject groups, it is unlikely to enjoy a second edition.

[52] World Wide Web pages such as those of Oxford University and the U.S. Army War College, and a June 2003 telephone interview with Dr. J. Michael Waller, Annenberg Professor of International Communication, The Institute of World Politics, Washington, DC.

[53] Some Sandinistas in overt politics were assassinated after their party lost. Others still active in politics include the once-feared secret police chief Lenin Cerna. Former interior minister Thomas Borge is among the Sandinistas now grown wealthy from business, according to Dr. Waller (op. cit.).

attained complete governmental power during the twentieth century, include the Bolsheviks, the Maoists, the Castroites, the Algerian FLN, and the Khmer Rouge.

The suggestion that terrorism may succeed prompts the question: "What is success?" As noted earlier, there are important forms of partial success. One is to gain effective sway over regional or national affairs without holding state office. Another is to assume state power temporarily. Another is simply to bring down the current state structure, even if the terrorists cannot themselves replace it. Like other human organizations, violent groups may have ultimate objectives and also intermediate ones. They may deem partial success worth having.

FARC has been a violent opponent of Colombian democracy since the mid-1960s. Its leaders may well think it enough to have survived and flourish in large swaths of that state, even if they are unlikely to break the government in Bogotá. Their cadre live in, and even administer via shadow governments, large "liberated" zones, including for several years a region the size of Switzerland that the last executive, President Pastrana, in a shocking abandonment of sovereignty, demilitarized and vacated. For famed FARC boss "Sure Shot" ("Tirofijo") Marulanda Velez, this may be victory enough. He is said to be vigorous for his years – three-fourths of a century. He is a hero to hundreds of thousands, one of the richer men in the country, and his word means life or death for all those within his power. Undoubtedly, he would prefer to hold national power, but his "state within a state" is doubtless a compensation and a good living. Counterinsurgency manuals sometimes state that, for the guerrilla, "to survive is to win." Although that limited form of success may not satisfy all, it satisfies many guerrillas and terrorists.

"Revolutionary Organization November 17" made virtually no outward progress during a quarter-century in the Greek underground. It had some two dozen hardcore members in 1975 and no more when the millennium ended. Often employing the same Colt 45 pistol in its murders and known for lengthy Marxist-Leninist proclamations, November 17 survived during all those years as a burr to authorities and a standard bearer for revolution. Its persistence and secretiveness kept fear alive in Greece and in NATO, a favored target of its assassinations. Gradually, the legacy came to include quiet international contempt for a Greek government which could not or would not stamp it out. No member of November 17 was arrested until the group botched a bombing in June 2002, and then, in subsequent arrests, informed on one another. By that year's end, the Greek government had arrested nineteen men.[54] But for decades, no member had defected in discouragement.

---

[54] U.S. Dept. of State, "Patterns of Global Terrorism," Washington, DC, April 2003, p. 46.

THE FUTURE OF TERRORISM

"Three rapid attack craft and three supply ships belonging to the Sri Lankan Navy were damaged in this historic offensive launched by the Black Sea Tigers at 0130 yesterday morning. Nine Black Sea Tigers, including two women ... embraced martyrdom from the LTTE side while carrying out this successful surprise attack. This attack was a joint operation. ... Swimming underwater the Black Sea Tiger frogmen attached bombs to the ships and blasted them. ... At the same time, a speedboat of the Black Sea Tigers entered the port swiftly and attacked the buildings in the port complex with rocket-propelled grenades. ... At that time, there was fierce fighting between the Black Sea Tigers and Sri Lankan naval forces inside the harbor area. The fact that the Sea Tigers can penetrate the enemy's security zone with weapons in groups and launch offensives has frightened the Sri Lankan authorities. A correspondent from Colombo reports that the nightmares of Sri Lankan authorities have come true."[55]

The Tamil success suggests much about the near-term future. First, the Liberation Tigers of Tamil Eelam, one of the world's most lethal killers of civilians, but also a group very adept at guerrilla war, released the previous statement. The LTTE have made the transition from terrorism to insurgency, and do both with facility, as Hezbollah does. Second, this attack and others by LTTE suggest much to armies and navies about force protection. Suicide boats or frogmen had sunk more than a few Sri Lankan naval vessels by the time of the suicide attack on the *USS Cole*. A third feature is that this was a press release, issued on the World Wide Web. A fourth is its boastfulness about its women as killers. LTTE also has used child killers in large numbers in the past, but recently ceased boasting about that morally awkward subject. Others may derive further insights from this brief statement by Tamil publicists.[56]

Modern history makes it evident that terrorism has a future. What can be said about that future? Social sciences are as much art as science; technically, they cannot offer predictions. That is why contributors to this volume have said so much about what history "suggests" and so little about what it ordains. It ordains nothing. Moreover, trends in evidence today may change or even reverse themselves tomorrow. Trend analysis is a touchy and unreliable subject. But it is clear that terrorism has a future. Even the current global war on terrorism led by the United States and Britain cannot and will not extirpate it. It has been with the international community for decades. All living citizens recall its sting because they all have been part of

---

[55] Tamil Eelam News Web posting of April 13, 1996, trans. and repr. by the Foreign Broadcast Information Service, June 10, 1996, p. 80.

[56] A theme of my own publications is that the spoken and written words of active terrorists are far more revealing and useful than many social scientists think.

its designated audiences. Terrorism, in its durability, is akin to crime – it is successful enough so that it will always be with the world, and there will always be hopefuls who take up the method as an alternative to peaceful politics or for the power it gives or promises.

What cannot be foreseen is the level of global terrorism. One measure is incident levels. Currently, these average some 300 to 400 transnational acts a year. Another measure of terrorism is its reach. George W. Bush and his administration's campaign has from the beginning properly aimed at all "terror groups with global reach," not simply all terrorists, for that would be impossible. A third measure of terrorism's strength is the duration of the deadliest groups. One scholar probably errs in generalizing that "statistically, most guerrilla and terrorist campaigns last between 13 and 14 years."[57] Revolutionary Organization November 17, for example, lasted for more than a quarter-century, suffering not a single arrest. Were the generalization true, al Qaeda, which originated at the end of the 1980s, would now be dead. Instead, al Qaeda retains many personnel, including several key leaders. Even if further battered, it may still revive in unexpected places.

A related way to measure terrorism's endurance is to turn away from individual groups and take the long view of a state or states. Several governments such as Iran have for decades been outright sponsors of violence abroad. Iraq has been on the State Department's list of sponsors of terror since 1979. Only the forcible deposition of Saddam Hussein finally changed that pattern. Recent public discussion has focused on Iraq's limited linkages to al Qaeda, but the state's long-standing relations with the secular Palestinians Abu Nidal and Abu Abbas provide a clearer picture of Iraq's terrorist relations.[58] North Korea has always accentuated guerrilla war, but it has done more. Its agents have carried out terrorist attacks abroad – by assaults on South Korea, by kidnappings in Japan, and by bombing an airliner and a foreign Cabinet meeting in Burma. North Korea has already had a "regime change," but the successor to the "great leader" is the man reputed to have directed several of Pyongyang's worst terror attacks.[59]

The Republic of Yemen is a state of a wholly different sort, but also one associated with terrorism. Its pattern has been more of change than continuity. From 1970 onward, South Yemen was in the public eye as a member of the Soviet bloc, which itself fostered terrorism. That bilateral policy and the

---

[57] Rohan Gunaratna, *Inside Al-Qaeda: Global Network of Terror* (New York, 2002), p. 13. This may be an error that even Gunaratna does not defend because his book makes it evident he thinks al Qaeda remains very powerful and dangerous. Gunaratna has since released a mid-2003 edition. He is in the unusual position of a scholar in great demand by academics, police, and media in Europe, the United States, and other regions, and his high repute is richly deserved.

[58] Nidal died in Iraq shortly before the war of 2003; Abbas was arrested when the Allies invaded.

[59] Kim Hyun Hee, *The Tears of My Soul* (New York, 1993).

country's remoteness and geographic advantages contributed to further international problems. The PLO trained pilots there, according to one report.[60] There were camps for foreign gunmen such as those loyal to George Habash, who led the PLO splinter group PFLP. The regime did not merely tolerate this; it gave every appearance of approval. Hijackers often sought refuge there.

South Yemen disappeared after the USSR did, when war broke out between north and south. Since reunification, the Yemeni state has been making its way back into the world community. Yet, by the late 1990s, united Yemen was again known for violence, its current phase characterized by criminal kidnappings for ransom, general lawlessness in certain areas, and the presence (but not necessarily sponsorship) of international terrorists. This homeland of Bin Laden's father yielded militants seeking jihad.[61] Moslem radicals also came to Yemen for training – this known by the end of the 1990s. Today, the country is not on the State Department's list of sponsors of international terrorism, but it remains under an international microscope. Absence of strong central government, ideological and familial sympathies with active terrorists, and geography all make the small state one to watch. Yemen's last several decades offer a case study in the way terrorism rarely dies; it may linger, or reemerge later, in new ways.

Similar problem states are Afghanistan, Lebanon, and Sudan. Some of the new "stans" are likely to continue adding to the transnational terrorism phenomenon. Jihadi training of youngsters now takes place in schools in the Fergana Valley connecting Uzbekistan with two of its neighbors.[62] Apart from such "gray area" states, there will always be states which are outright exporters of violence. Some have prospered through the use of terrorism, and others will attempt the same for their own interests. This factor has been a harsh challenge to international law and organization. The authors of the UN Charter did not dwell on the low-level purposeful export of violence by states. But the half-century since has demonstrated the need for counteraction.

There are many other reasons that terrorism will persist, having to do with transient but powerful underlying political causes, with the persistence of human problems, or with the intrepid nature of many ideologies. Terror's utility as a method of insurgents is yet another reason terror will endure. Terrorism was a tactic of Red Chinese insurgents and militia from the 1920s onward. After World War II, insurgents inspired by Mao such as the Huks,

---

60 Owned by Jane's, *Foreign Report* was perhaps the best open-source periodical covering terrorism in English; later, it was bought by *The Economist*.

61 For example, when the USS *Cole* was blown up in harbor, it emerged that perpetrators may have had identification documents via a Yemeni official of a low level, friendly but unofficially.

62 Martha Brill Olcott and Bakhtiyar Babajanov, "The Terrorist Notebooks," *Foreign Policy*, March April 2003, pp. 30–40.

the Malay Communists, the Vietcong, and the Khmer Rouge, all used terror in their struggles. In the 1980s, Maoist methods brought Sendero Luminoso to power in large swaths of Peru, and there was Maoism evident in some violent parts of India. Since 1996, there has been a revolutionary war in Nepal by indigenous self-described Maoists.[63] Terrorism as a tool of insurgency thus is a well-founded pattern in history, as well as the product of clear and extremist political ideas of Maoist character.

Terrorism thus stays on, but it does not stay the same. Occasionally, there *are* new things under the sun. There are new political movements, new circumstances giving rise to violence, and new cults. Since 1968, the counterterrorist community has seen no other group like al Qaeda. There is no precedent for this powerful and cohesive international multiethnic terror organization.[64] Yet, because that is well recognized in the British and American capitals and other places, and because of the war underway since late 2001, the Islamic radical threat may soon seem less frightening to newspaper readers than some new rival, even as responsible governments soldier on. A decade from now, the concern may well be some new kind of terrorism – a fusion of nationalism with organized crime, or legions of agitators for a Kurdish state, or a dramatic and pervasive assassination campaign, worldwide, against providers of abortion.

The world will occasionally be surprised by new technologies. Once dynamite was invented, anarchists such as Germany's Johannes Most immediately found it a thrilling and effective way to announce themselves and their cause. In the late twentieth century, Sendero Luminoso rediscovered this simple weapon in Peru. If engineers and mechanics create a light portable automatic rifle that any fifteen-year-old girl can carry, produced in sufficient numbers to be affordable, terrorists are likely to examine and adopt this new weapon, as they have others in the past. Most terrorist acts are committed with fire, a knife, dynamite or other explosives, or with personal automatic weapons. The majority of these are at the "low-tech" levels. The change in this respect, and a strong recent concern, is increasing sophistication with remote detonation methods. These are disturbingly easy to arrange and can give new life to a deadly old standard, the vehicle bomb.

"Midtech" threats (to which the author drew attention in 2000) include the "dirty bomb" of nuclear waste dispersed by conventional explosive, the ultra-lite aircraft, and the shoulder-fired anti-aircraft missile. The last two already have been used, and SAMS were fired again at an Israeli aircraft leaving Nairobi airport in 2002. By the following year, popular literature

---

63 One excellent source on the Communist Party of Nepal (Maoist) and the Naxalites of India is the Web site of the South Asia Terrorism Portal, where one finds original party documents and articles by such writers as Dr. Ajai Sahni and K. P. S. Gill.
64 Gunaratna, *Inside al-Qaeda*, pp. 1 and 11.

had blossomed on the danger to commercial air travel. Use of a full airliner as a weapon was a powerful and imaginative stroke in the mid-tech range, suggested by a 1994 plot by Algerian extremists and realized successfully on September 11, 2001.[65] Police can imagine such scenarios without end. Clever ideas for evil uses of technology come easily to calculating minds, when they are inspired by their own needs, read of other groups' successes, or link plots with new technologies to imaginative theory in well-known handbooks, such as *The Minimanual of Urban Guerrilla Warfare* by Carlos Marighella, circa 1969, *The Turner Diaries* of white supremacist William Pierce (1978), and *Military Studies in the Jihad Against the Tyrants*, by al Qaeda (c. 1998). There is always new – something instructive and destructive – on the World Wide Web.

At the highest level are the potential and actual weapons of mass destruction, which must be taken profoundly seriously. Perhaps the best American analyst of terrorism, senior RAND political scientist Brian Jenkins, wrote a quarter-century ago that "terrorists don't want a lot of people dead; they want a lot of people paying attention." Even before September 11, 2001, he revised that thesis in a new essay.[66] Perhaps Aum Shinrikyo's nerve gas attack and its other attempts to kill with biological weapons were the most apparent reason for reconsideration. Now there are others. Al Qaeda has demonstrated an interest in ricin and other chem/bio weapons. In the United States, anthrax has been weaponized and used to terrorize and kill. It is, indeed, fortunate that an atomic bomb is so complicated and so expensive to make.

Yet, there is no clear reason to expect enhancement of the recent trend toward greater lethality in the attacks. Much discussed, that trend has been real, but logic and experience show how trends may divert or die away. The use of gas by Germany against its Western enemies did not occur in World War II just because it had occurred in World War I. Thus far, the actual use of nuclear weapons has been a singular event in human history; 1945 set no pattern of use, only of research and development. Ricin was used in the 1978 murder of an émigré in London, and the U.S. White Power movement of the 1980s and early 1990s showed great interest in it. But ricin is not easy to administer, and despite continued interest in the toxin, apparently has never again been successfully deployed in political murder. Terrorism is commonplace on the globe's surface, but the average terror incident will remain a focused, small-scale, low-tech affair, still featuring a telephone threat, use of a knife, murder by pistol or rifle, or placement of a time bomb. Judged only by numbers of incidents and the technology employed, there has been far

---

[65] Pages 54 and 196 of *Terrorism Today*; chap. 4 deals with other "mid-tech" threats; terrorism writer Ronald Payne chose to highlight these in his review of the book in *TLS* (London), Aug. 18, 2000. But I did not explicitly predict an attack like that of September 11.

[66] Brian M. Jenkins, "Will Terrorists Go Nuclear? A Reappraisal," chap. 13 of *The Future of Terrorism: Violence in the New Millennium*, ed. Harvey W. Kushner (Thousand Oaks, CA, 1998).

more continuity than change. The lust for lethality stunningly demonstrated on September 11 is not of itself proof of a dark future world. One might just as reasonably foresee different terrorist patterns, such as emergent campaigns for the environment or animals. These would capture new attention and might involve hundreds of individual attacks and actions, but occur at the level of sabotage, not killing. Killing in such cases could be deterred by the sentiments, concerns, and ideologies of the perpetrators thenselves, who see themselves as prolife. Such campaigns are likely, and they are most likely in relatively wealthy countries. People will not care about them as much as they do about al Qaeda, but such practices will be a part of the terrorism picture.

For the same reasons of logic, there is no assurance that the 1990s' rise in religious terrorist groups will continue. A brief period of Sikh fascination with terrorist spectacle ended in the 1980s. The Christian Identity movement spawned several terrorist actions in the United States but today has quieted. *Madrassas*, a pronounced threat to world peace, continue to enroll thousands of potential recruits to militant Islam. But even that pattern of graduates comes from perhaps a dozen countries, whose nationals are increasingly subject to police scrutiny worldwide. In the United States, Bin Laden's crimes may inspire violence by a few dozen moslem Americans and hot rhetoric from a few political zealots, but in this author's view, al Qaeda's mass murders are a painful embarrassment for most American moslems. Aum Shinrikyo has not spawned new religious terrorists in Japan or Russia, despite a wide following of the cult in both countries and a prevalence of available "root causes" in each place, including economic crisis and deep discontents. Religion will remain a source of much terrorism, but it need not become worse.

A pattern that will predictably intensify is the internationalization of terrorist causes. One may expect many twenty-first century rivals of "past masters," such as the nineteenth-century Anarchists or mid–twentieth-century Algerian FLN. The world will grow accustomed to such recent phenomena as a Tamil Web site used by global readers or a TV station run by Hezbollah for the attentions of its state sponsors and the Levantines. Indeed, it will be deemed notable, and perhaps odd, if a successful group more than two or three years old does *not* develop a Web site. From its first days of operation, it is likely to use the international post, satellite-aided cell phones, the transnational arms market, and so on.[67] Globalization, seemingly unstoppable,

---

[67] "What changed with 9–11 was that the threat was internationalized ... " says a spokesman for the London-based World Markets Research Center (WMRC), upon release of a new report. This is of course only a matter of emphasis; historically, terrorism has often gone international, and for over three decades now it has been a fully international phenomenon. The WMRC report is one indicator of new concerns in the business community about the global character of threats to them. "9/11 Style Attack Predicted in Next Year," AP story of August 18, 2003, courtesy of Mr. Jim Holmes of the Institute of World Politics.

allows for airing of discontents and for violent action against the innocent to publicize such discontents. Finally, many virulent ideologies are internationalist by nature, and when ideologies yield up terrorists, globalization will only support the pattern.

One example is violent Irish nationalism. In the 1850s, at the time of the founding of the Irish Republican Brotherhood, the supportive "Fenian Brotherhood" originated in the United States. A century later, in the 1950s and 1960s, such men as George Harrison, Cathal Goulding, and Joe Cahill labored to keep up the eastward transatlantic flow of money and weapons. The Irish Northern Aid Committee registered for official status with the U.S. government. Very unofficial, clandestine methods doubtless were even more useful. In the 1990s, the IRA Provos had representatives in the eastern United States trying to buy shoulder-fired missiles – a potential reply to British air power. Already in the new millennium, IRA operatives have turned up in Moscow to buy new sniper rifles, and in Colombia to teach FARC more about homemade mortars, a Provo specialty for many years. Members of the IRA have also attended many international terrorist summits on the continent of Europe. One should conclude that both the IRA's own history and the latter twentieth-century phenomenon of international terrorist summits bringing together distant and disparate groups indicate that internationalization of terrorism is a trend that will continue. Globalization and emerging communications technologies will assist the pattern.

CONCLUSION

The foregoing has suggested some conclusions about terrorism although some of them are limited, interim, or offer only a small a window on the future. Strictly speaking, the social sciences cannot predict. But we may hope that, in accord with Carl von Clausewitz, a diligent student of human nature and the past can unlock certain secrets and prepare his mind well for what the future may present. Perhaps that is enough.

Scattered pages of *On War* by Clausewitz offer a useful distinction between the "nature" of war and its "character." Nature is permanent and so always present – by degrees of visibility – in all times and places; "all wars are political," and so on. The character of a war may evolve, be similar to the last war, or change from one war to the next. Terrorism is no mere label and in no way ambiguous. It too has a nature, which is the deliberate use of violence against the innocent. Its objective is political power. It attacks the will, often by inflicting harm on a third party, and thus aims at a wide audience more than an immediate material purpose. It is more psychological than most forms of war; one archetype is the hostage drama that may never do physical damage. Terrorism has only limited similarity to guerrilla war: certain weapons and tactics, and its emphasis on reconnaissance, stealth, and surprise. The nature of terrorism is exceedingly political, even if the announced objective appears to have most to do with a particular economic issue, social question, or religious matter. The end is power – power over a regime, over a people, on behalf of a foreign government, and so on.

The character of terrorism is variegated and malleable. Its styles have changed, and will do so again, as history stretches forward. Named groups can and sometimes do change their mode of operation or their targeting. In the last decade, observers *have* noted movement from psychological drama toward mass casualty acts. One symbol is Hamas, which began with the knife and now specializes in major suicide bombings. There *has* been less terrorism by secular political groups and more by religiously motivated groups in the last decade. Yet, there are more half-trends and whole illusions than things dramatically new. Three examples offer themselves. Today, terrorism is more internationalized in its effects and operations than ever, but it is not playing a *different* kind of role in global affairs than did transnational terrorism in 1968 or 1998; its political and psychological workings are essentially similar. Second, terrorism is not increasing, despite present concerns. For example, far fewer international terror attacks succeeded in 2002 than in the preceding year. Third, it has not been shown that organizations are more ad hoc or loose today than before. Today's Hezbollah and IRA Provos seem to run with ruthless discipline. In contrast, the principle of "leaderless resistance" was developed by a white power advocate in the United States a quarter-century ago, and when one reconsiders the violent Italian left of the 1970s, that was never well organized at the national level.[68]

In considering the future, one thus begins with the logic that present trends do not deserve to rivet the attention of analysts and policy makers. Only some groups follow cultish tradition. Many more evolve or innovate. There are always entirely new groups arising, as well as new methods of operation and attention grabbing. Predictions of terrorism, which rest on such rubrics as poverty and oppression are not useful; history does not support the linkage, and neither does the existence of massive slums in Latin American states, where there is virtually no revolutionary terrorism at all. It is clear that terrorism will never be eliminated; it can only be reduced. One should not regard it as a natural fact of life, but it is certainly a pattern in contemporary politics and most likely to persist. The reasons for that include a plethora of human problems, political obsessions such as hypernationalism, and the camp, insurgency, which often turns to terrorism as a tool, choice by

---

[68] My first journal article on terrorism (in 1982 in *Grand Strategy: Countercurrents*, from The Claremont Institute) concerned Giangiacomo Feltrinelli, heir to the Italian publishing firm, who promoted leftist militant books and aided certain terrorists, fostering indigenous militants but also a very loose international network. Recently, Dr. David Tucker of the Naval Postgraduate School has used such well-known past networks to question the new conventional wisdom that al Qaeda is wholly revolutionary in how it operates.

individuals and individual groups, and state practice. Special technology is not the holy grail of future terrorism. The dagger served the medieval Assassins well in the Middle East and was reintroduced by Hamas in the 1980s for similar effects. Past patterns of success, or limited success, will also continue to drive terrorists onward.

What is most evident about our future is that terrorism in some form will continue, and continue to attack moderate states and the democracies, which must in turn maintain the resolution and solid sense to resist terror by comprehending its manipulative methods and by defeating its worst outbursts. The year 2003 saw the unexpected reopening of files on convicted terrorists in Peru, a country that narrowly defeated the scourge in 1992 and has since become both calm and fully democratic. Peru's legal and judicial self-critique of the present moment is a vivid reminder of how terrorism puts democracies at risk: initially by horrific violence, then by the requirement for governmental response with sweeping legislation and force, and then again by the later patterns of relentless self-criticism and even shame. It must be hoped that Peru will prove an example of democratic strength, instead of this new self-examination encouraging or renewing terrorism, making Peru an example of *How Democracies Perish*.[69]

---

[69] This is a reference to the admirable volume by Jean Francois Revel; another such study preceded it, and was at least as good: Harold W. Rood's 1980 *Kingdoms of the Blind*.

14

History and future of civil–military relations: bridging the gaps

FRANCIS G. HOFFMAN

As the small group of insiders filed out of the president's office, they were sure one of them would never be back. It was November 1938, and President Franklin Delano Roosevelt had just met with his most trusted advisors and military leaders. He had called the meeting in the aftermath of the Munich debacle to find a way of deterring Hitler's apparently insatiable ambitions. Roosevelt proposed to build 10,000 airplanes a year as a strategic deterrent. He suggested no other increases to American defenses – neither ground forces nor the requisite aviation support. As he went around the room, the president's personal advisors seemed to be in complete support. Wrapping up the meeting and pleased with the apparent consensus, Roosevelt turned to the only individual who had not spoken, asking, "Don't you think so, George." The newly minted Army deputy chief of staff, Major General George C. Marshall, responded, "I am sorry, Mr. President, but I don't agree with that at all."[1] The president appeared startled, and the other participants were surprised at Marshall's blunt candor. They believed he had committed a serious gaffe and that his career prospects were over. But the one advisor with the temerity to suggest that the president was wrong would not have considered any other answer. He was merely stating his professional judgment as requested.

As events soon proved, everyone underestimated Roosevelt. Marshall's long selfless career had not reached its end. A year later, the president personally selected Marshall to become the next Army chief of staff. On the eve of global war, Roosevelt reached down below thirty more senior officers, and selected a man he could count on to provide honest, forthright advice. Their remarkable partnership would prove a major factor in the successful

---

[1] Forrest C. Pogue, *George C. Marshall, Education of A General, 1880–1939* (New York, 1963), pp. 322–3.

248   *Francis G. Hoffman*

development and execution of U.S. policy and military strategy during World War II.

Some observers do not believe that such a partnership is achievable today. The inestimable Marshall was from the old school, one that adhered to a professional creed that has seemingly faded from memory. Marshall had a deep understanding of what he called the "sacred trust," the bonds that exist between the military and the democratic society it protects.[2] This soldier's ethos guided Marshall's sense of duty throughout the war.

Scholars today fill the security literature with debates over the divisive problems of civil–military relations. Many argue that the end of the Cold War coincided with an erosion in the relationship between civilian authority and the military.[3] Retired officers admit that the professionalism of the military has markedly declined since the end of the Gulf War, while recent studies have warned about a growing partisanship among officers, a sharper identification with party, and resentment about the imposition of society's liberal values on their unique culture.[4] Pundits question the wisdom of having military "proconsuls" as principal actors in the day-to-day management of America's foreign policy. Such critics suggest that the military influences national policy to too great an extent.[5] More broadly, others warn about a growing "gap" in values between American society and its military, with the attendant dangers of creating a military profession isolated from the society it serves.

One should not underestimate the significance of the debate. Civil–military relations, even in the post–Cold War era, have considerable implications for America's security and civil liberties. History contains numerous examples of strategic failure that resulted from divided policy councils and dysfunctional relationships between soldiers and statesmen. In the end, democracies must strike a balance between the functional imperative of security and the societal imperative to preserve democratic values and political institutions. Nations that fail to develop such a balance "squander their resources and run uncalculated risks."[6] History offers insights into the dangers and

[2] Forrest C. Pogue, *George C. Marshall, Organizer of Victory, 1943–1945* (New York, 1973), pp. 458–9.
[3] Richard H. Kohn, "The Erosion of Civilian Control of the Military in the United States Today," *Naval War College Review*, Summer 2002, pp. 9–59.
[4] Don Snider, "America's Postmodern Military," *World Policy Journal*, Spring 2000, pp. 52–3.
[5] See, among others, Richard H. Kohn, "Out of Control: The Crisis in Civil–Military Relations," *The National Interest*, Spring 1994, pp. 3–17; A. J. Bacevich, "Civilian Control, A Useful Fiction?" *Joint Force Quarterly*, Autumn/Winter 1994/95, pp. 76–9; on how the military perceives itself relative to the rest of society, see Thomas E. Ricks, "The Widening Gap Between the Military and Society," *The Atlantic Monthly*, July 1997, pp. 66–78; Ole R. Holsti, "A Widening Gap Between the U.S. Military and Civilian Society? Some Evidence, 1976–1996," *International Security*, Winter 1998/1999, pp. 5–42. On the military's influence in foreign policy, see Dana Priest, "The Proconsuls: Patrolling the World," *Washington Post*, Sept. 28, 29, and 30, 2000.
[6] Samuel P. Huntington, *The Soldier and the State* (Cambridge, MA, 1957), p. viii.

implications of dysfunctional civil–military relations. That relationship is important both to the security of democratic states and the profession of arms.

CIVIL–MILITARY RELATIONS AS STRATEGIC CULTURE

As a group, historians have not paid sufficient attention to the influence of civil–military relations on strategic effectiveness.[7] This is somewhat surprising because civil–military relations represent an important subset of strategic culture.[8] All conflicts are products of the societies involved, and of course, war has a reciprocal influence on social institutions and government. The study of culture, representing the nexus of historical experience, attitudes, beliefs, and values, is now a recognized and growing area of study.[9] History, myth, and perceived lessons have a particularly strong influence on how societies defend themselves. Americans, in particular, have their own preconceptions and imperatives, conscious and unconscious, that influence strategy and produce a unique national approach to war.[10] Thus, the study of strategy and civil–military relations is indivisible. It involves the interaction of those preconceptions about the nature of war and politics, and the irresistible but often contradictory impulses that emerge from their interaction.

The main lines of American strategic decision making are difficult to assess because of the inherent complexity of its strategic culture. Strategic cultures are not necessarily perfect, rational, or correct. In fact, one strategist suggests they can be entirely dysfunctional."[11] Whether functional or not, they reflect the aggregate distillation of a country's experience and approach to war. Because strategic culture is a product of the reciprocal relationships between social values, political institutions and processes, and government bureaucracies, civil–military relations represent an expression of that culture.[12]

Yet, strategic culture remains an undeveloped area of strategic study. As one commentator has observed, "recent theoretical writing on strategic

---

[7] A charge levied by A. J. Bacevich, "The Paradox of Professionalism: Eisenhower, Ridgway, and the Challenge to Civilian Control, 1953–1955," *Journal of Military History*, April 1997, p. 304.

[8] On the importance of culture, see Victor Davis Hanson, *Carnage and Culture: Landmark Battles in the Rise of Western Power* (New York, 2002); and John A. Lynn, *Battle: A History of Combat and Culture from Ancient Greece to Modern America* (Boulder, CO, 2003).

[9] The best study of this issue is Colin S. Gray, *Modern Strategy* (Oxford, 1999), pp. 129–51.

[10] Colin Gray, "National Style in Strategy: The American Example," *International Security*, Fall, 1981, pp. 2–42.

[11] Gray, *Modern Strategy*, pp. 146–7.

[12] Earl H. Fry, Stan A. Taylor, and Robert S. Wood, *America the Vincible: American Foreign Policy in the Twenty-First Century* (Englewood Cliffs, NJ, 1994), p. 133.

culture leaves much work to be done."[13] If true, civil–military relations remain an even further underdeveloped area for military historians. "Strategic thinking and behavior does not occur in a vacuum, it represents a complex process influenced by the intangibles of culture, contingency, and personality." [14] What academics have not yet addressed is how civil–military relations, the confluence in which the various players, institutions, and agencies interact to develop strategies and plans, impacts strategic effectiveness. If it is true, as another commentator claims that "the study of the relationship between the soldier and statesmen lies at the heart of what strategy is all about," then history has much to offer on the subject.[15]

CIVILIAN–MILITARY RELATIONS VERSUS CIVILIAN CONTROL

Civil–military relations represent a complex issue, especially within fractious democracies. The Founding Fathers took special pains to ensure the military instrument would be responsive and accountable to civilian authority. They were conscious of the internal and external dangers the new republic would confront. They were also aware of the difficulties faced by the Greeks and Romans. They had read Thucydides and Plutarch and could quote Cicero from memory. The Declaration of Independence includes specific grievances about unchecked military power not subordinated to civil political control. The Federalist Papers set out the need for defense and a professional military, juxtaposed against concerns about the dangers of a standing military establishment. James Madison, in Federalist 41, acknowledged that "the liberties of Rome proved the final victim to her military triumphs."[16] Thus, military officers of the American experiment were to be responsive to the elected representatives of the people. Executive control by a commander in chief was to rest on a single elected civilian, while Congress retained sole authority to raise and maintain the armed services. To assuage fears of a standing army, the Constitution also established a militia system. Thus, from the founding of the United States, the legal and structural aspect of American civil–military relations was an issue."[17]

---

[13] Gray, *Modern Strategy*, p. 148.
[14] On the importance of culture to military effectiveness, see Williamson Murray, "Does Military Culture Matter?" *Orbis*, Winter 1999, pp. 27–41.
[15] Eliot A. Cohen, *Supreme Command: Soldiers, Statesmen and Leadership in Wartime* (New York, 2002), p. xii.
[16] *The Federalist Papers* (New York, 1982), p. 205.
[17] Contrary to Huntington's assertion in *Soldier and the State*, p. 163. For influences affecting the creation of the military in the early days of the United States, see Richard H. Kohn, *Eagle and Sword: The Beginnings of the Military Establishment in America* (New York, 1975), especially pp. 1–13, 73–88; Don Higginbotham, *The War of American Independence, Military Attitudes, Polices and Practice, 1763–1789* (Boston, 1983), pp. 1–56.

But civil–military relations are more than just the ability of civil leaders to "control" the aimed forces. Civil–military relations, properly defined, encompass how society views its military forces, as well as how the professional military identifies with the broader civil society it defends. Also included within a broader definition of civil–military relations must be the mutual respect and understanding between civilian and military leaders, the exchange of candid views and perspectives in the decision-making process, and effective follow-through by military subordinates.

Effective civil–military relations are harder and more important than "civilian control," which only addresses the degree to which civilian policy makers control the making of policy, and not the overall quality and effectiveness of the policy in the first place.[18] One can have superb levels of civilian control, with the military blindly obedient to decisions that make no military sense. Too narrow a focus on civilian control risks ignoring the overall quality of the decision-making processes. Decisions, not processes, are the ultimate output of effective civil–military relations, and they determine the quality of strategy. In the end, the ability of accountable decision makers to integrate functional and societal imperatives during periods of great stress is the real issue involved in civil–military relations. Thus, like strategy, one can best view civil–military relations as a process.[19]

DEFINING AND BRIDGING GAPS

For almost the entire last decade, much professional literature in the United States has focused on a purported rift in civilian–military relations. From initial claims about the existence of a "gap," a significant body of research has emerged.[20] Early claims maintained that a potentially corrosive gap existed between mainstream America and its military culture. More specifically, the U.S. armed forces were supposedly becoming more insular in their attitudes, values, and makeup than civil society. Such a cultural divide might weaken the support the military enjoys among the body politic or threaten the peace as the military begins to think of itself as both distinct from and superior to the society it protects.

Some defense experts suggest Americans should accept this gap.[21] They argue that reducing it by making the military a mirror of society would

---

[18] Michael Desch, *Civilian Control of the Military: The Changing Security Environment* (Baltimore, 1999).

[19] Kohn, "The Erosion of Civilian Control of the Military," p. 16.

[20] See, particularly, Peter D. Feaver and Richard D. Kohn, eds., *Soldiers and Civilians: The Civil–Military Gap and American National Security* (Cambridge, MA, 2001).

[21] John Hillen, "The Civilian–Military Gap: Keep It, Defend It, Manage It," *Proceedings*, Oct. 1998, pp. 2–3; Mackubin T. Owens, "Gaps, Real and Imagined," *Washington Times*, Nov. 1, 1999.

compromise a culture and ethos that contribute to the military's functional effectiveness. The military's unique culture represents a set of values, rituals, and behaviors that help preserve the country's security. Rather than weaken the military, the argument runs, American society understands the need for the armed forces and accepts the need for distinctive attitudes and values. History suggests that such an approach is an appropriate response because the warrior caste in society has often represented a unique sub-element with distinct values. As one commentator notes:

> Soldiers are not like other men. They are those of a world apart, a very ancient world, which exists in parallel with the everyday world but does not belong to it. Both worlds change over time, and the warrior adapts in step to the civilian. It follows, however, at a distance. The distance can never be closed.[22]

Yet, although concerns about this particular "gap" may not be on the mark, scholarship suggests Americans should not ignore or dismiss the issue. The issues that detract from effective civil–military relations run deeper and are corrosive. These gaps can and will impair America's strategic performance. They include

- A *culture gap* that significantly degrades communications and understanding between political and military leaders
- A *role gap* that creates a false distinction between civilian and military spheres based on a distorted view of civil–military relations
- A *concept gap* that promotes a purely military perspective and a restrictive set of criteria that subverts Clausewitz's dictum that policy ends are the preceptors of policy means
- A *values gap* that creates strains between the professional military ideal and the perspective of many of today's officers on their duties and obligations

These gaps exacerbate what is an already complex and tension-filled process. Each has historical precedents that underscore its potentially deleterious impact.

CULTURE AND KNOWLEDGE GAP

The first gap exists as a result of the distinctly opposing cultures of statesmen and soldiers. The politician is a man of words, comfortable with fluid constituencies, shifting loyalties, partisan agendas, and ambiguous priorities. The general is a man of deeds, lifelong study, and preparation for a day of battle that may never come. His world is more orderly, structured, and hierarchical. More important, his loyalties and allegiances are constant – so,

---

[22] John Keegan, *A History of Warfare* (New York, 1993), p. xvi.

too, his priority, a disciplined readiness to manage violence. Given the gulf in culture and competencies, a systemic inclination toward mutual miscomprehension and miscommunication is inherent in the relationship.[23]

Related to the cultural gap is another source of friction that significantly impairs the collaborative discourse. One might term this the knowledge gap because it reflects what one might call the "reciprocal ignorance" of two worlds, each lacking the perspective, background, and knowledge to appreciate the other.[24] As the complexities of conflict and demographics grow, so also does the potential for mutual ignorance. The cultural frameworks of the two parties in the civil–military exchange thus are not converging, but rather diverging.[25]

Unlike those of earlier generations, politicians today rarely have military experience or even interest in military affairs. Demographic trends suggest that even fewer will possess such an experiential background in the future. Since the end of the Cold War, fewer civilians appear interested in working in the Pentagon, and even fewer are studying military history or defense policy in America's universities. One result of increasing deaths among the World War II and Korean War generations is that fewer citizens in the general population or in positions of responsibility possess an appreciation for military culture or the military way of life.

Despite the close association of statesmen and military leaders of his day, Clausewitz made explicit his belief that the former must possess a feel for the nature of the military and not ask of it something foreign to its nature.[26] This feel for military matters is declining within American society as a smaller military, civilian demographics, and popular disinterest in public service all chip away at the edifice. Moreover, today's elites are much less interested than their predecessors in military or governmental service. This trend has actually been developing for some time, accelerated perhaps by the Vietnam conflict. More recent research highlights dramatic declines in the number of veterans in Congress. Only one-fourth of today's legislators have had any military experience, and most of those are among the most senior.[27]

Of course, one can overrate military experience. Two of America's greatest wartime presidents, Abraham Lincoln and Franklin Roosevelt, were not combat veterans. Yet, they excelled at strategy, coalition building, dealing

---

23 Samuel Huntington, "The Clash of Civilizations," *Foreign Affairs*, Summer 1993.
24 Gray, *Modern Strategy*, p. 61.
25 John Hillen, "Servants. Supplicants, or Saboteurs: The Role of the Uniformed Officer and the Changing Nature of America's Civil–Military Relations," in Douglas T. Stuart, ed., *Organizing for National Security* (Carlisle, PA, 2000), p. 218.
26 Carl von Clausewitz, *On War*, Michael Howard and Peter Paret, eds. (Princeton, 1986), p. 608.
27 William T. Bianco and Jamie Markham, "Vanishing Veterans: The Decline of Military Experience in the U.S. Congress," in Feaver and Kohn, eds., *Soldiers and Civilians*, pp. 177–98.

with difficult generals, and economic mobilization. Lincoln did have a brief exposure to militia duty, while Roosevelt served as assistant secretary of the navy for almost eight years, thereby acquiring an astute grasp of the Navy's culture and bureaucracy. In fact, military experience among senior leaders appears to have had little correlation in the past to strategic effectiveness or smooth civil–military relations. Nevertheless, some grasp of military culture and realities would appear beneficial, and the costs of a learning curve are steep if one waits until elected before learning about the basic security institutions and their function.

If one cannot count on military experience, can Americans count on brilliant national leaders who have devoted considerable study of philosophy, international relations, or political history? Robert Kaplan suggests that Americans cannot. He warns that the long peace will not prepare future political leaders for the coming conflicts and anarchy.

> A long peace would rear up leaders with no tragic historical memory, and thus little wisdom. Nor would such future leaders be fortified by a life of serious reading to compensate for their lack of historical experience; permanent peace with its worship of entertainment and convenience, will produce ever-shallower leaders.... Such shallow leaders and advisers would by the very virtue of their lack of wisdom and experience, eventually commit the kind of ghastly miscalculation that would lead to a general war of some kind.[28]

The knowledge gap is not entirely the responsibility of the civilian world. Future military professionals will have to be well read in the fundamentals of their profession and international affairs. Most of today's officers possess a background in the military arts and sciences. However, the system of professional military education in the United States provides little study of the fundamentals of the American society they protect. In particular, military education largely ignores the study of civil–military relations. At best, it is an elective subject in most military schools.[29] Nor do military professionals have significant opportunities to interact with civilians from other agencies of government. Closing this particular gap requires educational programs that prepare civilian and military participants for future strategic challenges.

ROLE GAP

There is a second source of political–military tension: the role gap. This gap has resulted from an accommodation that has grown up over the years. One

---

[28] Robert D. Kaplan, *The Coming Anarchy: Shattering the Dreams of the Post Cold War* (New York, 2000), pp. 183–4.

[29] Judith Hicks Stiehm, "Civil Military Relations in War College Curricula," *Armed Forces and Society*, Winter 2001, pp. 273–94.

of the myths in the American way of war is the belief that there is an inherent division of labor between the civilian and military spheres. Believers in this myth holds that civilian leaders should focus on setting forth clear policy aims and then avoid close supervision of plans or the conduct of war. It partly rests on Samuel Huntington's theory of civil–military relations that asserts the existence of distinct spheres for civilians and military leaders. On one side, civilians are supposedly responsible for creating strategy and political objectives; and on the other, the military is responsible for military objectives, training, doctrine, and war.[30] Moreover, the myth contends that acknowledging this autonomous sphere for the military enhances military professionalism and civilian control.[31]

This gap also exists because of an erroneous interpretation of the lessons of Vietnam and several recent conflicts. This myth reduces the role of civilian policy makers to the setting of policy objectives and minimizes their role in asking hard questions about military means. Supposedly, civilians should avoid micromanagement of military operations and leave the details to the professionals.[32] To a considerable extent, this view rests on the Vietnam War's postmortems and the bitterness of officers at the impact the war had on their institutions.[33] The toll the war took created a collective belief in a generation of officers, best captured by Colin Powell's oft-quoted statement that his generation left Southeast Asia with a conviction that they would not sit idly by and acquiesce in a similar debacle. As Powell commented in his memoirs, "when our turn came to call the shots, we would not quietly acquiesce in halfhearted warfare for half-baked reasons that the American people could not understand or support."[34]

The Vietnam debacle had many proximate causes, but the flawed processes of strategic deliberation was the principal one. During the "policy-making process," generously described, that led to the incoherent slide into Vietnam, the Joint Chiefs of Staff (JCS) had limited opportunities to inject views into the processes of decision making and failed to exploit those they had. The Secretary of Defense, Robert Strange McNamara, excluded the JCS from strategic policy discussions and minimized military advice so he could control the debate. The planning and advisory process rested on untested assumptions and a "cozy implicit agreement on fundamentals," from which "never

---

[30] See Don M. Snider, John A Nagl, and Tony Pfaff, *Army Professionalism, The Military Ethic, and Officership in the 21st Century*, (Carlisle, PA, 1999), p. 15.

[31] "The essence of objective civilian control is the recognition of autonomous military professionalism." Huntington, *Soldier and the State*, p. 83. For critiques of Huntington, see Cohen, *Supreme Command*, pp. 225–48.

[32] The existence of this myth is Eliot Cohen's principal thesis in *Supreme Command*, pp. 1–14.

[33] David H. Petraeus, "The American Military and the Lessons of Vietnam: A Study of Military Influence and the Use of Force in the Post-Vietnam Era," Ph.D. dissertation, Princeton, 1987, pp. 116–17.

[34] Colin Powell with Joseph Persico, *My American Journey* (New York, 1995), p. 167.

was heard a disparaging word."[35] Instead of rigorous debates, National
Security Council meetings, which excluded military advisors, were nothing
more than tiny enclaves of those who acquiesced in decisions already made.
The military were merely "technicians whose principal responsibility was
to carry out decisions already made rather than fully participating in the
planning and advisory process."[36]

From this disaster emerged the myth that the Johnson Administration
had micromanaged the war and should have let the professionals deal with
the war. Ironically, both sides of the civil–military divide now ascribe to
this myth. The ghosts of Vietnam influenced the conduct of military operations and civil–military relations during interventions in Beirut in the early
1980s and Panama in 1989.[37] Operation "Just Cause" was successful from
a military perspective, and reinforced post-Vietnam perspectives about the
proper role of civilian leaders. The inputs into the campaign came exclusively from the military, while even civilians in the Pentagon had little role
in the planning. The president approved the Joint Staff plan with no modifications or discussion. In the words of a retired military officer, "Just Cause"
"showed what professional soldiers can accomplish when allowed to do their
jobs without micro-management and secondguessing."[38] Thus, Panama was
supposedly unlike Vietnam, "where the civilian leadership hadn't been willing to commit the force necessary to accomplish the military objectives."[39]
Despite atrocious flaws in planning for postconflict stability, senior military
leaders concluded that the lack of civilian involvement was instrumental
in operational success.[40] One general claimed that "Mr. Cheney's biggest
contribution to the invasion was to get out of the way."[41]

During the Gulf War, the president clearly avoided any appearance of
micromanaging the military.[42] As a result, the U.S. military has come to see
Operation Desert Storm as a model of proper civil–military relations. The
civilians provided the policy aims and requisite resources, and then stayed out
of the way. One postwar assessment noted, "every American commander in
the Gulf conflict expressed gratitude and satisfaction over the fact that their

---

[35] Townsend Hoopes, quoted in Bernard Brodie, *War and Politics* (New York, 1973), p. 210.
[36] See McMaster, *Dereliction of Duty*, p. 305.
[37] John Prados, *Keeper of the Keys, A History of the National Security Council from Truman to Bush* (New York, 1990), p. 471.
[38] Benjamin F. Schemmer, "Panama and Just Cause: The Rebirth of Professional Soldiering," *Armed Forces Journal*, February 1990, p. 5.
[39] Bob Woodward, *The Commanders* (New York, 1991), p. 163.
[40] Caleb Baker, "Army Officials Credit Success in Panama to Planning, Few Bureaucratic Obstacles," *Defense News*, Mar. 5, 1990, p. 8.
[41] "Inside the Invasion," *Newsweek*, June 25, 1990, p. 28.
[42] President Bush claimed to have learned from Vietnam "where the political leadership med-dled with military operations." George H. W. Bush and Brent Scowcroft, *A World Trans-formed* (New York, 1998), p. 354.

president and commander-in-chief had allowed them to fight the war as they saw fit."[43] Bush had no inclination to disagree with the military and made no major decisions that contradicted their advice.

However, the conclusion that civil–military relations were effective during the first Gulf War has to overlook major failures in war termination. Once again, the military delivered "loose assumptions, unasked questions, and thin analyses" to a president who accepted them without any challenge. The same president who did not want to be perceived as micromanaging the military only succeeded in achieving a Pyrrhic victory.[44]

The myths of Vietnam continued to influence military operations throughout the 1990s, especially in Somalia where civilians remained out of the loop. The debacle of October 1993 still did not reverse the widening gap. One former Clinton Administration national security advisor captured the prevailing conception during a battlefield staff ride at Gettysburg. His visit was "an extraordinary opportunity to reflect on Lincoln's relationship with his generals and to reaffirm our general pattern in which the White House *offers strategic guidance* and direction, and makes sure the missions are clear; but does not get into tactical decisions which are best left to professional military men [emphasis added]."[45]

This statement evidences an astonishingly poor grasp of history. It perpetuates the image of Lincoln as a cross between St. Francis of Assisi and Ghandi, instead of the ruthless and engaged leader of an imperiled state that he was.[46] Beyond its historical inaccuracies, the comment also reflects a weak understanding of policy's proper role. Leaders must do more than *offer* guidance. The fact that this statement came from an official involved in the inept handling of Somalia explains much.

The current president is also prone to overdelegate his responsibilities to the military. On two occasions, one during Afghanistan and later during Operation Iraqi Freedom, he publicly announced that

> My timetable is going to be set by Tommy Franks...we won't be making political decisions about what to do with our military. I gave [General] Franks a mission; it was a well defined mission. When Tommy says, "Mission complete, Mr. President," that's when we start moving troops out.[47]

43 U.S. News and World Report, *Triumph Without Victory. The Unreported History of the Persian Gulf War* (New York, 1992), p. 400.
44 Bernard E. Trainor, *The General's War: The Inside Story of the Conflict in the Gulf* (New York, 1995), pp. 413–26.
45 Anthony Lake, quoted in Bill Gertz, "Today's Top Generals March on Gettysburg," *Washington Times*, Mar. 4, 1995, p. B3.
46 See D. W. Brogan, "The United States," pp. 167–85, in Michael Howard, ed., *Soldiers and Governments: Nine Studies in Civil–Military Relations* (Westport, CT, 1978).
47 George W. Bush, Washington DC: The White House, at www.whitehouse.gov/news/releases/2001/12/20011228-1.html, p. 5.

The complexities of modem war do not allow such a simplistic delegation to a theatre commander, no matter how proficient or loyal he might be. How then do we resolve the dilemma, and how are the responsibilities for policy development, decision making, and supervision to be divided among civilians and military professionals? One noted political scientist has argued that policy makers must

> [i]mmerse themselves in the conduct of their wars no less than in their great projects of domestic legislation; that they must master their military briefs as thoroughly as they do their civilian ones; that they must demand and expect from their military subordinates a candor as bruising as is necessary; that both groups must expect a running conversation in which although civilian opinion will not usually dictate, it must dominate; and that conversation will cover not only ends and policies, but ways and means."[48]

History suggests civil–military relations must be a reciprocal process and military professionals need to demand the same disciplined and comprehensive search for viable solutions from their overseers. There are not separate and distinct spheres at the strategic level – *the roles overlap* as suggested by Churchill's famous dictum, "at the summit strategy and policy are one." Answers to questions generated by the process should form part of a continuous dialog, "a running conversation" at the strategic level.[49] Despite the desire for autonomy by military professionals, these running conversations certainly do involve ways and means. The melding of ends and means must be a two-sided and interactive process. This interaction might be cordial, but it must be intense and comprehensive. It can be a process of cooperative engagement if possible, but if necessary it can be a process of *collaborative confrontation*.

THE CONCEPT GAP

The third gap results from the nature of the security environment likely to confront policy makers and the armed forces for the foreseeable future. This security environment will pose demands that are substantially at odds with prevailing conceptions of the mission in today's military. It also presents a context for the application of force that runs counter to the existing military culture. This concept or doctrine gap is particularly wide and was the principal source of tension in American strategic discourses throughout the 1990s.[50] The tensions reflects the lingering ghosts of Vietnam, and

---

48 Cohen, *Supreme Command*, p. 206.
49 Ibid.
50 Christopher M. Gacek, *The Logic of Force: The Dilemma of Limited War in American Foreign Policy* (New York, 1994), pp. 250–93; David Halberstam, *War in a Time of Peace: Bush, Clinton, and the Generals* (New York, 2001).

significantly framed many debates about the use of force in the Gulf, the Balkans, Africa, and Haiti.

The new American "way of war" reflects the military's predispositions and preferences. Its operating paradigm evolved from painful lessons acquired in Vietnam and Lebanon.[51] Secretary of Defense Caspar Weinberger in 1984 and later General Colin Powell codified and publicized this approach during debates preceding American involvement in Bosnia.[52] The essence of the Weinberger/Powell criteria include clear political objectives; no "mission creep"; the use of force only as a last resort; the employment of overwhelming military forces only to secure vital interests, unrestrained by the civilian leadership; the establishment of political support prior to military intervention; and immediate withdrawal after victory in accordance with a predesigned exit strategy.

These conditions reflect the lessons drawn from Vietnam and Beirut; the military exists to "fight and win the nation's wars," defined as conventional and large scale, fought to secure vital interests. Underlying this intellectual construct is the belief that the United States should not employ its military in uncomfortable, messy, or ambiguous situations. The preference is to overwhelm the opponents of the United States in conventional combat and leave expeditiously, lest the nation find itself in a quagmire. This formulation has drawn justifiable criticism as an "all or nothing" approach, less than useful in situations short of a Soviet offensive through the Fulda Gap.[53] However, despite external critics, the military has internalized the Powell Doctrine as an article of faith.[54] Such a bias would not be harmful were it not at odds with the current security environment. As Paul Valery once observed, "Never has humanity combined so much power with so much disorder, so much anxiety with so many playthings, so much knowledge with so much uncertainty."[55]

The result has been that American military culture and leadership have not prepared themselves to address the disorder, anxiety, and uncertainty of the present and likely future environment. As September 11 underlined, America's military clout may be unassailable, but there are new players with new means that present stark dangers. The diffusion of various forms of advanced technology has lowered barriers to the effective use of force for some competitors and raised the risks of an attack that would directly strike

[51] Hoffman, *Decisive Force.*
[52] Weinberger's doctrine can be found in Weinberger, *Fighting for Peace* (New York, 1990), pp. 159–60, 445–57. For the Powell Doctrine, "Challenges for U.S. Forces," *Foreign Affairs*, pp. 32–45.
[53] Les Aspin, "Role of U.S. Military in Post–Cold War World," address before the Jewish Institute for National Security Affairs, September 21, 1992, pp. 1–6; Editorial, "At Least Slow the Slaughter," *New York Times*, October 4, 1992, p. E16.
[54] Marlin L. Cook, "The Proper Role of Professional Military Advice in Contemporary Uses of Force," *Parameters*, Winter 2002–2003, pp. 21–33.
[55] Paul Valery, cited in Peter Schwartz, *The Art of the Long View* (New York, 1996), p. xvii.

the United States. The staggering conventional military superiority of the United States not only serves as a deterrent to some, but also induces interest in asymmetric techniques and tactics, and lowers the threshold for the use of weapons of mass destruction.[56]

The new American way of war is seriously out of sync with a number of dangerous security challenges. This was clear during the 1990s in the Middle East, Africa, Southwest Asia, and particularly the Balkans. Tensions of nationalism and ethnic fanaticism, fragmentation produced by globalization, and the insidious emergence of Islamic fundamentalism heralded a dramatic rise in instability. Yet, over the last decade, the U.S. military has to a considerable extent chosen to ignore this environment.[57] Instead of selective engagement employing forces designed and trained to impose order on an unruly world, it has preferred not to engage at all. It has sought restrictive conditions and well-defined exit strategies. And not surprisingly, it has clung to a comforting but false "checklist illusion" in an increasingly disorderly world.[58]

The preconceptions in the Powell Doctrine are at odds with the era. Policy makers confront a world of angry individuals, undeterrable warriors, and constant conflict.[59] In fact, the prospects for even greater violence are inherent in today's global environment. Today's world pits Hegel's "last man," driving a sleek Lexus, against Hobbes's "first man" clinging to an olive tree. History has condemned the latter to a poor, nasty, brutish, and short life, and neither he nor his clan is very happy about their fate.[60] At least some of the Army's strategic thinkers have concluded that "[t]he first two decades of the 21st century will be dominated by protracted, complex, ambiguous armed conflicts rather than short, politically and ethically clear ones leading to decisive outcomes."[61]

These are not the types of conflicts for which fixed objectives, purely military means, and quick "exit strategies" are appropriate.[62] These are conflicts of "savage wars of peace."[63] They can be protracted and ambiguous. They

---

[56]   For a superb study of asymmetric options, see Lt. Col. K. Frank McKenzie, *The Revenge of the Melians, Asymmetric Threats and the 2001 QDR* (Washington, DC, 2002).

[57]   This trend was first debated by Martin van Creveld, *The Transformation of War* (New York, 1991).

[58]   Donald Kagan, "Roles and Missions," *Orbis*, Spring 1997, p. 192.

[59]   The phrase "super-empowered individuals" is Thomas L. Friedman's, *The Lexus and the Olive Tree: Understanding Globalization* (New York, 1999), pp. 14–15 and 401–5.

[60]   Kaplan, *The Coming Anarchy*, p. 24.

[61]   Steven Metz and Raymond A. Millen, *Future War/Future Battlespace: The Strategic Role of American Landpower* (Carlisle, PA, 2003), p. 14.

[62]   For critiques of the Powell Doctrine, see Russell Weigley, "The Soldier, Statesman, and the Military Historian," *Journal of Military History*, Oct. 1999, pp. 807–22; Michael R. Gordon, "A New Kind of War Plan: Powell Idea on Force May Not be an Option," *New York Times*, Oct. 7, 2001, p. 1.

[63]   Max Boot, *The Savage Wars of Peace: Small Wars and the Rise of American Power* (New York, 2002).

require discriminate force tightly controlled to support broad policies. To be ready for this sort of conflict, the American military might well dust off the Marine Corps' *Small War Manual*. There was in fact a past where "small wars [were] conceived in uncertainty [and] conducted with precarious responsibility and doubtful authority, under indeterminate orders lacking specific instructions."[64] The Savage Wars of Peace are not neat and idealistic. Persistence, patience, and resolve may constitute "decisive force" in such affairs, and exit strategies will depend on results, not predetermined time tables.[65]

Clausewitz warned the statesman to be wary of rigid doctrines, particularly in such uncertain times. He noted, "no prescriptive formulation universal enough to deserve the name of law can be applied to the constant change and diversity of the phenomena of war."[66] Yet, for over a generation, a rigid and prescriptive formula has taken hold. Although officers read Clausewitz in military schools, his subordination of military actions to the precepts of policy is not a dominant element in U.S. military culture. In fact, that culture is tacitly anti-Clausewitzian.[67] Although Clausewitz is certainly read in America's military schools, it is the spirit of von Moltke, Emory Upton, and MacArthur that resonates.[68] One hears the echoes of von Moltke's debates with Bismarck when officers invoke the Powell doctrine as "professional judgment." Von Moltke claimed that "politicians should fall silent when mobilization begins," that "the course of war is *predominantly* governed by military strategy," and that military strategy functions "*completely independent*" of policy in its actions."[69] This independence and autonomous professional judgment did not serve the German Empire well, nor has it served the United States well over the course of the past two decades.

In the end, one cannot divorce any discussion about war from the political rationale lying behind the war. Clausewitz's counsel that politics must be the guiding intelligence does not sit well in today's military culture. As Bernard Brodie noted in the aftermath of Vietnam, Clausewitz's "absurdly simple theme has been mostly ignored and when not ignored, usually denied."[70] Force does not have its own logic, as much as the military might prefer their own grammar and autonomy.[71] Clausewitz properly insisted that the

---

[64] U.S. Marine Corps, *Small Wars Manual* (Washington, DC, 1940), p. 9.
[65] Gideon Rose, "The Exit Strategy Delusion," *Foreign Affairs*, Jan./Feb. 1998, pp. 56–67.
[66] Clausewitz, *On War*, p. 152.
[67] For an argument on this point, see Antulio J. Echevarria II, *Globalization and the Nature of War* (Carlisle, PA, 2003), p. 5.
[68] Russell Weigley, *The American Way of War* (Bloomington, IN, 1975).
[69] On the Bismarck and Von Moltke debates, see Gunther E. Rothenberg, "Moltke, Schlieffen and the Doctrine of Strategic Envelopment," in Peter Paret, ed., *Makers of Modern Strategy: From Machiavelli to the Nuclear Age* (Princeton, 1986), pp. 296–325.
[70] Bernard Brodie, *War and Politics*, p. vii.
[71] Although some try to make the case. See Gacek, *The Logic of Force*. For an effective counter, see Suzanne C. Nielsen, "Political Control Over the Use of Force: A Clausewitzian Perspective" (Carlisle, PA, 2001).

political object will not only initiate a conflict, but will also pervade all operations and actions in a conflict. It is not just a matter of determining the *why* of a conflict. The *why* must dominate deliberations on the when, where, and how as well.

VALUES GAP

The fourth gap involves the normative values and ethos forming the foundations of a professional military. The moral dimensions of civil–military relations receive insufficient attention in the current debate. Civil–military relations rest on two pillars, one structural, the other ethical. The structural component is clear: civilians have the constitutional and legal authority to control in the making of decisions. However, the moral dimension is less clear. The normative values and ethics embodied in any profession are supposed to define its essence and frame its purpose and limits. The military defines itself as a profession and meets the characteristics of a profession, with the exception of an explicit code of ethics. Some scholars have suggested that the state of professionalism in today's military is declining. One observer argues that "fundamental concepts of military professionalism in the United States have eroded, at times to an alarming degree."[72]

Samuel Huntington's *Soldier and the State* still casts a long shadow over how American officers define professionalism.[73] Huntington defined three elements in the military profession: its *corporateness* or self-identity and commitment; *expertise* or competence in the management of violence; and finally, *responsibility* which acknowledges that the profession provides an essential function, the client for its service society itself. This last characteristic is the component of professionalism that contains normative values and the potential for ethical dilemmas. The nature of the profession of arms mandates that its employment be reserved for socially approved circumstances, and on behalf of society. Within democracies, elected civilian authorities determine the timing, scope, and purpose of that employment. Like doctors and lawyers, military officers only advise their clients on how to employ the military instrument, but the final decisions remain for the client. There are differences among professions, of course. Doctors and lawyers can dispassionately counsel their clients. The military professional can attempt to keep a sense of detachment but is hard pressed to be dispassionate about decisions that may inevitably lead to the death of those he or she commands.

Like other professions, the military desires autonomy. That autonomy is the source of much tension in civil–military relations. Yet, the military cannot

---

[72] Eliot Cohen, "Why the Gap Matters," *The National Interest*, Fall 2000, p. 39.
[73] Edward Coffman, "The Long Shadow of the Soldier and the State," *Journal of Military History*, January 1991, pp. 69–82.

be completely autonomous. Within a democratic system, military officers are the servant of the statesman and subordinate to civilian direction. But there are no exact ethical guidelines to establish the relationship between the officer and the state. Instead, the officer's oath of commission and the customs and traditions of the armed forces reflect the Constitution.

As a result of the actions of some senior officers, the professional military ethos of the past has faded. In particular, the obligations that required obedience to civil authority and selfless service to the nation have eroded.[74] Marshall exemplified the professional military ethic in his understanding of the "sacred trust." This ethic did not mean Marshall was apolitical or isolated from political discussions. Instead, it meant that his participation was within a larger context, the American democratic system and values. Part of that understanding included the bringing up of unpleasant truths in council, a responsibility that Marshall never shirked. This ethic also required officers to stay out of partisan politics and eschew involvement with or open identification with existing political factions or individuals. It also precluded Marshall from resisting those decisions made by Roosevelt, with which he strongly disagreed, including decisions to provide resources to Britain in 1940, and most famously, Roosevelt's decision to undertake "Torch," the invasion of North Africa in 1941.[75] Contrary to the Marshall ideal, the military now addresses the public on policy matters. Prominent scholars and influential former officers urge today's leaders to speak out in the public square in policy debates.[76] Instead of being a passive and neutral participant in the political system, the U.S. military finds itself engaged in open forums.[77]

This new norm has not gone unnoticed by a number of prominent academics with military experience. "The undeniable fact is that many officers today think they have a right that goes well beyond the soldier's clear duty to present his views frankly and truthfully when asked to do so by his civilian superiors," notes one veteran.[78] Another contends that America possesses a "highly politicized military establishment that feels no compunction whatsoever about inserting itself into the partisan arena when it sees its own interests at stake . . . the U.S. military today has become a powerful and quasi autonomous force in American politics."[79]

---

[74] This has been well captured and described in Snider, Nagl, Pfaff, "Army Professionalism."

[75] See Kent Roberts Greenfield, *American Strategy in World War II: A Reconsideration* (Malabar, FL, 1979).

[76] Sam C. Sarkesian, "The Military Must Find Its Voice," in John F. Lehman and Harvey Sincherman, eds., *America the Vulnerable: Our Military Problems and How to Fix Them*, (Philadelphia, 1999), pp. 96–114.

[77] Sam C. Sarkesian and Robert E. Connor, Jr., *The U.S. Military Profession into the Twenty-First Century: War, Peace and Politics* (London, 1999), p. 167.

[78] Mackubin T. Owens, "Soldier's Voice, Wartime Policymaking," *National Review Online*, Sept. 23, 2002.

[79] Bacevich, "The Paradox of Professionalism," pp. 305–6.

Thus, it appears American military culture has adopted norms quite at odds with the Marshall ideal. This will undoubtedly exacerbate civil–military tensions in the future. If, in addition to fulfilling its obligation to provide professional advice, senior officers shape policy debates external to their legitimate role in deliberations, the society will perceive them as pressuring policy makers. Such perceptions could undermine the policy-making process by giving additional weight to purely military perspectives and aggravate the burdens on policy makers who must ultimately account for a range of political factors, including short- and long-term issues, foreign and domestic policy goals, risk, and coalition dynamics. An advocacy role will weaken the military profession because its professional judgment will appear to be colored by its self-interest. Agencies that cannot subordinate their preferences to the greater national interest cannot serve society. When the officer corps forgets or loses sight of its proper role and underlying ethic, it is time to reconsider the profession, its fundamental ethos, and its professional education.

Marshall's sacred trust" incorporates a higher standard and example. Unless both sides of the civil–military relationship restore a balance between the functional, societal, and moral imperatives inherent in effective civil–military relations, serious results will most certainly follow. Huntington warned of the consequences of such a divide decades ago. "Unless a new balance is created, the continued disruption of American civil–military relations cannot help but impair the caliber of military professionalism in the future. A political officer corps, rent with faction, subordinated to ulterior ends, lacking prestige but sensitive to the appeals of popularity would endanger the security of the state."[80] That warning was appropriate in the 1950s, not long after General Douglas MacArthur had gone well past the legitimate boundaries of his authority, and is still appropriate today. Until Americans address the broader issues inherent to civil–military relations and reinforce old norms central to the professional military ethic, they will run incalculable risks.

Such a gap is unmanageable and unacceptable. As one American statesman put it to an assembly of Marine officers, "I pray that when the time comes for you to answer the call to arms, the battle will be necessary and the field well chosen. But that is not your responsibility. Your honor is in the answer, not your summons."[81]

CONCLUSION

Winston Churchill once quipped that the history of coalition warfare was a litany of mutual complaints. One could note the same of civil–military

[80] Huntington, *Soldier and the State*, p. 464.
[81] Senator John McCain, cited in Robert Timberg, *The Nightingale's Song* (New York, 1995), p. 462.

relations. History does afford insights to alleviate the problems inextricably produced by the interaction of policy ends and military means. The task of drawing the right lessons is never easy. As Michael Howard observed, "Clio is like the Delphic oracle; it is only in retrospect, and usually too late, that we understand what she was trying to say."[82] One does not need an oracle, however, to appreciate the crucial importance of proper civil–military relations to the development of strategy and conduct of military operations. Nor should Americans look back in retrospect, belatedly, to understand the potential danger incurred by not grasping what history has to offer. The implications are clear. Effective civil–military relations, in the future as in the past, require judicious reflection and intensive engagement by civilian policy makers, the intimate correlation between policy aims and available means, candid and frank inputs from military advisors, and a renewed professional military ethic.

Furthermore, civil–military relations are just as important in peacetime as during global wars because those periods shape future leaders and military doctrines. The management of the relationship and the underlying cultures, codes, and concepts of the military is also the purview of civilian leaders and strategists. Failure to shape these elements before war is a recipe for serious strategic miscalculation. Civil–military relations is a critical component of security policy. The lessons of history need to be continuous threads in the educational programs that prepare both civilian and military leaders. As Clausewitz suggested, "The first, the supreme, the most far-reaching act of judgment that the statesman and commander have to make is to establish ... the kind of war on which they are embarking."[83]

---

[82] Michael Howard, "The Use and Abuse of History," in *The Causes of War and Other Essays* (Cambridge, MA, 1985), p. 195.
[83] Clausewitz, *On War*, p. 88.

Index

Lightning Source UK Ltd.
Milton Keynes UK
UKOW051143200312

189257UK00001BA/6/P